In *Mending the Heart, Tending*
meditator, Gail Albert, guides us
Books of Moses, the Torah/Pentateuch. Her emphasis on psychology
brings forth rich interpretations of material on each page....Dr. Albert
has done a marvelous job in demystifying profound subjects in a way that
open gateways to hidden mysteries for readers of all backgrounds. Her
approach offers a new and powerful way to experience the gems and depths
of wisdom available in the exploration of popular Biblical study. Highly
recommended for all spiritually oriented readers.

- Rabbi David Cooper, *God Is A Verb.*

Gail Albert returns to the ancient way of encountering sacred scriptures....
With Albert's help, we once again find the original purpose of these holy
texts: to lead the one who reflects upon them on a sacred journey of
transformation.

Albert takes us slowly, contemplatively, through the layers of meaning that
these stories offer. We are brought into the mystery of scripture ever deeper:
from head to imagination, to heart and action, and to the depths of soul. It
is the classic pattern of *Lectio Divina* practiced by medieval monastics, and
Albert makes this practice fresh again. For those who enter the journey,
these sacred stories take on new, and potentially life-changing, vitality.

- Brian C. Taylor, *Becoming Christ: Transformation through Contemplation*

A fresh and insightful reading of the Judeo-Christian scriptures which
makes them relevant not only to their followers, but also to those of us who
have come to the spiritual practice by way of other traditions.

- Jose Reissig, dharmaseed.org, formerly teacher at Insight Meditation Society

Mending
the Heart,
Tending
the Soul

DIRECTIONS
TO THE
GARDEN
WITHIN

Gail Albert, PhD

iUniverse, Inc.
Bloomington

Mending the Heart, Tending the Soul
Directions to the Garden Within

iUniverse books may be ordered through booksellers or by contacting:

iUniverse
1663 Liberty Drive
Bloomington, IN 47403
www.iuniverse.com
1-800-Authors (1-800-288-4677)

ISBN: 978-1-4759-1600-3 (sc)
ISBN: 978-1-4759-1599-0 (hc)
ISBN: 978-1-4759-1598-3 (e)

Library of Congress Control Number: 2012907392

Printed in the United States of America

iUniverse rev. date: 10/31/2012

In the Bible, Jews are called the "children of Israel," and in Hebrew, the word *Israel* is translated as "G-d wrestler." This book is for G-d wrestlers of all faiths and traditions.

Contents

Book 1

Introduction

The book you are holding presents a year's worth of weekly teachings rooted in the earliest Jewish/Christian Wisdom text, the Five Books of Moses, also known as the Written Torah[1] or the Pentateuch.

At the core of the Jewish Bible and the Christian Old Testament, the Torah/Pentateuch takes us from the moment of creation at the start of Genesis to the edge of the Promised Land at the end of Deuteronomy. The stories in this part of the Bible are compelling, and many of the commandments that are given lie at the center of our moral teachings.

But the Torah/Pentateuch is even more meaningful when the text is not taken literally but as an allusion to a reality that lies beyond words. When we approach the narrative as if it were written in the language of dreams, we discover a new story that follows a path toward a different Promised Land, a place outside geography, a state of mind in which inner and outer worlds are all expressions of the one indivisible Source of All that we call G-d.

In this reading of the Bible, each of the five books—Genesis, Exodus, Leviticus, Numbers, and Deuteronomy—is resonant with a hidden story that is expressed through imagery and word play and symbol, as in dreams. Each book adds its own plot line to the larger narrative, and each plot develops sequentially as the chapters follow one another week by week.

These hidden narratives address our consciousness as we navigate in the world, and they offer a path out of suffering, negativity, and alienation, regardless of the physical circumstances of our lives. Read in this way, the five books are a guidebook for psychological growth and spiritual transformation.

The five books work together to make a single complex and coherent story that is premised on a belief in our inevitably conflicted nature as human beings. In the metaphor of Genesis, our bodies are created from the dust of the earth. We are inescapably fragile, in need of care and protection, and it is all too easy to become enslaved to the desires and fears that arise from our vulnerability. But we have also been brought to life by the Divine breath, so that we yearn for a deep connection to something larger than ourselves, to a source of love and compassion that we often call G-d.

The hidden narrative slowly takes us out of enslavement by our self-centered fears and cravings, journeying through the wilderness until we approach the place of inner freedom that we call enlightenment. In this deep reading, the Promised Land awaiting us at the end of Deuteronomy is the state of mind in which we come to *know* that everything and everyone is holy, in which we act with loving-kindness toward all creatures, and in which we feel ourselves in the presence of the living G-d that is both outside us and within.

By the first century of the Common Era,[2] such enlightenment was already referred to as a return to the inner Garden, to the state where we live with G-d, as in the paradise of Eden. If we took to heart the teachings of the Five Books of Moses week by week, we would approach this Garden Within, the mystical Promised Land, by the time we reach the end of Deuteronomy, just as the Israelites stand at its geographic edge in the literal story. For this part of the Bible can be read as a guidebook offering step-by-step instruction for transforming ourselves spiritually.

How to Read This Book

The first part of this book starts at the beginning of Genesis and proceeds straight through to the end of Deuteronomy, with the text divided into fifty-four sections. The second part of this book contains background material, which you can read at any time and which may answer questions you have.

You may want to start at the beginning of Genesis, because that will make the overall structure of the narrative clearer. But you don't need to explore each section in sequence to be changed by the teachings offered. Sections can be skipped and you can begin anywhere. What is certain is that the more you grapple with the ancient wisdom of this Bible narrative, the closer you come to the kind of contemplative process that leads to an altered consciousness of yourself and the rest of the universe, for the narrative offers answers for these big questions: "Who am I? What is life about? How should I live each day? Where is G-d? How can I find peace?"

Wherever you begin the readings, you will see that I've started each of the five books with a general framework, designed to help you know what to expect. Each section within each book then has its own overview for a quick orientation, after which comes a fairly detailed summary of the literal text for readers who have no Bible readily accessible, or for whom the details of the text are overwhelming. The summaries are generally quite specific so as to give you a clear sense of the basis for the interpretation that I then offer.

This interpretation is the most important part. After you read it, let yourself play with its meaning, however you do that. You may have questions that arise, or connections you make to other reading or experiences. If you allow yourself to hold the interpretation in your awareness as you go about living your week, you are likely to begin to notice it having an effect on you. And the more you wrestle with it, the more you immerse yourself in it and bring it into your actions, the more will happen. (Of course, you may well find other ways of construing the Biblical text than the ones given here, for the Torah is an astonishingly complex piece of writing that calls for endless interpretation. There is no single "correct" understanding.)

After the interpretation, I offer a specific meditation. Rooted in the interpretation, the meditation can be very powerful, able to take you immediately to experiences that go way beyond intellectual understanding. I strongly recommend trying the meditations because they offer a very direct path to the Divine Presence; and I recommend working with each one for a week if you can. But it is also quite true that you can definitely follow the spiritual path of these teachings without doing them.

Finally, I've followed each suggested meditation with one of my own experiences with it. In the group I facilitate, we each talk about what we've experienced during the meditation session, and our sharing of these images, thoughts, and feelings has helped us all move forward on our respective paths. Likewise, I offer myself to you as a partner on the journey. You will probably notice that my path, like yours, has many ups and downs. But the trajectory remains.

How This Book Divides the Bible Text and Names Each Section

For more than two thousand years, most Jewish congregations have read the Torah at Sabbath services, progressing from beginning to end in each calendar year. For this reason, the text of the Five Books of Moses has been divided into weekly portions that have been standardized at least since the eleventh century CE.

Because the Jewish calendar is lunar, with a month added periodically to adjust to the solar calendar, there are as many as fifty-four Sabbath days in a year, and so there are a total of fifty-four portions.[3] These weekly readings are called *parshot* (singular: *parshah*) and they section the text very differently from the partition into chapter and verse that comes out of medieval Christianity, although many Jewish Bibles also indicate these for purposes of easy reference. In this book, I've numbered each *parshah* in sequence within its book (e.g., "Genesis, 2, Noah" for the second *parshah* in Genesis), and I've given the traditional chapter and verse as a reference for any quotations. Most *parshot* contain many such chapters; in a different usage of the word *chapter*, I have also, at times, called an entire *parshah* a chapter.

Every *parshah* has a name by which it is known in the Sabbath reading, the name being the most important word or phrase in the line of text with which it begins. And each of the five books has the same name in Hebrew as its first *parshah*. For example, the first *parshah* of the Book of Genesis begins with the line that is commonly translated as "In the beginning, G-d created heaven and earth." Thus, the Hebrew name of this *parshah* is "In the Beginning,"[4] or *B'reishit*. *B'reishit* then becomes the Hebrew name for the entire book of Genesis.

These first Hebrew words are crucial to our reading of the text; in traditional Jewish understanding, they point to a deep interpretation of what is to follow. This understanding is often different from what we'd expect from the English title, which is based on an idea of the overall meaning of the book as found in the ancient Greek translation that was ultimately retranslated into English. Thus, the Greek name "Leviticus" refers to the laws that fill the book, but in Hebrew the book is named *Vayikra* ("And [G-d] called"), which refers to a daily relationship with G-d. I have kept the Hebrew names for each book and *parshah* (alongside the English) to remind you of the meaning imbedded in the first sentence.

Throughout this book, I have taken each *parshah's* title and its first line from Friedman's *Commentary on the Torah with a New English Translation and the Hebrew Text*,[5] unless otherwise noted; and the English transliterations of the Hebrew titles come from Plaut, *The Torah: A Modern Commentary*.[6]

What Do We Mean by G-d?

I've been talking about G-d without much explanation. Yet I'm sure that you have certain expectations about what I mean when I use the word, most likely based on what your own ideas are, although not necessarily. Many of us, for example, grew up with the image of an old white man with a long beard looking down upon us from somewhere above. Some of us still have that image, either as our primary belief or held somewhere in the back of our mind, faint but not completely erased. But this is not the Divine Presence we are seeking in this book.

As you immerse yourself in the teachings or try the formal meditations offered in this book, I hope that you will have some direct experiences to add to the images or ideas you now hold; for so many of us know G-d only through the filter of other people's experience as described in the Scriptures. This is a secondhand experience, truly requiring faith, for we are asking ourselves to believe what someone else says without knowing it for ourselves. Asking this of ourselves seems a lot like expecting someone who's been blind from birth to experience the color red, because faith without direct experience gives us only an idea, or concept, of G-d. My hope is that you will need much less faith as you read this book, instead experiencing for yourself the compassionate, living presence of the Divine permeating your world—and mine.

I feel some need at the start to offer a few comments on what I understand the Bible text to mean by G-d. First, let's remember that this part of the Bible incorporates a number of different views because its roots go back to the tenth century BCE or even earlier. As Karen Armstrong has documented in *The Great Transformation: The Beginning of our Religious Traditions,*[7] our understanding of the Divine Presence has changed over the centuries. G-d may remain the same, but we do not.

So we have an ancient undertone to much of the literal text, in which the Divine Presence is often described in anthropomorphic terms, with feelings, emotions, and even a [temporary] physical appearance. Thus, G-d in Genesis is simply present, walking among men, asking questions, intervening in our lives. Just as Abraham is visited by angels at his tent, so might any of us be so blessed; just as G-d appears as destroyer of Sodom and Gomorrah, so might we be destroyed. In this tradition, which seems to go back to the earliest known roots of humanity, there is no real separation between earthly and divine realms, and divine characteristics don't seem all that different from ours.

But other views of G-d lie alongside this one, particularly as we follow the hidden narrative as our guidebook. I'd like to clarify here the paradox of G-d's transcendence—being beyond our comprehension—and G-d's immanence—being somehow present within the world and even within our deepest being.

Transcendence and Immanence

G-d has created the physical world and everything in it, but G-d is more than the physical world. G-d existed before the beginning of anything physical, even before the creation of time and space; exists to infinity in both these planes; and is unbounded and unlimited, in no way a thing of any kind. No image of the Divine Presence can be made, even if we wanted to make one, because any image automatically creates limitation.

In the Bible, even the name of G-d—YHVH—is unpronounceable, to remind us that no true image of G-d can be made. (The English letters are transliterations of the Hebrew letters *yud*, *heh*, *vuv*, and *heh*. They are the source of the Christian "Jehovah" as the name of G-d.) In fact, the meaning of these letters in Hebrew, while there is no exact translation possible, has to do with the verb "to be," so that the letters point to action or process, rather than relating to a noun. Although no correctly grammatical translation can be made for the name of G-d in Hebrew, the closest approximations are "I Am Becoming What I Am Becoming," "I Am That I Am," "I Will Be Who I Will Be," or even "I Am That Endures." There is also "The One Who Brings Things Into Being." For myself, I always think of the Christian and Buddhist phrase "The Ground of Being."

Moreover, this unnamable, infinite Divinity is not simply transcendent and outside of us, but is also in some way within each of us, at our very core. In the metaphor of Genesis, G-d breathes the Divine essence into us and so brings us to life. And the Hebrew word for breath, *ruach,* is also one of the words for soul. So that we are animated, ensouled, by the very being of YHVH, and we carry this Divinity always with us.

In Exodus, this idea is carried further as we are asked to make a holy place in which G-d can settle among us. Later commentators have translated the text to also mean that each of us individually is to become a Sanctuary for the Divine Presence. If we strive to follow in G-d's ways by embodying the Divine attributes of compassion, we will somehow find G-d within ourselves.

Some commentators have taken this understanding of G-d's immanence yet further. In these interpretations, it is not just humans who carry Divinity within themselves. We have a special relationship with YHVH, inasmuch as we are seen as uniquely able to choose moral action over immoral; and we are the only creatures in the Torah who are specifically animated by G-d. But we are not the only creatures permeated by the Divine.

In these teachings, the whole physical world of lions, trees, geraniums, volcanoes, mountains, and earthworms somehow contains the glory of Divinity. G-d is both transcendent—far beyond anything we can grasp—and inextricably present in the minutest aspect of the here and now. Whatever we may mean by the word *G-d,* we need not choose between transcendence and immanence, and any apparent contradiction is somehow nullified.

In some teachings, the world we live in is simply a manifestation of G-d. In medieval Kabbalistic language, the unitary G-d somehow unfolds through ten planes of reality (called *sefirot*), although calling them *planes* gives them a physical and fixed status which isn't really accurate. In some impossible-to-define way, these planes form a hierarchy, with the lowest plane, called *malchut* ("kingdom"), corresponding to the physical universe that we inhabit. Some of the planes, or facets of reality, just above *malchut* can be experienced in altered states of consciousness such as meditation, while the highest are considered to be beyond our perception as long as we live in physical bodies.

In Kabbalistic teachings (explicitly taken up by Hasidism in the eighteenth century CE and by the modern Jewish Renewal movement), there is nothing but G-d, and it is G-d's continuing presence that sustains existence moment by moment. Thus, the entire world is divine, and everything in our physical world is sacred; it is only our lack of awareness that keeps us from this realization. We can regain this awareness by traveling inward, to our hearts.

In writing this book, I have sometimes emphasized the Torah's view of G-d as simultaneously transcendent and immanent in each of us. At other times, I emphasize this later view—which arises spontaneously in meditation—that there is nothing but G-d, and that everything is an expression of Divinity.

A Note on the Word *G-d*

Because the G-d I recognize is neither male nor female, I have avoided all use of the pronouns *he* or *she*. I've also placed a hyphen in the word *G-d* to remind us that I am referring to an essentially unnamable Mystery. For the same reasons, I have tried to restrict myself to the following names: G-d, the Divine Presence (or simply the Divine or Divinity), the Mystery, the Source of All, or the unpronounceable YHVH.

A Note on Style

In general, I have taken all quotations as they were written, using whatever name for G-d (such as "The Eternal One") is used in the quote. However, there are exceptions to such exactness. For the sake of consistency, in all quotes that refer to G-d as He, I've changed the word back to G-d or an equivalently neutral term, and I have also spelled the word as G-d even if it was spelled God in the original text. I have however, retained the word *God* when it's part of a book title or Buddhist teaching.

When quoting from Elliot Friedman's *Commentary on the Torah,* I've also taken the liberty of changing the spelling of the name of G-d from YHWH to YHVH, which is closer to the Hebrew. Otherwise, I have tried to follow standard usage in capitalizing the various names of G-d and such terms as *the Flood, the Sanctuary, the Tabernacle, the Tent of Meeting,* and so on; I have also used the standard spelling of such familiar names as Rebecca. When standard usage seemed divided, I have chosen what seems right to me.

In addition, I've included a few terms that come from the language of meditation practice and differ from standard English, such as "Follow your breath," or "Open yourself to...."

About the Author

I was raised in an Orthodox Jewish home, but I had little connection to Judaism as an adult until I moved to Woodstock NY in 1999 to supervise the clinics offered by the county's Mental Health Department. But then I found a spiritual home in the Woodstock Jewish Congregation. I became a regular at Sabbath services and Sunday adult education classes, for the rabbi of the synagogue, Jonathan Kligler, was the best teacher I've ever met. Extraordinarily inspiring, he presented a spiritual and joyous Judaism never before known to me. When I went into full-time private practice as a psychologist a few years later, I was able to flex my schedule to come to the rabbi's weekly Torah class. I'd never studied Torah before, and I was stunned by the complexity and sophistication of the writing as Rabbi Kligler and members of the class explored it.

Meanwhile, a friend had passed on a brochure from a meditation center called *Chochmat Halev* (Wisdom of the Heart) in Berkeley, California, describing an intensive (largely long-distance), three-year program in Jewish mystical and meditative teachings throughout history. Although it made little sense to apply, I felt as if a searchlight beam were coming out of Berkeley and aiming directly at my heart; and I entered the program.

About a year after I began the *Chochmat Halev* program, I began facilitating a meditation group that met for an hour before Saturday morning synagogue services. Because we were going to be reading the weekly Torah portion at services, I began meditating on the week's *parshah* for phrases and ideas to work with during the hour that our group met. As time went on, I began to experience each *parshah* as having an overriding, central theme that could be— even should be—the focus for the hour. Often, my rabbi would pick the same theme for his teaching at the Saturday service, which I found most reassuring. As the weeks passed, it also began to seem as if the weekly themes that I was finding built into a coherent narrative as each one added its contribution to an overall plot. When we finished Genesis, I did not expect to find another continuous narrative in the next book, Exodus, but I did, and ultimately had the same experience with Leviticus, Numbers and Deuteronomy. Each book had its own underlying metaphoric story, built *parshah* by *parshah*.

By now, I was reading lots of books on Jewish mysticism, meditation practice, and Torah, both within and outside of the *Chochmat Halev* reading list. In addition, I'd been using two or three different translations of Torah, each with its own extensive footnotes and commentary, and I'd been checking all along with several online sources of Torah interpretation[8] to see if my interpretations were found in traditional sources somewhere. I was delighted each time I found my chosen theme in another source, although interpretations generally focused on a single line of text and not on the whole portion; neither did they suggest a continuous underlying narrative.

After the first cycle ended, our group continued for several more years, and I was able to further clarify the interpretations. This subsequent book is rooted in contemplative meditation; although I've added enough references to show that it is consistent with traditional teachings, it is not meant to be an academic work on Torah.

As to background, my PhD from Johns Hopkins University was in experimental psychology, and my dissertation involved the neurobiology of the brain. I left research and academia after a few years to become a writer and novelist, and am currently a licensed psychologist in private practice with specialty training in treating personality disorders. I am sure that my own writing has sensitized me to narrative structure and the nuances of language, while my training and experiences as a psychologist cause me to see the world through the lens of psychological and symbolic processes.

In addition, I helped to create, and was director of, an outreach program in New York City in the 1990s, in which psychiatrists provided care to mentally ill homeless people who would otherwise have gone without the treatment they needed. I can imagine no work to make one more aware of the needs of the powerless and of the commandment to be thy brother's keeper.

Acknowledgments

I am profoundly indebted to Rabbi Jonathan Kligler for opening the world of Torah to me, and for his enormous support and encouragement throughout this project. It would never have been completed without him, and his ideas are inevitably reflected in this book, although he is in no way responsible for any errors in it. I am also extremely grateful to Rabbi David Cooper, my long-term Jewish meditation guide and compassionate critic of this manuscript; and to the creators of *Chochmat HaLev,* Nan Gefen, and Rabbi Avram Davis, without whom this book would never have come into being. Although I have never met him, I am also most grateful to Reb Zalman Schachter-Shalomi, the founder of the Renewal movement, in which this book finds its place, and I offer this book as a gift to him.

Finally, I am indebted to the various members of my meditation group, many of whose ideas have been incorporated into this work; to Esther Rosenfeld and Sandy Gardner for their careful reading, comments, and enthusiasm in our weekly writing group; to Jose Reissig for his loving support as my teacher of *Vipassana* meditation; and to Alfred Levine, for his always incisive comments on the manuscript, for his boundless encouragement, and for always being there for me throughout the years of writing this work.

I have relied on Richard Elliott Friedman, on W. Gunther Plaut and David E.S. Stein, and on Robert Alter, whose Torah translations and commentaries have been essential[9]—and any errors of understanding are all mine. I am also particularly indebted to the writings of Aviva Zornberg, Mary Douglas, and Jacob Milgram[10] for their insights, and am grateful to Rabbi Shefa Gold, whose book *Torah Journeys*[11] gave me the confidence to continue on my own path of interpretation.

Dedication

The Judeo-Christian world has an extraordinary text in the Five Books of Moses, which is central to its spiritual heritage—a text that teaches that we are to love both our neighbor and the stranger. But few of us can see through the surface of the writing to its consistent and deep message of love, and Jews and Christians have too long been divided.

I have two sons, and both of them have married wonderful women who also happen not to be Jewish. I am dedicating this book to the four of them and to their children. I hope it will help them to honor their joint heritage and bring its mystical spiritual teachings into their lives.

To them and anyone else reading these words, this book is a guide. As it decodes the ancient text that makes up our shared Wisdom book, it leads directly to G-d and to living in a way that can heal our lives and create a paradise on earth for all.

1

General Framework of Genesis/*B'reishit*

The English title of the first book of the Bible is Genesis; in Hebrew, the title is *B'reishit*. The meanings are essentially the same, for the Hebrew name means "In the Beginning," from the opening phrase of the book's first sentence, commonly translated as "In the beginning, G-d created heaven and earth."

Genesis seems to have an odd beginning for a holy book. Cain murders his brother Abel in the very first section, and Noah gets drunk after the Flood and curses his grandson, the son of Ham. In later chapters, Jacob takes his brother Esau's birthright and then steals his father's blessing, flees so that Esau not kill him—and then is tricked into marrying Leah, the woman he never wants, instead of Leah's sister, his beloved Rachel. And much, much, much more.

When I first read Genesis, I was horrified by the behaviors described. But I gradually realized the question that was being put to us: can we humans, who seem naturally dominated by the instincts of self-preservation and self-concern, somehow rise above ourselves to live in this dangerous world as guardians of its resources and of each other?

In the very first chapters, G-d reaches out to us, calling to Adam in the Garden of Eden after Adam and Eve have eaten from the Tree of

Knowledge; later, G-d asks Cain where his brother, Abel, is after Cain has killed him. But Adam and Eve try to hide from G-d, and Cain tries to lie. "I do not know. Am I my brother's keeper?" Cain asks, in a line that reverberates through all of the rest of Torah.[1]

From the opening pages, we are shown how hard it is for us to be open to G-d's call. While Genesis hints at YHVH being a moral force, it doesn't read like a morality tale in which we demonstrate our goodness. Rather, it is an unblinking view of our general failure to remain in relationship with G-d, or to behave well once we break that connection.

The basic structure of creation is set out in Genesis. G-d is the creator of this physical world, and a special relationship exists between G-d and humans. In one version of creation, all creatures, including humans, are created simply by the act of Divine speech. In the other version of creation in Genesis, we are made from the dust of the earth, becoming alive only after G-d breathes Divine essence directly into us. Either way, only we are said to be made "in the image of G-d."[2] Either way, we have an earthly, physical nature that is somehow permeated by the Divine.

In particular, we are the only beings on earth to have choice. We alone can choose to mimic the qualities of G-d, to obey or disobey the desires of the Divine, to know, even, that we *can* choose. We are given the task of responding to G-d's call to Cain about Abel by choosing just *how* we live in the world.

We are asked by the Divine to guard creation.[3] Even more, the Cain and Abel story implies that we are, indeed, to act as our brother's keeper. This implication is spelled out later in the Torah as the central commandment: to love your neighbor as yourself.

The narratives of Genesis then illustrate what we actually do.

As we move more deeply into Torah, we will see even more clearly the dilemma laid out. Each of us is asked to emulate the Divine qualities of compassion, mercy, and love while living in this world in a vulnerable physical body that has needs, desires, and a drive to preserve itself and its offspring. While our spiritual essence may be made in the Divine image, our bodies are necessarily concerned with *self*-protection, and with consequent *self*-concerns, looking out primarily for what benefits *us*—what is sometimes called our "little *i*."

And we have good reason to be *self*-centered. For it is bad enough to know that we are mortal, but it is even worse to know that terrible things can happen to us at any time, even if we do not die because of them. We know that bad things happen even to good people, and that they can happen despite our best efforts at self-protection.

The bulk of Genesis traces our efforts to cope with the awareness of our vulnerability.[4] The text uses concrete imagery to make clear that we are bound by our physical limitations, describing us as being made from the very dust of the earth. In fact, the very name for human, which is *adam,* means "earthling" in Hebrew, for the word for earth is *adamah.* So we are an inextricable mix of G-d's essence and the dust of the earth. And our dual nature places us in inevitable conflict with ourselves.

We may be able to express G-d's qualities of love, mercy, and compassion if we choose, but how well do we really do if we are left to ourselves? The answer of Genesis is that we generally do pretty badly.

Genesis/*B'reishit* Week by Week

Genesis/*B'reishit*, 1, "In the Beginning"/*B'reishit* (Gen. 1:1–6:8)

"In the beginning of G-d's creating the skies and the earth...."

—Gen. 1:1

Interpretive Overview: The opening of the Book of Genesis sets the frame for the rest of the Torah in its stories of the creation of the world, the expulsion of Adam and Eve from the Garden of Eden, the first murder—of Abel by his brother Cain—and the continued bad behavior of the following generations. Through its image of G-d breathing life into humans, who are made of the dust of the earth, it offers a way to see ourselves as physical and spiritual beings who are inevitably conflicted, caught between our lower and higher selves.

Summary of *Parshah*: This most famous chapter depicts G-d's creation of the world in six days, with the seventh a day in which G-d rests. (In Hebrew, G-d is "re-ensouled.") The creation of man and woman is also described, but in two conflicting versions that are presented without comment. In both versions, the man and woman are placed in the Garden of Eden, where the Divine tells them that they can eat of every tree except the Tree of Knowledge. But the serpent tempts Eve, who eats of it, and gives some to Adam, who also eats.

Immediately thereafter, they become aware that they are naked, and make clothing to cover themselves. When they hear G-d in the Garden, they hide because they know that they are naked, and G-d accuses them of having eaten of the Tree of Knowledge. Adam then blames Eve, she blames the serpent, and G-d curses them all: the serpent to crawl on his belly on the ground and be hated, the woman to have the pain of childbirth, and the man to have a life of hard work.

Commenting that the humans might also eat now of the Tree of Life and become immortal, the Divine then banishes them from the Garden of Eden. Sometime after this, Cain, and then, Abel are born. Cain grows up to be a farmer, while Abel becomes a herdsman; Cain offers "some" of his crop as sacrifice to the Divine,[1] while Abel offers one of the "choice lambs of his flock."[2] When G-d approves Abel's offering, but not Cain's, Cain murders his brother in jealousy. When G-d then asks Cain where Abel is, he answers with the famous words, "Am I my brother's keeper?"[3] In response, G-d curses Cain with unending wandering, never to settle in one place.

After this comes a listing of Cain's descendants, the birth of Eve's third child Seth, and the naming of Seth's descendants down to Noah's three sons, Shem, Ham, and Japheth.

Finally, the chapter nears its finish with a statement about (unexplained) divine beings mating with the daughters of men, giving birth to giants called the *Nephilim*. In its final lines, G-d decides that it was a mistake to make humans because they behave so wickedly, and gets ready to destroy humanity, except for Noah.

Parshah **Interpretation:** "Where are you?" G-d cries to Adam and Eve after they've eaten from the Tree of Knowledge.[4] And they hide in shame. And when G-d asks Cain where his murdered brother is, Cain too hides— his answer defensively evasive.

The question is not, "Have you sinned?" Because, of course, we have. Rather, one of the eternal questions of Genesis is simply, "Where are you now?" Because G-d is calling to us every moment to become more than our most limited selves.

In the literal reading of this *parshah*, G-d appears to be an external presence that is in some way separate from us. The Divine creates the world, breathes life into Adam, judges, and punishes. But later on, in the book of Exodus/

Sh'mot, G-d is described not simply as an external presence, but as, in some way, internal. For Exodus asks each of us to become a dwelling place for the Divine; the text says that G-d can somehow be within each of us. And the apparent contradiction, like so many other contradictions in Torah, is simply accepted.

Later parts of the Hebrew Bible expand on each of these views of G-d, and Jewish tradition has for millennia contained the whole range, from fully transcendent—and external to us—to fully immanent, and internal. But humans have a unique role in all cases, for we are the only creatures described as having awareness of ourselves as distinct beings with moral choices.

In the metaphor, Adam and Eve eat of the Tree of Knowledge and suddenly know that they are naked. The metaphor is describing the fact that we are not simply immersed in *being*-ness, the way animals are. The lion hunts the zebra because that is the lion's nature, with no morality attached. But we are not as bound by instinct, although we have animal needs. Like Adam and Eve, like Cain, we have consciousness of ourselves existing in a moral sphere. Having eaten of the Tree of Knowledge, we know that some acts are good and others are bad, and we can choose which way we go. Unlike the lion, we are making a choice in a moral dimension when we kill. As Cain chose.

So here we are, selecting one action over another in this realm of *malchut*, filled with our egos, with our cravings and emotions and *self*-concerns, while at the same time, we are, in some way, manifestations of G-d.

For Formal Practice: Whatever your beliefs about the nature of G-d, please use the metaphor given in this chapter of Genesis for today. As you meditate, ask what it means to be made both of the dust of the earth and of the breath of the Divine.

When you are ready, inhale and allow yourself to feel the Divine breath filling you and permeating every cell of your body.

As you exhale, release that blended essence of Divine breath and physical self.

Inhale again, allowing yourself to feel the Divine breath filling you and permeating every cell of your body.

As you exhale, release that blended essence.

As you continue to inhale and exhale in this way, have your intention hover over the question, "What does it mean to be made of both the dust of the earth and of the breath of the Divine?"

Remember that this is a contemplative meditation and not an intellectual exercise. Just let your attention hover over your question without letting yourself think your way to answers.

As you try to stay with the meditation, you will notice ways in which your mind distracts you with its concerns: with thoughts about finding a right answer, worries about whether you're doing this meditation the right way, reminders of "To Do" lists, and other fears and distractions. Remember that these concerns are all part and parcel of being in physical bodies that require our protection. For this *is* our essential problem: the apparent conflict of being made of both the dust of the earth and of Divine essence.

Each time you notice yourself thinking, gently return to the image of G-d breathing into you and melding with you. Notice what appears to you and let it go.

Throughout this week, see if you can return to the question, "What does this image mean to me? What does it mean to be human?" Don't think about it. Just see what comes to you. Experience your deepest nature.

In My Own Practice: *As I begin to breathe in and out, I see a clear image of a baby being born. Its skin is dotted with what looks like grayish clay. It* *takes a deep breath and begins to cry. It has become separate and it has become aware of separateness, both at the same time. And with separateness comes fear. The thought appears to me: But I can take G-d in with each breath. I am not really alone.*

I picture G-d's breath moving into me and through me and out. And again. For a moment, I see that there doesn't have to be conflict. As it passes into each cell of my body, the Divine breath melds with my physical being. Each permeates the other, cooperating and joining together. Even uniting. In this moment, there is no conflict. This is what it truly means to be human.

Genesis/*B'reishit,* 2, "Noah"/*Noach*
(Gen. 6:9–11:32)

"These are the records of Noah: Noah was a virtuous man."

—Gen. 6:9

Interpretive Overview: The destruction of the Flood is brought on by the violence and corruption of the generations after Adam and Eve. While the waters cover the land to erase all signs of what has taken place, Noah rests in the safety of the ark on the limitless sea. When the Flood ends, the Divine makes a covenant with Noah, telling humans to forgo violence and promising never to wreak world destruction again. Metaphorically, we read that we can always come back to the infinite sea of the Divine, supported by G-d, no matter how far we've strayed from G-d's call for love and compassion.

Summary of *Parshah:* At the literal, narrative level, this second *parshah* begins ten generations after Adam and Eve. G-d says that the behavior of humanity has gotten steadily worse, and the Divine wants to erase us from the earth to start again with Noah, who is "a virtuous man."[1] After the Flood, G-d blesses Noah and his sons, and makes a covenant with every living being that, "I will not again strike down all livings things as I did."[2] In addition, humans are told to forgo violence toward one another.[3] This high point of the narrative is followed immediately by Noah getting drunk, after which some kind of sin occurs, probably sexual, that involves some action with his son Ham, whose son Canaan he then curses.[4] Then comes the story of the Tower of Babel, whose construction is described by G-d as sinful, arrogant, and something to be punished. The chapter closes with a naming of the ten generations from Noah to Abraham (just as there were ten between Noah and Adam), many of the names being identified with different nations of the Middle East. (Archeologists currently agree that at least some of the history appears to go back as far as 1300 BCE.)

Parshah **Interpretation:** The frame of this second *parshah* is the same as for the first, for it is the general frame of Genesis. We are an inextricable mixture of the dust of the earth and the breath of G-d, and both aspects of our nature are to be cherished. Thus, at the end of the creation story, "G-d saw everything that G-d had made, and, here, it was very good."5

In the traditional understanding of Torah in Judaism, our needs for self-preservation, self-aggrandizement, and protection of our physical selves gives us the energy for all of our own acts of creation, procreation, and invention. Thus our needs are a necessary and valuable part of us. (Freud would agree.) But it is also true that these physical needs give rise to our selfish, fear-driven, arrogant, and nasty impulses too. Our task is to be aware of our violent and destructive tendencies and tame the impulses to act them out.

As we read the narrative of the Flood, we see that it can be interpreted with this understanding in mind. Rather than accept the story in terms of punishment—as described at the simple, literal level—we can choose to read it as a metaphor for the actions of what we might call fate, or life, rather than the actions of G-d. Bad things happen. Sometimes they just happen, and sometimes they happen as an inevitable consequence of our bad behavior.

By our behavior, we can create the destruction of our worlds. Our physical world, our homes, our families—all of these can be drowned in the flood of our own untempered self-centeredness and arrogance. And, as this *parshah* implies, after we start again—after the Flood—we inevitably err again. It is inherent in our nature to struggle with that part of us that, in Hebrew, is called the *yetzer harah,* which is generally translated as "the evil impulse," even though this impulse is also understood to be the root source of our drives for survival and material well-being.

The deep, mystical lesson of Noah is that we can always return to the place where *all* parts of ourselves are simply with G-d. Again and again we err, and again and again we can choose to return.

The ark is described as a box, using the same word in Hebrew that is used for the cradle in which Moses is placed upon the water as an infant to escape Pharaoh's decree of death. Noah's Ark, however, is a closed container three floors high, with an opening only at the topmost level, to the heavens. Like a womb, the box holds Noah safely enclosed as he rides on the waves of the unending ocean, awaiting rebirth.

At the literal level, we have the animals at the bottom, Noah's human companions in the middle, and the opening to the sky on the third level. These are symbolic of the three aspects of our own selves: animal, human, and that which is close to the Divine. In Jewish tradition, these are the first three levels of soul.

Noah is in a kind of time-out, present with his animal needs (level 1), his human relationships (level 2), and the part of him that is most consciously close to the Divine (level 3). Here he is in these endless days and nights, in a box on the waters, just as Moses was, under the protection of G-d. Here Noah is, waiting to be reborn so that he can create his life anew.

For Formal Practice: When you are ready, picture yourself in Noah's Ark upon the waves of an endless ocean, an ocean that is an image of G-d, as you are held and protected in every aspect of your being. Let yourself breathe in and out, in and out, without thought, as you are rocked by the waves. If you are distracted and lose your focus, just return gently to the sense of being rocked by the waves of G-d.

Now quietly listen for the sound of animals, and feel the presence of your own animal nature—of hunger, thirst, physical discomfort, or other needs. Let yourself feel rocked by the waves.

Now hear the sound of human voices and let yourself feel your human needs as you are rocked by the waves.

Finally, rise to the topmost level, look through the skylight, and feel the part of you most consciously connected to the Divine.

Feel the waves rise and fall in the undifferentiated landscape of the ocean, and feel yourself cherished. As thoughts or feelings arise, just notice them and return to the sense of being rocked on the ocean of G-d. Feel yourself riding the waves, totally accepted as you are, held safely in the Divine Presence until you are ready to begin again, ready to start over and act with love and compassion for others and yourself.

Whenever you lose focus, gently return to the sense of being rocked and held and totally accepted in all aspects of your being—the animal, the human, and the part nearest to G-d—with all your losses and disappointments and regrets.

In My Own Practice: *I feel comforted as soon as I begin to feel myself being rocked. When I focus on my bodily sensations, I am aware of pain and discomfort in many parts of my body. As I let the sensations into awareness, while still being held, I am shocked by the physical sense of relief. It is all right to feel pain. It is acceptable. I can still be rocked. I feel like crying as I relax into the motion of the waves.*

As I move to the next level of my being, the memory of a recent meeting arises. I am certain I was disliked. I let myself ride the waves with that feeling. Somehow, I can turn it over to the ocean. I am surprised that the ocean accepts it. I want to cry as I let it go.

For a while, I have no thoughts. There is only the rocking. Being held and cherished.

Genesis/*B'reishit*, 3, "Go"/*Lech L'cha*
(Gen. 12:1–17:27)

"And YHVH said to Abram: 'Go from your land and from your birthplace and from your father's house to the land that I'll show you.' "

—Gen. 12:1

Interpretive Overview: We face choices once we emerge into life from the infinite Divine sea out of which we come. Some choices are major ones that we know will take us away from our familiar life, whereas most are imbedded in the daily routines of our lives and go unnoticed. But at each crossroads, large or small, we can choose to be like Abram (i.e., Abraham), open to G-d's call with its risks of unknown possibility, or we can shut down and stay in the routines of habit and upbringing.

Summary of *Parshah*: The *parshah* begins with G-d speaking to Abram, who is to be renamed Abraham near the end of this *parshah,* as his wife Sarai is to be renamed Sarah. Commanding Abram to leave his native land to settle instead in an unnamed place, described only as "the land that I'll show you,"[1] YHVH promises to bless him and make him and his descendants a great people, who will, in turn, be a blessing to all the peoples of the earth. Abram, who is seventy-five years old, obeys without question, going forth to the unknown from Haran with his beautiful, sixty-six-year-old wife Sarai, his deceased brother's son Lot, and their servants. He and Sarai have no children.

The group quickly reaches Canaan, which G-d now promises to Abram's descendants. But he and Sarai encounter famine as they travel farther and turn into Egypt for food. In an episode that has generally troubled Torah commentators, Abram now tells Sarai that the Egyptians will take her because of her beauty, and that she must pretend to be his sister so that he will not have to die in a futile effort to defend her. Pharaoh's ministers do, in fact, take Sarai for Pharaoh's house, and while the text says nothing about what happens to Sarai, it does say that Pharaoh rewards Abram. G-d then sends a plague to Egypt in punishment, which leads Pharaoh to realize that Abram has deceived him. In injured innocence, he lets Sarai go, and Abram and Sarai then return to Canaan.

Now, after Abram has demonstrated obedience to G-d by leaving his homeland, the text begins to demonstrate his ethical qualities. When Abram's herders begin to quarrel with Lot's over grazing land, Abram suggests that he and Lot move apart rather than fight, and he offers Lot first choice of where to settle. Lot takes the plain near the sinful people of Sodom; Abram remains where he is. Then YHVH again promises all of Canaan to Abram and his descendants, adding that they will be too numerous to count.

Immediately afterward, a large-scale war takes place between several different kings; Sodom is overrun and Lot is taken prisoner. In a second demonstration of ethical qualities, Abram and his retainers fight to rescue Lot, and Abram refuses any booty for himself after he wins.[2]

After this, G-d yet again promises Divine favor, but Abram points out that he is still childless. Using another metaphor, YHVH says that that Abram's descendants will be as many as the stars, and then gives Abram instructions for performing a ritual animal sacrifice (historically known to have been used throughout the Middle East of that era for marking a contract).[3] Abram then falls into a deep sleep, in which G-d tells him about the eventual slavery of his offspring in an alien land and their liberation at G-d's hands. And in the darkness of the night, amidst mysterious smoke and flames, G-d completes the formal covenant, promising him Canaan for his offspring.

The focus of the chapter now shifts to the personal, as Sarai gives her maid Hagar the Egyptian[4] to Abram to have a child, because she believes that doing so will, in some way (unclear to modern readers), change Sarai's barrenness. But Hagar begins to look down on Sarai once she becomes pregnant (with Ishmael). Sarai complains to Abram, who refuses to intervene, telling her to "do to her as you please."[5] The text says that Sarai then "degraded"[6] Hagar, so that Hagar flees into the desert where an angel (or G-d—the text says both) reassures her and tells her to go back. Abram is eighty-six when Ishmael, his first child, is born.

And at the end of this very full chapter, when Abram is ninety-nine, YHVH appears to him again[7] and explicitly tells him to walk in G-d's ways; that is, to be G-d's servant. Then the Divine announces another covenant in which the earlier promises are reiterated, changes Abram's name to Abraham, and demands that Abraham and his descendants mark this covenant with circumcision. G-d also announces that Sarai will be the mother of these descendants and changes her name to Sarah. Abraham laughs—in most interpretations, joyously—aware of their agedness, and reminds G-d of his first son, Ishmael. The Divine promises to reward Ishmael too, but repeats that it is Sarah who will have the son that Abraham has been repeatedly promised. In the final piece of text, all the males undergo circumcision as G-d has commanded, as a mark of their commitment to the covenant.

***Parshah* Interpretation:** Last week, we saw Noah in the metaphor of the ark, held safe on the waves despite the tensions created by his tangled, three-part nature: animal, human, and divine. With Noah, we were ten generations beyond Adam and Eve, waiting to be reborn to begin a new and more godly life. With Noah, G-d was planning to start anew, but Noah failed as soon as he reentered daily life, for he immediately became drunk and involved in some kind of sin.

Then came ten more generations of badly behaved humanity. In this week's reading, G-d is ready to try for the third time, through Abraham.

At the narrative level, the story looks like so many others in which the hero leaves his parental home to enter the unknown upon a quest, experiences a variety of adventures in which he demonstrates his heroic attributes (or growth from boyhood into heroism), and finally is rewarded with treasure at the end. We see tribulations involving his leaving his homeland, family, and all he knows; the dangers of travel; rivalry over land; and full-scale war, with each successive narrative describing conflict on yet a larger scale. We also have the purely personal conflict within the family around childlessness, which ends with the reward of a promised son to Sarah: Isaac.

At the deeper level, this adventure is not about overt acts of heroism, but about inner growth as Abraham tries to follow G-d's will, struggling to channel into holiness his human impulses that focus on self-preservation and endless desire. Thus, he is both a frightened man who lies about Sarah being his wife, a passive bystander allowing Sarah to mistreat Hagar, and, later, a thoughtful and ethical warrior who tries to avoid unnecessary conflict and who seeks no material gain.

With Abraham, we are again addressing our struggle with a human nature that is (metaphorically) made of both the dust of the earth and of the Divine breath. But with Abraham, we are no longer in the oceanic womb, awaiting rebirth like Noah; we are already in this physical plane, out in the world where decisions are required. For Abraham's journey begins at a place called Haran, which translates as "crossroads."

Moreover, Abraham is asked to leave "your land, your birthplace, your father's home, [to go] to the place I will show you." (Gen 121:1) At the metaphoric level, he is asked to let go of tradition, of everything he has been taught, and even of his basic instincts, to find his own way on the path of righteousness by looking for a sign from G-d at each choice point. From the text, it appears that G-d speaks to him (i.e., he remains connected and aware of the Divine Presence) when Abraham acts truly as YHVH's servant.

Each of us reading this *parshah* is an Abraham. Like him, each of us lives life and passes through trials in a journey that leads always to the unknown—to unknown places. We are always at a crossroads, but unlike Abraham, we seldom know that we are journeying with G-d. Neither are we trained to listen for Divine guidance.

In some teachings, the opening phrase of this *parshah* is translated not simply as "Go!" but as "Go into yourself!" In this interpretation, we are asked, like Abraham, to go inward and search our own hearts to look for G-d's path, to discern at each crossroads whether we are making choices of mercy, love, and compassion for ourselves and for those around us.

For Formal Practice: Put yourself into Abraham's shoes, wandering through unknown territory to an unknown place, and know that this is your journey too. This is life as we live it out in the world. Only now, with Abraham, we are trying to listen for the Divine voice, trying to follow behind G-d, to be guided in some way. Make this your intention as you do the meditation this week.

When you are ready, try to imagine yourself following YHVH—whatever that means to you—as you move through your life, listening for signs indicating the choices you should make. Imagine yourself walking through your life now, with G-d before you.

However you hold this image of yourself walking behind G-d, add to it the following phrase from the Jewish prayer book: "I place G-d before me always." (In Hebrew, *Shiviti Hashem l'negdi tamid.*) Divide the phrase in half so that you say "I place G-d" on the in-breath and "before me always" on the out-breath. Gently return to the phrase whenever you realize that your mind has wandered.

If you are comfortable with the Hebrew, take the same phrase, *Shiviti Hashem l'negdi tamid,* holding the first word on the in-breath, the second on the out-breath, and so on. Gently return to the phrase whenever you realize that your mind has wandered.

As your mind quiets, let yourself drift back to crossroads in your life, to decisions you have made or perhaps to decisions you need to make now. They can be large, or they can be the small decisions of daily life. Go inside yourself, into your heart, and notice how different the sensation is when you choose the path of love and compassion instead of the path of fear or greed. This difference in sensation is G-d speaking.

If your mind wanders, return to the phrase until it quiets again. Then go back into your heart. Feel G-d guiding you.

In My Own Practice: *I've had a lot of trouble with this contemplative meditation.*

I keep trying to use it to make a decision about a big question in my life, but I still can't see what to do. I can't tell if I am hearing G-d's voice or the voice of my conflicted ego.

But today, the experience is different. As soon as I begin, I realize that I cannot use the meditation to make my decision. I am being asked only to go inside and notice what I feel.

Each moment is a crossroads offering me a new possibility of awareness. Therefore, being present is what is asked. To be. Like the Divine, the I Am That I Am, the I Am Becoming What I Am Becoming. G-d as verb[8]: I Was, I Am, I Will Be.

If I pay attention to my experience over enough time, I may eventually be able to make my large decision. But now, the meditation asks simply for attention to moment-by-moment experience. In this moment, am I on a path of love and compassion, or a path of fear? For I can feel a sense of freedom in one direction and a sense of constriction in the other. The feeling is in my body, around my heart, in my chest, sometimes in my stomach, and in the muscles of my body.

This is the crossroads: to know my path in the process of moving from one moment to the next, to feel mood shifts from moment to moment, to have different—and even conflicting—thoughts and feeling come to consciousness.

Doing this over the years, I have become less attached to my mood shifts, seeing them more as surface phenomena, like ocean waves that follow one upon another, changing form and intensity quite dramatically as situations shift—or sometimes for no apparent reason at all—while the underlying deep ocean remains unruffled.

Over the years, even my sense of "I" has become less fixed, and at times, almost transparent. Some other part of me observes the waves calmly without becoming so involved in them. Yet I am, at the same time, more joyful, more spontaneous, more present, and more aware of the changes in my body that tell me when I am on the path of compassion or not.

Lech L'cha: *Go inside yourself. Unlike Abraham, I cannot know the outcome. G-d is making no promises to me. But I can know that some paths open the heart while others close it down.*

Genesis/*B'reishit*, 4, "And G-d Appeared"/*Vayeira* [1] (Gen. 18:1–22:24)

"And G-d appeared to him at the oaks of Mamre."

—Gen. 18:1

Interpretive Overview: This is the pivotal story of Genesis, in which Abraham hears G-d telling him to sacrifice his son Isaac, but is stopped by an angel just as he is about to kill him. Reverberating through all that follows, the narrative can be read symbolically as Abraham's experiencing the deep truth that everything we have really belongs to G-d and is ours only on loan. Because he is fully open to the Divine call, he can accept this truth about the inevitability of impermanence and loss, and keep going forward into the unknown. Like other mystics, he experiences safety in G-d's presence no matter what befalls him in the world. He is even ready to let go of all other desires to be with G-d.

Summary of *Parshah:* The *parshah* begins with Abraham sitting outside his tent by the oaks of Mamre[2] when three men appear. He is extremely hospitable and insists that they stay, telling Sarah and a servant to prepare a fine meal, choosing a calf for the meal, and then serving the men. They ask where Sarah is, and then one of them says that she is going to have a child. Sarah is listening at the entrance of the tent and laughs in disbelief, after which G-d seems annoyed by her skepticism, so she denies it. (G-d seems to be present throughout this scene, as if the three men and G-d are interchangeable.) The men begin to leave, pausing to gaze down upon Sodom, with Abraham accompanying them in farewell.

Using the literary form common to the Bible, in which the intention is not stated overtly, but indicated by juxtaposing one narrative against another, the text then inserts a series of stories that illuminate Abraham's godliness through contrast. For in the next section, the chapter turns to the tale of Sodom and Gomorrah.

G-d decides to tell Abraham, whom G-d expects to be teaching his descendants "to keep the way of the Eternal, doing what is right and just,"[3] that Sodom and Gomorrah are about to be destroyed for their sinfulness. Abraham then pleads with G-d until the Divine agrees not to destroy the cities if they contain even ten good inhabitants. From here, the scene moves to Sodom, where two of Abraham's visitors (here called angels rather than men) are now going. Although Lot offers them hospitality, the townspeople want to sexually attack them, and Lot offers his two virgin daughters instead. (This behavior has provoked much rabbinic consternation and subsequent interpretation. According to Maimonides, the twelfth-century sage, and others, the story shows Lot's evil heart.)[4] The townspeople attack Lot's house anyway, but the angels prevent them from entering and tell Lot to flee with his family before the city is destroyed. At dawn, Lot escapes with his wife and two virgin daughters (but his married daughters and their husbands laugh at him and stay). His wife looks back (despite being warned not to) and turns into a pillar of salt, as fire and brimstone rain down on Sodom and Gomorrah.

Sometime later, in a story reminiscent of Noah, Lot's daughters get him drunk so that each can get pregnant by him because "there's no man in the earth to come to us."[5]

Then comes an episode in which Abraham again travels with Sarah as his sister, just as he did in the prior *parshah,* when they went to Egypt. This time, it is King Abimelech who takes her, rather than Pharaoh, but in this instance, the text makes clear that Sarah is never approached sexually.

We now return to the main story. After Sarah is returned to Abraham, she becomes pregnant and gives birth to Isaac. But her rivalry with Hagar over their sons continues, until she says, "Throw this slave girl and her son out. The son of this slave girl is not going to share in the inheritance with my son Isaac!"[6] Abraham does not want to abandon Ishmael and agrees to send him and Hagar away only after YHVH commands him to do it, at the same time guaranteeing that Ishmael's descendants will also become a great people. The text then describes G-d's saving the lives of Hagar and Ishmael after they are banished, after which Abimelech reappears to make a covenant with Abraham, saying, "G-d is with you in all that you do."[7]

And now comes the narrative in which G-d "tested"[8] Abraham by telling him to offer his son Isaac as a sacrifice on a mountain to which G-d will direct him. Abraham takes Isaac up the mountain, binds him, and is about to kill him with his knife when he hears an angel call out for him to not harm the boy. Instead, a ram appears, caught in a thicket, to be the one taken for sacrifice. The angel (i.e., understood to be either a messenger of G-d or a manifestation of G-d) then announces G-d's declaration to bless Abraham and his descendants *because* Abraham obeyed the command to offer Isaac up.

The *parshah* ends with genealogy, including the birth of Rebecca (who is to become Isaac's wife), who is a granddaughter of Abraham's brother, Nahor.

Parshah **Interpretation:** This chapter includes the extraordinary and profoundly disturbing story of Abraham's near-sacrifice of Isaac: what is known in Hebrew as the *akedah* (i.e., the "binding" [of Isaac]). Because it raises so many questions, this story has garnered endless commentary, not only within biblical circles but in philosophy and literature; and we will trace its ramifications through most of the remaining chapters of Genesis.

We will begin our approach indirectly, with the basic issue of the Torah. Over and over, explicitly and implicitly in the text, we are asked to emulate G-d's qualities of love, mercy, and compassion. Later in the Torah, we are explicitly commanded to love our neighbor as ourselves, and we are given this command even though we are living in physical bodies that are wired to keep our attention on *self*-preservation and *self*-satisfaction of all sorts of desires—what are sometimes called the needs and cravings of the "little *i*." As we seek to become holy, we are inevitably faced with internal conflict precisely *because* that's the set-up: we are made both of earth and of G-d's divine breath. And each generation, and each one of us individually, has to struggle with this conflict.

In the last *parshah,* we followed Abraham as he chose his responses to the various challenges confronting him after he left his birthplace, at YHVH's command, for an unknown land. Of course, we all face choice-points in some form in our own journeys, but Abraham is notable because of his extraordinary devotion to G-d and his generally high level of holiness.

In this week's *parshah,* Abraham has moved farther on his journey. The chapter begins with his extremely expansive welcome to three strangers who appear in front of his tent. And when they tell him that Sarah will have a child within the year, he expresses no skepticism—unlike Sarah— trusting in G-d. After that, he bargains with G-d for the survival of Sodom and Gomorrah, if only ten just people are found there, arguing that it is immoral to "sweep away the innocent along with the wicked."[9]

By implication, the chapter then offers a contrast to Abraham, through stories of selfishness, fear, and lust in the narratives about Sodom and Gomorrah, Lot's drunkenness, and his daughters having sex with him. Even Abraham sins by being afraid to tell Abimelech that Sarah is his wife (although G-d does not seem to hold him accountable). As is typical in Torah, the contrast is unspoken, made through juxtaposition of narrative and repetition of certain words and phrases.

After this, the narrative returns to the fully personal, as Sarah demands that Abraham exile Hagar and Ishmael, probably to their deaths. But Abraham has largely overcome his self-concerns to become a channel for the Divine will, agreeing only after G-d explicitly orders him to go ahead and promises their safety.[10] And then, the Divine tests him still further—to the limit—by commanding that he sacrifice his remaining son, Isaac. And Abraham obeys G-d's will without hesitation, even getting up early in the morning to begin the task.

In all his long life, he has had only two children: Ishmael and Isaac. He has already given Ishmael up at G-d's bidding, and now he is being asked to kill his other child, who is called in the text "your son, your only one, the one you love."[11] And if he kills Isaac, he also loses all that Isaac represents; Isaac will leave no offspring if he dies now, provide no descendants to fill the Promised Land. Abraham is giving up his own future in giving up Isaac.

As such, this test can be read as an ultimate statement about giving up attachments to anything but the Divine Presence—giving up everything we own, everything that we think of as ours, everything we might care about beside G-d. It is, indeed, the ultimate test.

In the literal reading of this narrative, it is often said that Abraham is following a tradition of child sacrifice, existent at the time in the worship of other gods, and that the point of this *parshah* is that his particular god, YHVH, does not accept such sacrifice. In some interpretations, Abraham may even misunderstand the meaning of G-d's command, which can mean simply "bring him up" instead of "sacrifice him as a burnt offering." In this latter reading, G-d never intended that the test of obedience call for Isaac's death; Abraham was being asked only to bring Isaac forward, to have him stand before G-d.

But tradition and liturgy both say that we are asked to accept G-d's will. To understand that all that we have comes from the Divine and that it is not ours to own. We are asked to be grateful while understanding that everything is on loan—even our beloved children. And the text seems to find Abraham to be holy precisely because he understands and accepts this truth.

As long as we stick to the literal narrative, the horror of the story makes this underlying meaning hard to see. It is easier if we read it metaphorically. Then, we can more easily comprehend that Abraham is being asked—or believes he is being asked—to give up that which is most important to him. Renouncing the part of him that is made of the dust of the earth, he is being asked to be like an angel, expressing only that which is Divine in himself. As Abraham raises the knife, we are to see it as the extreme of asceticism.

We can understand the yearning for obedience—particularly if we don't take it to such extremes. It is easier in many ways to give up our independence, to follow the rules (as we perceive them) without question. It is often harder to accept responsibility for ourselves than to do what we are told—even without G-d entering the picture. And once we add the Divine Presence, we may feel ecstatic as we surrender all of our human desires. Certainly, such ascetic ecstasy is often part of a spiritual path.

But the text says that such renunciation is not being asked of us. It may even be Abraham's misunderstanding in thinking it ever was asked. The task set by Genesis is to somehow serve G-d by fusing the human and the Divine that is in us—and not to simply deny the human.

We can even read the text as implying that Abraham is so holy precisely *because* some part of him rebels at the extremity of the sacrifice. A number of rabbinic commentators have stated that the crucial point is that he is able to hear the angel calling for him to stop. Others might not have heard that Divine call. At the literal level, Abraham hears the angel and comprehends that he needn't give up his beloved son. And at the metaphoric, that he need not give up his humanity in renunciation of his physical being.

Abraham is rewarded for his devotion and unswerving desire to accept the Divine will; even so, both Abraham and the rest of us can understand from the *akedah* that the path of devotion and service is not through extremes of asceticism.

For Formal Practice: The intention of this contemplative meditation is to enable you to feel any craving you may have to merge with the Divine, letting go of all your desires so that you can disappear into a place of peace. Notice, also, whether you feel you *ought* to entirely renounce all kinds of yearnings rather than treasure your physical being.

When you are ready, focus on the response Abraham gives when G-d calls to him in this *parshah*. When G-d calls, first to test him, and then, through the angel, to stop him from the sacrifice, Abraham says simply, "Here I am." (In Hebrew, *Hineini.*)

When you are ready, begin to follow your breath. As you breathe out, say, "Here I am," in English or Hebrew. Notice how your body feels. Does it have discomfort anywhere? And then just listen in silence as you breathe in. Notice the thoughts that occur to you as you repeat the phrase "Here I am." Then let the thoughts go and return to the phrase.

Who is that "I" who says, "I am"? Does that "I" have needs? What about those needs? Let the questions float by without letting yourself think. "Here I am." *"Hineini."*

In My Own Practice: *I feel intense craving to be taken up by G-d as soon as I begin. As I call out, "Here I am." "Hineini," I want only to lose that "I," to give it up, to dissolve into the peace of the silence. The silence feels so comforting.*

Then comes the thought that I am supposed to stay here, working away, repeating, "Here I am." I hate this work. Then the words separate, split up. "Here." "I am."

I don't like this. I don't want to be here. It's too hard.

Time passes.

I notice that my neck is tense, extended, pulling my whole body forward. I breathe, trying to bring my neck back atop my spine. I breathe out. "Here I am."

The thought appears: I don't have to try so hard. I don't have to call out with such effort. I can just be. Be here.

"Here I am." With no agenda. Just here. Nothing more is asked.

Genesis/B'reishit, 5, "Sarah's Life"/*Chayei Sarah*
(Gen. 23:1–25:18)

"And Sarah's life was a hundred years and twenty years and seven years...."

—Gen. 23:1

Interpretive Overview: The intergenerational narrative continues, beginning with the death of Sarah, going on to Isaac's arranged marriage to Rebecca, and ending with Abraham's death. Throughout the narrative, Isaac's profound passivity is implied. At a deeper level, the story is about the aftermath of Abraham's near sacrifice of his son, suggesting the damage to mother and son created by Abraham's finding Isaac expendable in the face of his devotion to G-d.

Summary of *Parshah:* Sarah's death follows immediately after the story of the *akedah,* in what seems like a typical piece of Torah commentary through juxtaposition. (As I've said before, Torah's comments are rarely overt. Instead, they depend on placing one bit of narrative next to another, or having a phrase in one section echo a phrase somewhere else. For more than two thousand years, Torah readers have made inferences from these juxtapositions. The meaning of Sarah's death has provoked particular discussion.) After Abraham mourns Sarah, he negotiates to buy land near Mamre (the text also calls it Hebron) that contains the cave of Machpelah to be used for Sarah's burial site.

In the next section of narrative, Abraham sends his senior servant to find a wife for Isaac back in Abraham's homeland, rather than among the Canaanites where he lives. When the servant reaches the city of Nahor, he asks G-d to point out the right woman by having her offer to water all ten of his camels as he stands at the well—and Rebecca does just this. The servant then asks her about her family, discovers she is a patrilineal descendant of Abraham,[1] thanks the Divine for leading him, and puts jewelry upon her. She takes him back to her family, where her brother Laban welcomes him. The servant immediately recounts his mission and the ways the Divine has guided him, and Laban and her father accept the marriage as G-d's will. In the morning, the servant wants to leave with Rebecca, although her brother and mother want to wait ten days. They ask Rebecca, who is ready to leave immediately, and so they do.

Isaac sees them arrive (and she sees him, as well, after he has "been meditating in the field,"[2]) toward evening. He runs toward them, hears the story from the servant, and brings her immediately "into the tent of Sarah his mother and took Rebecca as wife. And he loved her and Isaac was consoled after his mother's death."[3]

In what seems a kind of coda to the rest of the narrative, the text then says that Abraham takes another wife, Keturah, with whom he has six sons, whose many descendants include the Midianites,[4] one of whom will become the wife of Moses.[5] Giving these six sons gifts, he sends them away from Isaac to the land of the East.[6]

Abraham finally dies at the age of one hundred seventy-five, and Isaac and Ishmael together bury him in the cave of Machpelah alongside Sarah. (The text makes no comment on their meeting again for this purpose.)[7]

The chapter closes by listing the twelve sons of Ishmael, all of whom become chieftains, and ends with Ishmael's death.

Parshah Interpretation: In this chapter, we hear Abraham arranging for Isaac's marriage; we hear the servant recounting the story; and we hear briefly from Rebecca and her brother Laban. But the chapter is most notable for its silences. We never hear from Isaac himself. We never hear from Sarah. We never hear from Isaac's half-brother Ishmael.

Yet the silence resonates with what has gone before, primarily with Abraham's near-sacrifice of Isaac, the *akedah;* and perhaps even with an undertone about the near-murder of Ishmael by Abraham and Sarah when they banished him to the desert with his mother. In fact, the entire *parshah* can be read as the flip side of the last one.

Thus, the chapter begins with Sarah's death, with no mention of whether time has passed since the *akedah*. Because of the juxtaposition, there are many commentaries that assume she dies in horror of what might have been, as soon as she hears the news. For we understand that Sarah, who has been racked by barrenness all her life, experiences Isaac as her laughter and joy. In Hebrew, his name, indeed, *means* laughter. If he were to have been killed by Abraham, she would have no more reason to live. And even though Abraham didn't complete the act of sacrifice, he began it. How can she now go on being with him; how can she go on living?

Meanwhile, Isaac, poor Isaac, lives with the knowledge that his father intended to kill him. Abraham may have believed that he was supposed to give Isaac up as proof of his devotion to G-d. But his belief led him to treat Isaac no longer as the beloved son of his old age, but merely as an object, as if Isaac could not have desires quite independent of Abraham's—as if Isaac's life were of no importance to Isaac.

The text does not explain why Isaac let himself be tied up by Abraham. (In many commentaries, he is believed to be an adult man in his thirties, and not a child. The text gives little indication of age.) Neither does the text indicate what Isaac thought as he faced the moment of his death, nor what he felt about G-d when he was saved.

The text is even ambiguous about whether Isaac accompanied Abraham off the mountain or ever spoke to him again. In any case, Sarah's death right after the *akedah,* and Isaac's silence, raises the question not so much about YHVH's compassion as about Abraham's lack of it. Bible commentators frequently assume that Abraham came from a world in which children were regularly offered as sacrifices to the gods; nevertheless, we might expect him to have had a moment of hesitation.

Perhaps he hoped for a reprieve; perhaps not. But the obedient, unquestioning man who binds his son on a funeral pyre and lifts the knife to kill him is the same man who argued with G-d to save innocents in Sodom and Gomorrah.[8]

Both Isaac and Sarah (and perhaps Ishmael) have seen the abyss: the possibility of being considered expendable in the face of someone else's passion or need—even someone we love and trust. In the face of this possibility, Sarah dies and Isaac somehow goes on—but in silence. (In this context, the *parshah* can even be seen as pointing toward the story of the later Egyptian enslavement and of the command throughout Torah that we are never to forget what it means to be at the mercy of another's power.)

When we focus on Abraham, we can talk about the *akedah* metaphorically, in terms of a path of asceticism in devotion to the Divine. But the question remains about the effects of Abraham's asceticism on his family. In the narrative, we can perhaps assume that Abraham is trying to help Isaac find a way back to life by arranging for his marriage. And Isaac does find comfort in Rebecca's arms. Yet, we hear the persistence of the abyss in his silence.

Abraham is the first patriarch in the Judeo-Christian-Muslim traditions. He epitomizes obedient faith, and the text seems to say that he is treasured by G-d for his devotion. He has proved his worthiness by his unquestioning willingness to do whatever is asked, regardless of the cost. Yet it is exactly such an unswerving sense of mission that has led to some of the most horrifying actions in human history. And in this post-Holocaust era of endless new genocides and terrorism, we hear the reverberation even more.

For Formal Practice: I would like to focus on the value of each life, and of life itself everywhere on the planet, in all its manifestations. When you are ready, follow your breath for a minute or two as you inhale and exhale.

Now let yourself now go back to the scenes of the *akedah*.

Walk with your father for three days, until he tells the servants to stay, while you and he go ahead.

Feel him put the wood for the sacrifice on your back, and take the knife and firestone for himself. Walk up the mountain alone with him.

Ask him, "Father, where is the sheep for the burnt offering?"

Hear him tell you, "G-d will see to the sheep for the burnt offering, my son."

Watch your father build an altar and lay out the wood.

Now feel him bind you and lay you atop the wood.

See him pick up the knife to kill you.

Stay with this image for a bit as you breathe in and out.

Now hear the angel call to him, "Abraham! Abraham!" and hear him answer, "Here I am."

Focus on the words of the angel: "Do not reach out your hand against the lad, and do nothing to him, for now I know that you fear G-d and you have not held back your son, your only one, from Me."

Let yourself feel the words of the angel. Just notice what arises as you contemplate the scene—Abraham with his knife raised to strike, the angel stopping him.

In My Own Practice: *The intent of the angel seems so clear: you cannot harm another in the fulfilling of your own sense of mission.*

I think suddenly of having just been a dinner guest at someone's house. The hosts did not know me, but I had been brought by someone very close to them, and they welcomed me warmly.

They had served chicken, and I am vegetarian for ethical reasons.

I considered not eating it, as I usually would not, but this time it seemed hurtful to refuse. They were offering openhearted hospitality, and refusing to accept it in the name of my spiritual path felt self-contradictory. If I came again, I would tell them beforehand that I ate no meat, but here, now, at this table, it felt like wielding a knife to their spirit.

Such a trivial matter, I think. And yet, not. The angel is clear. My devotion, my desire to serve the Divine is understood. Accepted. But I should not do harm to another as part of my service.

Genesis/*B'reishit*, 6, "Records"/*Tol'dot*
(Gen. 25:19–28:9)

"And these are the records of Isaac, son of Abraham: Abraham had fathered Isaac."

—Gen. 25:19

Interpretive Overview: This chapter traces the rest of Isaac's life, but it is most famous for the story of the rivalry between his twin sons, Esau and Jacob, which culminates in Jacob's theft of Esau's birthright and blessing. The chapter can be read as a continued exploration of the aftereffects of the *akedah,* showing that Esau and Jacob have shut down entire parts of themselves as they try to adapt to the reality of their father's experience. Each is fractured, only half a person; in the symbolism of twinship, each is the other's missing part, needing to merge into a single identity to become whole. In this reading, the chapter is looking at our own splintered selves, as we acknowledge many different, even warring, strands of identity in our struggle to survive alongside one another.

Summary of *Parshah:* The chapter begins with a familiar motif, for Rebecca is barren (as Sarah was) for twenty years, so that Isaac prays to G-d for a child. When Rebecca finally becomes pregnant with twin sons, they compete with each other even in the womb, so that she feels despair. G-d tells her that two nations shall come of them, and that the older shall serve the younger.[1] When they are born, Jacob—the younger—comes out clutching Esau's heel.

Esau, Isaac's favorite, is red and hairy and grows up to become a man "who knew hunting, a man of the field,"[2] while Jacob, Rebecca's favorite, "was a simple man, living in tents."[3] One day, a very hungry Esau comes in from the outdoors and asks for some of the lentil stew that Jacob is cooking. In what many people find yet another morally disturbing exchange in

Genesis, Jacob gives it to him only after the famished Esau gives up his birthright as the firstborn son[4] in exchange for the meal.

Then the narrative returns to Isaac as he replicates—but in a less intense, truncated manner—many of the episodes of Abraham's story. In what looks like the same anecdote, for example, he travels to the court of Abimelech (like Abraham) to escape famine, pretending that Rebecca is his sister (as Abraham did with Sarah), so that he need not fight for her if she is coveted by the king. As in Abraham's story, Abimelech discovers the truth and sends them away.

The text then reports that Isaac prospers as a herdsman, as his father did; it also details his digging of wells at the same sites Abraham had dug.[5] Finally, G-d appears to him at night to bless him and his descendants, after which Abimelech comes to him to makes a treaty saying, "We've *seen* that YHVH has been with you...."[6] All of his experiences were like Abraham's.

Then Esau, at the age of forty, takes two Hittite wives, creating "bitterness of spirit to Isaac and Rebecca."[7]

Finally, in the long dramatic episode of this chapter, Isaac feels himself near death and asks Esau to hunt game and prepare for him the kind of meal he loves, so that his soul can bless Esau before he dies. When Esau leaves for the hunt, Rebecca, who has overheard, tells Jacob to pretend to be Esau. He is afraid Isaac will discover the trickery and curse him; she tells him that she will take on any curse and that he should just do as she says. So he brings a kid for her to cook, and she gives him Esau's best clothing to wear and covers his hands and neck with goatskin so that he will feel hairy like Esau.

Jacob goes to Isaac, who is blind. Isaac asks who he is, and Jacob answers, "I am Esau, your firstborn."[8] But Isaac continues to doubt, thinking that the voice is Jacob's. Yet when he touches Jacob, the goatskin feels like

Esau, and so he gives a blessing. Even then he is doubtful, asking yet again if he is really Esau, and Jacob again lies. Isaac eats his meal and, still uncertain, kisses Jacob and smells his clothes (which he says has the aroma of a field blessed by G-d). Only then does Isaac give him the blessing of the firstborn.

Immediately after Jacob leaves, Esau arrives with his dish of game. Isaac asks who he is and trembles as he realizes the deception. When Isaac confesses what has happened, Esau cries out and begs to be blessed as well, but Isaac says that Jacob has stolen the blessing. Stating that Jacob has now stolen both his birthright and his blessing, Esau then asks if there is any blessing saved for him, and a distraught Isaac answers, "And for you: where, what, will I do, my son?"⁹

Weeping, Esau then cries, "Is it one blessing that you have, my father? Bless me, also me, my father."¹⁰ Isaac does find a blessing, but says Jacob will be Esau's master.

The chapter ends with Esau vowing that he will kill Jacob as soon as the period of mourning for Isaac ends. Rebecca hears of the vow and tells Jacob to flee to her brother Laban. Then she tells Isaac that she is afraid Jacob will marry a Canaanite woman; so Isaac, too, tells him to go and find a wife from among the daughters of Laban. Jacob leaves, and Esau, hearing of their marriage wishes for Jacob, realizes their disapproval of his wives, and takes another wife from Isaac's brother, Ishmael.

Parshah **Interpretation:** At the narrative level, the chapter is once again very disturbing. Jacob mistreats Esau and lies, and then he is rewarded. Most interpretations say that the underlying principle is that the will of G-d is being carried out, regardless of how the morality looks to us.

On the other hand, later chapters imply that Jacob is indeed punished for his trickery. Despite his rewards, he too will suffer horribly as he, in turn, becomes the victim of deception in his own life.

But we can also read this week's chapter in an entirely different way, as yet another phase of the continuing narrative of the *akedah*. For it opens by looking backward: "And these are the records of Isaac, son of Abraham." In this reading, the question is still about what happens when we come face to face with the abyss of what humans can do to each other in the conviction of their righteousness.

We can also read the *akedah* story even more broadly, to represent the first time we are confronted with the awareness of the absolute fragility of life, for Isaac would be dead if G-d had intended his death to be the outcome, just as people die all the time of disease, accident or natural catastrophe, whether by what we call the hand of G-d, or fate ... or life.

In response to his traumatic shock, Isaac, who never protested his sacrifice, seems to barely exist, able to do little more than repeat his father's path. His physical blindness is symbolic of his inability to visualize a life of his own, to *see* a future.

Meanwhile, his sons are also bound: Jacob withdraws into the tent, not living in the physical world at all, while Esau is so aware of the possibility of the abyss that he has no trust in the possibility of a future of any kind. Living only in the moment, as a hunter, he sells his birthright for a meal when he is hungry, because all that he can count on is the *now*.

Sarah dies, Isaac is barely alive. Jacob hides from the world in a tent, and Esau sees no future. Such is the fruit of the *akedah*.

But there is more to this *parshah* than hopelessness, for Genesis is adamant that we must go on, despite full awareness of the possibility of life ending at any instant.

The rivalry between brothers also has a deeper meaning here than the usual Torah narrative of sibling rivalry. In light of the legacy of the *akedah*, we can read the story of Esau and Jacob in terms of the symbolism of twinship, in which each twin represents the missing half of the other.[11] To be whole, to be complete, they need to merge. The pivotal moment of this *parshah* is when Isaac asks Jacob who he is, and Jacob says, "I am Esau, your firstborn."[12]

Our physical being craves to live, even if there are no assurances. The desire to survive is part of our very essence as beings made of the dust of the earth; it is what keeps us going despite catastrophe. In taking on Esau's identity to obtain his father's blessing, Jacob melds together the physical vitality of Esau with his own inwardness and moves on, knowing that the abyss exists but living as if it doesn't. He suffers for his deception all his life, but he does create the future.

Moreover, in Jacob's triumph over Esau, we have the elder "serve the younger," as G-d tells Rebecca during her pregnancy,[13] and we can read this in terms of our own internal struggle. We need to exist in the world in all the complexity of our humanness, bringing to our lives both the Esau and the Jacob parts. But Esau cannot rule. While we must have the vitality of our physical, earthly being, the Esau part of us is too simple to exist alone.

For Formal Practice: The intention is to ask, "Who is that 'I' who I am? How am I Jacob? How Esau? Who else am I?"

When you are ready, try out the phrase "I am (<u>your name</u>)." Now begin to let yourself become aware of the different faces of this "I."

As you breathe, let yourself become aware of a needy aspect of your being. Then let your awareness move onto a greedy aspect. Let the awareness move about to different components without clinging. Notice an impulsive part of what you call you. Or a deceitful part.

Notice parts of you that feel like Jacob. Like Esau.

Notice, and then let go. As you breathe in, feel the richness of your complexity. As you breathe out, say your name. "I am…." Notice how different you feel now.

In My Own Practice: *I see Jacob bullied by his mother into stealing Esau's blessing. I also see Jacob taking Esau's birthright as the firstborn son.*

I see Esau holding the bowl of lentil porridge, totally in the moment as he takes the steaming dish. Consequences have no meaning for him. There is only now. And Jacob—Jacob is all about consequences. Always weighing what might happen if….

I am Esau when I dance, or cook, or make love. Immersed in the immediate physicality of my experience.

I love being Esau. My Esau is joy.

And my Jacob, poor Jacob, takes up too much of me. Jacob the worrier, Jacob the planner.

It is Jacob who picks up the pieces and copes after Esau too exuberantly says yes to still another project. Esau always says yes, and sometimes the rest of me has to pay too high a price in energy and time.

But Esau listens to my heart's desire. While Jacob tries to reason his way to decision.

I need them both—Esau to recognize the heart's desire and Jacob to navigate desire's path with skill.

Esau for spontaneity. Jacob for judgment.

Genesis/*B'reishit*, 7, "And He Left"/*Vayeitzei* (Gen. 28:10–32:3)

"And Jacob left Beer-sheba and went to Haran. And he happened upon a place and stayed the night there because the sun was setting."

—Gen. 28:10

Interpretative Overview: As Jacob flees from Esau to his uncle Laban after stealing Esau's blessing, he dreams of angels going up and down a ladder to the skies, waking to the awareness of G-d's having been present without his knowing it. The other well-known episode of the chapter is Jacob's working for seven years in order to marry his beloved Rachel, only to be tricked into marrying her sister Leah instead. Like us, Jacob is intermittently aware that G-d is always present, but he generally does not see the Divine in the midst of a world laden with deceit and betrayals—including his own.

Summary of *Parshah*: As the *parshah* opens, Jacob comes to an unnamed place just as the sun is setting. Stopping there to sleep, he sets a stone as a headrest and has a visionary dream. "And here,"[1] the text reads, stood a ladder that reached from the ground to heaven, with angels climbing up and down it. "And here,"[2] was G-d standing over him, once more promising the land to him and his descendants, and adding, "Through you and your descendants, all the families of the earth shall find blessing."[3] G-d also promises to watch over Jacob always.

Jacob wakes in awe, looks around, and says, "Indeed, the Lord is in this place and I did not know!"[4] He takes the stone of his headrest for an altar, calling the site G-d's house (in Hebrew, *Beth-El*), and promising to make YHVH his G-d *if* YHVH protects him on his journey and brings him back "safely."[5]

He walks on. "And he looked, and here was a well in the field and here were three flocks of sheep...."[6] But the well is covered by a heavy stone so that the sheep cannot drink. Meanwhile, the men at the well tell him that Rachel, daughter of Laban, is on her way. As soon as Jacob sees Rachel, he goes over to the well, rolls off the heavy stone, waters all her sheep, and kisses her.

After this, he tells her he is her cousin. She runs to tell Laban, and he comes out to welcome Jacob, who then stays with him. After a month, Laban asks him what he wants as his wages, and Jacob asks for Rachel, offering to work seven years for her.

At the end of seven years, a feast is held to celebrate the marriage, but Laban deceives Jacob, bringing Leah to the marriage bed instead of Rachel. Jacob discovers the deception in the morning: "and here she was: Leah!"[7] But when Jacob goes to Laban, Laban says it is not the custom to have the younger take precedence over the older in marriage (making us think of Jacob having stolen his older brother's Esau's blessing through deception). Laban then tells Jacob he can have Rachel after a week, but must promise to work seven more years for her after that, and so Jacob promises.

In recompense for Jacob not wanting her, G-d makes Leah fertile. In the course of the marriage, she becomes pregnant seven times, giving birth to six sons: Reuben, Simeon, Levi, Judah, Issachar and Zebulon, and to a daughter, Dinah. But Jacob's beloved Rachel, like other women in these stories, is barren. In despair, Rachel gives Jacob her maidservant Bilhah to have children for her (just as Sarah originally did with Hagar),[8] and Bilhah gives birth to two sons: Dan and Naphtali. Leah does the same with her maidservant, Zilpah, who also gives birth to two sons: Gad and Asher.

Now that ten sons have been born to Jacob by three other women, the Divine remembers Rachel, who finally becomes pregnant and gives birth to Joseph, who will become Jacob's favorite. After all this, Jacob tells Laban that he wants to be paid for his years of labor by being allowed to take every brown lamb and white-speckled goat in the flock. Although Laban agrees, he deceives Jacob yet again by sending all such animals off to his sons. But Jacob manages to end up with all the healthy animals he wants, while Laban gets the sickly ones (by techniques that strike us as magic but were part of folk belief at the time the Torah was written down), and Jacob prospers.

Jacob sees that Laban and his sons have become resentful of his growing wealth. Meanwhile, G-d calls, Jacob answers, "I'm here,"[9] and the Divine tells Jacob to go back to his father's home. Jacob calls Rachel and Leah to him, complains about Laban's mistreatment of him after all his hard work, and says that he obtained Laban's livestock through G-d's intervention (without mentioning his own efforts). When he tells the two women that G-d has told him to go back to the land of his birth, they immediately agree, for they too are angry at Laban. Without telling Laban his plans, Jacob then leaves with all his family and retainers and property.

Laban comes after him, but on the way, G-d tells him not to harm Jacob. He catches up, complains that he would have sent them all off with proper ceremony if he'd been asked, and adds that certain household idols[10] have been stolen. With Jacob's permission, he searches through all of Jacob's possessions, except for the saddle on which his daughter Rachel sits. Jacob, not knowing that it is Rachel who stole the idols, vows in his innocence that whoever has stolen it will die (a promise he is to pay for later when Rachel dies by the roadside after giving birth to their second child, Benjamin).

Nothing is found, and an angry Jacob asks how Laban can treat him so badly after he has worked so hard for him for twenty years, adding that Laban would have sent him away empty-handed if not for the protection of YHVH. But Laban and he make peace with each other, going their separate ways in the morning, after which angels come to Jacob, who says, when he sees them, that the place he is in is a camp of G-d.

***Parshah* Interpretation:** Jacob, fleeing his home after stealing his brother Esau's blessing, now begins his journey into adulthood. As soon as he goes into exile, night falls, and he has his first vision in a dream in which he sees himself stretched out in the symbolism of the ladder. In traditional reading, he is rooted in the ground, made of the dust of the earth, while, at the same time, his essence partakes of the heavens, of Divinity. Even more, this Divinity extends to all parts of Jacob, intermingled with every aspect of his being, for the angels, who are manifestations of G-d, are present at all levels of the ladder.

In the last chapter, Jacob merged with Esau in response to the intergenerational dilemma posed by the *akedah*. Instead of splitting off parts of himself in a defensive shutting down, Jacob took on the task of combining into one being all of the different aspects of personality that these twins represent. Thus, he merges the active, in-the-moment physicality of Esau with his own intelligence and quick-wittedness. And in the image of the ladder on which angels go up and down, he can be seen to contain the possibility for expressing both the earthly and the Divine in each one of these Esau-Jacob fusions.

A central question of Genesis is whether we can express the earthly parts— for Jacob and for each of us—in ways that simultaneously manifest the Divine. Can we follow our passions and lusts—as we must, as long as we are in physical bodies—without also acting with deceit and betrayal?

In this chapter, Jacob takes on the challenge of continuing his spiritual journey after the dream of G-d's promise to protect and be with him always. Jacob wakes from the dream and cries, "Indeed, the Lord is in this place and I did not know!"[11] And in that moment, he has no fear *because* he is aware of G-d's protective presence; for the fact of being open to G-d's presence in itself reduces—even eliminates—our need for earthly self-protection.

In the chapter, the phrase "and here" occurs again and again. It seems to express the quality of being simply present in the moment, experiencing its astonishing *is*-ness without, for once, being distracted by concerns about self-preservation and self-aggrandizement. In these sentences, Jacob is without thoughts of what might have been or what may yet happen, simply experiencing the action of that moment. But this is what it means to open to the *being*-ness that we mean by the word *G-d*. And in those moments, there is no fear.

Jacob's challenge—and ours—is to manage the integration of the human and the Divine while being fully immersed in an active and engaged life that offers unpredictable loss and pain alongside rewards. Jacob's dream provides a vision for each of us on the journey.

For Formal Practice: Our intention is to realize that YHVH is present anywhere, at any moment, if only we enter a different state of consciousness. For the Divine Presence can be experienced no matter what we are doing, whether peeling potatoes or praying. We need not give up our physicality to have G-d present.

Take Jacob's phrase "G-d is in this place." When you are ready, just follow your breath as you inhale and exhale. Repeat the words "G-d is in this place," as you allow yourself to feel your breath coming into your body, going through it, and out.

Let yourself become aware of different areas of your body, and repeat the phrase "G-d is in this place" for each area.

Picture your surroundings and repeat the phrase. As your consciousness moves outward to include other people, repeat the phrase over and over.

When distractions occur, repeat the phrase again and return to your breath. Let yourself move into silence if you can.

In My Own Practice: *My own experience sitting with our meditation group was to feel a subtle weight permeating the room. I felt as if I had somehow set aside my intrusive I-ness from the scene and so had made a space in which this* *quality could be readily perceived. I realized that it was always there; I just needed to give it freedom to be seen.*

It was everywhere. And then, when I focused on the other meditators in the room, I was overcome with love for them. They were so beautiful. They were to be cherished.

I was aware that it wasn't me who was doing the loving. I was merely a passive conduit for the love to flow through. But in being the conduit, I, too, felt love, and was permeated by that love.

"And Jacob sent messengers ahead of him to Esau, his brother...."

—Gen. 32:4

Interpretive Overview: In his years with Laban, Jacob's life—like many lives—becomes complicated and filled with unpredictable twists and turns. As he now prepares to meet the brother whom he betrayed so long ago, he wrestles all night with a man/angel.[1] At dawn, he is given the new name of Israel, meaning "G-d wrestler," and for the moment, he has overcome his baser instincts of greedy desire and fearful self-protectiveness. He has, at last, become whole, greeting Esau with unrestrained love, and he is so open to the Divine that he sees G-d shining through Esau's face. But the rest of the chapter takes us back to our inability to remain conscious of G-d's presence, as it describes all-too-human episodes of rape, deceit, murder, and loss.

Summary of *Parshah:* As Jacob begins his journey back to the land of his birth, he sends messengers to his brother Esau to announce his return. When the messengers tell Jacob that Esau is coming toward him with four hundred men, Jacob assumes attack is likely. In anguish and fear, he divides his camp in half, so that at least a portion will survive, and prays for the protection that G-d has promised him. Sending servants ahead, each with his own herd of animals to give to Esau, he tells them to spread out so that Esau will have time to relent. And then he sends everyone else he has brought with him to the other side of the river, and spends the night alone.

During the night, a man/angel/G-d wrestles with Jacob. Although unable to overcome him, the being injures Jacob's thigh in some way, so that he walks with a limp afterward. At dawn, the angel tells Jacob to let him go.

Jacob refuses until he is given a blessing, and the presence tells him that his name is now changed to Israel (which means G-d wrestler), "For you have struggled with G-d and with human beings and you have prevailed."[2] And Jacob says "I have seen G-d *face*-to-face, yet my life has been spared."[3]

And then he looks: "And here,"[4] Esau is coming close with his four hundred men. Jacob has each of his wives walk behind him with their children, with Joseph and Rachel last, and he walks in front, bowing seven times until he comes up to Esau. Esau runs to him and embraces him, and they both weep. Jacob then introduces his wives and children, and offers Esau his gifts. Esau says that he has a great deal already and adds, "Let what's yours be yours."[5] But Jacob says, "I've seen your face—like seeing G-d's face!"[6] and he insists that Esau takes these gifts as his blessing because "G-d has been gracious to me and because I have everything."[7]

Esau wants to travel on with Jacob, but Jacob asks instead to meet later at Seir. Esau goes to Seir, but Jacob, in fact, goes on to Shechem, already falling from his spiritual epiphany back into deceit. Destruction follows.

The son of Shechem's chieftain has illicit sex with Jacob's only daughter, Dinah (Leah's daughter). Because the son also yearns to marry Dinah, his father, the chieftain Hamor, meets with Jacob and her brothers to ask for the marriage as well as for general peace and intermarriage. Meanwhile, his son offers to do whatever they ask. Jacob's sons speak deceitfully because they are enraged at what they see as Dinah's defilement, and say that the entire tribe of Shechem must be circumcised before any such agreement. Three days after all the men are circumcised, Simeon and Levi sneak into the city, kill all the men, and take and despoil all their wealth, including women and children. Jacob is furious, in large part because their action will have made enemies of the other inhabitants of the area, who outnumber them, but his two sons are unrepentant.[8]

Then G-d tells Jacob to go on to Beth-El—where the ladder, its angels, and G-d had first appeared to him when he was fleeing Esau. Jacob has all his retinue purify themselves and leave their foreign gods[9] before setting off. The Divine Presence protects them from the tribes they pass on the journey, and Jacob finally builds the altar he'd promised to G-d at Beth-El at the beginning of his exile so long before.

Then comes a line about the death of Rebecca's nurse, Deborah, and her burial beneath the oak at Beth-El, after which G-d appears to Jacob, telling him again that his name is now Israel, and repeating the promises about the land and the multiplication of Jacob's seed.

Finally, as they are on the road from Beth-El, Rachel goes into labor and dies giving birth to Benjamin (fulfilling the curse unwittingly laid on her by Jacob in the last chapter in regard to stealing Laban's idols). She is buried by the road.

Immediately after, comes a line about Reuben having sex with Bilhah, his father's third wife (and Rachel's maid), and Jacob hearing of it. Then the twelve sons' names and lineage are repeated.

After that, without comment, Jacob finally reaches his father Isaac at Mamre. Isaac dies at the age of one hundred and eighty, and Esau and Jacob bury him.

The chapter ends with the records of Esau and his wives and children, along with a statement that Esau leaves Canaan for Mount Seir because he and Jacob have too much property between them to live together.

Parshah **Interpretation:** When Jacob first left his home, he had a dream/ vision of G-d promising to be with him always. In turn, Jacob offered his fealty only if he could succeed in completing his exile and returning home *b'shalom,* or whole. (The Hebrew carries the meanings of "whole, balanced, complete" and, as such, is also the word for peace.) Then he woke up with the realization that G-d had been present and he had not known it.

As this chapter begins, twenty years have passed since Jacob left home. In that time, Jacob has prospered economically, and he has acquired four wives, twelve sons, and a daughter. But he has also slaved for his father-in-law[10] Laban, and in regard to that service, the Torah uses some of the same language used in regard to the Israelites' Egyptian slavery. Jacob has been deceived into marrying Leah, when the only one he ever wanted was Rachel, with the sisters' rivalry disturbing all the years that follow. Even when he marries Rachael, their relationship is troubled, for he loves her far more than she seems to love him.

So his life, described in great detail, shows us the impossibility of simplicity in this world, as well as the impossibility of guarantees. Nor does the account include what is yet to come: the rape of his only daughter, death and destruction, the death of Rachel, and, soon, the catastrophic loss of his beloved, favorite son, his son by Rachael: Joseph.

Jacob's challenge is ours: given the inevitable losses life deals us, how do we become able to accept our vulnerability, so that we can stop trying to protect ourselves by adding more and more possessions or achievements? And how do we stop envying our brothers and sisters, and taking what is theirs in the endless and futile pursuit of safety?

In the aftermath of the *akedah,* Jacob lives with full awareness of this central dilemma of human existence. After merging with Esau, he struggles throughout his life to create wholeness out of the disparate aspects of himself, so that he can become fully alive despite fear and the full knowledge of his unavoidable vulnerability.

In this chapter, Genesis carries the spiritual struggle to a new plane, for we are expected to act as channels for the manifestation of the Divine qualities of love, mercy, and compassion *even though G-d's presence in the world does not keep us from loss and pain.* Near the beginning of Genesis, Cain asked, "Am I my brother's keeper?" And now Jacob is returning to the brother he has cheated and fears. How will he behave?

When Jacob first left Haran, he dreamed of a ladder—himself—extending from earth to heaven. He woke to the awareness of G-d's presence and to the Divine's promise to be with him throughout his life. But YHVH is a fearful presence to Jacob after the *akedah,* as well as a loving one, for the G-d of the *akedah* brings us face to face with our inability to control so much of what happens to us.

For twenty years, he has tried to come to terms with his sense of G-d, as he struggles to become whole. Now he has a second night vision, as he fearfully waits to once again meet Esau, the brother he has cheated. In these last hours before the confrontation, G-d comes to him in the form of a man (i.e., as an angel), and they wrestle in a literal, physical, dream-metaphor way, just as Jacob has wrestled figuratively with his own mixed nature: Jacob/Esau, human/Divine. In the narrative, these two dreams serve as bookends for these twenty years of his life.

He comes through this second vision in a different state; he is simply in the *now,* no longer haunted by memories of the past or fear of the future. He's given the name *Israel,* which means "G-d wrestler," for he has wrestled with the unnamable G-d who stands for *being*-ness/*becoming*-ness, for the I Am That I Am, and for the I Am Becoming What I Am Becoming, the names that G-d will reveal to Moses in the Book of Exodus. In this state, Jacob is ready to meet Esau with love.

He cannot maintain this awareness, however. By the time his sons massacre the inhabitants of Shechem, he has already lost it.[11] Like most of us, he reverts to his usual imperfections and deceitfulness.

But at this high point of his spiritual life, he can manifest G-d's love within himself; fully awakened, he is even aware of the reality of G-d's presence immanent in each of us. And so when he finally meets Esau, he says, "I've seen your face—like seeing G-d's face!"[12]

For Formal Practice: We all partake of both the earthly and the Divine. Using the metaphor from Genesis as our guide, we accept that G-d is always present in each of us. In many mystical traditions, including Kabbalah, G-d is more than simply present in us; instead, the whole physical world—including us—is a manifestation of G-d.

When you are ready, begin to follow your breath with the intention of feeling the presence of the Divine within you. When you are ready, move on to sensing the presence of the Divine in someone you love, and open yourself to the face of the Divine in this person. If you wish, think of someone with whom you have been struggling and see if you can see the Divine in him or her.

In this meditation, it is often helpful to place the letters of the unnamable name of G-d on the head and body of the person you are seeing in your mind. The letters in Hebrew are printed in Appendix B of this book, because visualizing them is a standard Jewish meditation that I recommend many times in the course of these pages. The intention here is not so much to use the letters as a mantra as to use them to help you focus on the idea that G-d is manifesting in the world through each one of us. (If you feel more comfortable, you can try this meditation using the word *G-d* or *Divine Presence*, etc.)

When you lose the thread of concentration, return to your intention and/or to these words or letters.

In My Own Practice: *As I sit in the meditation group and place the letters of the name of G-d on each person, I see their bodies glow in my mind's eye. There is so much light pouring out of them that I can hardly tolerate the intensity of the vision. Then, when I shift in my mind to people outside this room, I see the light as dimmer, as constrained and partly hidden by habitual crusts of self-concern and self-protection. I turn to myself in my mind and see the crust plainly, see it keeping the Divine light from showing clearly, trapping it in a shell of deadness. As I continue to follow the breath and let go of thought, the shell thins, and more light shows through. When an image of my baby granddaughter arises, I see nothing but light.*

Genesis/*B'reishit,* 9, "And He Lived"/*Vayeishev*
(Gen. 37:1–40:23)

"Jacob now settled in the land of his father's sojourning, in the land of Canaan."

—Gen. 37:1[1]

Interpretative Overview: Jacob wants only to settle down in peace, but instead is mired in grief when his favorite son, Joseph, appears to have been killed by a wild animal. In fact, Joseph's jealous brothers have sold him, so that he goes from being the favorite son to being a slave in Egypt. There, Joseph's fortunes again go up and down, and the chapter ends with him in prison, struggling to accept his changed identity. Yet he remains open to G-d's messages as they appear in dreams, and uses whatever opportunities arise to get himself freed. Unlike Jacob, Joseph remains aware, flexible, and present to the moment as he responds to life's unpredictable challenges and pain, including an assault on his very sense of who he is.

Summary of *Parshah:* This is the *parshah* in which Joseph's brothers throw him into the pit and sell him into slavery.

Opening with Jacob, the chapter moves immediately to Joseph, who is now seventeen. Jacob loves him best of all his sons, so that Joseph's brothers hate him in their jealousy. Moreover, Joseph has carried back to his father tales about his brothers' poor behavior (about which no details appear in the text); he also insists on telling his family about two grandiose dreams that he has had, in which his brothers and father and even "the sun, and the moon and eleven stars were bowing down" to him.[2] At this, even Jacob is angered.

Then Jacob tells him to see how his brothers are faring some distance away as they pasture his flocks, to see if they are *shalom,* meaning "whole, well, complete, at peace."³ Joseph answers his father's summons with the memorable word *Hineini* or "Here I am, "⁴ after which he sets out while wearing the special, embroidered tunic (commonly translated as the "coat of many colors") given him by his father. On the way, he meets "a man,"⁵ perhaps an angel, who directs him to his brothers. But when his brothers see him coming, most of them want to kill him and pretend an animal did it. Reuben argues that they should merely throw him into a nearby deep pit (possibly a dry cistern), for he hopes to rescue him later.

When Joseph reaches them, they tear off his robe, throw him into the pit, and sit down for a meal. When a caravan of Ishmaelites/Midianites (both words are used) then approaches, Judah asks the brothers to sell Joseph to them rather than kill him, for "he is our brother, our own flesh."⁶ They sell him for twenty pieces of silver, and Reuben (who has been gone) is horrified when he returns, and rends his clothes. But it is too late.

They then kill a lamb, dip Joseph's robe in the lamb's blood, and go back to Jacob to ask if he recognizes it (reminding us of Isaac trying to recognize his son Esau, in order to give him his blessing). Immediately grief-stricken, Jacob cries that a wild beast has torn and killed his beloved son. He will remain inconsolable for many years after, for as long as he believes Joseph to be dead.

At this juncture, a contrasting tale about vows and obligation and deceit is interposed. Judah has three sons, and the oldest marries a woman named Tamar, but then the son dies because of G-d's displeasure with him. (No reason for such displeasure is given.) The second son, Onan, now marries Tamar in a tradition in which a child then conceived would be treated as his dead brother's. But Onan spills "his [seed] on the ground"⁷ rather than impregnate her in his brother's name,⁸ and G-d is again displeased and has him die too. Fearful of losing his third son in a marriage to Tamar, Judah sends her back to her father's house, ostensibly to wait for the third son to grow up. But this son reaches adulthood without marrying her. Wronged and wanting a child, she hears that Judah will be in the area, and she waits for him by the road as if she is a prostitute. He is recently bereaved himself and has sex with her. When she asks for his seal, cord, and staff as pledge of his payment, he gives them to her. But when he sends someone to pay her afterward, no one knows of any such prostitute.

About three months later, Judah is told that Tamar is pregnant and orders her to be burned as a harlot. But she sends him back his pledges with a message that they belong to the father of her child. Recognizing them, he admits his sin in not having her marry his son. She then gives birth to Judah's twin sons, Perez and Zerah. (King David and thus the messiah will be descended from Perez.)[9]

The chapter then goes back to Joseph, who has been sold to an Egyptian official named Potiphar. The text says that YHVH "was with Joseph"[10] and makes him successful, and that Potiphar puts Joseph in charge of his own house because he senses YHVH's involvement. For a while, all goes well. But Joseph is handsome and Potiphar's wife soon desires him. He rejects her repeatedly, saying it would be sinful and against G-d to have sex with her. The final time this happens, she tears off his robe as he flees from her and uses it as evidence that he has tried to rape her. He is thrown into prison—and Joseph uses the same word for it as for the original pit into which he was thrown by his brothers.[11]

Even in prison, the text says that G-d favors him, so that the chief jailer soon puts him in charge of all the prisoners. Then Pharaoh's baker and cupbearer are also imprisoned, and each has a distressing dream. Seeing their worry, Joseph offers to interpret their dreams, saying the interpretations will come from G-d. He tells the baker that his dream means he will be beheaded, and the cupbearer that his means he will soon be restored to his position. He also asks that when the cupbearer is restored, that he put in a good word for Joseph with Pharaoh. Both dreams come true, but the cupbearer forgets all about Joseph, so he remains in "the pit."[12]

Parshah **Interpretation:** Because this chapter begins with Jacob's return from exile and "the generations of Jacob," it appears to be a continuation of Jacob's story. But it is also the beginning of Joseph's story. So this is their combined tale. From another vantage point, it is the beginning of the story, for each one of us, of our possible spiritual growth from being Jacob into being Joseph. (Judah's story also begins here, but its importance isn't apparent until much later in the narrative.)

At the literal level, the chapter is once again about sibling rivalry and deception, which are the recurring themes of Jacob's life from the time he stole the birthright and blessing of his brother Esau. The story also implies punishment for wrongdoing, with Jacob suffering the loss of Joseph because of his own treatment of his brother Esau so long ago.

At a deeper level, however, the *parshah* is continuing to explore the question of how we experience what happens to us in an unpredictably changing world. In this chapter, Jacob's beloved son Joseph vanishes, presumably torn apart by a wild beast. With this event, Jacob's lifelong fear is realized. He had returned from a twenty-year exile with the hope that he was finally settled in safety (i.e., *shalom*), but now his life has again been turned upside-down in one calamitous moment. Indeed, the loss of Joseph eerily echoes the symbol of calamity, the *akedah,* that we have been following all through Genesis. For it, too, is about the loss (or possible loss) of a beloved child. The parallel is emphasized by the fact that it is Jacob himself who sends Joseph into danger when he tells him to seek out his brothers.

Jacob had thought he was finally settling down in peace. But his peace, his hard-won *wholeness,* is lost, torn away from him. Except for the brief moment of his meeting with Esau, it was never totally achieved anyway, and so he was marked (after he wrestled with the man/angel/G-d) by a limp of imperfection. For Jacob represents each of us in our own unfinished spiritual work.

In fact, Jacob loses his child because his other sons are jealous of Joseph's status as Jacob's favorite. It is Joseph who is the son of the beloved Rachel, and Joseph to whom Jacob gives a special coat. Joseph then makes things much worse by his own self-centeredness, carrying tales of his brothers' bad behavior back to Jacob, and later telling them all that he's had two dreams in which they all bow down to him. In response, his brothers tear off his coat, throw him into a pit, and sell him into slavery. Joseph is not killed, but he is no longer who he has been; in no more than a moment, he has gone from favored son to slave.

This chapter is filled with images of being torn asunder, of being rent by pain or thrown into a pit of blackness. Jacob is torn from his expected state of peace and rends his clothes upon seeing Joseph's bloody clothing. Joseph is torn from his special position in his childhood home to go into exile as a slave, with the ripping of his coat a symbol of the tearing away of his identity. Later, he becomes not only a slave but a prisoner, when Potiphar's wife accuses him of rape, and she too tears off a piece of his coat. The images are concretizations of our inner experience when the rug is pulled out from under us, when our sense of specialness is challenged, when what defines us suddenly vanishes. Whether it be our relationships, our possessions, our achievements, our power, or something else, we use them to label our place in the world. If they suddenly disappear, if they are ripped away, we are no longer comfortable in our skin, no longer feel we are ourselves. Our very identity is gone; likewise, in the phrase used repeatedly in this *parshah,* Joseph "is not."[13]

However, Joseph remains largely present despite his lost identity. He not only continues to hear G-d's prophecies in his dreams, but seeks to take advantage of his position as dream interpreter to get Pharaoh's attention. Yet he is not fully present, for he is still looking backward to his brothers' betrayal and to the false accusations that have imprisoned him now. While his father mourns at home, Joseph is in the pit. Each is still mourning the passing of what was, and grieving for the way their lives "ought to be."

At the symbolic level, the narrative is still about us (as is every character in this *parshah*). We know that there is the possibility of wholeness, of integration of all parts of ourselves when we can accept whatever happens in our lives. But too often, we feel torn apart and lost even to ourselves as we experience the losses, injuries, and disappointments the world brings.

Too often, we feel ourselves lost and in darkness, even cast into a pit of despair from which we see no clear exit.

G-d may be there with us, but we do not feel it as long as we tell ourselves stories about "what should have happened" in the past and "what might yet happen" in the future—or stories that say, "I am stupid," "It's my fault," "It's his/her fault," "The world is out to get me," "Good deeds never go unpunished," and so on.

For Formal Practice: In this chapter, Joseph is thrown into the pit by his brothers and then sold into slavery. Later, he is cast into an Egyptian prison when Potiphar's wife accuses him of attempted rape. Although the text states that G-d is with Joseph (and we know that Joseph will be released in the next chapter), he is still struggling with the theft of his identity.[14]

While acknowledging Joseph's inner conflict, let us dwell on his ability to be aware of the Divine even in times of extreme darkness, trying, also, to open to that Presence deep within us. In this state of remaining fully present in the world, we can somehow accept whatever befalls us, experiencing our pain yet receptive to what comes next. In some writing, this practice is labeled "radical acceptance."

When you are ready, let yourself go to some experience in your life in which you feel frustrated, stuck, or even hopeless.

As you follow your breath, notice whether you keep trying to change the experience by going back to the past to see what you might have done differently. Notice whether you go to worrying about the future and what might yet happen. Let yourself notice other secondary thoughts and judgments about the experience.

Each time you see yourself go to past or future or to other judgments, let the thought go, and return to your breath. Notice how your body feels as you do this.

Just let the experience rest there in the moment, freed from the phantoms of your ideas about it.

If your mind goes back to judgments, return again to the moment as you follow your breath.

When you are ready, begin to offer your whole self to whatever happens. When you notice that you've lost concentration, return to some variant of the phrase "May Thy will be done."

Notice how your body feels. Feel your heart—be aware of it opening and softening.

"May Thy will be done."

In My Own Practice: *Today, I took the Amtrak on a six-hour trip down to Washington D.C., and I took my laptop with me to work on the train. I even paid for business class so that I could more easily keep the computer charged and usable for the whole trip. But I discovered that I'd left the charger home as soon as I began to work.*

As I do this week's contemplative meditation, I take this incident for my focus, and I notice that I am not berating myself as I once would have. It is a fairly trivial example, hardly a life-altering event, but at one time, I would have thrown myself into a pit of black self-recrimination and judgment. And this used to be so much the texture of my daily experience.

But as I meditate, I notice that even my disappointment is muted. As the meditation continues, I turn myself over to the present moment, to possibility, to the G-d whose self-description is, "I Will Be What I Will Be." What else can I do? What should I do? What is calling to me?

May Thy will be done. May Thy will be done.

Possibilities abound. I have my laptop for two hours even without the charger. I have paper and pen. And I can meditate. I can treat the train ride as a retreat—at least part of it. I sit here treasuring the expanse of possibility.

Thy will be done. Thy will be done.

I suddenly feel light. I don't have to work. I am not simply the work I do. I can just be. I feel the rhythm of the train throughout my body. I feel myself softening as the shell of workaholic ego breaks open. My mouth turns up in a smile.

"At the end of two years' time, Pharaoh had a dream…."

—Gen. 41:1[1]

Interpretive Overview: Joseph interprets Pharaoh's dream as meaning that a famine will strike Egypt, and Pharaoh makes him vizier to cope with what is coming. But the life Joseph has put behind him unexpectedly comes alive after he recognizes his brothers when they come before him to beg for food. Although part of him wants to embrace them, another part remains enraged at their betrayal; and so he acts unpredictably, continuing to hide behind his role as vizier as he alternates between hospitality and a variety of accusations, threats, demands, and traps. We can all understand Joseph's feelings, for we have all been betrayed at times by someone we've loved.

Summary of *Parshah:* This is the *parshah* in which Joseph interprets Pharaoh's dreams and is made his second-in-command to prepare for the coming famine, and in which he meets his brothers (but hides his identity from them) when they come to Egypt for food.

At the start of this *parshah,* two years have passed. Joseph is still in prison when Pharaoh has two dreams. In one, seven fat cows come up from the Nile and are eaten by seven scrawny cows that come up next. In the other, seven years of full fat grain are swallowed up by seven years of thin, scorched grain. When none of Pharaoh's magicians can interpret the images, his cupbearer remembers Joseph's skill at reading dreams. He informs Pharaoh, who then orders Joseph to be brought to him from prison.

Telling Pharaoh that his gift comes not through his own power but through G-d's, Joseph then explains the dreams as the Divine's warning that seven years of plenty will be followed by seven years of famine. He tells Pharaoh to find a wise man to begin storing food during the seven good years. Pharaoh responds by saying, "Is there anyone like this to be found, a man with the spirit of G-d in him?"[2] And then he appoints Joseph as the wise man. Given more power than anyone but Pharaoh himself, Joseph (who is now thirty years old) marries an Egyptian women, Asenath.[3] In the course of the next seven years, he has two sons by her. The first he names Mannaseh, meaning "for G-d has *made me forget* all of the troubles I endured in my father's house."[4] He names the second Ephraim, to mean "G-d has *made me fruitful* in the land of my affliction."[5]

When the famine comes, it strikes everywhere. Jacob sends ten of Joseph's brothers to Egypt for food, keeping only Benjamin (Rachel's remaining son), "Lest a deadly mishap befall him."[6] Joseph recognizes his brothers when they arrive, as all of them bow to him, "noses to the ground,"[7] as in the dream he had as a youth.

But they do not recognize him, even as he questions them closely about their father and family, even as he accuses them of being spies. Denying the charge, they insist on their honesty and call themselves Joseph's servants.

They explain that they are twelve brothers, although one is "no more,"[8] and the youngest is at home with their father. But Joseph insists they are spies, puts them in prison for three days, and then tells them to return with Benjamin if they want more food. They exclaim to one another that this is happening because of what they did to Joseph even after he'd pleaded with them, and the eldest brother, Reuben, reminds them that he'd begged them not to sin against "the boy."[9] Although Joseph weeps as he secretly listens to them, he still shackles Simeon (the second oldest) to keep as hostage, and sends the rest on their way with grain.

Without telling them, he also has all the silver that they'd spent for food put back in their bags. They discover the silver while they are on the road, and exclaim that they do not know what G-d has done to them. When they return to Jacob with the full story of what happened, he at first refuses to let them take Benjamin, saying he cannot bear to lose him, too, not after losing Joseph. They argue back and forth without convincing Jacob, but he finally gives in when Judah says that they will all die [of hunger] if they don't bring Benjamin back to Egypt with them.

As soon as they return to Joseph's house with Benjamin, along with gifts and double the silver, they anxiously tell his steward about finding the silver in their bags. He tells them not to worry, for it was done by their god and their father's god, and he frees Simeon. Joseph then greets them, asks again how their father is, sees Benjamin, "his brother, his mother's son,"[10] and has to leave to hide his tears. After this, he sits down to feast with them, giving Benjamin a portion five times greater than he gives any of the others.

Finally, he sends them on their way once again, but this time he hides his special cup in Benjamin's bag. After they leave, his men chase them and accuse them of theft. Proclaiming innocence, the brothers say that if the cup is found anywhere, the person who has it should die. And then Benjamin is discovered to have it.

They all come back to Joseph, falling to the ground, and Judah says, "By what shall we justify ourselves? G-d has found your servants' crime."[11] Joseph responds by saying he will keep Benjamin as a servant, and he tells the rest of the brothers to go back to Jacob in peace.

***Parshah* Interpretation:** In general, Joseph operates at a high spiritual level, open to the Divine call, at least in part because he is centered in each moment, present to the *is*-ness of now instead of losing himself in memories of the past or fantasies of the future. Like Joseph, we are asked to remember that G-d's name is simply I Am That I Am.

Joseph even names his children in terms of letting go of his past life to take on his new one. But when his brothers come to him to beg for food, it does seem as if he has perhaps buried his past instead of integrating it into his new identity. For Joseph subjects them to his unpredictable, even irrational, behavior much as he was subjected to the whims of those whose slave he was (and even now his status depends entirely on pleasing Pharaoh). As he secretly watches the reactions of his brothers, he also sets up for them experiences akin to his: of having unexpected catastrophe happen, of having fortune abruptly reverse itself, of seeming to be saved only to be pulled down again. Even more important, he challenges their very identity by insisting that they are not what they claim to be, but are spies instead.

He was only seventeen when they sold him, and now he is approaching forty—more than half of his years have been spent in Egypt. Yet he has not forgiven them for wrenching him from the life he had. Despite his efforts to let go of the past, he reacts to his brothers not so much as the powerful man that he has become, but as the victimized boy they sold into slavery and, presumably, oblivion. Although traditional commentators have written that he is merely testing his brothers to see if they have changed,[12] the text seems to plainly indicate his deep ambivalence toward them, as he feels both the desire for revenge and the yearning for reconciliation. For beneath his anger is hurt and the desire to love and be loved, the universal human craving to restore his sense of connection and wholeness, to repair the fabric of his life. And so he listens in on their private conversations, hoping to hear that they have changed, that they can be trusted now with his yearning. As he hears them proclaiming their guilt for what they did to him, his heart begins to soften, but he is not yet ready to let down his guard and reveal himself.

For Formal Practice: Even when we are moving forward on our spiritual path, old hurts often remain. Because these hurts are not part of our current life, we may not think of them often. But they are still part of who we have been, and of who we are now, simply awaiting the right circumstance to come back alive.

When you are ready, let yourself go to an experience in which someone you cared about seemed to betray you. Choose an experience that is still painful when you recall it.

Let yourself sit with your feelings, just noticing what they are.

If you can, see the other person in the matrix of his or her own life, with all its limitations. If you can, glimpse your own limitations in the relationship the two of you had. Just notice what happens.

In My Own Practice: *I go immediately to an experience that occurred more than thirty years ago with a cousin-by-marriage, who had become a close friend. She and I spoke on the phone two or three times a week, our families visited often, and our children grew up together. Then, at her daughter's* bat mitzvah, *there was a ceremony, a common one at the time, in which the adults important to her child were asked to come up to light a candle. Members of her family were called up. Friends were called up. But I was not.*

I was stunned, humiliated, betrayed. When I asked her later, she had no explanation. And I've never been able to ask again, because she was killed in a car crash a little while afterward.

When I go back to the memory now, I feel a hard knot in my chest. I sit with it, forcing myself to sink into it. Immediately, I feel enraged. I see myself at the ceremony, shooting her, shooting her husband. I feel so good killing them that I play the scene several times.

After this, I feel relief, a letting go of tension. The knot has dissolved, as if a pus-filled wound has been lanced. I am surprised by the degree of the rage. Then I realize that I feel as Joseph did, enraged at betrayal by someone I love, someone I trusted. No wonder he tormented his brothers.

As I sit, I also feel the deep question: "If you did this to me, then who are you really? And who am I if I am not your beloved friend?" For the ground shifted with her betrayal, my very sense of myself went into question. That is what makes the betrayal so profound.

I go back again, my anger less intense now, as I understand why I feel so bereft. But I also feel another deep truth: I had buried the experience, moving on as if I had put it behind me. But it had not really gone away. Like Joseph with his brothers, I cannot trust her again. I cannot open my heart to her.

A Note: When I look at this meditation the next day, I realize that I have finally let go my anger. I still would not trust her with my heart, but having allowed myself to sit with the memory of her betrayal has somehow reframed the experience. Now, it no longer feels like a personal attack, but more like the lion devouring the zebra. It is in our nature to do hurtful things to one another at times, consciously or through inattention. That's just the way it is.

Genesis/*B'reishit*, 11, "And He Went Over"/*Vayigash* (Gen. 44:18–47:27)

"And Judah went over to him and said, 'Please, my lord, let your servant speak something in my lord's ears, and let your anger not flare at your servant, because you're like Pharaoh himself.' "

—Gen. 44:18

Interpretive Overview: In this climactic *parshah,* Judah pleads with Joseph, begging him to spare Jacob further grief by not taking Benjamin from him. Judah's extraordinary compassion and empathy for his father hints at the central role compassion will take in later books of the Torah, as it causes Joseph's heart to break open so that he finally reveals himself and forgives his brothers. In this scene, Joseph also says that that his brothers are without blame, because G-d was behind their selling him to Egypt, in order for them to be saved from famine. Presenting a mystical view in this speech, Joseph brings to the fore questions about determinism and free will that continue to this day.

Summary of *Parshah:* The *parshah* begins with a long plea by Judah to Joseph, in which Judah poignantly insists that Jacob will die if he loses Benjamin, because he has already lost Joseph, the other son he had with Rachel. Insisting that he can't go back to Jacob without him, Judah begs that Joseph keep him as servant instead of Benjamin. Joseph can no longer restrain himself, and asks everyone except his brothers to leave. Weeping uncontrollably, he reveals himself, once again asking his brothers if Jacob is really alive. They are terrified of him, but he assures them that he has no anger, because it has all been part of the Divine's plan to preserve life despite the famine. He tells them to hurry back to tell Jacob that G-d has preserved him and that they must now settle near Joseph in the land of Goshen, where he will provide for them. Weeping, he embraces Benjamin and then all of his brothers.

When Pharaoh hears what has happened, he tells Joseph to tell his whole extended family to come to Egypt, where they will be given the best Egypt can offer. Joseph sends his brothers back to Canaan with many provisions, and they reach Jacob and tell him Joseph is alive and rules all of Egypt.[1] But Jacob does not believe them until he sees all the wagons that Joseph has sent. With this belief, Jacob's "spirit came alive,"[2] and he leaves for Egypt.

Under the name of Israel,[3] Jacob now comes to Beer-sheba and offers sacrifices to "the G-d of his father, Isaac."[4] In a night vision in the same passage, G-d calls to him, and he answers, "I'm here."[5] YHVH tells him, yet again, to be unafraid, that he will make him into a big nation in Egypt and will also bring him back up (to Canaan).

And so all of Jacob's children and wives and grandsons and granddaughters leave with all of their property and households. All of their names are then recorded in the text, with a total of seventy people[6] from Jacob's clan going to Egypt.

Upon their arrival, Jacob sends Judah ahead to tell Joseph he is coming. Joseph then goes out to meet his father, after which they tearfully embrace and Jacob (here again called Israel) says that now he can die. After this, Joseph presents five of his brothers to Pharaoh, who, in turn, gives the family the best land in Egypt, appointing the most able of them to be in charge of Pharaoh's livestock.[7] Then Joseph brings Jacob to Pharaoh, and Jacob blesses Pharaoh, who asks his age. Jacob answers that he is one hundred and thirty years old, and says that his days have been "few and bad,"[8] and fewer than Abraham's and Isaac's. Then he blesses Pharaoh again.

As the famine continues, Joseph collects for Pharaoh all of the silver in Canaan and Egypt, for people sell their silver to buy the grain that Joseph has stored. By the second year, the people have sold all of their livestock as well, and then they sell their land and are moved off into the cities. Finally, they sell themselves, to be sent back to work the land and to give one-fifth of their earnings to Pharaoh forever. And for all of this, the people are grateful to Joseph, because now they will live.

The *parshah* ends with the comment that Joseph's family stays on in Egypt, holding onto their property, and that they prosper and multiply.

Parshah Interpretation: Judah's plea for Benjamin is unparalleled in its expression of empathy for Jacob's grief, particularly in light of Judah's clarity about his own inferior status with his father. Fully aware that Jacob truly loves only his two sons by Rachel, Joseph and Benjamin, Judah puts himself aside to beg for his father's well-being and wholeness. Offering himself instead of Benjamin, he also appears (by implication) to take full responsibility for the sin of casting Joseph into the pit, just as he took public responsibility for his daughter-in-law's pregnancy earlier.[9]

Judah has an extraordinary capacity to accept the way things are. Acknowledging now the reality of Jacob's limitations (just he acknowledged his pledge to his daughter-in-law), understanding that Jacob is simply not capable of loving him more, he can let go of how Jacob "ought to be," and feel compassion for Jacob as he is. In reading his speech, we may also remember that Judah has lost two sons himself; presumably, he knows just what the loss of a child means. But he makes no reference to his own loss; indeed, he transcends all thought of himself in his compassion for his father.

Until now, Joseph has spoken coolly, restricting the arena to issues of justice before these supposed spies and thieves, for he has been unable to open his heart to his brothers. In part, he cannot allow himself to be vulnerable, as long as he fears to be met yet again with their hatred of him. But there is even more, for his own heart has become encrusted in the process of his coping with the betrayals he has experienced.

He has moved on as best as he could, attempting to put what happened behind him. As we saw in the last *parshah,* he even named his sons for that process of letting go of the past. Yet, he has not so much let go of the past as he has walled it off, barricading himself away from the pain. He toys cruelly with his brothers, not merely to discover who they have become, but also because his pain is still alive behind the barricade. Joseph is finally able to open his heart, because Judah shows that he can be trusted as he transcends his own needs in his compassion for Jacob.

In a prefiguring of what is to be the central theme of Torah teaching, both Joseph and Judah, in that moment, are released from the bondage of self-absorption and egoistic concerns, from the insistence that the world be the way they want it to be. They are then able to manifest G-d's compassion in the world by becoming, quite literally, their brothers' keepers—the overt theme of the remaining four books of the Torah.

The *parshah* also brings to center stage the question of free will and destiny, which the last *parshah* hinted at, as Joseph insists that his brothers' actions are to be forgiven because they served the Divine plan.[10] To Joseph, all of his suffering, all his experience of loss and pain, are now understood to be in the service of preserving life. Indeed, all of Joseph's suffering has taken place so that he can protect his family—and by implication, be the keeper or guardian of all humanity.

The story of Joseph's manipulation of his unwitting brothers, and of the twists and turns of Joseph's own life, mirror the larger truths of all of our lives. We are always imbedded in an immeasurably complex world system that inevitably restricts our possibilities and shapes the choices we have. We may choose to exert power as if we were Pharaoh, as Joseph did with his brothers, or we may choose to act with compassion, as did Judah. But our lives take place in a much larger play that we do not control.

Torah's language goes further, making the assumption that all has been pre-ordained by the Divine Presence.

The truth of this is not, of course, provable; but it is not uncommon to feel ourselves embedded in a pattern that has great meaning beyond our comprehension, inarticulately glimpsed and essentially mysterious, even if we do not label it G-d's plan. And certainly, many of us, as we look back on our lives, find value even in our worst experiences, seeing that they have led us to good places we never would have found otherwise. Such reframing doesn't make the bad experiences good, but it does give them welcome significance.

In fact, Torah goes yet further, alluding to the mystical experience that occurs when the heart opens to the reality of the I Am That I Am, to the holiness of what is in front of us all the time. In these experiences of deep acceptance, there is the sense not only of being embedded in an infinite space-time tapestry, but of that tapestry being, in some utterly indescribable way, perfect. All is divine, and all that has happened (including all suffering) is then exactly as it should be. (This statement, however, is inexplicable to those who haven't experienced it. Nor can it be understood by the rational mind, even for those who have had the experience.)

For Formal Practice: When you are ready, begin by visualizing the chain of earlier generations that has led up to you: all of the choices of partners that led to your mother and father, to their mothers and fathers, going back as far as you can. Any change anywhere, no matter how far back, would have led to someone with a different makeup—someone other than you.

See your own existence, then, as a tiny bit of weaving in an endless tapestry in time and space. Let yourself begin to feel the immensity of the tapestry of which you are a part.

Now let yourself hear the words "Holy, holy, holy," or in Hebrew, *Kadosh, kadosh, kadosh.* All the world is filled with Divine glory. Just notice whether you sense anything purposeful to the tapestry.

In My Own Practice: *In imagery that is as much a feeling as a visual perception, I see the generations extending back in time, in a kind of thick* *ribbon. As I continue to look, these generations go back further, beyond the human, beyond the primate, beyond anything I can see, to the very beginning of life, to the very beginning of the universe, beyond the capacity of any image, but in some way felt.*

When I turn, then, to this particular moment of time, the pattern flattens out in some way, as if on a different axis; but it, too, extends through an infinite space. Anything I choose to focus on, whether my jacket or the tea in my cup or the chair on which I sit, each is the result of a set of choice points that extend back through all of history.

The whole matrix is lit up with choice points, and each choice point opens to another glittering avenue of possibility. As I turn in my mind to one avenue, the others disappear in a shower of star-like sparkles. But there are always more choice points. I can't believe, in this moment, that the future is ordained. But I do know that we follow the path of the Divine Presence when we act with love and compassion. The tapestry shimmers with light.

Kadosh, kadosh, kadosh. *Holy, holy, holy.*

Genesis/*B'reishit*, 12, "And He Lived"/*Va-y'chi* (Gen. 47:28–50:26)

"And Jacob lived in the land of Egypt seventeen years."

—Gen. 47:28

Interpretive Overview: The story of the patriarchs closes in this last section of Genesis. Before dying, Jacob adopts Joseph's sons Mannaseh and Ephraim, and blesses them and his twelve sons. Jacob is fully alive in these scenes, finally without fear, aware that G-d has been with him from the moment of his birth. At the very end of the *parshah,* Genesis closes with Joseph's death, leaving all his extended family thriving in Egypt. Although it is now the site of their prosperity, the stage is set for what will follow: the literal and metaphoric Egyptian slavery of the Israelites, and their exodus toward freedom under Moses.

Summary of *Parshah:* Jacob has reached the age of one hundred forty-seven. As he gets ready to die, he asks Joseph not to bury him in Egypt but in the burial place of his fathers. Joseph agrees and later brings his sons for blessing. Rousing himself to sit up in bed, Jacob tells Joseph that G-d appeared to him long before to promise the land of Canaan to his descendants for eternity. And so Jacob wants to adopt Joseph's sons, who were born in Egypt, so that they too will be directly in line for the inheritance, just like, for example, Reuben and Simeon. Then Jacob refers to his having buried Rachel on the road as they traveled from Beth-El.

When Joseph presents his two sons for their blessing, Jacob kisses them, places his hand on their heads, and blesses them. Joseph notices that he has placed his right hand on Ephraim's head, although he is the younger one; he tries to correct Jacob, but Jacob says it is intentional, that Ephraim will be the greater, even though he is the second-born. (Another example of the pattern we've seen throughout Genesis.) Then Jacob says he is dying, calls to all his sons, and gives each one of the twelve a different blessing (although these blessings may not all strike the reader as blessings).[1] Among the most important are the following:

- The demotion of Reuben from the position of firstborn, because of his defiling Jacob's bed by having sex with Jacob's concubine Bilhah;

- The condemnation of Simeon and Levi as violent (referring to the massacre they committed at Shechem after their sister was taken), to be scattered among the other tribes.[2]

- The giving of praise and domination to Judah, the fourth-born, (the son whom later books of the Bible reveal to be the ancestor of King David through his child by Tamar).

After bestowing his blessings, Jacob asks again to be buried in the cave at Machpelah with his ancestors and his first wife Leah, and he dies. He is embalmed and his death is mourned throughout Egypt (presumably because he is Joseph's father) for seventy days, after which Joseph gets permission from Pharaoh to go to Canaan to bury him. He leaves with his whole family (excepting infants), and with the elders of Egypt and the servants of Pharaoh, crosses the Jordan into Canaan, and buries Jacob in the cave; then they hold a seven-day funeral.

When they get back to Egypt, the brothers are afraid Joseph will kill them now that their father is dead. They inform Joseph that Jacob had commanded them to tell him that he must not retaliate for the sin they committed against him,[3] and they fall down in front of him, offering themselves as slaves. Joseph only weeps. Telling them not to be afraid, he says that even though they did something bad, it was G-d's will to have it happen so that everyone would be kept alive. He then promises to protect them.

Joseph lives to be one hundred ten. As he is dying, he tells his brothers that G-d will remember them and bring them back to the land they have been promised. After asking them to bring his bones with them when they leave Egypt, he dies. They embalm him and set the body in a coffin in Egypt, from where his bones will ultimately be taken back during the Exodus.

***Parshah* Interpretation:** In this week's chapter, Jacob is dying but fully alive spiritually. As he lies on his deathbed, Joseph comes with his two sons, Manasseh and Ephraim, and the text says "and he [Jacob] blessed Joseph and said, 'The G-d before whom my fathers, Abraham and Isaac, walked, who shepherded me from my start to this day, the angel who redeemed me from all bad, may He bless the boys.' "[4]

So Jacob has finally gotten past the terror of the *akedah,* able to live with the uncertainties of life; and yet he feels that somehow he has been watched over and protected, despite all appearances. Jacob, our stand-in in Genesis, has at last reached the state of mind that Joseph possesses.

In Torah language, G-d is Jacob's protector, but we know that Jacob's life has not been easy or free of disaster. Using different language, we can say that Jacob has become aware that G-d is ever present, and in that awareness can live life with an open heart, somehow transcending the fear and cravings of his small self to be immersed in the experience of the large I Am That I Am as it creates the world, second by second, in all its complex causal chains.

For Formal Practice: At the end of his life, Jacob experiences G-d as shepherding him from birth. Let us try to experience the Divine Presence in this way.

When you are ready, begin by visualizing the letters of the unnamable name of the Divine. (The Hebrew letters *yud-heh-vuv-heh* of this standard Jewish meditation are found in Appendix B; I owe thanks to Nan Gefen for introducing this meditation to me.[5]) Or, if that feels uncomfortable, use some other word that is relatively free of anthropomorphism, such as Divine Presence.)

See yourself at the moment of birth and place the letters, in Hebrew or English, or the word you are using, upon yourself. Place the same letters or word also in the physical space around you at birth and on any other people who may be present. Now, extend that imagery to other moments in your life, including very difficult or painful moments, placing the letters or word upon yourself, into the surrounding physical space, and upon other people as you see them in your mind in these moments.

Place them wherever you can in the image in order to have the presence hovering around you and with you. As you keep following your breath, do the same, eventually, for this moment, here today. Place the Divine Presence with you, hovering in the chairs, along the wall, in whomever else may be in the room, in plants outside, in the light coming in the windows, in the very air.

The intention of this meditation at the end of Genesis is to feel as Jacob does: that the Divine has always been present, shepherding you from birth through this moment, guarding you despite whatever may seem to be happening.

In My Own Practice: *I have had trouble doing this meditation. Nothing has happened when I've gone through the imagery. Until today. I am on a weeklong silent retreat, and today is different.*

As soon as I begin, I see that it is obvious that G-d has been with me since birth. Because all is YHVH. There is nothing but G-d. Everything and everyone is G-d. The whole process by which one event follows another is all G-d unfolding.

There is much more to G-d than this physical realm, but in this realm there is nothing outside of G-d. Nothing external to G-d exists.

But why is this comforting?

Because all is holy. All is holy because all is Divine. There is only G-d's glory. All of the universe shines with G-d because it is G-d. Holy, holy, holy.

If I'd been able to see this as a child, the people who frightened me would have been less frightening, because, in some way that I can't articulate, my physical body is an illusion. Or, rather, it is only a temporary form that G-d takes in this time and place.

Somehow, the "I" that I normally experience falls away in this moment. Behind that apparent "I" is the reality of G-d. I am G-d.

In this moment of awareness, there is only G-d viewing G-d.

Nothing that befalls the physical self ultimately matters, for it is only a temporary shelter through which the mysterious Divine moves.

As I write these words after the meditation practice, I realize that they go far beyond where Torah seems to go. But this is my experience.

Interpretive Summation of Genesis/*B'reishit*

Genesis begins with a metaphor of humans as made of both the dust of the earth and of the Divine Essence. Adam and Eve then leave the state of undifferentiated union with the Divine—in which everything is good—when they eat of the Tree of Knowledge. They had already displayed free will when they disobeyed G-d's command to not eat of the tree. But it is with this action that they become self-aware and differentiated from G-d, and now they are ejected from the blissful perfection of the Edenic Garden to live in a lower realm, in the real physical world of imperfection and incompleteness that necessarily distinguishes between Good and Bad (which is the other name of the Tree of Knowledge).

In the Cain and Abel story that follows the expulsion from Eden, Genesis then asks the question of how we are to use our free will to live as our brother's keeper in this imperfect world, when we are clothed in vulnerable physical bodies that have needs and desires, and that require self-protection.

In its early chapters, Genesis can be read as elaborating on our dilemma by using the near sacrifice of Isaac by his father Abraham, the *akedah,* as a metaphor for the experience of the uncontrollability of life. (It also points to the spiritual path in which we accept the impermanence of anything we possess, including our very lives.) For we often seem to have little or no power over what happens to us.

Indeed, we may experience pain and loss even when we try as hard as we can to avoid them, and we may behave badly as we try to protect ourselves. As the tales of the generations after Abraham and Sarah unfold, Genesis provides an extraordinarily frank narrative about the ease with which we hurt and deceive others as we try to control our destinies in a world that lacks the limitless abundance and innocent safety of Eden.

The narrative implies that our self-protective misbehavior often creates the very outcomes we want to avoid. Sometimes, the outcomes appear like directives from G-d, as in the Flood, or when the notoriously wicked people of Sodom and Gomorrah are destroyed. Sometimes the results are more subtle: Jacob, for example, reaps the results of his open preference for Joseph when his other sons sell Joseph into slavery and lead Jacob to believe he is dead for so many years. But it is also true that life is sometimes simply unpredictable.

And so the *akedah* raises another question that we all ask as we experience the vicissitudes of life: why do bad things happen to good people?

The simple answer is to believe that there are always causes for what happens and that there is some Divine balance sheet, so that seemingly good people must have committed sins that are unknown to us, but for which they are being punished. And yet Isaac appears blameless as his father ties him up for sacrifice; Esau, in the plain text, undeserving of being tricked out of his birthright; and Joseph, undeserving of the depth of his brothers' hatred or the slavery into which they sell him.

Neither do wicked acts seem to necessarily result in punishment. As the narrative progresses, Abraham is rewarded even though he banishes Ishmael; Sarah, even though she mistreats Hagar; Jacob, despite his stealing Esau's birthright; Joseph's brothers, despite them selling him into slavery; and so on. So we are each supposed to be our brother's keeper in the face of our vulnerability—and with the full knowledge that the good may suffer and the wicked thrive.

Now, we are at the end of Genesis, and, as well, finally at the end of the story of Jacob. We have been following his story, because Jacob—known also as Israel—is our namesake, personifying each of us. He sins when he betrays his brother Esau, just as we sin against our fellow human beings. He loves passionately both his wife Rachael and, later, his children by her (Joseph and Benjamin), with the intensity with which we feel love. He is betrayed by Laban into marrying Leah, just as we may have our trust in someone else betrayed. He also feels tremendous grief at the loss of his son Joseph, just as we grieve our losses, and so on.

As we do, Jacob also experiences some outcomes as explicable—as, more or less, straightforward results of earlier actions. This final chapter of Genesis emphasizes this aspect of life in the deathbed blessings he gives his sons, for the outcomes that he describes relate clearly (in at least several cases) to their prior behavior. Thus, Judah, who has behaved so well for most of the narrative, is rewarded, while others lose out. (And Jacob himself has had an unhappy life, with the implication being that his own betrayal of his brother Esau somehow contaminates all of his relationships down the road.) Actions do indeed have consequences.

But the text is grappling with the fact that good actions are not *necessarily* rewarded, nor are bad ones punished. Some of us, of course, may believe that the balance is corrected in an afterlife, when the good go to Heaven and the bad, perhaps, to Hell or some lesser place. Or, that suffering in this life is part of a chain of events that extends through many other lifetimes, in some kind of karmic dance in which the soul has many chances to grow and learn from different kinds of experiences. This is not only a Buddhist or Hindu belief, but is found in certain strands of Judaism that grow out of Kabbalah. But this is not quite where Genesis seems to be going.

Instead, the text specifically states that Joseph's experience of being sold into slavery by his brothers is intrinsic to a hidden Divine plan whose goal is our ultimate good. In part, the text also can be interpreted neutrally, to say that we are imbedded in chains of circumstance, with only limited freedom. Moreover, like Joseph, we can find meaning as we look backward, seeing ways in which we may treasure the shape of our lives, even if that shape grew out of suffering that we would rather not have had.

The next book, Exodus, begins with the enslavement in Egypt of the descendants of Joseph and his brothers. Its focus is their liberation from slavery in order to serve the Divine instead of serving Pharaoh, and to become, each of them, a *dwelling place* for G-d. At the deeper level, Torah believes that each of us can become such a dwelling place right now. The spiritual and meditative goal is to become totally immersed in the Divine, to be a conduit through which G-d manifests. Joseph is so remarkable because he seems to be such a conduit, feeling G-d's presence and trusting in the safety of G-d almost all the time, no matter how bad things seem. But the rest of us are more like Jacob. We never can see the infinitely complex tangle of events that creates what happens down the road; neither can we generally glimpse ourselves as safely imbedded in the Divine as we experience bad times. Few of us feel safe in G-d's protection when the *akedah,* or some other experience of loss and suffering, strikes. But it is possible.

The goal is to come full circle, back to the Edenic state, to see that the sense of separateness from G-d is illusory, even though we are in physical bodies. For the creation metaphor states that we are made, as well, of the Divine essence—inevitably, therefore, safe. In the language of Exodus, the idea is made explicit that we can find G-d deep within us, at our core, so that separation must be illusory. In later Jewish writing, including Kabbalah, the whole physical world, including us, is understood as a manifestation of G-d in this plane of reality. There is, then, nothing but G-d. When we know these truths, we are released from enslavement to our cravings, our fears, and our efforts at controlling the future, freely turning ourselves over to G-d's service instead, and, indeed, each of us becoming our brother's keeper.

2

General Framework of Exodus/*Sh'mot*

Exodus (in Hebrew, the book is called *Sh'mot,* meaning "Names")[1] is the second book of the Torah. In this book, the narrative moves from the first creation to a second beginning, further exploring the questions raised in Genesis about human nature and our relationship to the Divine.

At the literal, or *p'shat* level, G-d in Exodus starts afresh with humans by freeing the Israelites from slavery in the land of Egypt, so that they will enter into covenant with the Divine to be a holy people. And in the new beginning chronicled in Exodus, the freed slaves choose to accept this covenant when it is offered at Mount Sinai, pledging to follow G-d's will. The book then starts to detail the specific terms of their commitment as it permeates all the activities of daily life, with laws including the Ten Commandments as well as many more detailed ritual and ethical rules. Exodus also narrates how hard it is for the Israelites to maintain their pledge, how frightened they are of this new path, and how frequently they rebel—even, at times, saying they want to go back to Egypt.

We tend to forget that the freeing of the slaves from Egypt, the offer of covenant by G-d, and the Israelites' acceptance of that covenant is found in the spiritual sourcebooks of both Judaism and Christianity. While the religions diverge in later history over the acceptance of Jesus Christ as the messiah, Christianity came out of Judaism, and the inclusion of Exodus in both religious traditions reflects their shared history. Whether you consider yourself Jew or Christian, the tradition says that your spiritual ancestors were freed from slavery in Egypt to serve G-d.

Moreover, when we remember that the word *Israel* means "G-d wrestler," we can apply it to each of us who are exploring spiritual pathways, whether as an adherent of any of the world's formal religions or not. For when we move beyond specificity to the mystical level—as we will—the path, at its core, looks very much the same, no matter our starting point.

But if we begin with the literal, narrowest reading of Exodus, it is the story of the Israelites' redemption from slavery in Egypt to become the community of the children of Israel. If we focus on this aspect more than on the Israelites' covenant with the Divine, the story is a more-or-less straightforward history (albeit with miracles), documenting the creation of a particular people. Although we have no clear archeological evidence of its historical truth,[2] it is the central story of Judaism, retold each year at the feast of Passover, which commemorates that escape from Egypt. (In recent years, some American Christians have also begun to celebrate Passover.)

In the ancient tradition of Torah interpretation, Exodus can certainly be read more broadly as a narrative celebrating human freedom and opposing oppression for all people, everywhere. Thus, Dr. Martin Luther King Jr. took Exodus as his inspiration as he led the Civil Rights movement of the 1960's in the American South.

Exodus can also be interpreted as a story about the development of ethics, with the focus on the Israelites accepting the Ten Commandments as well as other, more specific, rules for behaving properly in the world. In this reading, the moral imperatives of Exodus/*Sh'mot* flow out of the chronicles of Genesis/*B'reishit,* which show humans behaving badly all too often. We may even choose to believe that many of the stories of Genesis are deliberately intended to be demonstrations of human failure in the absence of specific rules. In this reading, G-d in Exodus presents the Ten Commandments and other laws of behavior precisely because humans have clearly proven that they desperately need regulations.

At a more mystical level of Torah interpretation, Exodus is the second creation story. The first creation was about the physical world, both human and nonhuman, while the second creation focuses on the moral sphere. At this level of understanding, G-d is a moral force as well as the creator of the physical world, for G-d's very essence contains compassion, justice, and mercy. As this understanding is presented in Exodus, creation begins anew with the Israelites' acceptance of a moral covenant with G-d. In this second creation, humans truly become partners with the Divine to create a world of compassion and justice. Although they cannot maintain their commitment consistently, the possibility of partnership is now always present in their consciousness. Holiness has become a dimension of existence, shimmering in the Israelites' awareness.

Furthermore, Exodus can be read as a guidebook for each of us individually, for our psychological healing and spiritual enlightenment. In the ancient tradition of Torah interpretation, known as Oral Torah, Egypt is not a physical place at all—and it should never be confused with a physical place. Thus, in Hebrew, Egypt is called *Mitzrayim,* meaning "the place of constriction, the narrow straits." In psychological interpretations of Torah for more than two millennia, then, *Mitzrayim* refers to a state in which our spirit is constricted, in which our narrowness of vision leads us to be trapped in our habitual fears and desires. Feeling neither safe nor satisfied, we hide unhappily behind defensive walls, unable to open our hearts to love, unable to be channels for Divine compassion, and unable to perceive that G-d is always with us.

Moreover, the Torah, both oral and written, presents G-d as a force/presence/process that is not simply external to us. In Exodus/*Sh'mot,* G-d is portrayed primarily as transcendent, but G-d is also portrayed as immanent within us, found at our inmost core when we peel aside the layers of egoistic self-protectiveness. Indeed, in much of the traditional (including Kabbalist) understanding of Torah, the entire physical world, including us, is but a manifestation of G-d. In such mystical knowledge, there is nothing else but G-d.

The problem is that we lose awareness of this most of the time; we live our lives in a more limited state of consciousness. In our usual state, we live within the restrictive confines of ego and self-concern, as if physical reality and self-preservation is all there is.

In the tradition of Oral Torah, the whole story of Exodus is a metaphor, in which Egypt represents the psychological state of constriction. In this state of limited awareness, Pharaoh represents the rigidity and arrogance of my ego as I try to protect myself in a dangerous world in which I feel alone—in which my frightened ego says that I'd better take care of myself without giving much regard to anyone else (except, possibly, my family and closest friends). Exodus then presents us with a covenant in which we are asked to emulate G-d's qualities of love and compassion toward everyone—even enemies—even when we feel alone and unprotected, even when we are in the narrow state of consciousness known as *Mitzrayim.*

In the simple *p'shat* narrative, the children of Israel experience G-d presenting the Ten Commandments at Mount Sinai, and they vow to obey. The personal reading of Exodus says that it is we who are making this vow, each of us individually.

Like the Israelites, we then struggle to keep our commitment. While the literal text traces the external events of Exodus, a psychological reading traces our internal wrestling with the ego's constriction.

Furthermore, the Torah says that our emulation of G-d's qualities of love and compassion, both when it is easy and when it is not, progressively opens us to the awareness of the Divine Presence in each moment, pervading all existence, including ourselves. And we will feel safe in this awareness, regardless of what happens in the world. We will become holy, G-d says, and one meaning of the Hebrew word for holy (i.e., *kadosh*) includes "separate," for we will become separated from the world of egoist fearfulness and leave fear behind, even in the face of disaster and death.

Thus, the statement in Genesis that we are made in G-d's image refers not to the physical body but to actions. Made as he is in the image of G-d, Cain should not murder his brother. Indeed, the question he asks—"Am I my brother's keeper?"[3]—is supposed to be answered by each of us with a resounding yes.

In the metaphor of Genesis, we are made in the Divine image in terms of our capacity for expressing G-d's qualities of love and compassion in our own choices. This is the final message of Exodus.

Exodus/*Sh'mot* Week by Week

Exodus/*Sh'mot,* 1, "Names"/*Sh'mot*
(Exod. 1:1–6:1)

"And these are the names of the children of Israel who came to Egypt.... And Joseph and all of his brothers and all of that generation died."

—Exod. 1:1, 6

Interpretive Overview: At the literal level, Exodus begins with the Israelites enslaved in Egypt, so spiritually lost that they do not even remember their connection to G-d. But G-d in Torah always seeks a relationship with us. So when they cry out in despair at their burdens, G-d responds, calling out to Moses at the burning bush. The story of our spiritual Exodus begins similarly with our basic lack of consciousness, our not even knowing that we are missing the awareness of G-d. But we are asked by G-d to break out of the rigidity of the ego with *seeing,* by opening to the Divine Presence as Moses does.

Summary of *Parshah:* This first chapter of Exodus begins by naming the sons of Jacob who came down to Egypt. Then the text says that their descendants "were fruitful and swarmed and multiplied and grew very vast, and the land was filled with them."[1] But now a new Pharaoh, "who knew not Joseph,"[2] comes to power, and he is afraid that the Israelites will, with their great numbers, side with an Egyptian enemy in war.

Although he makes their labor more oppressive, they continue to multiply anyway, and Pharaoh goes on to decree that all male babies be killed at birth. When Moses is born, his mother hides him for three months and then puts him in a cradle on the Nile. Pharaoh's daughter finds him and takes him home, hiring Moses' mother as nurse at his sister's recommendation, without knowing who either mother or sister are.

Moses grows older, until "he went out to his brothers [the Hebrew slaves] and saw their burdens, and he saw an Egyptian man striking a Hebrew man, one of his brothers."[3] Moses looks around, sees no one watching, kills the Egyptian, and hides his body in the sand. The next day, when he tries to stop a fight between two Hebrew slaves, one angrily asks if Moses thinks he's in charge of everyone, and if he will kill him "the way you killed the Egyptian?"[4]

Moses then flees from Egypt to avoid Pharaoh's death sentence for the murder. Later, he rescues the seven daughters of the Midian priest, Jethro, as a band of shepherds keep them from watering their flock at a well. He stays with the priest, marries his daughter Zipporah, and has a son, Gershom.

After a long time, a new Pharaoh appears, the Israelites cry out from their bondage, and G-d hears and remembers the covenant made with Abraham and his descendants. As Moses is herding his father-in-law's flock in the far desert, by Mount Horeb (otherwise known as Mount Sinai), he sees a burning bush and approaches it, whereupon the Divine Presence calls out to him. Moses answers, G-d reveals the intention to rescue the Israelites, with Moses to act as G-d's agent; and Moses keeps arguing that the task is beyond his ability. G-d insists, demonstrates three miracles for Moses to show Pharaoh, predicts Pharaoh's resistance to the miracles, and at last agrees to let Aaron (Moses' brother, who has not appeared in the narrative before this time) be Moses' spokesman. In the course of their conversation, G-d tells Moses the true name of the Divine, which translates as "I Will Be Who I Will Be" or "I Am that I Am" or even "I Am That Endures" or "The One Who Brings Things Into Being." The English transliteration of the Hebrew name is given as YHVH.[5]

At the end of the chapter, Aaron and Moses speak to the elders of Israel, and go from them to Pharaoh, who responds by working the Israelites still harder. The Israelites complain to Moses for making things worse, Moses complains to G-d, and G-d tells him that Pharaoh will lose this contest.

***Parshah* Interpretation:** The Hebrew name of this first *parshah* (and thus of the whole book of Exodus) is *Sh'mot,* which means "Names," but the names referred to are those of the sons of Jacob who come down to Egypt. For the Israelites now are merely nameless slaves. They are fertile, for they "swarmed and multiplied and grew very vast and the land was filled with them,"[6]—words that return us to the creation story of Genesis. But the very word *swarmed* (in Hebrew, the verb is *sharats*) refers in Genesis to the swarming of creeping things, like insects. By implication, they are fertile like swarming animals, but not quite human in their enslavement. Certainly, they do not even know to call out to G-d at the start of this *parshah*. So the Israelite slaves can be seen as representing a kind of unconscious state, in which there is not even the awareness of something missing, not even an awareness of the absence of connection to the Divine Presence.[7]

And in their absence of awareness, G-d, too, seems absent. But when they cry out in the agony of their slavery, "their cry for help from the bondage rose up to G-d,"[8] and G-d "heard their moaning,"[9] and responded by calling out to Moses at the burning bush. So the exodus from slavery—from unconsciousness and lack of awareness of the Divine Presence—begins for each of us with a cry from the heart.

And the *parshah* goes further. Soon after Moses is born, his mother places him in a basket in the reeds by the bank of the Nile. There, Pharaoh's daughter "saw"[10] the basket; and she takes Moses from it and brings him to the palace, where he grows up. At some later time, he "saw"[11] the burdens of the Israelites and "saw"[12] an Egyptian striking a Hebrew slave. He then acts to protect the slave, and kills the Egyptian. When he discovers that the killing has been witnessed, he flees to Midian, where he marries and becomes a shepherd. And one day, he "saw"[13] a bush burning out in the desert. When he turns aside to "see"[14] it better, G-d calls out, and Moses says, "Here I am."[15] YHVH says to him that G-d has "seen"[16] the degradation of the Israelites and now will act to save them.

So this section of the *parshah* emphasizes the importance of paying attention, of actually *seeing* what is in front of us. We, like the Israelites, swarm mindlessly about our daily affairs, most of the time without consciousness. And without paying attention, without consciousness, we live a constricted life, enslaved to our habits and essentially dead to everything around us. But when we actually *see,* we have the possibility of opening to some entirely new way of being in the world.

This G-d who calls out to Moses has no form and no description. Indeed, when asked for a name, the Divine Presence gives an unpronounceable grouping of Hebrew letters (in English transliteration, YHVH), which derive from the verb "to be." In traditional understanding, these letters are meant to be unpronounceable, because any naming would impose limitation. Commonly translated as "I Am That I Am" or "I Am Becoming What I Am Becoming," the letters point to process and mystery and the inability to confine reality into rigid boundaries. So *seeing* offers us a way to relate to an unbounded, unconditional YHVH, a G-d of *being.* As we *see,* we have the possibility of freeing our spirit from the confines of the expected and the known, and so open ourselves to partake of the mystery of unlimited Divine Presence. But, of course, we resist, even as Moses does.

For Formal Practice: When you are ready, see yourself in front of the mysterious burning bush, standing with bare feet on holy ground, just as Moses stands. See the sun in the sky, and the almost blinding light pouring from that sun into your eyes, enveloping you and bleaching the whole landscape in its whiteness. Feel the dry heat of the desert hot on your skin, hurting your lungs as you inhale, burning the soles of your feet pressed on the rocky, sandy surface. See the bush on fire, see the flames coming out of the leaves and branches, and see how they remain green, strangely unconsumed. Look at it closely so that you really see how strange and wondrous that fire is. Let your heart open to wonder, even if you want to flee.

Like Moses, say, "Here I am. Ready to see. Here I am."

If you like the Hebrew, you can use the word *Hineinei* for "Here I am."

If you wish, allow yourself to come into the present exactly as you are. Begin to notice the sensations of your breath going in and out, as well as the sensations in different parts of your body. Notice the sounds in the room. Become aware of any aromas.

When you realize that your mind has wandered from such awareness, repeat the phrase "Here I am" or *Hineinei.* Then return to the experience of being in the moment, with the intention of committing your heart to full presence before the mystery of the Divine.

Here I am.

Hineinei.

In My Own Practice: *I am standing in the desert. I feel the sun, the heat of the air as I inhale, the burning of my feet on the rock. I gaze at the bush, just looking. It is so hard to see the fire while at the same time seeing that the leaves stay green. In my mind, they keep turning brown and shriveling. But they are not brown! They do not burn! For the moment, I can see that they are green. As the image shifts again to brown, I deeply realize how hard it is to see the impossible.*

Finally, I see the leaves are green, with fire dancing out of them. Somehow, the fire is not consuming. The thought appears: How can a fire not consume? What is this that looks like fire and is not?

It cannot be fire because it does not consume. Yet it is fire. The vision is impossible, but I see it. The miraculous. Awe overtakes me. I want to prostrate myself.

"Hineinei." I say it softly. The bush is too awesome for me. This is the realm not of the human, but of G-d. Again, I whisper, "Hineinei."

Exodus/*Sh'mot*, 2, "And I Appeared"/*Va-eira* (Exod. 6:2–9:35)

"And G-d spoke to Moses and said to him: 'I am YHVH.' "

—Exod. 6:2

Interpretive Overview: At the start of this *parshah*, Moses, the elders of Israel, and Pharaoh all resist G-d's call for change. The focus then shifts to Pharaoh's resistance to freeing the Israelites even when G-d responds with plagues throughout Egypt. At the metaphoric level, the chapter focuses on the way we protectively close down because of our fearful self-concerns, whether out of despair (like the children of Israel), fear of inadequacy (like Moses), or arrogance (like Pharaoh). The examples demonstrate how the ego's defensive constriction closes us off from the awareness of G-d's voice.

Summary of *Parshah*: YHVH repeats the promise to free the Israelites and bring them to the Promised Land, and tells Moses to inform the Israelite leaders. When they refuse to listen to Moses because their spirits are crushed by enslavement, Moses again tells G-d that the task is beyond him, and YHVH agrees to let Aaron speak for him. The Divine then tells them both to go to Pharaoh, adding that G-d will harden Pharaoh's heart. (This enigmatic phrase will be discussed in the interpretation of the next *parshah*.)

And then they speak to Pharaoh many times, saying only that they want the Israelites to go into the desert for three days to offer sacrifice to G-d. With each meeting, they demonstrate that YHVH is more powerful than Pharaoh's magicians. First, Aaron turns a rod into a snake. Then he converts the waters of the Nile into blood. After that, he calls up a plague of frogs, then one of lice, then one of insects; then calls forth the death of livestock; and finally calls up boils and then hail, until the whole land of Egypt is in ruins. This entire time, Pharaoh continues to refuse to let the Israelites leave, although he sometimes agrees, but then reneges on his promise as soon as the plague is lifted.

***Parshah* Interpretation:** Throughout the previous chapter, Moses strongly resisted his assignment to lead the Israelites out of Egypt. At the beginning of this chapter, he finally does speak to the leaders of Israel, but they refuse to listen to him. And so, he again argues with YHVH about taking on the task, saying, "Here, the children of Israel didn't listen to me, and how will *Pharaoh* listen to me?"[1] Then, for the remainder of the *parshah*, Pharaoh remains stubborn throughout the plagues.

Everyone is resisting G-d: the children of Israel, Pharaoh, and Moses. The *parshah* suggests that the children of Israel resist because they are ground into despair by their slavery; that Moses resists out of a sense of inadequacy; and that Pharaoh resists out of arrogance. None of them are fully open to the path of new possibility that comes through openness to YHVH.

Whatever the particulars, we are all resistant to being freed from the narrowness of our normal state of consciousness, to being open to the possibilities of the I Am Becoming What I Am Becoming that is the essence of G-d.

For Formal Practice: The intention of this meditation is to pay attention to your own unwillingness to open yourself to new possibility, whether that unwillingness be rooted in despair, as with the children of Israel; fear of unworthiness, as with Moses; arrogance, as with Pharaoh; or yet another emotion.

Pick some area in your life, or some issue, that you could in fact approach differently, but in which you find yourself stuck. It may or may not involve another person.

When you are ready, just let yourself pay close attention to the sensations of your breath for a few moments. After a while, let your attention return to the issue or situation you picked out (unless some other one now comes to the forefront of consciousness). Let yourself focus simply on the *feeling* of resistance—without thinking about the issue.

Note the sensations in your body as you feel the resistance. Just notice any place in your body that hurts or holds tension around this issue or situation, and let yourself simply *feel,* without comment or interpretation or naming. When you become aware of images or thoughts, just note them and let them go, resisting the urge to dwell on them.

Try just to be aware of your sensations, without commenting, without naming, without interpreting. Notice your resistance to doing this, as well; notice the way in which your ego tries to keep your mind busy with thought.

If you find that the resistance shifts in some way, just let it happen. If at some point, you feel ready to simply follow your breath without thought, go ahead.

Remember that any time you go from the place of thought (and resistance) to the place of simple awareness, you may also open to the experience of Divine Presence.

In My Own Practice: *In the meditation, I go to the resistance I have to calling an old friend I am angry at. I often feel attacked by her when I feel I have done nothing to hurt her, when I have simply spoken without self-consciousness. I experience her as getting mad at me because she feels in some way victimized by me. I picture myself at the telephone and feel the tightening in my chest and throat. Then I feel the surge of nausea, the emptiness in my belly. Fear.*

And then sadness, near tears. The image of my mother shouting at me, once again, for spilling milk on her newly washed kitchen floor. As if I'd spilled the milk to undo her hard work, her scrubbing away on hands and knees. She hated me, it felt like, because she believed I'd intended to hurt her. When I hadn't.

I feel my body. I am young. Less than eight. Maybe five? Six?

I am just clumsy. I would give anything not to spill that milk.

A thought appears: why didn't she carry the milk for me?

I let the memory go and stay with sensation and emotion. Just feel the fear, the nausea. The sadness. Then I see her face, distorted by fury, hating me in that moment. My friend's face reappears, the same tone in her voice, a tone of victimization.

I breathe, and follow my breath. Return to the phone conversation. The tension is less. They are not the same, my friend and my mother. And I am not five.

The thought appears: how terrible to feel so victimized.

For the moment, compassion appears. And then words to say next time: I am not trying to hurt you. Stop.

The tension is gone. I follow the breath without thought.

Exodus/*Sh'mot*, 3, "Come"/*Bo*
(Exod. 10:1–13:6)

"And YHVH said to Moses: 'Come to Pharaoh....' "

—Exod. 10:1

Interpretive Overview: The plagues continue because Pharaoh remains arrogantly certain that his power to control what happens is greater than YHVH's. He gives in only after YHVH kills all the firstborn children, and at that point, the Israelites flee. At the metaphoric level, we are to take Pharaoh's arrogance as a symbol of our own defensive unwillingness to acknowledge our vulnerability and our lack of control over so much of what life brings us. Like Pharaoh, we continue to act as if we can make events turn out as we want them to, and we may have to face disaster before we can admit to, and confront, our essential helplessness.

Summary of *Parshah:* At the opening of this chapter, Moses is told yet again that YHVH is hardening the heart of Pharaoh as Egypt is crushed in order to demonstrate YHVH's mighty power. The *parshah* continues with the last three plagues inflicted on Egypt: locusts, darkness, and, finally, death of all the firstborn. With the first two, Pharaoh repeats his earlier pattern of promising to let the slaves go and then reneging when the plague lifts. Then G-d tells Moses that all the firstborn of Egypt will be killed on the fourteenth night of the month to follow, and that the Israelites should mark their doorposts with lamb's blood so that their homes will be passed over when this plague strikes. After that, instructions are given for this fourteenth day to be commemorated forever with seven days of eating only unleavened bread (i.e., the holiday of Passover). Finally, Moses gives G-d's instructions to the Israelites; Egypt's firstborn are all killed; and Pharaoh, at last, tells the Israelites to leave. The Egyptians are eager for them to go, and six hundred thousand flee with their flocks and herds, taking with them all kinds of gold and silver objects that the Egyptians give them.

The chapter closes by saying that they had been in Egypt for four hundred and thirty years. It also gives additional rules for observing the Passover commemoration, and adds that each firstborn of the Israelites is forevermore to be consecrated to G-d: if an animal, it is to be sacrificed; if a son, he is to be redeemed from G-d by an animal sacrifice.

Parshah **Interpretation:** At the narrative level, the Divine's hardening of Pharaoh's heart is difficult for many of us to accept. But the problem may lie largely with the translation. According to Richard Elliot Friedman,[1] the better translation is that G-d *strengthened* Pharaoh's heart. In this reading, G-d merely enhances Pharaoh's existing inclinations, strengthening the direction toward which his heart already turns. But Pharaoh retains the capacity to choose the direction in which he goes. He could stubbornly choose to keep the slaves despite the plagues, or he could, with equal stubbornness, choose to let them go despite the impact on Egypt's economy and his own power. In this reading, our inclinations are constrained by our conditioning, by our past, by our temperament, by a host of factors that we all recognize; but, within those constraints, we have free will—we have choice.

At the literal level of this *parshah,* there is a contest between Pharaoh and G-d; G-d is simply demonstrating the greater power. At a more subtle level, the plagues represent the fact, presented yet again, that we have very limited control over what happens to us. We may believe that all comes about through G-d's will, or we may believe that what is described in the text as Divine intention can be read instead as simply an attempt to give a label to the inexplicable, to the way in which bad things happen in life for no apparent reason.

Or we can more mystically say that the plagues arise through unimaginably complex chains of causality woven across time and space in a tapestry far beyond human comprehension, knowable only at the level of the eternal and unnamable I Will Be What I Will Be.

For purposes of our own spiritual growth, let us begin with the opening words of the chapter, "Come unto Pharaoh." With these words, the *parshah* asks us to focus on our stubborn arrogance, as represented by Pharaoh. For Pharaoh is the embodiment of our own delusions of control, of our desperate unwillingness to acknowledge our inability to be in charge of life. Similarly, the plagues of Egypt represent the way in which we may have to have our hearts broken by life circumstance before we can admit to and confront our inevitable limitations. In this case, the final blow to Pharaoh is having the firstborn child in each household killed.

For Formal Practice: When you are ready, begin to "come unto Pharaoh" by briefly seeing the thick mass of locusts swarming everywhere, a moving carpet of insects devouring everything green, leaving the land barren.

Then feel the three days of suffocating darkness, a blackness in which you cannot see even your own hand.

Then, finally, the death of all firstborn.

Feel your utter helplessness.

And now focus on a current area in your life in which you are trying to maintain a sense of false control. It can be major or minor. It may involve health, a recent accident, a course of action, or another person.

Let yourself notice the tension in your body as you go to this issue in your mind. Follow your breath and try to let go of thought. Note the experience of fear as you acknowledge your vulnerability.

As you sit, breathing in and out, let your heart soften in its vulnerability around this issue. Try to let go of all thought. Simply be in the moment, open to the safety that only YHVH can provide in this space of alert nonthought. When you begin to think, return to your breath and the sensations of this moment. If you can, let your mind empty completely.

In My Own Practice: *Today, I have a potentially serious health problem. I am about to go for more tests for diagnosis. I am anxious, afraid of cancer. I am already playing out imaginary scenarios involving bad news.*

As I breathe in and out, focusing on my breath and the sensations in my body, I realize once again that we always have the moment we are in right now, and that it is in this space of now that I can feel G-d's presence as soon as I let thought go. And that all thoughts about the future are total illusion, a story we tell ourselves.

A phrase appears out of the space of nonthought: what will be, will be. I find myself deeply letting go, giving thanks for the moment, for the person sitting next to me in our meditation group today, for having her as my friend, for the glorious silence of the library where we are meditating at the synagogue, for having a place to meditate, for the sun behind me. Tears stream down my face in thanks. Later, I have a dental cleaning and take pleasure even in the pain, because it is, *and it is beautiful in its gritty* is-ness.

A few days later, I have one of the worst nightmares I have ever had. I am in a taxi going from Manhattan over a bridge. My driver says he is trying to avoid the traffic and takes a turn into what looks like a construction zone. He drives badly, and I tell him to be more careful. He drives farther and farther into a deserted area of blocked-off road. Then he stops and gets out of the cab, tying the cab to a pillar. I start to unbuckle my seat belt, to get out; he looks up at me from where he's crouching by the pillar, and says, "Aren't you worried? We're all alone here. Aren't you wondering what I'm doing?"

I am very afraid, but terrified of letting him know. I think that maybe I'll be all right if I pretend to be safe with him. "I'm not worried," I say. "You look nice."

He smiles threateningly. "I'm not."

I try to get out of my seat and then realize that a second man is now in the cab, up against my left side. He's dark-haired, his face unshaven, leaning toward me, ready to grab. And then, in front of me, a women with dark, curly, unkempt hair, laughing viciously.

I have no hope. There will be no rescue.

I wake screaming. It feels so real, I fear it's prophetic. It's still with me the next day. Finally, I realize that I've been meditating on helpless terror all week. My dream is so powerful because it embodies the experience. I try to return to the place of safety. What will be will be.

Exodus/*Sh'mot,* 4, "When He Let Go"/*B'shalach*
(Exod. 13:17–17:16)

"And it was, when Pharaoh let the people go, that G-d did not lead them by way of the Philistines' land—because it was close—because G-d said: 'In case the people will be dissuaded when they see war, and they'll go back to Egypt.' "

—Exod. 13:17

Interpretive Overview: As the Israelites begin their journey out of slavery toward the Promised Land, they are often frightened. Although they rejoice when the Red Sea parts before them and then drowns Pharaoh's oncoming army, they soon return to the constriction of fear. Often, they complain to Moses that it was safer to be in Egypt, and they blame him for releasing them. At the metaphoric level, the *parshah* accepts that spiritual growth is often halted by our existential doubt, no matter how clearly we sometimes feel the presence of G-d. The spiritual path is slow, with much backsliding.

Summary of *Parshah*: When the Israelites leave Egypt, the text states that G-d knows that they would flee back to Egypt if they followed a direct route that took them by the warlike Philistines, and so the Divine leads them on a roundabout route by way of the Red Sea.[1] And thus the armed Israelites march, with Moses carrying Joseph's bones with him, as promised long before.

Leading the Israelites in the form of a cloud by day and a pillar of fire by night, G-d tells Moses to have them camp by the Red Sea, adding that YHVH has once again strengthened (or hardened, depending on the translation) Pharaoh's heart, so that Pharaoh is sending an army, whose defeat will demonstrate YHVH's power. As the Israelites see the approaching Egyptian army, they blame Moses for taking them out of the safety of their slavery, but Moses reassures them of G-d's salvation.

At G-d's command, Moses reaches his hand over the sea so that it parts, and the Israelites walk between two walls of water on dry ground, with the column of fire leading them. Behind them, G-d stays as cloud and darkness over the Egyptians, throwing them into chaos until they try to flee. When Moses again reaches his hand out over the sea at G-d's command, the water flows back over the Egyptians to drown them all.

After this, the people sing a song of thanksgiving, proclaiming, also, that the power of YHVH is now known to the whole world. And Miriam, the "prophetess, Aaron's sister,"[2] takes a drum and leads all the women in dance and drumming as she sings.[3]

But then the Israelites' fear overtakes them three more times in this *parshah,* so that they argue that they were safer in slavery—and G-d responds with sustaining miracles each time.

First, they complain to Moses when they find only bitter water after three days of travel. He cries to G-d, who shows him a tree to throw into the water for sweetening. G-d also promises not to inflict on them any of the sicknesses that were set on Egypt, as long as they listen to the voice of the Divine Presence and observe the laws and commandments.

But on the fifteenth day of the second month after leaving Egypt, they enter another wilderness. In their second protest, they blame both Moses and Aaron for bringing them there to starve, saying that they were better off in Egypt where they had meat and bread. G-d tells Moses that food will rain down to be collected every morning, with a double portion on the sixth day, so that they need not collect on the Sabbath, the day of rest. Later, the food is described as tasting like a wafer in honey.[4]

When the food appears on the ground in the morning, like a fall of dew (in Hebrew, it is called *manna,* which means "What is it?"),[5] Moses gives the people instructions to take as much as they need, leaving none on the ground, and to take extra on the sixth day to hold over for the Sabbath. Of course, some of them disregard him, and he is angry.

Finally, as we near the end of the chapter, they once again have no water, complaining this time that Moses has brought them from Egypt to kill them. Overcome with frustration at this third criticism, Moses cries out to G-d, who tells him to go back to Mount Sinai[6] with some of the elders and to strike the rock there with his staff to release water. He does, the water reaches the people, and Moses names the site of their quarrel with him Massah and Meribah, meaning "Testing" and "Quarrel" respectively.

In the final scene of this chapter, the tribe of Amalek attacks them. Telling Joshua (who will eventually become his successor) to lead the battle the next day, Moses says he will stand on the hilltop, holding his staff aloft.

When the battle comes, Amelek loses every time Moses holds up the staff, and wins every time his hand falls. As he tires, he sits on a stone, while Aaron and Hur (the reference is not explained, but he is traditionally thought to be Miriam's husband or son) hold up his hands, one on each side. Joshua thus defeats Amalek.

In the final paragraph, G-d tells Moses to write down that YHVH will wipe out the memory of Amalek and will be at war against Amalek, Israel's enemy, forevermore.

Parshah **Interpretation:** Fear is primary and takes over even after we have had a taste of the Divine Presence, even when we have experienced what seems like a miracle in our lives. We are all dependent for our sustenance, our safety, and our very lives on forces outside our control just as the Israelites are; and we find this fact terrifying. We, too, give thanks when we are saved from some terrible disaster, or when an event that could have turned out badly turns out well, but we quickly move back to fear. For we know that bad things happen to good people without any apparent reason.

In the constriction of our anxiety, we lose awareness of the Divine. We can despair, as the Israelites repeatedly despair in this *parshah,* or we can attempt again to assert control as Pharaoh does when he sends his army in pursuit. Either way, we do not yet know how to live in G-d's presence always; we do not feel the safety of Divine protection in a realm that transcends our physical existence. In traditional mystical Judaism, the crossing of the Red Sea is seen as a symbolic birth, the beginning of our spiritual journey. But it is only the beginning of opening our consciousness to Mystery. Thus, in the first sentence of this chapter, G-d chooses not to take us on the direct path to the Promised Land, but orders a roundabout route, for we are not ready. It is a statement to each of us about the strength of our anxieties. Our paths may be punctuated by moments of revelation, ecstasy, or even blissful merging with the Divine, but these moments fade, becoming little more than remembered pointers toward a larger reality. In the end, spiritual change, the journey toward the Garden Within, is a slow process—the difficult work of gradually undoing our fearfulness and learning to trust in the Divine.

When Amalek attacks at the end of the *parshah,* appearing as Israel's implacable enemy, the traditional reading[7] is that Amelek represents doubt, the eternal enemy that is ever ready to pounce when we are weakened and fearful, an enemy to be slowly rooted out by our awareness of YHVH's presence with us.

For Formal Practice: Place yourself on the dry sand in the middle of the Red Sea, seeing the water towering above you on each side of the corridor G-d has made for your passage. Notice the dry sand on the path beneath you, the pillar of fire in front of you. Hear the sounds of the Egyptians behind you, frantic in the cloud and darkness. Hear them screaming as the sea closes over them. Hear the horses.

Notice again the water high around you on each side. Be aware that it can close in on you too at any moment. And yet, you are still walking safely on the path.

Let yourself turn to your vulnerability as you breathe. Perhaps to a current place of vulnerability in your life. Follow your breath as you continue to picture the scene of this miracle, and feel your vulnerability on the path as well as your safety.

If you find yourself thinking, return to your breath and this scene.

In My Own Practice: *I can see the walls of water quite clearly. They tower above me, frozen and unmoving, as if time has stopped, but I know that they can fall upon me at any instant. I follow the path, seeing the sand clearly beneath my feet. I hear the Egyptians screaming behind me and the sounds of chaos. I know my turn could come. It could be me.*

I turn to the effort involved in writing this book and the sense of loss it carries. It means giving up so much time, fitting it in after work or before. It has meant forgoing so many dinners with friends, so many chances to be connected; giving up time to just be present, time that cannot be made up. But most of all, it is an act of faith. I don't know how long it will take, or what will happen to it once I'm done. In the end, I may be the only person ever to read these words. But the very commitment to this study has placed me squarely on my path, taking me out of my own Mitzrayim.

I continue to walk along the dry sand. For the first time, I feel the presence of others on the path with me, although I do not see them. The path goes on. I feel safe on it, despite the water above my head on each side. The words appear to me: "What will be, will be." I breathe, feeling calmness. What matters is staying on the path. And I feel comforted by the presence of the unseen others.

"And Jethro, priest of Midian, Moses' father-in-law, heard everything that G-d had done for Moses and for Israel...."

—Exod 18:1

Interpretive Overview: In this chapter, YHVH tells Moses to offer the Israelites a contract: if they agree to follow G-d's commandments, they will become a holy people and a treasure to the world. After the people agree, YHVH speaks to them directly, with terrifying power, proclaiming what is known in English as the Ten Commandments. This is the pivotal *parshah* of Exodus, for the Israelites are able to be entirely open to the Divine Presence, hearing G-d's voice for themselves because they have let go of their self-concerns in committing themselves totally to Divine service. This is the path open to any of us—as is the resistance that follows.

Summary of *Parshah:* Jethro, priest of Midian and Moses' father-in-law, hears about what YHVH has done for Moses and the Israelites, and brings his daughter and grandsons to Moses at Mount Sinai. Moses comes out to meet him, they embrace, and Moses tells him all that has happened. Jethro rejoices for the Israelites, says that he knows that YHVH is greater than any of the other gods, and offers sacrifice to YHVH. Then Aaron and the elders share a meal with Jethro "before G-d."[1]

The next day, Jethro sees Moses acting as judge for the people the whole day, and tells him that he should teach G-d's laws and instructions to the people, but must delegate authority if he does not want to become worn out. Moses does as Jethro suggests, creating a whole hierarchy of chieftains, so that only the most difficult problems of judgment will henceforth be brought to him.

In the third month of their trek, all the Israelites come to Mount Sinai. Moses is already on the mountain; G-d tells him to tell the people that they have been freed by G-d, and that they will be a "treasure,"[2] "a kingdom of priests and a holy nation,"[3] if they observe G-d's covenant and listen to G-d's voice. When Moses tells the elders, all the people respond together, saying, "We'll do everything that YHVH has spoken."[4]

G-d tells Moses to tell the people to prepare for YHVH's words by having them consecrate themselves for three days, washing all their clothes and having no sex. After warning that the Israelites will die if they ascend the mountain when G-d is there, G-d comes to the top of Mount Sinai on the morning of the third day, amidst thunder, lightning, a heavy cloud, and the loud sound of a horn. The people stand at the foot of the mountain as it trembles in fire and smoke, and G-d calls Moses up, saying he must again warn the people not to ascend the mountain. Soon after, YHVH utters what, in English, are known as the Ten Commandments. In essence, they say:

1. I am YHVH, your G-d who has brought you out of slavery in Egypt.
2. You shall not have other gods or serve them. You shall not make a statue or any form of G-d.
3. You shall not make an oath to G-d and not fulfill it.
4. Remember the Sabbath and cease from all work on that day.
5. Honor your father and mother.
6. Do not murder.
7. Do not commit adultery.
8. Do not steal.
9. Do not give false testimony.
10. Do not covet *anything* your neighbor has.

As the thunder and lightning and smoke and sound of the horn continue, the people move back, saying to Moses, "*You* speak with us so we may listen, but let G-d not speak with us or else we'll die."[5] Moses then goes up the mountain to receive further instructions.

Parshah **Interpretation:** This is the sublime chapter of Exodus. Until now, we have been focused on human resistance to the awareness of Divine Presence. Today we enter a rare and different state, of complete openness to revelation from G-d.

The chapter begins with Jethro, the foreign Midianite priest who is Moses' father-in-law, as he comes to the Israelite camp. Having heard of the miraculous rescue from Egypt, he brings Moses' wife and sons back to him, and he offers up his own sacrifices to YHVH after listening to Moses tell the whole story. So YHVH is accessible to anyone who chooses to listen, whether Israelite or not. To anyone who wrestles with G-d.

Then the Israelites enter the wilderness of Sinai, where the Divine Presence offers a contract to them. Calling to Moses, YHVH tells him to declare to the children of Israel, "And now, if you will truly heed My voice and keep My covenant, you will become for Me a treasure among all the peoples, for Mine is all the earth. And as for you, you will become for Me a kingdom of priests and a holy nation."[6]

But G-d offers no details for Moses, and neither Moses nor the people ask. Instead, in an eternal moment of total openness to G-d's will, the people accept the covenant, declaring with one voice, "We'll do everything that YHVH has spoken."[7]

The chapter then moves into the climactic scene of Exodus, as all the Israelites who have fled Egypt stand at the foot of Mount Sinai to hear G-d pronounce the Ten Commandments—or what in Hebrew are called the Ten Utterances.

Here at Sinai, in this moment, traditional Jewish teachings say, stands every Jew who has ever lived (even if we believe the moment to be more mythical than historical). In my reading and in a few Jewish traditions, anyone—Jew or not—who wrestles with G-d can consider themselves to have stood at Sinai. (And of course, standing at Sinai is part of Christian heritage.) So here we all are.

Then, at Mount Sinai, G-d speaks directly to the waiting people. Using the formal contractual language of the ancient Middle East, YHVH sets out the terms of the covenant. "I the Eternal am your G-d who brought you out of the land of Egypt, the house of bondage. You shall have no other gods besides Me ... Honor your father and your mother .... You shall not murder. You shall not commit adultery. You shall not steal. You shall not bear false witness against your neighbor. You shall not covet your neighbor's house ... nor anything that is your neighbor's."[8]

And what is this G-d whose voice they see proclaiming clear moral obligations? YHVH: *being*-ness. I Am That I Am. I Will Be What I Will Be. The living force behind the miraculousness of every breath we take, the force sustaining the whole physical world. Not merely the G-d who splits the Red Sea, or sustains the Israelites on manna, but the G-d of each moment. As the liturgy says in the daily prayer service, in the prayer called the *Amidah:* "We acknowledge You, declare Your praise, and thank You for our lives entrusted to Your hand, our souls placed in Your care, for Your miracles that greet us every day, and for Your wonders and the good things that are with us every hour, morning, noon, and night."

For Formal Practice: When you are ready, place yourself in the camp in the wilderness of Sinai. You have been preparing for three days, and now it is morning. You become aware of "thunders and lightning and a heavy cloud on the mountain, and a sound of a horn, very strong."[9] You are standing with all the other Israelites at the bottom of the mountain, trembling. "And Mount Sinai was all smoke because YHVH came down on it in fire, and its smoke went up like the smoke of a furnace, and the whole mountain trembled greatly. And the sound of the horn was getting much stronger."[10]

And the voice begins to speak: ""I the Eternal am your G-d who brought you out of the land of Egypt, the house of bondage. You shall have no other gods besides Me."[11]

You have been taken out of Egypt, from the place of constricted awareness. What does accepting this covenant mean to you who are in this state of opened awareness? What does it mean to be a treasure to Divinity?

As you continue this meditation, focus on whichever of the Ten Commandments most strikes you now.

Ask G-d what is meant by the command that we not have other gods. Or not steal. Or not covet another's possessions. Ask G-d what we are to understand.

In My Own Practice: *When I did the meditation this morning, I was called to sit with the commandment against stealing. I don't steal, I thought. Where is the relevance? And then came the image of a child somewhere in the world looking for firewood. It is February 8th today and very cold where I live in Woodstock, New York, yet I am warm enough in my house. All I had to do was set the thermostat.*

In the meditation, the vision is very clear. I and the child are linked. We are in relationship. And there is only so much of the world's resources to go around. He has less and I have more, because I have taken more than my share. Without any intent on my part, I have stolen from this child. Yet I have no more right than he, for we are both made equally in the Divine image. I am a thief.

Exodus/*Sh'mot*, 6, "Judgments"/*Mishpatim* (Exod. 21:1–24:18)

"These are the rules that you shall set before them...."

—Exod. 21:1–2[1]

Interpretive Overview: The Divine now supplements the Ten Commandments with a large number of more detailed rules. The added laws provide specifics for acting with loving-kindness (in Hebrew, called *chesed*) in all parts of life, with the implication that the Israelites (and each of us) need more than generalities to overcome self-centeredness, even after committing to the spiritual path. In the language of metaphor, most of the community then stays at the foot of the mountain, while the elders (who are to be understood as further along the spiritual path) go partway up and have a vision of G-d. And Moses, whose ego is almost entirely subsumed to Divine service, enters the cloud at the top to be with the Divine Presence.

Summary of *Parshah*: This week's *parshah* moves to the next scene at Mount Sinai, where YHVH gives Moses additional rules of behavior for the Israelites. The rules, which are now known as the Book of the Covenant, at first involve categories of behavior that harm another: mistreatment of (Hebrew) slaves[2] (beginning with an implicit contrast to the Egyptian enslavement); acts of violence, whether the harm is intentional or indirect; contemptuous treatment, specifically in relation to parents; acts of thievery or damage to property, whether direct or indirect, intentional or not; and seduction of a virgin. It is understood that the Israelites will, at some time, break all these rules, despite their vows and intentions, for the commands specify the penalties for their violation.[3]

After this, we see a mix of commands, some of which refer to ritual practice, and most to creating a society in which all are treated equally before the law—and a society in which everyone, including the powerless and the stranger, is treated without exploitation. A few of these commands extend the range of required behaviors enormously. These include the command to actively offer help to your enemy when he is in trouble;[4] to neither wrong nor oppress the stranger;[5] and to not allow your judgment to be swayed by the opinions of those around you.

After this come a few commands related to ritual observance. Among them are (1) letting the fields rest from planting in the seventh year, (2) keeping the seventh day as a day of rest, and (3) celebrating before G-d three pilgrimages each year: one for the exodus from Egypt, one for the first harvest of the year, and one for the final harvest. Finally, G-d once again promises protection if all the commands are kept.

When Moses conveys all of G-d's words, the Israelites accept the covenant, answering with "one voice," and they say, "We'll do all the things that YHVH has spoken."[6] The next day, they offer sacrifices at the altar that Moses builds as a sign of their vow, saying, "We'll do everything that YHVH has spoken and we'll listen."[7] After this, the elders climb partway up Mount Sinai, where they feast and have a vision in which they see G-d. Leaving the elders with Aaron and Hur,[8] Moses ascends farther up the mountain to enter G-d's presence, where he stays for forty days and nights, hidden by a cloud.

Parshah **Interpretation:** What Moses has proclaimed this time begins very differently from the Ten Utterances the people have already heard, for G-d opens with a shift from the general to the specific.

Instead of the brevity of the Ten Utterances, the Divine makes known a long series of more specific rules designed to cover many of the situations inherent in human interaction. The shift in tone is both jarring and puzzling. Why does the narrative switch abruptly from the high drama of last week's *parshah* to the almost obsessive and—to the modern ear, at least—rather boring legalisms that begin this week's account?

125

Because, the *parshah* implies, we humans need the guidance of detailed rules in the daily routines of our lives. For we make choices all the time, generally without thinking much about them, and we usually make these choices from a place of constriction, from within *Mitzrayim*. Most of the rules come with penalties for their violation, because it is understood that we will often fail in our intention to observe them, no matter what we promise. The penalties represent the consequences for failure, and also warn us to stay on track.

Later parts of this *parshah* then switch back to more general commands, although even these commands are more specific than the Ten Utterances. Many of them have no punishment attached for failure, or call forth a response from G-d rather than society. Because they are mixed in with commands for ritual observances that are metaphors for opening our consciousness to the Divine, observing them seems to involve greater closeness to G-d than the earlier and more specific rules.

All the rules of this *parshah* seem simply to be statements of *is*-ness—of the way things really are—in those brief moments in which I am open to the blinding voice of YHVH. In that state of consciousness, I know with all my being that everything in the physical world is a manifestation of G-d. In that state, everything is to be cherished, even the gypsy moth caterpillar inching across my front step. There is only G-d, and G-d is One.

In such moments of revelation, loving behavior does not seem to depend upon a commandment but seems simply to be the inevitable response to recognizing the unity of all within the Divine Presence. In that state, unbounded loving-kindness is natural.

But we cannot stay in this place of direct communion for long. Nor are the memories of such communion generally able to keep us cherishing everything and everyone we encounter. Not when we fall back to earth. In this state—my normal mode of being—I am annoyed by the driver of the car ahead of me, inching down the road as slowly, it seems to me, as any gypsy moth caterpillar. In my impatience, in the isolation of my mind, I call him a moron.

We are given rules to follow for the times when we do not *feel* permeated by the compassion of G-d, when we feel separate and alone, when we are ruled by the small consciousness of the ego. And this is most of the time.

Indeed, the Israelites had begun to shut down by the end of the last *parshah.* While they had vowed to follow G-d's laws, they were already too much back in their skins to tolerate direct experience of the Divine, so that Moses had to serve as an intermediary. Indeed, the commands of this *parshah* are given within the context of the idolatry that is about to follow—despite all the Israelites' promises. For when Moses comes down from the mountain after forty days, he will discover that the people have created a golden calf to worship. And today, we are no different.

Most often, then, the best we can do—and this is a great deal—is to try to follow the rules that we are given for acting well, starting with those that are easier to manage. But the point is to *do,* regardless of how we feel. And to keep on doing, stretching our limits as we grow. For the more we try, the greater our closeness to the Divine, and the more we feel Divine protection.

And so, we can begin our personal climb to G-d, ascending Mount Sinai as the elders do.

For Formal Practice: When you are ready, stand at Mount Sinai on ground that may still be trembling with the power of YHVH. You can see the smoke and the fire as Moses listens to the Divine voice.

As Moses now tells you G-d's commands, let your attention move to the intent of these laws.

Let your attention hover over the following categories:

- Do not harm anyone or their property through your acts.

- Do no harm by your speech.

- Remain unswayed by your peer's opinions.

- Do not oppress the stranger, for you were a stranger.

- Do not harm another, even indirectly or inadvertently.

- Offer help to someone in need who dislikes you or you dislike.

As you sit and follow your breath, just let yourself notice some of the ways that you have failed to observe these commands.

If possible, pick a command that seems particularly difficult to follow. Imagine yourself carrying it out.

Notice how your body feels. Notice any resistance. Notice the thoughts that arise.

Return to an image of you observing this commandment. Notice how you feel, as you say, "I will do what YHVH has spoken." See if anything changes.

In My Own Practice: *I pick the commandment to offer help to someone I dislike. My first reaction is gratefulness that the person I'm thinking of doesn't ask me for help. Then I realize that I feel warmer toward her when I imagine helping her, at least with something small, like giving her a lift. I realize that it's easier in my mind if she asks than if I simply volunteer. But I'm surprised that I can imagine a range of helpful actions if the opportunity were to arise. As I sit with this contemplation, I can feel my heart softening. In my mind's eye, she has become more appealing. Then I realize that I've actually had this experience just recently, when I gave a ride to someone I haven't much liked.*

Exodus/*Sh'mot*, 7, "Donation"/*T'rumah*
(Exod. 25:1–27:19)

"The Eternal One spoke to Moses, saying, 'Tell the Israelite people to bring Me gifts…. And let them make Me a Sanctuary that I may dwell among them.'"

—Exod. 25:1[1]

Interpretive Overview: In this chapter, the Israelites are given meticulous instructions for the next stage of their spiritual journey, in which they are to construct a Sanctuary wherein G-d can dwell. The language of the text indicates that G-d is perceived as both transcendent and immanent, as an external force dwelling amidst the community and as an inner presence deep within each person's heart. Also, the materials for construction are to come from donations freely given by those so moved. At the symbolic level, we are asked to donate our gifts of service to create a place for the Divine within both our society and our hearts, using our talents to bring forward G-d's qualities of compassion, mercy, and justice.

Summary of *Parshah:* In the last *parshah,* Moses entered the cloud, joining G-d atop Mount Sinai for forty days. Now G-d gives him detailed instructions for building the Sanctuary, the *mishkan* (which is also known as the Tabernacle or Tent of Meeting), within which G-d will somehow dwell among the Israelites. It is understood that G-d's presence is not limited to the Sanctuary; but the Sanctuary is a special place set aside for G-d and the people to meet, wherever they may travel. The chapter begins by saying that each person will make a donation toward the construction as his heart moves him.

YHVH describes sumptuous gifts to be brought for the *mishkan's* construction: gold and silver and copper; blue, purple, and crimson yarns; fine linen fabric, goat's hair, and skins of ram and dolphin (the Hebrew is actually of unclear meaning); acacia wood; oil for lighting;

spices for anointing oil and incense; and gemstones. Then YHVH goes on to describe the construction at length, although the design of the construction is actually not made clear in the text. In a general way, however, the Tabernacle is described as consisting of a series of chambers of progressive holiness. As we come through the entrance of the Tent, we are in a forechamber that contains a sacrificial altar on which animal and grain offerings will be burnt. Behind this area is a smaller second area that holds a table for consecrated bread, a gold lampstand for oil, and an altar for burning incense. Yet further in is a curtained area—the Holy of Holies—which contains the Ark of the Covenant, made of acacia wood, overlain with gold; this is where G-d comes down.

***Parshah* Interpretation:** In the last two chapters, we made a covenant with G-d. We would become holy, a treasure, G-d said, if we accepted our moral responsibility to behave well. And we accepted the covenant.

Then, at the end of the last chapter, Moses ascended alone to the summit of Mount Sinai, and thence into the cloud with YHVH for forty days.

This week's chapter begins with utterances that YHVH makes to Moses during those forty days atop the mountain. Now Moses receives instructions for creating a portable dwelling place for YHVH, the *mishkan*. This is a holy place designated as a site for G-d to meet with the children of Israel, wherever the Israelites travel.

This holy place is a metaphor for the experience at Mount Sinai, for its three compartments are meant to mirror the three zones of holiness at Sinai. The area near the base of the mountain was open to the whole community, just as the forechamber of the *mishkan* will be; the middle area of the mountain was restricted to the elders (i.e., leaders) of the community just as the middle chamber of the *mishkan* will be restricted to the priests; and the top of the mountain was where the Divine Presence was to be found, just as the innermost chamber of the *mishkan* will be G-d's. Only Moses ascended to the top of the mount, just as the High

Priest will later be the only one to enter the innermost chamber. (The Temple in Jerusalem that was built by King Solomon also followed this three-part division, as did the Second Temple, built after the destruction of Solomon's.)

Moreover, the Hebrew is deliberately ambiguous, having YHVH say that the *mishkan* will allow G-d to dwell both among the Israelites and within each Israelite individually, implying that we may have an open channel— separately and together—for receiving the Divine Presence.

Indeed, the instructions in this chapter have many referents to parts of the human body, thus emphasizing the *mishkan's* meaning as both a concrete, physical construction for the entire community, and as something that exists in the heart of each individual. I am indebted to Rabbi Jonathan Kligler for pointing out this relationship between the human body and the terms used in the *mishkan's* construction, and for these examples: *yadot*=hands/handle;[2] *tzela*=rib/side;[3] *yarketayim*=femurs (or loins)/rear or lower section;[4] *bariyach*=clavicle/bolt or bar.[5]

The opening of the chapter also states that the *mishkan* will be built through gifts freely given by those whose hearts move them to donate. In the ancient world, the heart was the seat of the intellect, of intelligence as well as emotion. And our heart has free will, the Torah says. We always have a choice; we each choose the path we follow. If we choose to freely offer ourselves up to living a life of righteous action, we can create this dwelling place internally, within ourselves.

Yet we know that G-d is not limited to a certain space; G-d is everywhere in time and space. The entire physical world is an expression of G-d, shimmering with G-d's glory, if only we can open our hearts enough to see.

So what does it mean to choose to donate your gifts in order to make your heart a dwelling place for G-d?

For Formal Practice: The intention of this week's practice is to explore what gifts you can donate in order to make your heart a dwelling place for the Divine Presence. When you are ready, begin by trying to freely offer your promise of behaving with compassion, mercy, and justice. Notice any resistance you have to this general promise, and let yourself sit with the resistance as you breathe. Just notice where in your body you hold the resistance. Return to your breath if you lose focus. As you breathe, notice whether anything crosses your mind as you consciously experience these sensations. As you continue to breathe, let gifts that you might offer to G-d come into your mind.

Let yourself go to the specific, just as YHVH does in telling Moses what is needed for the *mishkan*. If you like, let yourself see someone with whom you have a troubled relationship. Let your mind offer a gift you can bring to this relationship, and thus to G-d. If you become distracted, feel yourself taking G-d in with each inhalation and breathing G-d out with each exhalation. Let G-d within you recognize G-d outside, in the other person, in everything around you, as you breathe.

In My Own Practice: *Today, it feels egotistical and wrong to offer to G-d any qualities that I may possess. In my mind's eye, it feels like bragging. Certainly, the whole sense of donating these qualities feels like ego in action—asking for praise, wanting to be noticed. At least it does today.*

As I sit with the meditation, waiting to see what might be brought, I realize that today I am being asked to bring simply my presence, my commitment. After all, this is the G-d that says, "I Am That I Am," "I Will Be What I Will Be." This is the G-d that emanates all existence, moment by moment.

Here I am. Thy will be done.

On another day that I sit with this meditation, a friend comes to mind; she is often, and unpredictably, critical of me. She is a good friend most of the time, but I never know when I am going to be attacked. I have come to dislike her and I find myself saying nasty things about her. I don't speak to her directly because I don't know how; I feel too hurt and betrayed. Often, I think I'll never speak to her again, but I keep returning, remembering how good a friend she can be. I avoid her and feel guilty that I am hurting her. I am sure she doesn't know her effect on me.

As I meditate, I see that the first gift I can offer is to see that she acts this way with others. Her attacks are not aimed at me. So I can offer objectivity as my first gift. Then I ask myself why I get so hurt. I know immediately: it reminds me of my mother, the unexpectedness of her anger, my wanting her to stop, to smile at me again, even my desperate acceptance of her accusations so as to make her stop. I am a child again, and I've lost my glasses. My mother is furious, telling me that I've lost them deliberately, that I've lost them to hurt her. I did not mean to lose them. I have no idea what happened to them. I would do anything to find them, but I don't know where to look. I keep saying that I'm sorry, but she doesn't stop. I feel so guilty. I am a bad child.

But this is me. My memory. My thought. The second gift of remembering.

And my third gift can be self-awareness. For I don't have to go to the past. My friend doesn't make me return to it. She voices a criticism in the present. I can accept it or not. I can apologize if I feel she's right, or I can tell her I don't agree. In the now. I feel incredibly freed. My heart feels open, light. I can see the letters of the name of G-d, YHVH, across both our bodies.

Exodus/*Sh'mot*, 8, "Command"/*T'tzaveh*
(Exod. 27:20–30:10)

"And you: You shall command the children of Israel that they shall bring clear pressed olive oil to you for the light, to keep up a lamp always."

—Exod. 27:20

Interpretive Overview: At the literal level, this *parshah* describes in detail the priests' clothing, the consecration ceremony yet to be performed, and a variety of rituals for which the priests will be responsible. At the metaphoric level, the ceremony symbolizes our own consecration to G-d in our awareness of our behaviors and intentions, and in our consciousness of the Divine Presence everywhere and at all times.

Summary of *Parshah:* The chapter begins with the command for keeping a lamp burning all night in the Sanctuary. Then the Divine gives Moses detailed instructions for making the priestly vestments for Aaron and his sons. (Aaron's vestments are the basis for those of priests, and particularly of bishops, in the Roman Catholic and Greek Orthodox churches.) The most striking feature of the vestments is the band of gold at the front of the priest's headdress, inscribed with the words "Holy to YHVH."[1] Also, the colors of the fabric are the same as those used for draping the *mishkan*.

After this, G-d tells Moses how to perform the consecration ceremony for Aaron and his sons, with additional instruction for the seven days after the ceremony.[2] (These instructions will be described and interpreted when we get to the next book, Leviticus. Please go to the Bible itself if you want more details.) Then instructions are given for the burnt offerings to be made each morning and evening once the Sanctuary is consecrated. Finally, G-d promises to be present to the Israelites at the *mishkan,* and says that the people will know that YHVH is their G-d, who brought them out of Egypt to dwell among them.

The chapter ends with instructions for building the altar on which incense is to be burnt, in the middle chamber just outside the Holy of Holies, with the statement that Aaron shall burn such incense morning and evening when he attends to the oil lamps, and not use "unfit incense."[3] And finally, G-d instructs Aaron to make atonement at the incense altar once per year. (This later became part of the ancient Yom Kippur service in the Jerusalem Temple.)

Parshah Interpretation: This week's chapter begins with the command for burning a lamp in the *mishkan* all night, using only the purest olive oil (with no contaminating solids); and it ends with G-d saying "I ... brought them out from the land of Egypt for Me to abide in their midst."[4]

If we move from the literal level to the hidden story, we must ask for the meaning of the lamp that shines in the *mishkan* existing within us. We can understand the lamp's light as representing the quality of awareness—that aspect of ourselves that is simultaneously self-aware, alert to our behavior and intentions, and at the same time aware of the self's immersion in the larger experience of Divine Presence.

Similarly, the purity of the olive oil that creates the light refers to the purity of our intention. For to be truly liberated from *Mitzrayim,* ready to be a Sanctuary for Divine Presence so that G-d can dwell within us, we must first have the intention to move in that direction. We must want to become a channel through which Divine Presence can express itself (via our actions in following the Ten Commandments and *mishpatim*).

As the chapter continues with rules of priestly dress, in which the priests' clothing must be of the same colors as those draping the *mishkan,* it hints at a ritualized, perhaps shamanic, merging of human with *mishkan,* and provides yet another clue that each of us is to take on the task, at the spiritual level, of actually becoming a home for the Divine.

And then, after a variety of other commands, the chapter states that the priest shall wear a gold plate on his forehead that is inscribed "Holy to YHVH."[5]

This image of the priest is reminiscent of the instruction of the most famous prayer of Judaism, the *Shema,* which says, "let them serve as a symbol on your forehead,"[6] to remind each of us of the prayer's credo that G-d is one—or, in our understanding—that everything in this world is a manifestation of G-d.

This whole *parshah* can be read at the literal level as being about the consecration both of a holy people and of the High Priest; or it can be read, instead, as pointing to the consecration of each of us individually if we choose to accept the covenant to love G-d, as the *Shema* says, "with all your heart and all your soul and all your might."[7]

For Formal Practice: When you are ready, continue to follow your breath with awareness of sensations in your chest, noting any constriction there or around your heart. If you can, be aware, as you breathe, of letting go of any such constriction, as you acknowledge your yearning to make your heart a place for the Divine Presence.

When you are ready, hold in front of you, as if it were a sign on your forehead, the intention of consecrating all your actions to YHVH. Use the phrase "I hold G-d in front of me always." (In Hebrew, the phrase is *Sheviti HaShem l'negdi tamid.*)

And slowly, as you relax into your breath, alternate that phrase whenever you like with the phrase "Holy, holy, holy" (in Hebrew, *Kadosh, kadosh, kadosh*), in regard to everything that falls into your awareness, including distracting thoughts, emotions and sensations.

In My Own Practice: *Yesterday, I wanted desperately to have a day off from work, and we had a huge snowstorm that would have made it easy for me to cancel my appointments. Yet I went out early in the morning, shoveled out my car, and left for my office.*

In sitting for this meditation, I am suddenly surprised by the realization that I had been offered a gift from G-d: the opportunity for the day off I so much wanted. The snowstorm hadn't been aimed at me, but its existence made possible an opportunity that I had ignored. I had spurned a gift from G-d because I hadn't been paying attention.

As I sit, I see through a different lens what it might mean to always hold G-d in front of me. Today, I see that it can mean seeing gifts showered upon me that I normally ignore. A snowstorm can be a gift, as can an unexpected free half-hour or a phone call from a friend or almost anything. As I sit, I see the world light up with bounty.

"And YHVH spoke to Moses, saying: 'When you add up the heads of the children of Israel....'"

—Exod. 30:11

Interpretive Overview: The Israelites now have a spiritual crisis in which they lose faith and build a golden calf to worship instead of the Divine. We, too, lose sight of G-d, creating our own golden calves of money, possessions, worldly power, beauty, or accomplishment; and the *parshah* is clear that none of these are more than idols—meaningless compared to the infinite Divine Presence. Indeed, YHVH cannot be grasped or defined, although G-d does declare a number of Divine qualities to Moses upon passing him as he shelters in the cleft of the rock. It is these Divine qualities that can be known and made part of us, so that we partake of G-d's holiness in our awareness and behavior.

Summary of *Parshah*: The *parshah* begins with G-d's final commands to Moses on Mount Sinai, after which Moses receives the two stone tablets that G-d has inscribed with the Ten Commandments. Moses has been gone for almost forty days, and the people are terrified that he'll never come back. When they ask Aaron to make them gods to lead them now, Aaron melts down all their gold jewelry, shapes it with a stylus, and makes a golden calf. And the people say, "These are your gods, Israel, who brought you up from the land of Egypt!"[1]

Aaron then builds an altar before the calf and calls for a festival to be held the following day to YHVH (rather than to pagan gods), which takes place with sacrifices and loud singing and dancing. Upon seeing what's happened, G-d tells Moses to hurry down, because the Israelites have already violated their covenant. G-d then vows to destroy them and turn over their promised inheritance to Moses.

Moses pleads for mercy, arguing that Egypt will say G-d intended to bring such an end all along, and reminding G-d of the promises made to Abraham, Isaac, and Jacob. G-d relents, and Moses sets off down the mountain with the stone tablets in his arms.

But when he gets close enough to see the golden calf and the dancing, he hurls the tablets in rage, shattering them in his fury. Taking punishment into his own hands, "he took the calf that they had made, and he burned it in fire and ground it until it was thin, and he scattered it on the face of the water and he made the children of Israel drink!"[2] Turning then on Aaron, Moses asks what the people did to him to have him bring such great sin upon them, and Aaron tells him what they said about needing gods to lead them. He also pretends not to have made the idol, saying that after the people gave him their gold, lo and behold, "I threw it into the fire, and this calf came out!"[3]

Seeing that Aaron has let the people fall into such disarray, Moses takes the punishment further, calling out, "Whoever is for the Eternal, come here!"[4] All of the tribe of Levi step forward, he tells them to kill the idolaters, and about three thousand men are then killed.

The next day, Moses tells the people that they have committed a great sin but that he is going to plead for them with the Divine. And he does, asking that he be erased from G-d's record unless YHVH forgives them. In return, G-d says that only those who have sinned will be erased, and sends a plague. (This chapter has a great deal of killing and punishment in it. Once we read the text metaphorically, we interpret punishment metaphorically as well. This will become clearer as we interpret Leviticus, Numbers, and Deuteronomy.) Then YHVH tells Moses to set out with the Israelites for the Promised Land, adding that an angel will lead them but that G-d will no longer go in their midst, so as not to destroy them. Hearing this, the Israelites take off their finery and go into mourning.

After a break in the narrative line having to do with the *mishkan,* Moses insists that he needs to know the "way" of YHVH if he is to be truly able to lead the people to the Promised Land; a few sentences later, he asks to see the very form of G-d, and the Divine answers that Moses cannot see G-d's face and live. But YHVH tells him he will be able to stand in a cleft in the rock and see G-d's back as the Divine passes before him. (At the literal level, the text is unselfconsciously anthropomorphic.) After this, Moses is told to carve two new stone tablets, upon which G-d will write the same words as on those Moses shattered.[5]

When Moses comes up the mountain with the tablets the next morning, G-d comes down in a cloud. Passing before Moses as Moses stands in the rock's cleft, G-d calls out what has become a famous passage in the Jewish High Holy Days liturgy: "YHVH, YHVH, merciful and gracious G-d, slow to anger and abounding in kindness and faithfulness, keeping kindness for thousands, bearing crime and offense and sin; though not making one *innocent*...."[6] And with that, Moses hurriedly kneels, asking YHVH to again dwell among the Israelites, forgiving their sin.

In a long response, G-d once again offers a covenant with the Israelites, with many commands attached to it. Moses then stays on the mountain for forty days and nights, and "he did not eat bread, and he did not drink water. And he wrote on the tablets the words of the covenant, the Ten Commandments."[7] When Moses finally descends with the new set of tablets, the skin of his face is so transformed that the people are afraid to approach him,[8] so that he wear a veil from then on, except when he speaks with G-d or reveals G-d's commands to them.

***Parshah* Interpretation:** In this chapter, the children of Israel lose sight of their connection to YHVH within forty days of Moses' disappearing onto Mount Sinai; and in their experience of being abandoned by YHVH, they turn to an image that they make: a golden calf.[9] This is the classic chapter about the ever-present possibility of losing faith—of having spiritual doubt.

Just as the children of Israel lose their sense of connection to YHVH as the source of their blessings, we, too, repeatedly experience apparent separation and disconnection from the Divine Presence. When we have lost this sense of connection to G-d, when we begin to even doubt its possibility, we, too, substitute other powers that we can lean on for blessing and safety. Not literally a golden calf, it may be the gold of money, or possessions, or worldly power, or beauty, or accomplishment of some kind. Sometimes our search for a substitute for the direct experience of the Divine Presence is even expressed through our becoming overly attached to the concreteness of ritual, including the ritual forms of religion.

But we must remember that G-d first appears to Moses as flame—a process, a presence without form. And YHVH gives a name that translates as "I Will Be What I Will Be," an action rather than a thing. Thus, Judaism uses the unpronounceable name YHVH to remind us that G-d refers to the unnamable, unknowable *being*-ness, the ground of reality that is beyond our comprehension. You can't pin YHVH down to any definition; you can't make any golden calf—physical or not. For this reason, the first commandment is "You shall make no image."

Yet this pure *being*-ness strives to be in relationship with us. Thus, G-d offers Moses a self-description that consists of attributes, such as mercy, grace, and faithfulness, that can only manifest through relationship and that are part of the very fabric of creation. Furthermore, the text says that we can directly experience Divine Presence as we emulate these qualities in our own actions.

For Formal Practice: Our intent is to experience the qualities of Divine Presence as they permeate the world, sustaining it.

When you are ready, place yourself at the cleft in the rock, as if you were Moses. As you follow your breath, going in and out, let yourself feel the Divine passing by you, calling out the qualities by which G-d is to be known.

As you breathe, imagine yourself taking in the qualities of the Divine, as Moses hears them:

"YHVH, YHVH, G-d merciful and gracious, slow to anger and abounding in kindness and faithfulness." (In Hebrew, *"YHVH, YHVH eyl rachoom v'chanoon, erech apayim v'rav chesed v'emet."*

G-d (*YHVH*)

G-d (*YHVH*)

G-d (*eyl*)

merciful (*rachoom*)

and gracious (*v'chanoon*)

slow (*erech*)

to anger (*apayim*)

and abounding in (*v'rav*)

kindness (*chesed*)

and faithfulness (*v'emet*)

Feel these qualities entering you as you inhale, and let them penetrate all the cells of your body, melding with them.

As you exhale, release the blended essence of yourself and the Divine qualities. Return them to the universe.

As you breathe, let these qualities waft toward you like the scent of the Divine *being*-ness, permeating all reality, inextricably woven into all existence and each of us. Follow your breath and let your mind open to any of these qualities as part of the very texture of your experience. Slowly let your mind empty to Divine Presence.

In My Own Practice: *As I sit with this meditation today, I can't feel the qualities. Then I realize that they do not—and perhaps cannot—stand alone. The words* kindness *and* faithfulness *are not truly nouns, for they have no separate existence of their own. None of these words stand alone. They can only describe the quality of an action, the emotional tone of an interaction. I can be given something with kindness, in a merciful and patient way.*

G-d is not a noun but a quality of action. Of Divine moving spirit.

Exodus/*Sh'mot*, 10, "And He Assembled"/*Vayak'heil* (Exod. 35:1–38:20)

"And Moses assembled all of the congregation of the children of Israel and said to them, 'These are the things that YHVH commanded, to do them: Six days work shall be done and in the seventh day you shall have a holy thing. A Sabbath, a ceasing to YHVH.' "

—Exod. 35:1

Interpretive Overview: In this chapter, the *mishkan* and its fittings are completed with great enthusiasm by the Israelites, who openheartedly donate even more than is needed. With the *mishkan* built, they are ready to move forward. But they (and we) need more than enthusiasm and intention if we are to follow a spiritual path. And so, at the beginning of the chapter, Moses repeats G-d's command that the Israelites observe the Sabbath as a day of rest. At the symbolic level, the command to rest—to simply be present in the moment without action—can be read as an instruction to let go of the ego's self-concerns and drive for control.

Summary of *Parshah*: Moses assembles all the Israelites to tell them what YHVH has commanded of them, beginning with the keeping of the Sabbath as a day without work, dedicated to G-d. He then states that G-d has asked for a donation from each of them "whose heart is moved [to donate]."[1] And he enumerates all the materials needed for the building of the *mishkan* (i.e., Sanctuary or Tabernacle or Tent of Meeting) and making of the priestly vestments.

Finally, he says, "Let everyone wise of heart among you come and make everything that YHVH has commanded."[2] And so the men and women bring their donations to Bezalel (whom G-d has told Moses to place in charge), and his helper Oholiab. The people bring more than is needed, so that those working on the project tell Moses to have them stop.

The remainder of the chapter describes in great detail the completion of the construction of the Tent of Meeting and everything belonging in it.

Parshah **Interpretation:** At the literal level, the story of the Book of Exodus begins with the Israelites' apparent disconnection from the Divine Presence, moves through their increasingly deep commitment to follow in the ways of G-d, and ends with their intimate, day-to-day awareness of YHVH's presence in the midst of their encampment. At the deeper level, the story of Exodus is a metaphor for our own spiritual growth, as we move from a secular existence—without YHVH in our life—to greater awareness of G-d's presence within and around us, as we attempt to emulate G-d's qualities in our actions. Despite our lapses, as chronicled in Exodus, we always have the possibility open to us of becoming able to feel the Divine Presence at all times.

Yet the path is a difficult one, despite our best intentions. In this deep reading of Exodus, this next-to-last chapter can be read as an explicit instruction for attaining such profound spiritual awareness.

"And He Assembled" begins with the commandment to keep the Sabbath as a day of rest for ourselves, just as it is a day of rest for YHVH. Even for G-d, the Sabbath is a time not of acting in the world—even for purposes that are good (such as building the Sanctuary)—but of simply *being*. And in Hebrew, the word for resting can also be translated as "re-ensouling." So G-d somehow is replenished, or re-ensouled, by stopping action.

We are told in Exodus that G-d is not reducible to any image whatsoever, and that the closest statement that can be made in giving the Divine a name is "I Am That I Am," or "I Will Be What I Will Be." If we attempt to emulate G-d by taking a day of rest, of pure *being*-ness, rather than of action, the text implies that we will come closer to knowing G-d's nature. And, in fact, a classic pathway to revelation is just to sit. Not to think, not to plan, not to look back or forward, but just to be sitting in the moment, moment by moment, coming closer to emulating pure existence—and in so doing, feeling YHVH as the pervasive underpinning of the world.

To be present in this way, without action or words or thought, is a fundamental meditative practice used in many spiritual disciplines to transcend the individual ego and open consciousness to the Divine Presence.

For Formal Practice: When you are ready, begin to follow your breath, noticing the sensations at your nostrils as you breathe in and out; or notice the movement in your chest or belly as you breathe. Be aware of your sensations without commenting, without naming, without interpreting. If a sound occurs, just let yourself hear it without comment or interpretation, and return to the sensations of breathing. And as you notice that you do begin to think, to name, to categorize, to plan, to worry, to do all the narrowing that the ego automatically does, return simply to awareness of sensation, not reaching for it but remaining open just to what *is.* You will probably find yourself thinking again and again, for this is what we do most naturally. Each time that you notice thought, gently return to sensation. As you open your awareness simply to what *is,* to *being* without *doing,* you may also open to the awareness of Divine Presence.

In My Own Practice: *More and more, I find that sensations do not seem particularly localized when I sit in meditation. If I make an effort—if I begin to do something with the sensations instead of simply noticing them—I can find which part of my body they are coming from. But if I just observe them, they are not connected to my body. There is, rather, a feeling of warmth somewhere below, an experience of pain somewhere behind and to the left, etc. The sensation remains very clear and very present, and can be quite intense, but it's not mine. It's just there. And so, the body that I inhabit seems insubstantial. Not quite there anymore.*

I follow the breath, feel the sensations, note sounds that I make no effort to identify.

No striking illuminations appear, no moment of clear Divine Presence. But calm and peace permeate the awareness.

I stand in the cleft of the rock as a living force goes past me, emanating ways of being in the world. As it passes, I am cradled, held for the moment, lovingly, mercifully. A force that is not so much slow to anger as patient with my failures. Endlessly patient, always ready to enfold me in love.

Exodus/*Sh'mot*, 11, "Accounts"/*P'kudei* (Exod. 38:21–40:38)

"These are the accounts of the Tabernacle, the Tabernacle of the Testimony, that were made by Moses' word...."

—Exod. 38:21

Interpretive Overview: In this last chapter of Exodus, the Israelites have completed the Sanctuary and are ready to move forward toward the Promised Land with the Divine Presence in their midst, for "YHVH's cloud was on the Tabernacle by day, and fire would be in it at night, before the eyes of all the house of Israel in all their travels."[1] At the deeper level of this story, we, too, are now carrying YHVH with us, within our hearts, and we, too, can be guided by G-d, for the Divine is always present, always available. We are traveling toward the Promised Land of enlightenment, the Garden Within, although we are not yet there.

Summary of *Parshah:* The accounts begin by saying that Bezalel made everything commanded by YHVH to Moses, and that Oholiab was with him. Then the sums are given of all the gold, silver, and bronze used, with specific notes in regard to exactly how the silver and gold were used in construction. A long section comes after this, detailing the making of the priestly vestments, some of it by "they" (i.e., Bezalel and Oholiab, and perhaps others) and some by "he," (not clear who). And when the Israelites finish making all the components of the Tent of Meeting and all the vestments, they bring what they have made to Moses, who blesses them upon seeing that they have done just as G-d commanded.

Then the Divine tells Moses to set up the Tabernacle, and everything in it (in detail), on the first day of the first month of the second year since leaving Egypt; when he's done, he is to consecrate the Tabernacle and everything in it. After this, he is to bring Aaron and his sons to the entrance, wash them, dress them in their priestly vestments, and anoint them so that they may function as priests in a lineage that will last forever.

Moses sets up the Tabernacle, as commanded, after which the cloud covers it and G-d's glory fills the Tabernacle so that Moses cannot enter. "And when the cloud was lifted from on the Tabernacle, the children of Israel would travel—in all their travels—and if the cloud would not be lifted, then they would not travel until the day that it would be lifted. Because YHVH's cloud was on the Tabernacle by day and fire would be in it at night, before the eyes of all the house of Israel in all their travels."[2] Thus ends the narrative of the Book of Exodus.

Parshah **Interpretation:** In this last section of Exodus, we complete the Sanctuary. While the text speaks of a physical structure, we are interpreting the *mishkan* in terms of psychological space, as we ready ourselves to be present to the Divine each day. For we have built a space within ourselves that opens our awareness to G-d's presence, creating it with great effort and cost, even if the cost is not measured in gold and silver and bronze, as it is at the literal level in this chapter. We have begun to clothe ourselves in holiness, even if not literally in priestly vestments. We have anointed ourselves not with holy oil but with the intention of following in G-d's ways, listening for the Divine voice.

As we try to make ourselves a channel for the Divine, we hope to receive G-d's guidance on our path, for in this moment of creation that is out of time and always accessible, YHVH is waiting for us: so that we can follow the cloud by day and the fire by night. But the way remains difficult, for neither fire nor cloud offer clear outlines. Both involve movement, even shape-shifting, rather than easy clarity, and sometimes the cloud does not seem to move at all, offering no guidance whatsoever in that moment.

For Formal Practice: When you are ready, focus on the image of G-d's presence in front of you. Let yourself sit with the image of a cloud by day, of fire by night.

If you need guidance in your life today, ask, and open your heart to hear whenever you are ready.

In My Own Practice: *Even though it's not the instruction, I begin with the mantra "I place G-d before me always."*

But there is too much I-ness in that. It's been helpful at other times, but now it doesn't work. I can't focus. Then I switch to the images of fire and cloud, as the instructions asked. The fire is life. But it is also destruction. It can go either way.

There are no guarantees in life.

I'm never going to know what happens next. Or what a choice will lead to. And even if something looks bad now, I don't know what good it may make possible. We never know the future. We have free will, but we can't control outcomes. I see my children, their wives, a new grandchild, another to come soon. I make my choices, trying to listen for guidance, but I have no control.

Yet, YHVH is still the fire in front of me. Offering far more than I get if I give in to despair or quiet resignation. The fire of life. Listen for vitality.

But the cloud blocks my vision. How can I move in the absence of sight? How do I dare? That's why they stay in camp, all those tribes of Israel. And yet I must leave camp, get out of bed in the morning, make choices.

Listen for the flame.

Interpretive Summation of Exodus/*Sh'mot*

Exodus is the story of rescue from slavery and the beginning of the journey to the Promised Land. Read literally, it revolves around three interwoven themes: First, G-d is revealed to the Israelites as a moral force, freeing them from slavery and the constriction of *Mitzrayim* (i.e., Egypt), so that they can serve G-d instead of Pharaoh by following the various commandments and laws. Second, G-d wants relationship, offering to be constantly present amidst the Israelites as long as they honor the covenant. Third, the mutual commitment of humans and G-d signals a new creation—that of a covenanted moral and spiritual world co-created by humans and G-d—, which is as important as the original creation of the physical universe.

At the deeper level, we are the Israelites, each of us individually. At this psychological level of Exodus, *Mitzrayim* is the state of mind in which we are bound up in the struggles of the ego to control reality. Whether we are arrogant Pharaohs who are certain that we can make happen whatever we choose, or despairing slaves who are convinced that we have no power at all, we are trapped in our own convictions of how the world works. In the course of Exodus, we begin to let go of this state of constriction, although we are frightened by the unknown in front of us and want often to return to our familiar habits of thought. In our best moments, we even commit ourselves to following G-d's path of compassion and loving-kindness, although we find the path extremely difficult and have many setbacks. But as we move into greater freedom from the ego's demands, our inner Sanctuary grows, and we can more easily be aware of the presence of G-d in each moment. As we become more able to enter the Garden Within, simply present to the *being*-ness that sustains all existence, we find our world to be filled with G-d's glory and holiness.

Yet, even at this culminating moment of Exodus, we can hear an implied warning, and that warning is true: we are still in the desert, far from the

Promised Land. Like the Israelites, we will repeatedly be plagued by doubt. And we can only glimpse G-d, the mysterious I Am That I Am, for G-d is always beyond our comprehension.

In the metaphor of the final chapter, the dilemma of our relationship with G-d is approached through the extraordinary imagery of fire and cloud—both the creative/destructive force of fire, alive but without form, and the impenetrable cloud, whose opacity must inescapably conceal the Mystery while seeming, also, to give it location.

And "YHVH's cloud was on the Tabernacle by day, and fire would be in it at night, before the eyes of all the house of Israel in all their travels."[1]

3

General Framework of Leviticus/*Vayikra*

The third book of the Torah is known in English as Leviticus, a name which emphasizes its presentation of the rituals and laws of the Levite priests. But the Hebrew name for Leviticus is *Vayikra,* taken from the opening sentence, "And G-d called…." I prefer using the Hebrew name because it takes us directly to the meaning we will be exploring: our relationship with the ever-present I Am That I Am.

Exodus set the scene for *Vakyikra,* as the Israelites built and completed the Sanctuary for the Divine to dwell not only amidst the community but within the heart of each person. *Vayikra* now continues the narrative as G-d remains a daily presence, a cloud by day and a pillar of fire by night, fundamentally beyond human comprehension, and yet somehow in the midst of the tribes clustered at the foot of Mount Sinai (and somehow present with us today).

What does it really mean, *Vayikra* asks, to be in covenant with this Divine force? What does it mean to actually have G-d in one's encampment, visibly present in one's life on a daily basis?

How do we behave when YHVH is living next door? How do we act toward each other if G-d is present? How do we act toward that awesome *being*-ness?

Turning to our inner experience, how does it feel to have full consciousness that YHVH is here and now, within us, when Divine power inspires both love and awestruck terror? *Vayikra* addresses a question that goes far deeper than following the ethics of the Ten Commandments, for it goes beyond rules of behavior to internal spiritual change as we each come to have direct experience of the Mystery we call G-d.

In exploring the nature of our relationship with G-d (whatever that word means to us), *Vayikra* provides instructions for self-transformation, so that each of us can become a holy Sanctuary (i.e., a *mishkan*) living in conscious communion with the Divine. As such, *Vayikra* can be read as the most mystical and rewarding of the five books of the Torah.

But *Vayikra* is also the most difficult book of the Pentateuch to understand— and, on its surface reading, probably the dullest. While it is a profound treatise on the meaning of holiness, its surface structure rises out of the mists of prehistory, and it is far less evocative to our modern consciousness than the mythic tales of Genesis or Exodus. Its perspective is so old, in fact, that it was already ancient, and its deeper meaning unclear, by the time of the rabbis who created the tradition of Torah interpretation during the Roman Empire.[1]

Vayikra has almost no stories, seems a jumble of ethical and cultic rules, and spends much of its text on ritual practices that, at the literal level, seem primitive, offensive, or—at best—incomprehensible. Since we don't feel comfortable completely discarding the text, we tend to ignore what we don't understand or agree with; in particular, we are likely to concentrate on the ethical commands. But while we may feel that ritual and biology are irrelevant to holiness, *Vayikra* does not. And so, if we look only at ethical rules, we are missing much of the meaning and intent of the total book.

In Vayikra's own understanding of deep spiritual work, ritual and ethical practices are inseparable in bringing us closer to, or further from, the holiness of G-d at every moment. In fact, ritual and ethics are intermingled in the text because they are both subsumed into another category entirely.

For *Vayikra* is imbedded in a worldview in which every aspect of life—including certain aspects of human biology—falls on a simple continuum that ranges from holy and pure at one end, to neutral in the middle, to profane and impure at the other end. In a general way, humans live in the middle realm, with most of what we do in daily life being neither holy nor impure, but neutral.

But the Divine is creator of all parts of the continuum. Because there is only one G-d, one source of power, G-d is the holy force that is both creative and destructive. On one end of the continuum, the Divine Presence creates all life, and sustains it moment by moment. At the other end, the Divine Presence also creates the awesome earthquake, and fire, and death. And mere humans cannot lightly trespass in either of these realms of power.

In fact, YHVH's realm of death and destruction is essentially forbidden to humans in its entirety. No calling up of spirits and no worship of the dead is allowed. To enter that lower realm is to die oneself. Even to come near this realm, even to handle a dead body, is to become impure. Rituals are needed, then, to cleanse us, to help us become neutral again. And at the symbolic level, we are told to practice love rather than destruction.

But we are also at risk if we cross the boundary—without adequate preparation—between our human realm and the realm of G-d's perfection. Only the High Priest can enter the innermost chamber of the Sanctuary, only once per year,[2] as commanded by the Divine—and only after many rites of purification. Even the middle chamber is limited to those specially prepared and named by the Divine, and failure to observe necessary ritual may cause death. Indeed, Aaron's sons die for just such a violation of ritual. Even the inadvertent coming into contact with a holy object will create a violation of boundaries that requires ritual undoing.

We are asked to purify ourselves so that we can safely approach G-d and open our hearts to YHVH's presence in our lives, committing ourselves to becoming conduits for G-d's compassion and love. For the Divine is calling us to come near so that G-d can manifest through us in the middle realm in which we dwell, through the moral sphere that belongs specifically to humanity.

In straightforward language, *Vayikra* asks us to be holy like YHVH by emulating Divine compassion in our own behavior in the world in which we live. It then sets forth a wide range of ritual and ethical practices that will lead us to this goal. At the core of the book is the impossibly general and demanding phrase "love your neighbor as yourself,"[3] which is followed soon after by an even more extraordinary charge to "love him [the stranger] as yourself."[4]

Despite the fact that we so often fail as a species to manage even acts of simple decency, *Vayikra* raises the stakes far higher. For *Vayikra* is not asking us to merely improve the way we behave. We are being asked instead to become holy, to imitate the Divine by treating others with loving-kindness and compassion because we see them through the lens of G-d's love and compassion for us. In Jewish tradition, this is the central teaching of Torah (as it is in so many other spiritual traditions); thus, a frequently quoted statement by Rabbi Hillel in the first century CE says "all the rest is commentary."[5]

Compassion is being demanded with full awareness of inevitable human fallibility. And so, *Vayikra* is filled with rules for both ritual and ethical behavior that will remove our impurities and increase our holiness. "You shall be holy because I am holy," says YHVH again and again, not in punishment, but as a statement of fact: if we are going to approach G-d, to reach for connection with YHVH, with Divine glory and power, then we must be holy ourselves or we will be destroyed. G-d's power will be too much for us to contain.

We tend to find *Vayikra* incomprehensible, because it espouses a worldview about ritual, purity, and holiness that is strange to us. But the text does not seem at all "primitive" once we begin to understand its deep meaning. As soon as we interpret the rules and rituals metaphorically, as we will while exploring each chapter, we can see that they speak to the very nature of the Divine as it permeates the universe. G-d is the source of life and death, and we are restricted to the realm of life. If we approach G-d too closely or without adequate purification, we ourselves become endangered and may even be destroyed; thus, we must be ritually cleansed.

In this metaphoric reading, we are not being asked to follow the literal and detailed rules *Vayikra* sets forth. Instead, we are being asked to bring into the human sphere those qualities of G-d that represent different components of the loving life force. These are such components as wholeness, integrity, balance (all aspects of the Hebrew word *shalom*), even perfection, as well as the qualities of mercy, compassion, and discernment.

The aspects of Divine holiness that we can approach are restricted to the middle realm, neither above nor below. Perhaps, a hint of such restriction to the middle realm comes into play in Genesis, after Adam and Eve eat of the Tree of Knowledge and are exiled from Eden before they can also eat of the Tree of Life and become immortal. *Vayikra* is struggling with making us holy in this world, where we exist in physical form, firmly placed in the middle realm of earthly life, asked to somehow imbue it with perfection—and this, despite full awareness of our fundamental imperfectability.

Leviticus/*Vayikra* Week by Week

Leviticus/*Vayikra*, 1, "And G-d Called"/*Vayikra*
(Lev. 1:1–5:26)

"The Eternal One called to Moses and spoke to him from the Tent of Meeting, saying: 'Speak to the Israelite people and say to them....' "

—Lev. 1:1[1]

Interpretive Overview: The Sanctuary is done, and the Divine is dwelling among us, but we need more guidance as to how to live in YHVH's presence on a daily basis. We are given instructions for answering G-d's call for constant relationship by offering several kinds of sacrifices in the Tabernacle. As the sacrifices are consumed by fire and transformed into smoke, they symbolize our commitment to serve G-d and let go of our baser selves so that we can bring G-d's compassion and loving-kindness into the human realm through our own intentions and actions.

Summary of *Parshah:* *Vayikra* begins with G-d's instructions for a variety of sacrifices that will continue to be mentioned throughout Leviticus, and that are central to our interpretation of the text. They include the *burnt offering,* the *grain offering,* and the *offering of well-being.*[2]

For them all, the person making the offering brings it to the outer courtyard of the Tent of Meeting, open to every Israelite. If the sacrifice is an animal (restricted to these domestic animals: bulls, sheep, or goats), the person kills it there by slitting its throat,[3] and drains its blood into a bowl for the priests, who then fling the blood on the altar. The text states, later on, that this is done because the blood holds the life force that must return to G-d.[4] (Thus, we are also forbidden to consume any blood from an animal.) The animal is always unblemished.

Meanwhile, the person who has killed the animal flays it, and cuts the body up so that the various parts may be distributed appropriately. The priests prepare the fire, and arrange the parts to be burnt on the altar.[5]

In the sacred ceremony of the *burnt offering,* all parts of the animal are totally consumed in the fire, going up to G-d as a "fragrant smell."[6]

In contrast, only a few organs and suet fat[7] are burnt up in the *offering of well-being.* The rest of the body is thought to have been shared out among family, friends, and priests (remembering that priests have no other source of meat). In fact, it appears that *Vayikra* sees animal life as so holy that the animal can be eaten only if it is killed in the context of a holy rite.

Then the text has G-d turn to the use of sacrificial offerings for atonement. First comes the ceremony of atonement to be made when someone sins inadvertently—whether a priest, the entire community, a leader, or an individual. In these cases, *the sin offering* (also called the *offering of atonement*)[8] is like the offering of well-being, except that no part of the animal is set aside as food; instead, everything not sacrificed on the altar is burnt outside the camp where ashes are normally spilled.[9]

This section on atonement closes with the sacrifice to be offered after knowingly committing a number of other clearly ethical breaches, such as stealing from someone or exploiting them. In these cases, payment must also be made to the person who has been harmed before the atonement sacrifice may be made to G-d. (Apparently, such penitential repayment was considered to convert the intentional sin to an inadvertent one.)[10]

***Parshah* Interpretation:** *Vayikra* begins just after the Israelites have followed G-d's instructions for building a holy place, a Sanctuary for the Divine to dwell in the midst of their community and within the heart of each of them individually. They are at a high point of commitment, ready to begin traveling through the wilderness, following the cloud of G-d by day and the fire of G-d by night.

But before they start their journey from Mount Sinai to the Promised Land, they need instructions on how to live with G-d on a daily basis. In this first chapter of Leviticus/*Vayikra,* G-d calls out to them, describing the various sacrifices they are to make at the altar of the Sanctuary.

The word we translate as "sacrifice," however, means something very different in Hebrew, in which "sacrifice" is derived from the verb "to come near."[11] So G-d is calling out, and our response is to come near, to approach, with our offering.

Thus, the sacrificial offerings can be viewed as metaphor. It is understood that G-d has no need to consume the offerings; instead, the sacrifice conveys our intention to draw near and make a place for YHVH within the heart of each of us.

The animal is always pure and unblemished: the best of ourselves. When we turn it all to smoke in the burnt offering, which is the first sacrifice described, we are ritually expressing our commitment to the path of holiness, metaphorically offering all of ourselves to G-d's service. As the entire animal burns, our lowest passions as well as our highest yearnings are to be consumed by fire, returning to the living, unnamable force of creation. The fire itself is a symbol of that unnamable source of life and death; and in the burnt sacrifice, we offer all that we are and all we can be, ready to be consumed in the flame of G-d, ready to be an open channel for G-d's presence on earth.

In the other sacrifices of this chapter, we burn only certain of the animal's innards—kidneys, part of the liver, and the hard layer of suet fat that lies over them and over the entrails and genitals. The reasons for sacrificing these particular parts have been lost for more than two thousand years; however, I am indebted to Mary Douglas'[12] discussion of the symbolic meaning of these organs, because her interpretations have led me to my own suppositions.

There seems to be deep significance to the parts of the body that are chosen for burning. If I think of the body in terms of zones, the kidneys and other inner organs that are covered by the hard suet fat seem to represent our passions (as they were thought to do in ancient times, and as the genitals still do), which are essential to our survival and capacity for creation. But our passions also give rise to the emotions of anger, fear, lust, and greed that we need to control if we are to serve G-d and open up to the Divine Presence.

In this imagery, the hard suet that covers these organs acts as armor, hiding the passions from the light of awareness, obstructing their exposure so that we remain unchanged, trapped in our egoistic needs and desires. The Torah uses the phrase "uncircumcised lips" and "circumcise my heart," as well as the rite of circumcision (i.e., the unsheathing of the penis), to convey in concrete terms this kind of resistant and self-protective encasement; and the covering must be addressed if we are to truly change our ways in order to answer the Divine call, *Vayikra,* with the response, "Here I am."

In the symbolism of the suet being peeled away and burnt, we are offering up our armor, exposing the inner organs so that we can begin to recognize the passions and fears that drive us away from loving-kindness.[13] Thus, the opening chapter of the Book of Leviticus recognizes both our desire to answer G-d and our resistance. The burnt offering represents our yearning as we offer ourselves totally to the Divine Presence; the other two kinds of offerings implicitly represent our conflict—our being torn between yearning and resistance as we peel away the suet covering to renew our commitment. (In the sin offering we are atoning for some kind of forbidden action that we have already committed; in the offering of well-being, we must make atonement for taking an animal's life if we are to eat it without committing a sin.)

For Formal Practice: Remembering that the word *Israelite* translates as "G-d wrestler," let us read the *parshah* as if it were written today for each of us as G-d wrestlers.

In this first chapter, "And He Called*"/Vayikra,* we will contemplate our inner conflict—our desire for communion with G-d and our simultaneous resistance.

As G-d calls out to us, let us respond with the phrase "Here I am" or *Hineinei.* When you are ready, begin the meditation practice by keeping the phrase in your mind, or chanting it, and then gradually let go of the word, while keeping the intent in your mind of saying yes to G-d. As distracting thoughts intrude, notice them as resistance and return briefly to the words: *Hineinei.* "Here I am."

In My Own Practice: *As I meditate today, I am filled with awe of the Divine Presence. And I am frightened to commit myself, because the demands for purification feel infinite. I will never satisfy them and I am afraid of judgment—even punishment—as I fail. I don't want to say, "Hineinei. Here I am." As I sit, I know that I have felt different at other times, far less afraid. But today is today.*

I give up on Hineinei, *try only to follow my breath, to be with my breath, to calm down, to just be. As I sit, I realize that I have been trying to say* Hineinei *to my vision of an all-powerful, completely transcendent being—my father, perhaps, when I was a little girl, now masked as the old man on the heavenly throne. How could I possibly say, "Here I am," to that? I just want to hide.*

But YHVH is the process, the I Am That I Am, the permeating presence within as well as without. As I sit, my mind gradually quiets until there is only the I Am. I am not apart from it. I am its manifestation in physical form. The whole world is that manifestation, even the air breathing in and out of this body. All. Hineinei. *Here I am. Here. Sitting, breathing. I am here.*

Leviticus/*Vayikra*, 2, "Command"/*Tzav*
(Lev. 6:1–8:36)

"And YHVH spoke to Moses, saying: 'Command Aaron and his sons, saying, 'This is the instruction....' "

—Lev. 6:1

Interpretive Overview: G-d commands that a fire be kept burning eternally at the altar, follows with further instructions for making the sacrificial offerings, and ends with the consecration of Aaron and his sons. At the metaphoric level, the whole *parshah* is a discourse on spiritual preparation and intention, as framed in the language of ritual: for we move from the eternal flame that symbolizes our awareness, to sacrificial offerings that represent our surrender of self-centeredness, to the consecration that marks our spiritual advance. In the symbolism of ritual, we are asked to be conscious of a renewed intention to serve G-d, not only by our behavior but within the depths of our heart.

Summary of *Parshah:* The *parshah* opens with YHVH's command for the priest to keep a fire burning at the altar at all times. (This fire became what is called the eternal flame, now an electric lamp found at the front of synagogues and many churches.) The text then supplies detailed instructions, yet again, for performing the sacrifices. This section also includes the reiteration of the command (without explanation) never to eat the fat or blood of an animal.

Then G-d has Moses assemble the people at the *mishkan* to witness the consecration of Aaron and his sons as priests. In this ritual, Moses washes Aaron and Aaron's four sons with water, dresses Aaron in the priestly garments as described in earlier chapters, puts anointing oil on the Tabernacle and on everything in it, and sprinkles the altar seven times. Finally, he brings forward Aaron's sons and dresses them too in their garments.

Now, Moses offers three sacrifices: a sin offering of a bull to purify the Sanctuary, then a burnt offering of a ram, and finally an ordination offering of a second ram to consecrate the priests. In each case, Aaron and his sons lay their hands on the animal before Moses slaughters it; then Moses kills the animal, cuts it up for sacrifice as has been commanded, and flings its blood on the altar.

In the ordination offering, Moses also puts some of the ram's blood onto the right earlobe, right thumb, and right big toe of Aaron and his sons, as G-d has instructed. (No explanation has been given in the text for why these places on the body have been chosen). Then he has Aaron and his sons hold up the parts of the ram to be sacrificed, along with some of the bread from the basket that is always in the Sanctuary, burns these offerings on the altar, and sets aside the ram's breast as food.[1] Finally, he completes the ceremony by sprinkling some of the anointing oil and some of the blood that has been flung on the altar onto Aaron, his sons, and their clothes.

After this, Moses tells them they must stay in the Sanctuary for seven more days, eating the meat (i.e., the ram's breast) and the bread from the basket.

Parshah **Interpretation:** The whole Torah is a spiritual workbook for each of us as individuals. So how can we read this chapter in terms of its meaning for us today, as we move into our own higher states of consciousness?

As already stated, the animal sacrifices that are being described in these rituals of purification and priestly consecration can equally well be seen as metaphors for our transformation of consciousness as we open our hearts to G-d. The animal is transformed into smoke, perhaps into the cloud of G-d, and the community and its priests offer themselves up to the service of G-d through the symbol of the animal sacrifice. In the burnt offering, they offer all of themselves, both good and bad. When only the fat and certain internal organs are burnt as in the sin offering, they are turning over to the Divine any self-centered resistance they may still have to serving YHVH. Either way, their intention is to symbolically transform their baser desires, as they commit to this sacrificial process.

But Leviticus is structured so that we move to higher and higher levels of holiness as it progresses. In this chapter, the focus shifts from the average member of the community to Aaron and his sons. As the priestly intermediaries between the people and the Divine, they are closer to G-d, and have to be at a higher level of holiness, each son single-pointed in his intention to remain conscious of his vow at all times.

In the course of their consecration as priests, Aaron, his sons, and the sacrificial altar are all doused with animal blood. With this action, they are being joined to the very essence of the Divine as physically expressed, for blood is the elemental life force, the force of creation. They have offered themselves through the metaphor of the eternal flame and animal sacrifice, and now they are transported into the realm of the Divine.

Of course, Aaron and his sons are not merely themselves in this narrative; throughout *Vayikra,* they also represent each of us as we progress in our spiritual development.

In this second chapter of *Vayikra,* their consecration may also stand for our position at the initiation of a new spiritual path. By linking the eternal flame with the priestly ceremony, the narrative perhaps represents the particularly focused and elevated state of consciousness we are in as we make a new commitment or renew an old one. Although it is very hard today for us to comprehend the meaning of ritual purity and contamination in Torah, we can have some feeling for it when we read that Aaron and his sons are to remain in the Sanctuary for seven more days and eat food that has itself been consecrated, food that is called the "holy of holies."[2] For we are somehow purified in the very act of making a new resolution, and must separate ourselves as much as we can, at least for a time, from whatever might distract or tempt us.

For Formal Practice: When you are ready, let us begin with a phrase from the Jewish prayer book: "I place G-d before me always." In Hebrew, the phrase is *Shiviti HaShem l'negdi tamid.*

Begin by singing this in your mind, or chanting it, in Hebrew or English, and then gradually let go of the words, while keeping the intent of them in your emptying mind. For our intent is to give ourselves over at all times to the service of G-d, so that we become shaped to G-d's will. As distracting thoughts intrude, return briefly to the phrase, in English or Hebrew, "I place G-d before me always."

This meditation can also be visualized as the burnt offering: transformed in the flame just as we are asking that our ego, in this meditation, be transformed. We are offering our small flame to become immersed in the larger flame of G-d.

In My Own Practice: *I have recently begun to ask the Divine Presence for help in very specific ways. Please G-d, let me find the hearing aid I've misplaced that is so expensive. Please G-d, help me to get more sleep this week. Like that. It's not that I expect a response. I don't believe in G-d coming to the rescue like the cavalry. But often, I get what I asked for: I find the hearing aid and someone decides to cancel an early morning session. And each time, I stop to give a moment of thanks.*

As I meditate today, the thought appears that this kind of prayer is part of service to G-d. I've been too arrogant to ask, keeping myself in some way separate and distinct from G-d, stubbornly wrapped in my own individual ego. To pray for help is to let go of that boundary line between us.

There is only G-d. The whole physical world is a manifestation of the one Divine Presence. I don't know what that means with my intellect; my intellect can't make any sense of those words. But I don't need to understand.

My intellect is convinced that the outcome is unchanged by my prayer. And in the course of my life, I've certainly had many prayers go unanswered. But none of that matters.

What matters is asking and what matters is giving thanks—and giving thanks for everything, whether or not the hearing aid is found or the working hours are fewer, for it is all G-d manifesting in my life.

"And it was, on the eighth day, Moses called to Aaron and to his sons and to Israel's elders."

—Lev. 9:1

Interpretive Overview: All is now ready to receive the Divine in the Tabernacle. But catastrophe occurs, for Aaron's two oldest sons cross a boundary that protects them from YHVH's overwhelming power, and they are consumed in the flame of Divine glory. Later in the *parshah,* YHVH tells the Israelites what foods may and may not be eaten; these instructions, like the story of Aaron's sons, speak to the issue of keeping appropriate boundaries as we each follow a spiritual path in our daily life. We must balance being present in the world with the experience of oneness with G-d; learn to differentiate our own desires from the promptings of the Divine; and pay close attention to what we ingest and make part of ourselves, psychologically and spiritually.

Summary of *Parshah:* Now that Aaron and his sons have been consecrated as priests, they are ready to call YHVH into the Sanctuary. Moses brings them together with Israel's elders, and tells Aaron to proceed by making atonement for himself and the whole people through appropriate offerings at the altar. Aaron performs the sacrifices as instructed and comes out of the Tent of Meeting with Moses to bless the people. The climax of the ceremony occurs as YHVH's glory appears to everyone there, while G-d's fire consumes the offerings. All the people see, and shout, and fall on their faces.

But then comes catastrophe. With G-d's glory fully present, Aaron's two oldest sons, Nadab and Abihu, "each took his fire pan, put fire in it, and laid incense on it; and they offered before the Eternal alien fire, which had not been enjoined upon them. And fire came forth from the Eternal and consumed them."[1]

Moses tells two of Aaron's cousins to carry the bodies of Nadab and Abihu outside the camp. After this, there are several exchanges in which Aaron and his remaining two sons are told, first by Moses and then by G-d (who speaks directly to Aaron for the first time since the beginning of Exodus), that they must continue with the prescribed ritual rather than go into mourning. If they do not continue, they will die and G-d will be angry at the whole people. In silence, Aaron and his sons appear to obey, but Moses finds, sometime later, that they have not eaten the food set aside for them as part of the sacrifices. When he becomes angry about this break with ritual, Aaron speaks at last, asking how it would have been good in the eyes of G-d for him to have eaten after his sons were just killed. And the text says that "when Moses heard this, he approved."[2]

Then the focus of the chapter shifts to the rules for distinguishing which animals can be eaten and which animals are forbidden to the Israelites. (These rules form the basis of the Jewish dietary laws about which foods are or are not *kosher*. They are given without explanation, and Torah commentators have never been completely successful in understanding the reasons for the choices that are made.)[3] G-d also says that a person or thing made impure by contact with the carcass of any of the forbidden creatures can be purified by washing and waiting until evening.

In the chapter's next to last paragraph, the text uses a phrase that will be repeated throughout *Vayikra:* "Because I am YHVH, who brought you up from the land of Egypt to be G-d to you, and you shall be holy because I am holy."[4]

***Parshah* Interpretation:** The opening of Leviticus has continued on the high plane with which Exodus ends, for its opening focus is on our holy commitment to serving G-d. In reading the story of Aaron's sons, we must bear in mind that the Sanctuary exists within each of us, for G-d is an internal Presence in the deepest part of us. So these events refer, as always, to our inner experience. But the chapter is ambiguous.

In some interpretations,[5] Nadab and Abihu are so caught up in their craving for union with YHVH that they want only to offer the fire of their individual selfhoods at the altar. The "alien fire" that they bring forward is their very being; and their essence is consumed as they merge into the larger consciousness of G-d, even though their bodies stay behind.

Anyone who has felt ecstasy in prayer or meditation practice knows how strong the desire is to be consumed—to stay in that state of selfless openness to Divine Presence. In comparison, it is so much drudgery to attend to the details and behavior of the daily here and now, to put into action G-d's commands on how to live in this world. But the message of Torah is always that we most truly carry out G-d's words as we live our lives in the secular world.

In other interpretations, Aaron's sons bring something new to the altar, something not commanded by YHVH, because they are motivated to do something "special" for this extraordinary moment. Thus, they may believe themselves to be pure in intention but, in fact, may be driven by personal ego, by the desire to stand out. As such, the story contains a warning about the destruction that can arise when we fail to distinguish the true voice of G-d from our own promptings.

In the second part of this *parshah,* the focus expands. For we not only need boundaries to protect us from the holy realm of YHVH's infinite and overwhelming power, as in the story of Nadab and Abihu; in the middle realm, in which we live, we also need boundaries separating us from the lower realm of death and destruction (which also belong to the Divine).

Thus, Aaron refuses to eat the holy food set aside for him in the *mishkan,* because his sons have just died, and Moses approves of Aaron's decision when he finds out. We can interpret Aaron's refusal as involving just this need to separate the realm of death (the impure) and the realm of the Sanctuary (the pure). Without commenting on the juxtaposition, the text then expands on this approach to separating pure from impure, providing a long series of laws about what we can and cannot eat.

This part of the *parshah* may be read as metaphor, referring to all that we ingest, to all that we allow to enter our being, with ingestion of the pure and holy heightening our harmony with G-d and ingestion of the impure and unholy taking us away from the paths of serving the Divine. What we eat, what we read, what we watch on TV or via computer or in the movies, what we allow into ourselves as conversation, what we ingest from another person or situation in the way of ideas or feeling or emotions all affect our state of holiness.

For Formal Practice: When you are ready, begin the contemplation practice by placing yourself under the protection of YHVH. You may choose to wrap yourself in white light or in a real or imagined prayer shawl (in Hebrew, *tallit*) held in the wings of G-d's presence.

Then ask these questions: "What is proper to ingest? What should I take in? What should I not accept into my being?" Quiet your mind by following your breath. As you continue to open your heart to the Divine Presence, ask again: "What is proper to ingest? What should I take in? What should I not accept into my being?" Breathe in and out, and wait quietly for any answers. Return to the question if you lose focus. Listen in the quiet for response.

In My Own Practice: *As soon as I begin contemplation practice, I see myself in a moment that I had with a friend last week. We are talking about an upcoming event. She is unenthusiastic, even critical of the person who is organizing it. I decide not to go. Why bother? It'll be boring. A waste of a day. Then the memory fast-forwards to the next scene. She is telling me that she did attend, and she had a wonderful time.*

I feel betrayed. I've been left out again.

I return to the contemplation, considering what to ingest, what to let in, what to keep out.

I see that I let in my friend's negativity and judgment. I allowed her annoyance to color my own feelings, even nullify them. I recognize that I am too easily influenced. Even worse, the other's judgment takes on a life of its own, becomes magnified, and obliterates my own sense. My friend wasn't even all that negative: after all, she went to the party.

I recognize the presence of what, in Hebrew, is called the lashon hara, *or the evil tongue. We are warned against it. No gossip permitted, no talking about a person not present. Because it is like taking in a spirit, a demon force. I become possessed. This requires a boundary: do not ingest.*

Another day that I sit with the meditation, I feel protected as soon as I follow the instruction of wrapping myself in the shawl of G-d's presence. I can feel G-d's love pouring into me.

I go to the contemplation, considering what to ingest, what to keep out.

Tears immediately well up. I keep out love. I just ignore its presence. I choose not to feel the other person's warmth or compassion or downright love. I hear the words, but don't believe them. I see the actions of love but don't connect them to the thing itself. And so I isolate myself. I keep out what should be embraced.

Leviticus/*Vayikra*, 4, "She Will Bear Seed"/*Tazria*
(Lev. 12:1–13.59)

"And YHVH spoke to Moses, saying: 'Speak to the children of Israel, saying, "A woman, when she will bear seed and give birth to a male, will be impure seven days." ' "

—Lev. 12:1

Interpretive Overview: While much of the last chapter focused on what is proper to take into ourselves from outside, this one does the opposite. For it concentrates on leakage from within the body to the outside, whether from the bleeding of a woman after childbirth, or from a variety of skin conditions. The chapter can be read symbolically in terms of our difficulty maintaining our spiritual concentration, so that our focus leaks away and our life force dissipates.

Summary of *Parshah:* This chapter distinguishes a variety of what it calls impurities of the physical self, along with instructions for purification practices. Once again, it uses specific physical examples to clothe its metaphoric meaning, presenting abstract ideas through limited examples. In language that is quite alien to us, the chapter focuses on two examples of physical impurity.

The first, a woman's impurity after childbirth, is referred to as similar to the impurity of her menstruation, and presumably, therefore, refers to the leakage of blood from inside her body.[1] In either case, she can neither enter the Tabernacle nor touch any holy thing until it is over; and her stint of impurity is ended with ritual sacrifice of a burnt offering and a sin offering.

The second form of leakage that leads to impurity seems to refer to a number of different skin disorders, which are lumped together under the rubric

173

of "leprosy" (although not what we mean today when using that word). In all cases, the priest repeatedly examines the afflicted person's skin and determines the state of purity as well as the necessary cleansing ritual, which is based on what the skin looks like. What is most notable is that a person can repeatedly alternate between pure and impure. Instructions are also given for the priest's actions when leprosy affects clothing of wool, linen, or leather, in which case the priest may burn the affected area or rip it out.

***Parshah* Interpretation:** We interpreted last week's food taboos as a metaphor for the issue of creating impurity in ourselves by taking in from outside what is taboo—or impure—psychologically and spiritually. This week's chapter instead raises the issue of becoming impure by letting out what should be kept in.

In these chapters, we are looking at impurity of self as we prepare to enter the Sanctuary within the heart (i.e., as we deepen our relationship with YHVH). In this context, skin lesions and bleeding after childbirth both involve an opening through which there is leakage of what is inside us, of what can be seen as life essence. In childbirth, in fact, the bleeding away of life essence can result in death if left unchecked. So the impurity may be seen to consist essentially of life essence being lost, and perhaps dangerously so.

The spiritual question here is not about sinfulness or punishment, but about diminishment of life force as one prepares to open one's consciousness to the Divine. I understand the examples to be metaphors for the psychological experience of losing one's concentration or focus, or of becoming inattentive. (We must remember that the language of Torah can be interpreted as if it were dream language that uses physical analogies for psychological statements, so that being in a sailboat that capsizes in the ocean is analogous to being overwhelmed by circumstance, or to psychologically drowning.)

If you've ever prepared for a new project by clearing your desk or your office, or if you've cleaned your house thoroughly before going on vacation, you may understand the psychological process we are discussing here; clearing the desk and cleaning the house are both acts that express, in physical form, the inner experience of clearing one's mind.

In this chapter, we are preparing to enter a different state of consciousness so that we can be open to the call of the Divine, leaving behind anything that does not belong to the realm of the sacred. As we focus our awareness on G-d, we want no leakage of life force, no weakening of intention. We want to be one-pointed, yearning for closeness with YHVH and offering ourselves in as whole a state as we can manage—in that sense, unblemished.

For Formal Practice: When you are ready, let yourself contemplate the metaphor of having your essential life force dissipate, feeling it trickling out of you, leaking away, wasted. Lost. Let the images come to you without thought as you follow your breath in and out. Notice them and let them go. When you are ready, offer yourself to the Divine Presence.

In My Own Practice: *Immediately comes the sense of busyness, of taking on too much, so that I have too little time to just exist—to be simply present. Then there is a sense of overwhelming fatigue and sadness—life force dissipating, vanishing. There is no end to the To Do list. Things to do to please others, to prove I am a good person. My mind is like a kaleidoscope, fragmented into compartments of obligation. To patients, to family, to friends, to self-improvement.*

I am still caught in childhood images of being judged and found wanting. I assume I am still being judged. I let that assumption cross into me. I ingest it.

And so I have my To Do lists. My life force leaking away as I try to please.

I return to the breath. The peace of being with the breath. No thought. Blue light begins to appear in the center of my vision, behind my lids. I breathe.

How to bring this peace into the world of action?

The answer comes: Stop ingesting fantasied ghosts of judgment. The past is over. It is I who make the judgments now, upon myself. Come into the living presence of the moment. The Divine is always here. Do each action for itself alone, and then there is no leakage. See it as holy or let it go.

Leviticus/*Vayikra*, 5, "Leper"/*M'tzora*
(Lev. 14:1–15:33)

"And YHVH spoke to Moses, saying: 'This shall be the instruction for the leper in the day of his purification....' "

—Lev. 14:1

Interpretive Overview: The focus now shifts to purification rites for conditions that occur repeatedly, with complex rites being offered for the serious disease called leprosy, and simple ones for the inevitable events of menstruation and the nocturnal emission of semen. Expanding on the concern with leakage of life essence, the metaphor seems to refer to habits that result in loss of focus and dissipation of spiritual energy. Some habits are more problematic than others and need more serious interventions, but even serious problems can be dealt with, for spiritual healing and a return to wholeness and purity can always take place.

Summary of *Parshah*: This chapter centers on the rules for purification from conditions that repeatedly occur, beginning with a variety of skin conditions that were called leprosy in the prior chapter. Leprosy can involve not only the person, but a house, in which case, it seems to refer to mold. The second group of impurities consists of genital discharges, whether because of illness or through the natural processes of semen emission by men and menstruation by women.

The ritual for recovery from leprosy is far more complex than that for impurities surrounding genital discharge. After the priest pronounces the leper healed, an eight-day purification ceremony, which has much in common with the priestly consecration,[1] takes place. After the details of this ritual are given, the chapter describes rituals for purifying a house that has leprosy, (which appears to be some kind of contaminating mold).

177

Once the house is pronounced healed, the ceremony is similar to that for purifying the leper, involving the same materials.

After this, purification rituals are described for genital discharges, whether from some kind of illness, from the discharge of semen,[2] or from menstruation. In the case of the emission of semen, all that is needed for purification is washing the person or anything the semen touches, and waiting until evening. Other discharges are treated more seriously, with washing being effective only after the discharge stops. Genital discharges (other than the normal emission of semen) and menstruation also call for a small sin offering and burnt offering of pigeons or turtledoves.

The chapter ends with YHVH saying that these rituals are necessary to protect those who become impure, "Lest they die through their impurity by defiling My Tabernacle which is among them."[3]

***Parshah* Interpretation:** The last two *parshot* have described the state of "impurity" that results from the leakage of bodily fluids when the boundary between inside and outside is ruptured. As our life force seeps away through the rupture, *Vayikra* places us on the forbidden side of a boundary line, on the same side as dissolution, decay, and even death. On the wrong side of the boundary, we become ritually impure and separated from G-d as creative force.

Reframing the ritual imagery in psychological terms, we can say that purity consists of being focused on becoming a channel for the Divine to manifest in this world. Impurity occurs when our energy dissipates into experiences of fear, anger, greed, etc. Our hope is to be freed of such little-*i* ego concerns—impurities—as we turn to the service of G-d or, at the least, become able to keep the passions of the little-*i* from leaking into behavior.

In this *parshah,* two of the ritual impurities are commonplace: menstruation and emission of semen. Because leprosy has been described in the prior chapter as appearing and disappearing repeatedly, it too may represent impurity that is an inevitable part of life, but it is far more serious, because now leakage of life force is everywhere, all over the body. It is so serious that it requires that the leper be sprinkled with blood—the essence of life force—at two different times, and in a manner that we have seen before, but only in consecrating the priests.[4]

So the examples range from those states of impurity that can easily be rectified to one—labeled leprosy—which is extreme. In the metaphor, such states speak to our going back and forth between times of greater and lesser focus, and greater and less dissipation of life force, because that is the nature of being human. We are, after all, made of the dust of the earth as well as of the Divine Essence. And sometimes our loss of focus is so extreme that it permeates all of our life, threatening us with spiritual death. Moreover, the dangers become greater as we progress along a spiritual path, for we feel our failures more as our standards rise.

The *parshah* suggests that we inevitably vacillate between states of greater and lesser purity, at different times acting as better or worse vessels for G-d's presence in our internal *mishkan*. The symbols also imply that coming back to G-d will be harder if we have erred more, but that coming back is always possible.

For Formal Practice: When you are ready, focus attention on your breath. When you are ready, go deeper into yourself, past the outer layers that you present to the external world. Bring your awareness to the Sanctuary within yourself, in which you yearn to be open to the Divine Presence.

When you are ready, let yourself become aware of habitual ways in which your life force gets dissipated. Let yourself open to some of the repetitive habits and patterns of your life that close off your awareness. Notice the physical sensations connected with the loss of life force.

Remember that it is fundamental to your nature as a human being to move back and forth between states of purity and impurity. Just observe.

In My Own Practice: *As soon as I attend to the feeling of dissipating my life force, I go to yesterday's experience of trying to have a clerk correct a large monetary error involving eventual retirement benefits. I'd received a letter saying I needed to act immediately if I felt changes were needed in the company's numbers.*

In the memory, I can feel my whole body tense, my blood pressure rise, my mouth tighten. I am afraid that I am being falsely reassured by the clerk helping me, that the error won't get corrected, even though she is making changes in the computer system as I sit with her. I feel that there is more I should be doing to make sure the error is fixed. My body is activated, ready to charge, sure that there is some other action I ought to be taking, but I don't know what it is.

I can feel the tightness in my shoulders and back, and know that this is dissipation of life force into fear and worry that I am not doing enough, or that I am doing something wrong. In the meditation, I go back to calm, feeling the difference as my internal space expands. This experience isn't about the now, about taking action as needed; it's about letting the little-i take over my feelings, going back into childhood experiences, and into fantasies about what might happen "if." I have lost my connection to the Divine; I have lost that focus. Instead of equilibrium and serenity with the clerk, I feel jagged, disjointed.

The body wants to defend itself. Inevitably.

But, instead, I follow my breath. Feel a return to calm as I let go of the fantasies of what might happen *and return to what* is happening. *The issue is about my focus, my internal state of purity.*

Leviticus/*Vayikra,* 6, "After the Deaths"/*Acharei Mot* (Lev. 16:1–18:30)

"And YHVH spoke to Moses after the death of Aaron's two sons—when they came forward in front of YHVH and died."

—Lev. 16:1

Interpretive Overview: This chapter brings to a close Leviticus' instructions for spiritual commitment and purity, as G-d mandates the ceremony for the annual Day of Atonement (known as *Yom Kippur*) and rededication to the Divine that is required of the entire people. All have contributed to a loss of holiness and the Tabernacle's consequent defilement; and now the High Priest enters the Holy of Holies, the innermost chamber where G-d dwells, to purify it and begin anew. By focusing on Aaron performing these dangerous rituals while still grieving over the deaths of his sons, the *parshah* emphasizes even more the high standard it proposes. For Aaron represents an ideal of focused selflessness as he puts his grief to the side in order to serve the Divine for the good of the whole community.

Summary of *Parshah:* This is the only day in which Aaron enters the Holy of Holies.[1] The text opens with a warning that Aaron must exercise great care and that no one else must enter any part of the Sanctuary while he is inside (in each case because of the danger of inappropriately coming too close to G-d's glory—as Aaron's sons had done only days before). Because the ceremony gives us some glimpse of the emotional power of the ancient rituals, I have summarized it in some detail below.

Aaron must rise at dawn, bathe, and dress in only the simplest clothing—a linen tunic, breeches and a turban—instead of his usual ornate vestments Then he is to bring a bull as a sin offering into the Sanctuary, to atone for himself and his household and all the priests. He must also choose two goats from the community, one of which will be the people's sin offering.

After slaughtering the bull, he is to take glowing coals from the altar, along with two scoops of incense, into the middle chamber of the Sanctuary, where he places them on the incense altar to make smoke. So blinded by the smoke that he cannot not see the Divine Presence, he can then safely enter the inner chamber, the Holy of Holies where G-d dwells, with a bowl of the bull's blood. There, he is to purge the Ark of the priests' accumulated impurities by sprinkling the blood, the holy life force, first directly on the Ark and then seven times on the floor of the inner chamber, as ritually prescribed.

After this, he is to exit the inner chamber to slaughter the goat that is the people's sin offering, and return with its blood to cleanse the Holy of Holies of the people's impurities in exactly the same way. Thus he is to purge the inner shrine of the "impurity and transgressions of the Israelites, whatever their sins."[2] Finally, he is to similarly purify the rest of the Tabernacle with the blood of the bull and goat.

When he is finished, he is to place both hands on the head of the second goat, confess all the sins and transgressions of the congregation over it, and then send off the goat with a man who is to let it go free in the wilderness, carrying all the people's sins away with it. (The goats are assigned to their roles by lot, and the goat sent into the wilderness is called "the goat for Azazel," which is unexplained in the text, but is probably the name, originally, of a demon.)[3]

Aaron is to then bathe in the Sanctuary, dress in his regular vestments, and end the ceremony by first offering up to G-d one burnt offering for himself and another for the people, and, second, putting on the fire the suet of the two sin offerings whose blood has already purged the Sanctuary.[4]

This section of ritual ends with G-d's command that this ceremony of expiation take place each year on the tenth day of the seventh month, with that day of atonement to be one of complete rest and self-denial.

The chapter concludes with two sets of rules that seem to revolve around respecting the holiness of the life force, with the first set involving restrictions on eating meat. The most important restrictions are, first, that animals be killed for meat only in a ceremonial sacrifice at the Sanctuary, where their blood is given over to G-d on the altar, and, second, that it is forbidden to eat the animal's blood. "For the life of the flesh is in the blood, and I have assigned it to you for making expiation for your lives upon the altar; it is the blood, as life, that effects expiation."[5]

The next set of rules involves a listing of forbidden sexual practices, seeming to disallow any kind of incest, adultery, homosexuality (although this reading is currently in dispute in many religious communities), or bestiality. Child sacrifice is also forbidden in this section, with the practice referred to in one translation as the giving "any of your seed for passing to the Moloch."[6] Again, the intent seems to be about seeing the life force or "seed" as holy, neither to be wasted nor used dishonorably.

Parshah **Interpretation:** Aaron's sons have died because they approached the Divine Presence without paying enough attention to what they were doing, so that they violated a boundary between pure and impure. Using ritual purity as a metaphor for devotion to the Divine, we have had three chapters on commitment that looked at what we take in spiritually, how well we maintain our dedication, and how we can always return to the spiritual path after a lapse. Here the whole community is held accountable for insufficient holiness, which necessarily defiles the sacred space that is the Tabernacle they have made for G-d.

Because lapses are not only inevitable, but leave behind the defiling aftereffects of our bad thoughts and actions, this chapter calls for a required, annual ceremony of atonement, purification, and rededication to the Divine, so that G-d can dwell with us in the world and in the Sanctuary of our hearts. As the essence of life force, the blood of the sin offerings is used to physically cleanse the Sanctuary of pollution, and the burnt offerings that follow symbolize our total commitment to take up the spiritual path anew.

Some Torah commentators feel that the text refers to conscious sins and transgressions rather than to impurities that result from unintentional or inevitable breaches of ethics or ritual (as with menstruation, nocturnal emissions, etc.).[7] Either way, it describes an annual ceremony for re-purification, with its focus on Aaron, the High Priest, as he performs the complex rituals to clear away the muck of our spiritual lapses—for Aaron alone enters the innermost chamber of the Sanctuary, where the Divine dwells.

Because this chapter begins with a reference to Aaron's eldest two sons having just died, it deliberately juxtaposes Aaron's grief with his acts of service as High Priest. So Aaron here embodies our giving up of self-concerns to serve G-d through action in the world. Perhaps it even refers to the purification of spirit that sometimes occurs after we experience very great loss.

In many commentaries, Aaron's sons are thought to have died as the result of joining YHVH in ecstatic union.[8] But the whole thrust of Torah implies that we are not supposed to choose this ecstatic path. In fact, we are not supposed to withdraw from the world either to seek such ecstasy or because we cannot bear our suffering here. Instead, our personal desires are to be subsumed in our commitment to Divine service. Aaron, in this *parshah,* represents us at our most devoted, not only because he is the High Priest, but because his selfless service just after his great loss represents the highest level of dedication and intention—the level that is reached, at least momentarily, in the yearly ceremony of atonement, the only day on which he is allowed to enter the innermost chamber.

And the ceremony of atonement is deliberately communal, for we are not only called to continue to act in the world, no matter what our wish for withdrawal, but to remain an intrinsic part of the larger community.

For Formal Practice: For today's practice, we are working with the intent of letting go of absorption in our own cravings and losses. Instead of focusing on our self-concerns, we are to practice selflessness, offering ourselves up to the service of G-d, emptying our hearts of all but G-d so that we can make the world holy and a fit dwelling place for the Divine.

When you are ready, let your mind go to some experience of great loss that you have had. If you can, remember how unimportant most of your usual concerns became. You may even remember the experience of feeling that the veil had been lifted from your eyes, so that you could see more clearly and knew what truly mattered.

Now picture Aaron performing the ceremony of atonement for himself and the whole community just days after the deaths of his two eldest sons.

See him slit the throat of a bull for his own expiation of sin.

See him catch the lifeblood of the bull in a bowl.

Watch him spread the smoking incense in the innermost chamber so that he cannot be destroyed by too clearly seeing the presence of G-d.

Stand with him as he sprinkles the bull's crimson life force onto the Ark, offering it up in place of his own as he stands amidst the smoke in the presence of YHVH, the awesome G-d of life and death.

Feel his concentration as he offers expiation for his transgressions. Feel his focus as he gives himself over to the service of the Divine.

Now let your mind hover around the phrase "I place G-d before me always." If you prefer the Hebrew, it is *Sheviti Hashem l'negdi tamid.*

Let the phrase hover in your awareness as you let other experiences, past or future, appear before you.

If you like, go into emptiness.

In My Own Practice: *I remember that I divided problems into three categories in the years that my husband was dying. There was life and death, which mattered. There was life-threatening, which mattered. And everything else was just various degrees of nuisance. Much later, I became willing to place a fourth category, quality of life, just below life-threatening, to at least recognize it as a category—but, even now, that often seems to contain difficulties that are, indeed, no more than annoyances whose importance I need not inflate.*

Then I see Aaron in the Sanctuary, sprinkling the blood, the life force, amidst the smoke.

I feel like coughing as I stand with him. His hands are shaking. It is so hard to concentrate in the midst of grief. And fear.

I am with him in the presence of the unnameable, the G-d of life and death. Anything can happen.

I am breathing with difficulty, my chest constricted.

I use the phrase "I place G-d before me always."

And then I see light. I suddenly begin to feel lighter.

What matters is to choose life, to choose love, to choose joy, to choose acceptance, and to let go of judgment. To be a channel for love and to see the bounty of the earth—despite the reality of loss and pain.

"And YHVH spoke to Moses, saying: 'Speak to all the congregation of the children of Israel, and you shall say to them, "You shall be holy, because I, YHVH, your G-d, am holy."' "

—Lev. 19:1

Interpretive Overview: After the preceding sections of *Vayikra* on building intention and purifying oneself as preparation for serving G-d, this *parshah* finally begins to outline what such service actually looks like. Filled with specifics, the chapter culminates in the extraordinary command to love one's neighbor as oneself, and this is followed by the even more demanding call to love the stranger as oneself. In the metaphor of Exodus, we have been freed from slavery, from the constrictions of the ego, for this purpose: we are to emulate G-d and manifest the Divine in the human realm by behaving with loving-kindness. In the process, we will also become holy beings.

Summary of *Parshah*: This chapter gives the Israelites a series of rules to follow so that they will be holy, both individually and as a community—and thus, allied with G-d. The chapter begins with the command that they be holy because G-d is holy (as stated at Mount Sinai, they have been freed from slavery under Pharaoh in order to become servants of G-d). Some of the rules that follow are restatements of the Ten Commandments. At the center of this chapter is the commandment "Love your neighbor as yourself."[1]

The rules include the following: honor your father and mother; keep the Sabbath; do not worship idols; do not steal, act deceitfully, or swear falsely by G-d's name; do not rob; do not "... insult the deaf or place a stumbling block before the blind";[2] do not favor the poor or show deference to the

187

rich; provide fair decisions; "do not profit by the blood of your fellow";[3] do not eat blood; do not turn to divination or soothsaying; do not consult ghosts; " … rise before the aged and show deference to the old";[4] do not give any offspring to Moloch; and do not commit adultery, incest, or other forbidden sexual acts.

Most important, perhaps, are these rules:

"And you shall love your neighbor as yourself: I am the Lord."[5]

And also:

"The strangers who reside with you shall be to you as your citizens; you shall love each one as yourself, for you were strangers in the land of Egypt: I the Eternal am your G-d."[6]

***Parshah* Interpretation:** In the last chapter, the Sanctuary—both the communal and the personal—was re-purified by our atonement, purged of the accretion of sins and transgressions committed during the prior year. In this chapter, we finally move from ceremonies of purification to rituals and behavior that are designed to keep us from sinning in the first place, so that we pollute neither the Tabernacle nor the entire land.

In the literal Torah narrative, G-d is external to us, but we are made in G-d's image, which is generally interpreted as meaning that we can manifest in ourselves qualities of holiness that belong to G-d. In a common spiritual metaphor, our souls are small candles next to the sun that is G-d: small, but akin.

But even the literal Torah narrative places G-d within us, as well, in a holy interior Sanctuary. For more than two thousand years, this *parshah* has been considered by Torah commentators to be the central chapter of *Vayikra* and of the entire Torah, for it directly addresses the question of transforming this internal Sanctuary into a true dwelling place for the Divine.

The chapter offers a mixture of ritual and ethical practices. Of these, the ritual practices seem, as always, to be essentially understandable as metaphors for coming down on the side of life rather than on the side of dissolution, decay, and death. The ethical practices are similar in that they refer to actions that are life-creating or sustaining, not only at the literal level of providing others with adequate food and physical sustenance, but also in terms of feeding other souls by acting toward them with loving-kindness. Ultimately, the chapter reaches its apogee in the command to love the other as oneself, even when the other is a stranger. (Bible translators often understand this command as calling less for the emotion that we call "love" than for us to act toward others with compassion, cherishing them, and treating them well.[7] One cannot command emotion; demanding behaviors of loving-kindness is challenging enough.)

When we follow these commandments, we manifest G-d's qualities of love and concern in the human realm. In the process, we transform ourselves, becoming holy vessels for the Divine. The ultimate goal is to have both our inmost being and the outer world become fit dwelling places for YHVH.

For Formal Practice: The intention of this meditation is to ask yourself in what way observation of the commandments in this *parshah* leads to holiness like G-d's. When you are ready, let your mind rove over some of these commandments:

Love your neighbor as yourself.

Love the stranger as yourself.

Honor your father and mother.

Do not steal, act deceitfully, or swear falsely by the name of G-d.

Do not rob.

Do not insult the deaf or place a stumbling block before the blind.

Do not favor the poor or show deference to the rich.

Provide fair decisions.

Do not profit from the blood of your fellow.

Do not eat blood; do not turn to divination or soothsaying.

Do not consult ghosts.

Rise before the aged and show deference to the old.

If you like, use the phrase "Holy, holy, holy," or in Hebrew, *Kadosh, kadosh, kadosh,* as you let different rules arise in your awareness.

In My Own Practice: *Today, I cannot stay with "Love your neighbor as yourself," much less with "love the stranger." Instead, my mind slips to "Do not favor the poor or show deference to the rich." I am to see the other without bias, not to be swayed by the category into which I may put them.*

I am to respond to others in all of their fullness, not as I reduce them by placing them in categories: young or old, rich or poor, pretty or not, etc.

Like shrubs in the desert, each of us is seen by G-d as a separate and complete and complex whole, each in our own individual space.

Each has our own history, both in our life and in the innumerable generations that led to the birth of our own unique self. Each is to be equally cherished in our unique aliveness.

To love my neighbor—or the stranger—as myself is not to blur the distinction between us, but to cherish others in all of their unique presence.

Leviticus/*Vayikra*, 8, "Say"/*Emor*
(Lev. 21:1–24:23)

"And YHVH said to Moses: 'Say to the priests, the sons of Aaron, and say to them: One shall not become impure....'"

—Lev. 21:1

Interpretive Overview: The *parshah* opens with more purity rules for priests. Because the priests symbolize us in our best moments, the rules seem to say that our actions must come down ever more stringently on the side of life rather than on the side of destruction and death, if we are to become more open to G-d's presence. The text then provides devotional practices to help us maintain focus on the sacredness of life throughout the year, and seems to be saying that spiritual progress is marked by increasing awareness of the Divine Presence filling the world in each and every moment.

Summary of *Parshah*: The chapter has three main sections. The first focuses on a variety of purity rules for the priests, with purity represented by physical perfection (e.g., they must have no physical defects and must marry a virgin) and avoidance of even indirect contact with death.

The second section focuses on purity rules related to the sacrifices that are consecrated for the priest to eat. First, the text states that the priest must be ritually pure before eating, or he will be "cut off"[1] from the Divine or "die."[2] Then it lists a variety of impurities from which he must be cleansed, indicates who else in the priest's household may eat the consecrated food, and closes with the reiteration that all sacrifices at the altar must be unblemished—again with a variety of specifics.

In general, these two sections have to do with the heightened level of ritual purity needed for both the priest and the food offered as sacrifice, for they partake of the holy realm of the Divine Presence. Also, the food itself becomes more potent once it is consecrated, so that only those of heightened purity can safely eat of it.

The final section of the chapter names the sacred holidays to be observed. This section is framed by references to the exodus from slavery in Egypt, beginning with G-d's words, "I am YHVH, who makes you holy, who brought you out from the land of Egypt to be G-d to you. I am YHVH."[3] And then G-d says, "These are My fixed times, the fixed times of the Eternal, which you shall proclaim as sacred occasions."[4]

Without further explanation, *Vayikra* then presents a path of devotional practice over the year. Starting with observing the weekly Sabbath as a day of rest, YHVH then specifies five sacred festivals between spring and fall that track both a spiritual calendar and an agricultural schedule. The first holiday is the spring festival of Passover; fifty days later, at the climax of the first grain harvest (probably barley) comes *Shavuot.*[5] Then there are three sacred occasions in the autumn that include the New Year,[6] the Day of Atonement ten days later, and the weeklong celebration marking the end of the autumn harvest that begins five days after that. In that seven-day holiday, the Israelites are commanded to celebrate and dwell in temporary housing, called *sukkot,* which give the holiday its name.

After the presentation of the yearly holidays, instructions are repeated (already given in the second *parshah* of *Vayikra*) for Aaron to keep an eternal fire burning in the Sanctuary, and for the bread and incense offering he is to make on the Sabbath. The *parshah* closes with a brief narrative about a man who is described as the son of an Egyptian man and an Israelite woman. He commits blasphemy, invoking G-d's name and vilifying it; the Israelites ask G-d what to do; and G-d demands that he be stoned to death, which they do.[7]

***Parshah* Interpretation:** The Book of Leviticus states that we become holy by following in G-d's ways of compassion and love. It then serves as an instruction manual, starting with rituals for declaring our intention to emulate these attributes, and moving onto guidelines for actually embodying them in our own actions. (Unlikely as it may seem, the final part of this *parshah,* on stoning the blasphemer, can also be interpreted in this light, as will be discussed below.)

In the last *parshah,* the whole community was given guidelines for becoming a "holy people." This week's chapter begins with requirements for ever more intense commitment, as symbolized by its initial focus on priestly matters and consecrated offerings (i.e., practices to follow if we are to be in the state of mind in which we are most open to the Divine).

As in the rest of *Vayikra,* the requirements are expressed in metaphor, using concrete terms to express abstract ideas. But the basic idea is that there is a zone of heightened purity around the Divine that works in two directions: anything coming into the zone needs already to be pure (whether people or offerings), and consecrated offerings (e.g., food) become more pure by their proximity to the Divine. The metaphor says that our offerings—our actions—must be holy if we are to approach the Divine. In turn, our holy actions serve to further purify us, so that we become channels for G-d to manifest in the world.

The next part of this week's chapter then turns back to instructions for the holiness of the community at large rather than of the priests alone. Starting and ending this section with references to liberating us from enslavement in Egypt, YHVH now tells us to set aside both the weekly Sabbath and five other specific holidays during the year for "holy gatherings." By creating times for specific observances throughout the year, G-d countermands our natural tendency to lose awareness of the Divine Presence as we become caught up in our daily affairs.

Each week, we end a seven-day cycle on the Sabbath, the day in which we leave behind work and striving; for the Sabbath is to be a day of rest, a day of simply being present and open to the miracle of existence. The annual cycle continues to honor the miracle of life as it follows the harvest; it simultaneously follows the path of spiritual growth that begins with Passover, as we are freed from internal enslavement to the freedom of serving G-d and creating a moral world. The spring celebration of life on earth, with the first harvest, comes next; after this is the autumn New Year, in which we atone for our sins and transgressions before starting over again on the path of holiness. The cycle closes with the holiday for the fall harvest (the Festival of Booths, or *Sukkot*), in which we also live outdoors in temporary dwellings to remember our wandering in the desert after leaving Egyptian slavery.

So this *parshah* begins by emphasizing that we must come down on the side of life rather than death, dissolution, and decay if we are to approach G-d; moves onto the purity required of our offerings; and then finishes by organizing time into an annual sacred cycle to help us maintain a state of mindfulness. And by ending the annual cycle with the Festival of Booths (i.e., *Sukkot*), in which we are told to live in temporary dwellings that are open to the wind and rain, the last part of this section reminds us that everything is temporary, on loan from G-d; and that our awareness of life's fragility makes it even more necessary to cherish each moment.

Thus, in the next section, the chapter repeats the command to keep an eternal fire going in the Sanctuary—to keep awareness alight. And the chapter ends with the scene of stoning a man to death for blaspheming G-d—a man who is described as the son of an Israelite woman and a man from Egypt/ *Mitzrayim,* the land that is the metaphor for the state of ego and unholiness. So he is a man of mixed nature, partway to holiness, but still trapped in the constrictions of the ego. And so his blasphemy is denial of the wondrousness of this world and of G-d's presence in our hearts: the denial of awareness. Stoning the man who blasphemes can be read as a metaphor for casting out that blind part of ourselves, the part we all have, so that we can *see* and be holy.

For Formal Practice: Let us try to experience awe and wonder today as our approach to purity. When you are ready, let yourself feel your way through the year, from season to season, beginning with spring. Just notice what arises in you as you experience the annual changes.

After a while, focus on the phrase "Holy, holy, holy," as you make your way through the year. If you prefer the Hebrew, use the same words in Hebrew: *Kadosh, kadosh, kadosh.*

"Holy holy, holy," the world is filled with G-d's glory.

G-d's glory is all there is.

The whole world is the manifestation of G-d's glory in this dimension of reality.

Follow your breath as you ask to see the holiness all around you. Let your mind empty. As you notice thought, return briefly to the phrase "Holy, holy, holy," or in Hebrew, *Kadosh, kadosh, kadosh.*

In My Own Practice: *Today, I find this a difficult meditation. The day is dark and cold, and I am low in energy. But then my mind stops at the holiday of Sukkot, when we are to live in temporary shelters. I can see the sun pouring down in the desert, the whole scene filled with light. I can feel the heat of the desert rock and sand.*

I am conscious that I am still wandering in the desert, not yet in the Promised Land. My house is temporary, because all shelters are impermanent and open to the winds of chance. I cannot know what will happen tomorrow.

But I can feel the sun and the heat. I can feel G-d's presence pouring in.

Then I see that the answer is always about being present to the moment, to the richness of what is. My rational mind doesn't have to understand.

As I breathe, my body calms, and I am losing the boundary between myself and what is around me. There is only the Divine.

Leviticus/*Vayikra*, 9, "On the Mountain"/*B'har*
(Lev. 25:1–26:2)

"And YHVH spoke to Moses in Mount Sinai...."

—Lev. 25:1

Interpretive Overview: This *parshah* opens with the Divine Presence commanding a yearlong Sabbath from farming every seventh year and follows with the command for a Great Sabbath after every seven times seven years, in which land goes back to its first owners. The chapter ends with a command, yet again, about renouncing idolatry and observing the Sabbath. Throughout, we are told that all belongs to G-d, including us; the land, our prosperity, and our very lives are given us on loan. And if we are to be in covenant with the Divine Presence, we are to serve only the Divine—the Source of All—turning away from all idolatry, including the worship of human wealth or power.

Summary of *Parshah*: B'har begins with the command to let the earth rest from farming every seventh year, having its own Sabbath. It then gives instructions for the Great Sabbath, or Jubilee, every fifty years—one year after every seven times seven years.[1] In the Jubilee, everyone is to go back to his family and to the original holdings of fifty years before (thus redistributing wealth to prevent the creation of a society of the very rich and the very poor).[2] For the land "must not be sold beyond reclaim, for the land is Mine; you are but strangers resident with Me."[3] Then a variety of rules are given for redeeming dwelling places for the Jubilee.

After this, the text goes to a long section that focuses on the way to treat fellow Israelites who have fallen on hard times: bringing them into one's home, lending them money without charging interest, and providing free food. And if, despite all efforts, one Israelite is sold to another, he must not be treated as a slave but as a laborer; and he must be free to go back to his family and original family holdings in the Jubilee year. If an Israelite becomes enslaved by a resident alien, his family must buy his freedom if possible; if not possible, he must be permanently freed at the Jubilee year. "For it is to Me that the Israelites are servants; they are My servants, whom I freed from the land of Egypt. I am the Eternal, your G-d."[4]

In the final paragraph of the chapter, the text once again forbids making any idols or bowing down to any image or pillar or carved stone. And we are to observe the Sabbath and feel awe for the Tabernacle.

***Parshah* Interpretation:** The final chapters of *Vayikra* bring us to a new level of communal commitment to act as servants of G-d. For we are commanded to create a society that expresses G-d's compassion and loving-kindness through our own actions, particularly toward those who are most needy or powerless.

Last week, we were told to observe the Sabbath and five festivals during the year to keep us remembering that the glory of the Divine Presence fills all the earth, sustaining creation. With *B'har*, the timeframe lengthens. While the last *parshah* stressed the weekly observance of the Sabbath and the annual round of festivals, this one commands us to keep a yearlong Sabbath of the land every seventh year, so that the land may rest. And after every seven times seven years, we are to have a completely new beginning, a jubilee in which we do not seed or harvest, and in which all accumulation of property is voided.

The *parshah* is named *B'har*, meaning "In the Mountain." At the center of creation with YHVH.

If we read the text metaphorically, it is speaking to all of us who wrestle with G-d as if we are at the start of creation all over again. We can always regain our lost innocence, be back in a kind of Eden again, where we act as the keeper of all our brothers and where, in turn, the Divine Presence will have provided for us. "And the land will give its fruit, and you will eat to the full, and you will live in security on it."[5]

"The land is Mine,"[6] says the Divine. And, "For it is to me that the Israelites are servants; they are My servants, whom I freed from the land of Egypt. I am the Eternal your G-d."[7] And then in the last words of the *parshah*: "You shall not make idols for yourselves, or set up for yourselves carved images or pillars, or place figured stones in your land to worship upon, for I the Eternal am your G-d. You shall keep My Sabbaths and venerate My Sanctuary, Mine, the Eternal's."[8]

All say the same thing in very strong language: All is YHVH's—the land, the world, the animals, each and every one of us. And we are offered the chance to start again—and again and again—both as individuals and as a whole community; for it is only by turning ourselves over to YHVH, and not to money or power or any idol of worldly success, that we are truly secure.

For Formal Practice: The intent of this meditation is to recognize that all belongs to the Divine, that everything that we have depends on the Divine, that every moment of existence is permeated by the Divine, and that our very existence depends on that Presence sustaining this world.

When you are ready, imagine yourself at Mount Sinai. Its peak is hidden in a cloud that contains the Divine Presence. As you climb, you are unable to see what lies ahead. Yet you can feel the awesome power of the Divine emanating from it.

Hear the words, if you can: "The land is Mine," says the Divine. "To me, the Israelites are servants." Freed from enslavement to Pharaoh to serve the Divine.

For the moment, give up your efforts to make things come out the way you want.

For the moment, acknowledge that all that you possess is on loan, and that nothing belongs to you.

If you can, let yourself feel G-d's presence creating, sustaining, and permeating all existence. The very ground of being.

Offer yourself to the Divine, even if you don't understand what that entails, emptying yourself.

When you lose concentration, return to the image of yourself in the cloud, approaching the peak, acknowledging that you own nothing and that all belongs to the Divine.

In My Own Practice: *I can feel the small, loose stones underfoot as I climb the path. There are low, blue wildflowers on both sides of the path and very green blades of grass. We are high enough for that, high enough to be out of the desert landscape. And as I enter the cloud, I can smell the moist freshness of water in the coolness.*

All is on loan. Nothing is mine.

I feel very small and insignificant.

I am imbedded in history, and the very process of history is G-d unfolding in time.

I am imbedded in place and time. My very body is given to me. My mind, my appearance, my genes, where and to whom I was born—all that was given to me. I haven't created it any more than I choose to breathe. It is given to me.

Yet I am told to choose how I behave. And somehow I do choose. I don't understand, but I know that I choose whether to behave well or badly. That is all that is mine—that choice.

The rest is given, and all that is given constrains so much of my choice: about where I live, how I earn my living, whom I am likely to marry, how my life turns out in so many ways. But I am always free to choose how I react, how I behave. That is my significance; that is my meaning.

Leviticus/*Vayikra*, 10, "If You Follow My Laws"/*B'chukotai*
(Lev. 26:3–27:34)

"If you follow My laws and faithfully observe My commandments, I will grant your rains in their season so that the earth shall yield its produce and the trees of the field their fruit."

—Lev. 26:3-4[1]

Interpretive Overview: This final chapter of *Vayikra* describes the consequences of serving the Divine—or not—in terms of literal reward or punishment, with the stipulation that we can always turn back to G-d and be welcomed. At the metaphoric level, punishment is experienced as exile from G-d's presence, so that we feel alone and afraid in a world that feels empty. But when we subsume our egos to serve G-d, we are rewarded by finding ourselves in a place of peace and plenty, no matter what befalls us, knowing that all of existence is simply another manifestation of the Divine Presence.

Summary of *Parshah*: In this final chapter of *Vayikra,* the Divine Presence sets out the consequences for obeying or disobeying the laws and commandments. If we obey, the earth will give us ample food, we will live in peace, and we will thrive and multiply. G-d will be ever present within our midst, and we will be G-d's people, freed from slavery and "standing tall."[2] If we do not follow the ways of YHVH, we will suffer disease, fail to multiply, and be overcome by our enemies. And if we still resist, the punishments will get worse and worse, until our cities are in ruins and our land devastated, with those who survive living in fearful exile amidst their enemies.

But when we finally repent and return to the ways of the Divine, G-d will not spurn us, for G-d will never break the covenant. This section ends with the words "These are the laws, rules, and instructions that the Eternal established, through Moses on Mount Sinai, with the Israelite people."[3]

Then comes a coda about assessing the value of certain kinds of offerings to G-d.

***Parshah* Interpretation:** At the literal level, this chapter describes the rewards for following G-d and the punishments for turning away. Many modern commentators prefer to interpret these statements in terms of earthly cause and effect rather than divine intervention. In this interpretation, the path of love and compassion naturally leads to peace and prosperity; turning away from that path leads to war and desolation.

At the metaphoric level, the consequences are internal. If we become vessels for the Divine by following the commandments, we will automatically come to cherish the world and everything in it, just as YHVH does. In the literal reading of Torah, we will also be protected in our physical bodies: the earth will feed us and our enemies will vanish. But at the mystical level, we come to understand that there are no guarantees in the physical realm. In this world, all is on loan to us: our health, our wealth, our families, our very lives. We will all die at some time, and the only safety lies in being fully present to YHVH in each moment, so that we feel ourselves immersed in YHVH's compassion and love.

In this final chapter, we are told that serving the Divine by following the commandments will create in us a state of consciousness in which we *know* that all is G-d and full of G-d's glory, so that each moment is rich and full and filled with compassion. Or, we can choose to ignore that knowing, to shut ourselves off from it, in which case we will live in a world of dryness and emptiness and fear.

Again and again, the Torah says to choose life, and to choose life by serving G-d, for this is the path that brings us to the awareness of G-d's presence and love permeating the world. This is the radical teaching that *Vayikra* has been leading to: the service of G-d leads to this state of consciousness. Thus, in Jewish lore, Rabbi Akiva[4] could joyously recite the central prayer of Judaism at the moment of his martyrdom: "Hear O Israel, G-d is One and G-d's Name is One." (Deut. 6:4-9)

For Formal Practice: When you are ready, go to the words of the *Shema*: "G-d is One and G-d's name is One."

As you breath in and out, just let your mind hover over the idea of oneness.

What does it mean that G-d is One? Is that different from G-d's name being One?

Let yourself imagine all of physical reality as an emanation of the Divine. If you like, let your mind hover over the idea of the whole world being in some way the body of the Divine.

In My Own Practice: *I do this meditation during a long, silent retreat, in which I am more receptive than usual. As soon as I begin, I experience a certainty that there is only G-d, and nothing exists outside the Divine: there is one vast, inexhaustible, boundless awareness that is, was, and will be. This Mystery predates all beings, predates time and space itself, and will still be there after the entire cosmos, all of the physical universe, ends.*

G-d's name, for me, is the physical universe itself, a sort of body that YHVH has chosen to appear in, in the realm of space-time—a sort of costume. And the physical universe—that name of G-d—is also One, begun in the primordial moment of creation in the Big Bang, and expanding outward ever since, becoming more differentiated, more complex, as the laws of the physical universe play out. The process unfolds both through randomness and the determinism of the laws of cause and effect in ways that are incomprehensible to us. As more creatures appear in more ecological systems, the intertwinings are too complex to unravel. But I can see that they create a single organism whose parts all mesh into one tapestry developing in time and space.

The organism is the physical universe that started as nothing more than an undifferentiated point.

It is more than interconnectedness of the parts that I see; it is the weaving of a dynamic tapestry that is this physical world.

Interpretive Summation of Leviticus/*Vayikra*

While the Book of Leviticus takes us back to an archaic world, its awareness is profoundly adult, for it squarely faces the experience of a G-d who is not "nice" at all, but is rather the primal source of both life and death. For there is only one Source, one I Am That I Am, and from that Divine Presence flows creation and destruction, the whole dance of existence in all its complexity and paradox.

Yet this unnamable YHVH calls out to us, commanding that we come near, commanding that we bring morality into the middle realm which we inhabit—the human domain. The Book of Leviticus is concerned with the command "You shall be holy, because I am holy."[1]

Both the most mystical and the most practical book of the Torah, it then sets outs the means for achieving holiness, offering a manual of rules and rituals that can serve to transform our consciousness and behavior, so that we ultimately can become beings alight with G-d, holy vessels for the Divine, living daily with YHVH.

In its rituals, the eternal flame symbolizes our consciousness; the sacrificial animals symbolize our own commitment to holiness; and their blood acts as a purifying life force. The rules for purity can be seen as symbolizing what we allow to influence us, how well we maintain focused commitment, whether we come down on the side of wholeness and life. In its annual ceremony of atonement, *Vayikra* allows us to be cleansed of our lapses and start fresh, and its detailed rules of ethics guide us in translating our intention and focus into the behaviors of daily life.

Vayikra begins just after the Sanctuary is completed, on the first day of the first month of the second year after the exodus from Egypt. During the month that follows, the Sanctuary and the priests are consecrated so that formal worship can begin. But there is almost no narrative, and the text takes place in large part in a space without time, in an eternal present in which a utopian vision is laid out—of a society in which we act with loving-kindness toward one another, even to the stranger and the dispossessed and the powerless. It is a text that outlines what it looks like to be a servant of the I Am That I Am, to become a channel for the Divine to manifest holiness in the world, to make one's heart a Sanctuary for the Divine Presence that is the unnamable YHVH, to create a holy society. It is a text that understands that we will fail, that we will have lapses, and that we will try again.

When it ends, we return to the world of time and movement. Now that we know what it looks like to live in the presence of G-d at all times, we are ready to move on. In the next book, Numbers/*B'midbar,* the Israelites begin the trek toward the Promised Land, marching forty long years in the wilderness before they finally reach its physical border. As we will see, Numbers also documents an inner journey to a state of mind, to the interior Promised Land—the Garden Within—that is sometimes referred to as enlightenment.

4

General Framework of Numbers/ *B'midbar*

In English, the fourth book of Torah is called Numbers, in reference to the very practical census taken in the first chapter to count the number of available fighting men as the Israelites march through unknown territory. In Hebrew, the book is called *B'midbar,* which translates as "In the Wilderness." As with the other four books of the Torah, the Hebrew title is taken from the opening sentence, which states: "And YHVH spoke to Moses in the wilderness of Sinai in the Tent of Meeting in the first day of the second month in the second year of their exodus from the land of Egypt...."[1] Because the Hebrew name has more emotional resonance, I will use it preferentially.

At the literal, simple level, Exodus and *B'midbar* can be read as the continuing narrative of the physical journey out of slavery of the twelve tribes of Israel. After escaping from servitude in Egypt, they swear an eternal covenant at Mount Sinai to serve the Divine; and they build a holy place, the Tabernacle, for G-d to dwell amidst the community and within each person individually. Exodus ends by looking forward to the Book of Numbers, describing how YHVH leads them toward the Promised Land of Canaan as a pillar of fire by night and a cloud by day.

Leviticus then intervenes, and for the most part, it takes place out of time, concerned with rules for holiness and purity that the Israelites must follow if they are to become, each of them, a channel through which the Divine can manifest. There is some narrative, as well, involving the consecration of the Sanctuary and the ordination of Aaron and his sons in preparation for the traveling that is described at the end of Exodus. *B'midbar* picks up the story again as they prepare to begin the journey one month after the start of Leviticus/*Vayikra*.

But what is this Promised Land supposed to be? At the literal level, of course, it is a physical place, the land of Canaan. Much of the land, but not all, is what we now identify with the modern State of Israel. At this level, it is worth noting that archeologists have found no evidence for the conquest of the Promised Land; instead, there appears to have been a gradual assimilation of the inhabitants with the people we call Israelites.[2]

The Promised Land is also a metaphor for the internal state in which we each serve as a holy Sanctuary for G-d's presence, in which we are truly able to act as servants of YHVH rather than of Pharaoh. In this state, we act with compassion and loving-kindness for each other and for ourselves. Thus, the Promised Land is also a symbol of the kind of world we would create if we could really allow ourselves to be channels through which Divine love could manifest in the human realm.

In this state, we let go of our own efforts to control fate and simply become present in the moment, open with each breath to the *being*-ness, the Mystery, the Source, YHVH, that we label G-d. In this state, we inevitably feel G-d's compassion flow through us, and we automatically become conduits for Divine love. In this state, we cannot be servants of Pharaoh: we behave well not in obedience to a set of rules, but because it has become natural for us. If we could reach this state, we would be in the Promised Land, the Garden Within, and our actions would create a perfected world—a new Eden.

However, *B'midbar* is still describing the journey through the wilderness of pain and suffering, symbolically and literally. By the time *B'midbar* begins, the Israelites have not only been given detailed rules for how to live in holiness, but have had many experiences of YHVH in action. They have seen the plagues in Egypt, heard G-d at Mount Sinai, eaten the sustaining manna, and also witnessed the punishment for rebellion after the episode of the golden calf. And yet, despite the overt presence of the Divine, the people cannot keep their promises to follow in the path G-d asks. Now, as the Book of Numbers continues, they see more miracles, but continue to stumble.

And they have a very long way to go, for most of their journey takes place in this book, as they wander for almost forty years after they leave Mount Sinai. *B'midbar* recounts the endless trek across the desert, as the ex-slaves age and give way to the next generation. At the literal level, they are led at all times by the Divine, appearing to them as fire or cloud, and providing them with food and water. They should feel safe in G-d's presence, but they don't, for the wilderness is still a hostile environment: they have minimum physical comforts, and they are marching into territory controlled by other groups.

They are squarely faced with the reality of their total dependence on the Divine for survival, and of their own lack of any control or power. So they live in fear and yearn to return to the known safety—and even physical comfort—of Egypt, despite its enslavement of them. As they repeatedly rebel against YHVH, they are repeatedly punished. Worst of all, the entire generation of ex-slaves is forbidden to enter the Promised Land; it is their punishment to wander in the wilderness for forty years until all they all die out. As Richard Elliot Friedman points out, the Book of Leviticus assumes that living in G-d's presence offers both safety and danger, and *B'midbar* plays this vision out in its narrative.[3]

As we return to a symbolic reading of the text, we can see *B'midbar* in terms of our individual spiritual development over the course of our lives. The symbolism is imbedded, as always, in very concrete narrative and description that easily seduces us into simple, literal reading. But I believe that many of the chapters are similar in structure to a kind of puzzle I used to do as a child. Called a rebus, the puzzle consisted of a sequence of pictures. The challenge was to decode the meaning, first by discovering the word each picture stood for, and then by lining up all the words in order to make a sentence.

Most of *B'midbar* can be read in a similar way, as if each small section is itself a symbol—or rebus—for a simple concept. When the concepts are lined up in sequence, the metaphoric narrative of the text appears.

At this symbolic level, then, *B'midbar* is concerned with our personal struggles as we journey toward the Promised Land. As we grow spiritually, we try to behave well in the world and act with loving-kindness. We also seek to regularly feel the Divine Presence as the underpinning of the physical world, as the larger reality behind the physical, as the very ground of reality permeating all existence—including our own. As we more often approach the Garden Within, we have more moments in which we *know* that G-d is the fundamental reality, and our individual selves no more than temporary channels through which the Divine manifests. In these moments, compassion comes naturally. But we lose this awareness and return to old behavior patterns no matter how clearly visible YHVH may sometimes be.

Our goal is to have this *knowing* become our everyday experience, so that we feel safe in G-d's presence and effortlessly allow Divine love to flow through us. The Promised Land, at the mystical level, is simply a metaphor for this state of realization, but the bulk of our existence is, at best, slow progress across what seems an endless wilderness of fear and yearning.

At the mystical level, *B'midbar* is, in part, a commentary both on our setbacks and on the various obstacles to be overcome once we have committed ourselves to the spiritual path. In Hebrew, the obstacles are called *klippot,* or shells, the husks around the divine spark at the center of our being, the husks that are inevitably part of the human condition, for we are made of the dust of the earth.

As we advance, our *klippot* change somewhat; we get stuck in different ways. Because the Book of Numbers comes after the tribes set out from Mount Sinai, it can be read as occurring later in the spiritual journey than the Book of Exodus. Thus, most of *B'midbar* can easily be read as pointing to a sequence of internal stumbling blocks we must surmount as we make progress spiritually in opening to the Divine and emulating YHVH's qualities.

Although it is not the subject of this book, I have found such extensive similarities between the mystical reading of Torah and Buddhist teachings—in my quite limited knowledge of Buddhism—that I keep wondering about the common influences on both Torah and Buddhism, and the exchanges between them. They, in fact, appeared at approximately the same time in lands that were connected to one another by open trade routes.[4] After feeling my way into a metaphoric reading of *B'midbar,* moreover, I unexpectedly came upon some utterly surprising and detailed parallels that were particularly relevant to my interpretation of the Torah text: the obstacles of the Six Realms described by the Buddha seem extremely similar to the *klippot* described in *B'midbar.* (I am indebted to Mark Epstein's *Thoughts Without a Thinker*[5] for a particularly clear rendition of the Six Realms.)

As a last comment, *B'midbar* is inclusive in tone: all the tribes are to be treated equally before G-d. And it seems to me that we—with our global awareness—can choose to fully expand this inclusivity. *Any one of us on this planetary home can choose to cleave to G-d. Anyone can become a holy Sanctuary for G-d's loving presence.* Taken metaphorically, *B'midbar* is our story now, today. Like the tribes of Israel, we are all in G-d's presence always, sustained by YHVH for every breath, for the very existence of air and food and water. Indeed, we are inseparable from G-d, both within and without.

And yet we are too often blind to the Divine Presence, so caught up in our defensive strivings that we unintentionally shut down our awareness.

Wandering in the wilderness, lost, seeking a Promised Land of safety and peace and happiness, we may be unable to realize that we exist as part of G-d, that we are safely *with* YHVH already and at every moment—and therefore need not fear, no matter what happens.

Numbers/*B'midbar* Week by Week

Numbers/*B'midbar*, 1, "Numbers"/*B'midbar*
(Num. 1:1–4:20)

"On the first day of the second month, in the second year following the exodus from the land of Egypt, the Eternal One spoke to Moses in the wilderness of Sinai, in the Tent of Meeting, saying: 'Take a census of the whole Israelite community....'"

—Num. 1:1–2[1]

Interpretive Overview: As the Israelites prepare for their trek across the desert from Mount Sinai, G-d tells Moses to take a census.[2] The Divine also gives instructions on how the tribes are to be arranged around the Tent of Meeting at the center of the camp, with each tribe having its own banner, and the Levites (who include Moses, Aaron, and Miriam) to be closest to the Tent, protecting it. At the metaphoric level, the census represents a call to each of us to follow our spiritual path wherever it leads. The Levites, who are placed closest to the Sanctuary, may also represent that part of us that is most open to the Divine Presence.

Summary of *Parshah:* The Tent of Meeting was set up at the end of the Book of Exodus, just a year after the Israelites fled Egypt. The events of Leviticus then took another month, and now *B'midbar* begins. The Israelites are still clustered at the foot of Mount Sinai, but they are soon to begin their march through the wilderness to the Promised Land.

In preparation for the journey, G-d commands Moses to take a census, counting every male, from age twenty up, who can bear arms. Those responsible for the count are named for each tribe, and the exact count is then given tribe by tribe, for a total of 603,550 men.[3] The Levites are the only group not counted for the army, for their responsibility is purely to the Tabernacle, protecting it from violation, taking it up and down, and carrying it on the march. Any outsider who encroaches will be put to death.

Next, G-d gives instructions for the Israelites to form a protective square around the Tabernacle as they camp and march. Each tribe, with its banner, is told exactly where to place itself in the square, which is composed of four divisions, each made up of three tribes. The tribes of Judah, Reuben, Ephraim, and Dan are each in charge of one of the four divisions, while Moses, Aaron, and his sons stay in front of the Tabernacle's entrance. (There are still twelve tribes, even without the Levites, because Joseph's two sons have each contributed a tribe.)

In the next section, G-d says that the Levites are to serve the priestly line of Aaron and his remaining sons Eleazar and Ithamar,[4] for the Levites are specifically consecrated to G-d's service in the Sanctuary. The Divine then tells Moses to count all the male Levites who are more than one month old,[5] outlines the duties of each clan of the Levites in regard to the Tent of Meeting, and says just where they should camp around it.

Finally, G-d asks for a different census, specifically of men between the ages of thirty and fifty, for the Kohathite clan of the Levite tribe. After describing in detail how Aaron and his sons are to pack up the Ark and other sacred objects for travel, the Divine repeats that the Kohathite clan will then carry the most sacred objects on the journey, adding that they must never see or touch them uncovered, or they will die.

Parshah Interpretation: We have committed to the covenant with the Divine, and begun to live with G-d as a daily presence. But we must continue to grow spiritually if we are to really approach the internal Promised Land.

In this first chapter of *B'midbar*, G-d tells Moses to take a census of all the tribes, sets aside the Levites as the particular guardians of the *mishkan* in the center of the camp, and gives instructions for how the other tribes are to arrange themselves around the Levites as they travel.

At the literal level, each able-bodied man is being called on to serve in the army as the Israelites journey through alien, and often hostile, territory. But the text stresses that each man is to be counted individually in his tribe. Each man—and in our era, it would be each person—is treated as a distinct being rather than as one of the nameless slaves of Egypt.

When the Book of Exodus began, the enslaved Israelites were described as "swarming,"[6] a word taken from Genesis to refer to crawling creatures; they were barely human. But the language of this *parshah* suggests that they have grown as they've left slavery behind, becoming more individualized and more able to choose to follow G-d rather than other idols. As we read the text in terms of our own spiritual growth, we are being reminded that each of us must stand up individually, making a personal commitment to emulate the Divine as we journey through the wilderness of life.

We can also choose to focus on the meaning of the different tribes each being given its own location vis-à-vis the Tabernacle, with the Levites in the center. The Levites thus represent in us that part closest to G-d, that part most yearning to enter the *mishkan.* The other tribes can be seen to represent other parts of us that serve both as defenses and as barriers around the heart.

For Formal Practice: When you are ready, let yourself meditate on the fact of G-d's calling out to you, asking you to stand up and be counted in all your individuality. Asking you to commit yourself to carrying the Divine Presence into the world by embodying it in yourself. Let yourself imagine the Divine call as fully as you can, feeling it entering you.

When you are ready, shift your attention to your reaction. Note your yearning to answer the Divine. Note, also, your resistance, without judgment of it. Remember that resistance has served a purpose for you, offering some kind of protection that you have needed, just as each clan in *B'midbar* serves a defensive purpose.

Just notice what arises without thinking about it. Let it go.

Go back to the Divine call if you become distracted, and then again to your yearning and your resistance.

As always, let yourself go into emptiness if you are ready to do this.

In My Own Practice: *I have been meditating on this* parshah *all week. Somehow, the idea arose that I need to move toward the people I would like to be closer to, that the path of holiness means connection to other people in this world, not simply to some disembodied Divine Presence.*

Often, I feel too shy, but most of the time my excuse is busyness. Today, I truly realize it is all resistance, behind which is fear. But if I am to commit to the Divine path, I am asked to ignore my fear and try to embody the loving-kindness of G-d. I must reach out just as the Divine reaches out to me.

My life is a journey toward the Promised Land. So I need to move, to act, not to keep sitting with the same paralysis. By the end of this week, I have made a number of phone calls.

Numbers/*B'midbar*, 2, "Add Up"/*Naso*
(Num.4:21–7:89)

"And YHVH spoke to Moses, saying: 'Add up the heads of the children of Gershon, them as well, by their fathers' house, by their families.'"

—Num. 4:21

Interpretive Overview: At the surface level, this *parshah* seems a hodgepodge of rules. At a metaphoric level, the rules can be understood as describing the whole range of spiritual experiences we encounter as we continue on our journey—from disconnection with the Divine through increasing possibilities of closeness. At the literal level, the chapter ends with each tribe offering the exact same gifts to G-d, just as each of us is to offer the same gift at the metaphoric level: to do our best to cleave to G-d and emulate G-d's compassion. In so doing, we each become a channel through which the Divine manifests, and the Priestly Blessing that is given at the end of this *parshah* becomes ours both to give and to receive.

Summary of *Parshah*: Near the end of the last *parshah*, G-d commanded Moses to count the number of men between the ages of thirty and fifty in the Levite clan of Kohath. This *parshah* begins with the same command in regard to the two other Levite clans and similarly outlines their particular duties for the Tabernacle. The count is then given for each of the three Levite lineages, with a total of 8,580.

Then come instructions for having any person, whether male or female, leave the camp if impure from leprosy, genital emissions, or contact with a dead body, so "that they not defile their camps in whose midst I abide."[1]

After that, there is a short passage—again for male or female—about confessing wrongs done to other people and then paying recompense to the wronged person before making an atonement offering in the Sanctuary.

This is followed by a long description of the trial by ordeal for a woman whose husband suspects her of adultery, despite lack of evidence.[2]

In the next section, instructions are given for anyone who vows to set himself (or herself) apart for G-d for a specific time. These individuals, called Nazarites, vow not to cut their hair—which is consecrated to G-d—drink alcohol, or eat anything off the grapevine. Neither are they to come near corpses (not even those of parents or siblings).[3]

After this, G-d dictates the blessing Aaron and his sons are to recite over the Israelites in what is the first ritual prayer in the Bible:

> May YHVH bless you and watch over you.
> May YHVH make the Divine face shine to you and be gracious to you.
> May YHVH raise the Divine face to you and give you peace.[4]

Finally, the chapter flashes back to the prior month, just after Moses finished setting up the Tent of Meeting, as the text describes the dedication offerings the tribal chieftains then made. The most important point is that the offerings are exactly the same for each tribe, and that each tribe's offering is described separately and in detail, even though they are all the same.[5]

The chapter ends by saying that when Moses came into the Tent of Meeting to speak with the Divine, he heard G-d speaking to him from between the two cherubs on the Ark.

Parshah Interpretation: At the surface level, this *parshah* seems all jumbl. At the symbolic level, however, it seems to follow a narrative line that moves us through different states of holiness and commitment to the Divine. In this sense, it expresses all the ambivalence as well as the different possibilities for us, which the rest of the Book of Numbers will expand upon.

The *parshah* opens with a count of the Levite lines of Gershon and Merari, who carry parts of the Tent of Meeting when the Israelites break camp, except for the most sacred objects. They can perhaps be seen as standing for that part of us which is largely, but not totally, committed to G-d. Perhaps we perform the ritual without the called for intensity of feeling, or perhaps we cleave to the Divine not so much by an act of free choice but through accidents of birth and tradition.

The next sections of the *parshah* read, at the literal level, as if different bits of text were cobbled together at random. Perhaps, they were indeed cobbled together, but not at random. Even if the stitching shows, the bits can be seen symbolically to follow a progression: beginning with complete disconnection from the Divine, the incidents take us through states of increasing closeness, to a moment of rapturous harmony.

The first reference is to exile, to being forced to leave the encampment because of a form of ritual impurity that we interpreted in Leviticus as representing loss of focus and dissipation of life force, even of coming down on the side of death rather than life. So we can interpret this section as metaphor for the experience of feeling separated from G-d—exiled from the camp—when we have lost our focus and squandered the life force given us by the Divine.

Then comes a short piece on making atonement for [perhaps inevitable] human failings, and re-approaching G-d. For most of us, this is the normal human state in which we repeatedly fail to follow in the Divine path of loving-kindness, make recompense, and then fail and make recompense yet again. Our impurity exists but is not so extreme that it leads to exile.

And then comes the ritual involving the possibly adulterous wife—the wife whose faithfulness we truly do not know. In traditional interpretations, the wife stands for the Israelites who have become betrothed to G-d in accepting the covenant at Mount Sinai. Frequently they are unfaithful, but they never entirely forget G-d. And for each of us today, lack of certainty about the wife's infidelity can be interpreted as our own state of spiritual uncertainty, as we vacillate between commitment and disconnection, teetering in the middle like the wife who may or may not be innocent.

After that, in the description of the Nazarite, we progress further toward communion with the Divine, looking at the parts of our being that most clearly long for a spiritual life, and not because of upbringing and conditioning. For the Nazarite is not like the Levite who is born into the service of G-d; the Nazarite chooses the spiritual path.

At this point in the narrative, we have moved from the impure state in which we are banished outside the camp, seemingly separated from YHVH, to the state of devotion symbolized by the Nazarite. And so we receive the Priestly Blessing, the blessing of awareness, of perceiving the Divine Presence shining on us.

And finally, in the reciprocal relationship that we have with G-d, we bring our gifts—each chieftain, representing each tribe, bringing the same donations.

Here is a very deep teaching.

On one hand, we each come to G-d individually. Whether we come as members of a tribe or of a religious community in prayer services, we remain responsible for ourselves. We may pray the same words, the same text, but each of us is asked separately to love the Divine.

But we are also each asked to make the same commitment, no matter where we come from, who we are, or how close we feel to G-d on a given day. We may come to the Divine as individuals on our own tortuous paths, but in the end we are asked to make the same offering: to cleave to the Divine and emulate G-d's loving-kindness to the best of our ability.

When we do this, manifesting G-d's compassion through our own actions, we begin to hear G-d speaking both through us and to us. The Priestly Blessing is ours both to receive and to offer:

May YHVH bless you and watch over you.

May YHVH shine the Divine face upon you and grace you.
May YHHV raise the Divine face to you and give you peace.[6]

For Formal Practice: When you are ready, turn your attention to the words of the Priestly Blessing: "May G-d shine the Divine face upon you and grace you."

Notice any resistance you may feel to opening yourself to this blessing. Notice any places of tightness or resistance in your body.

Now return to one of the places in your body where you felt the narrowing of resistance. As you follow your breath, slowly repeat, "May G-d shine the Divine face upon you and grace you," and let yourself feel G-d reaching out to you.

If you can, see what the tightness is about, see if it is part of a pattern in your life that may go back years and years, and move between the resistance and the sense of G-d reaching out to you.

At any point, you can simply return to full focus on the words, repeating them slowly as you breathe in and out, and going with them as far as you can.

If you are distracted at any point, return first to the breath, focusing just on the inhale and exhale, and then add the words, repeating them slowly as you breathe so that you can feel G-d's loving-kindness.

If you like, you can also turn your attention to your bringing the gift of loving-kindness to others and notice the feelings of resistance that arise in regard to a particular person or situation. Picturing the scene, very slowly repeat yet again, "May G-d shine the Divine face upon you and grace you," and notice what happens.

At any point, you can simply return to full focus on the words, repeating them slowly as you breathe in and out, and going with them as far as you can.

In My Own Practice: *When I began to meditate on the Priestly Blessing, I had trouble pulling air into my lungs. It was an odd sensation, as if the muscles were too weak, as if I had Lou Gehrig's disease or something like it. Midway through the meditation, I realized that the day before had been the anniversary of my mother's death and that she had died because she was in the final stage of multiple sclerosis. I felt that I was, quite literally, feeling some of the struggle she had by the end of her life to simply breathe. It wasn't quite compassion, but it was an approach to compassion through physical empathy.*

Today, as I meditate on the words of the Priestly Blessing, I feel resistance in terms of my being unworthy.

I did not show my mother the loving-kindness I would show her now. In a moment of horrified shock, I sit bolt upright. Whatever was in my mind that I didn't stay with her in the last week of her life?

She had refused food or water because she wanted to die. I knew it was the end, I had no doubt. But I kept going to work instead of sitting with her in the nursing home.

WHAT WAS I THINKING?

I return to the words of the Blessing. It goes out to both of us.

She had failed me, too. It had never occurred to me to stay because she had closed down so many years before. She was always absent when I tried to reach her.

I return to the words of the blessing, knowing that I would come to the hospital now even if she ignored me. But it is ten years later.

The thought arises that I was who I was. It never even occurred to me. I was who I was. I am different now.

I return to the words.

The thought arises that she, too, had responsibility. But now the words of the blessing wash over us both as if she is here with me now.

The thought arises that she, too, was who she was.

This is what happened. At least I held her hand as she died.

In silence, the peace of the Divine Presence enfolds us.

Numbers/*B'midbar*, 3, "When You Put Up"/*B'haalot'cha* (Num. 8:1–12:16)

"And YHVH spoke to Moses, saying, 'Speak to Aaron and you shall say to him, "When you put up the lamps...." ' "

—Num. 8:1

Interpretive Overview: This *parshah* begins with final ritual instructions to ready the Israelites for the march from Mount Sinai across the wilderness, but the Israelites rapidly lose their enthusiasm once they set out. Although the surface narrative seems disorganized, the deeper story can be read as a highly structured account of our spiritual journey as we move from preparation and initial fervor to the kinds of lapses that commonly follow: fear, desire for familiar comforts, and self-righteousness. These all lead to our feeling cut off from the Divine Presence, an experience that is described in the surface narrative as punishment.

Summary of *Parshah:* The last *parshah* closed with a flashback to the end of Exodus, when the twelve tribes made their dedication offerings in the newly finished Sanctuary. This *parshah* continues the flashback, as the Divine gives a final set of commands, opening with directives for Aaron's setting up the sacred, seven-branched lampstand (i.e., *menorah*) in the Tabernacle;[1] followed by instructions for consecrating the Levites so that they can safely perform their duties for the Tent of Meeting;[2] followed by a ruling that the Passover observance be celebrated a month late if people are unable to participate at the usual time.

G-d also adds that every Israelite is obliged to offer the Passover sacrifice and that a stranger residing in the Israelite community can choose to take part, following the same rule and rites.[3] In a remarkable sentence, the text says: "There shall be one law for you, whether stranger or citizen of the country."[4]

Completing the flashback, the text then says that the cloud of G-d covered the Tabernacle on the day it was set up and continued to rest upon it "in the likeness of fire"[5] all through the night. Thereafter, the people remained encamped whenever the cloud rested on the Tabernacle, (either in the form of cloud by day or fire by night), traveling only when it lifted and guided them.

In the final instruction of this *parshah,* G-d tells Moses to make two silver trumpets to be used for signaling travel, for bringing down Divine protection in warfare, and for commemorating G-d while offering sacrifices at festivals. Only then, on the twentieth day of the second month of the second year after leaving Egypt, does the cloud lift from the Tabernacle, and the Israelites set out.

Now the order of the march is given, tribe by tribe, with the names of each commander. Then Moses asks his father-in-law Jethro to come with them.[6] When Jethro refuses, saying that he is going back to his own land and birthplace, Moses asks him again, saying that Jethro knows the way when the Israelites do not, and that Jethro will be rewarded. But no answer is recorded.[7]

So the march begins, with the Ark of the Covenant in front and the Divine cloud above for three days. Then comes the inevitable disconnection from G-d, for the people begin to bitterly complain. YHVH is incensed and sends down fire at the outskirts of the camp, and then the people cry out to Moses, who prays, and the fire dies down. But in the next paragraph, the complaints begin again. "The riffraff in their midst"[8] feel a gluttonous craving for meat, saying, "We remember the fish that we used to eat free in Egypt, the cucumbers, the melons, the leeks, the onions, and the garlic. Now our gullets are shriveled. There is nothing at all! Nothing but this manna to look to!"[9]

As anger spreads through the camp, Moses hears, G-d is enraged, and Moses also complains, saying that G-d has mistreated him by giving him responsibility that he does not want, for people he cannot satisfy. "I cannot carry all this people by myself, for it is too much for me," he says,[10] and he begs G-d to kill him rather than continue to force upon him the burden of sole leadership.

YHVH tells him to have the seventy elders come to the Sanctuary to have G-d fill them with some of the same spirit that fills Moses, so that they can take over some of Moses' burden. Then G-d tells Moses to have the Israelites purify themselves (in preparation for eating meat), adding that there will be meat the next day—and the next and the next—for a whole month, "until it comes out of your nostrils and becomes loathsome to you. For you have rejected the Eternal who is among you, by whining before [G-d] and saying, 'Oh, why did we ever leave Egypt!' "[11]

The language remains pungent as Moses doubts G-d's ability to feed 600,000 men plus their families. And the Divine responds with equal tartness, saying "Is there a limit to the Eternal's power? You shall soon see whether what I have said happens to you or not!"[12]

So Moses reports G-d's words to the people and gathers the elders, who speak in ecstasy when the spirit that had been only on Moses enters them too.[13] After this, a wind sweeps in, depositing quail two cubits deep all through the camp. As the Israelites begin devouring the quail, with the meat "still between their teeth, not yet chewed,"[14] a furious G-d sends down a murderous plague. After that, the tribes set out for the next destination, Hazeroth.

And when they arrive at the end of this *parshah,* we have a new falling away from the Divine. But this time, it is not the riff-raff or ordinary Israelites who complain, but Moses' sister and brother, Miriam and Aaron. In a famous passage, we hear them criticize Moses for marrying a Cushite woman.[15] Then they complain about him making too much of himself when they are as close to G-d as he is. For they say, "Has the Eternal spoken only though Moses? Has [G-d] not spoken through us as well?"[16]

YHVH immediately hears, and the text sets the scene for G-d's response with a phrase that implicitly raises Moses above all others: "And the man Moses was very humble, more than any person on the face of the earth."[17]

The Divine then comes down in a column of cloud and tells Aaron and Miriam that prophets hear YHVH through dreams and visions, but that YHVH's servant Moses is greater than that. For the Divine speaks to Moses "mouth to mouth, plainly and not in riddles, and he beholds the likeness of the Eternal."[18] Incensed, the Divine then asks how they dare speak against Moses, and leaves.

As the cloud withdraws from the Tent of Meeting, Miriam's skin turns snow white. (This seems related to the skin diseases that were called leprosy in Leviticus.) Aaron instantly begs forgiveness for their sin, pleading that she not be mutilated, while Moses simply cries out: "Oh G-d, pray heal her!"[19] G-d answers that she must bear her shame for seven days, during which time she must be shut out of the camp. And so she is, and the people wait to march until she is readmitted. Then they leave Hazeroth and camp in the wilderness of Paran.

***Parshah* Interpretation:** Like the prior *parshah* in *B'midbar,* this one looks almost randomly cobbled together if we read it literally. But it makes narrative sense when we decode the sections, looking at their symbolic focus rather than at their word-by-word details. In essence, the symbolic story begins with our final preparations for an intense spiritual journey, moves into the grand beginning of the journey when we have high hopes for success, and then interrupts with three experiences of distraction from the goal—which the Torah sees as inevitable, as long as we are in human bodies.

Thus, the *parshah* begins by referring to the *Menorah,* the seven-branched sacred lamp in the Tabernacle. Plantlike in its form, the lamp has always been understood to represent some kind of tree, perhaps even the burning bush; its seven lights remind us of G-d's calling to us each day. The text then moves to the consecration of the Levites, where the Levites may stand for that part of us most yearning to cleave to this ever-present YHVH and to follow in YHVH's ways of compassion.

Then comes the reminder of Passover, our metaphor for the continual possibility of being freed from the enslavement to egoistic self-concern that keeps us from being with G-d. And then there's a final point, about remembering Passover at a later time if we have for some reason been unable to perform the traditional observance. Symbolically, we can read this section as implying that we will at times be unable to remember our vow to free ourselves from enslavement—and that we can always reconfirm that commitment at the next opportunity. Any of us, Israelite or not.

With all that in place, G-d awaits in the Sanctuary, ready for us to continue on our journey.

But first comes yet one more bit of instruction. For here, we read about the trumpets carrying messages, and about needing assistance from Moses' father-in-law, who already knows the land the Israelites will be marching through. So the text is reminding us that we need G-d's guidance on the path, but that we also want a teacher who has been on the journey before us and knows the route—and that teacher may come from anywhere, not necessarily from within the community, just as Jethro comes from outside.

Finally, we do set out, trying to follow where the Divine cloud leads us, holding in front of us, as one always available guide, the Ten Commandments and other rules of behavior that sit in the Ark. And in just three days, we encounter our first spiritual obstacle, for the Israelites complain bitterly as they enter unknown territory. No reason is given in the text, nor do we need one, for we know that it is always frightening to turn from our habitual life, in which we have at least an illusion of control. Even if the price of habit is slavery, we are frightened by the unknown, for it is hostile to all our desires to take charge, to predict, to plan.

The second spiritual obstacle is more specific, as the tribes yearn for the food of Egypt—despite its cost being their enslavement—preferring it to the manna provided by G-d. This is one of the more famous episodes in the Torah, and it represents another universal human experience.

As we first commit ourselves to change, the more animal parts of ourselves rear up in fear. (In traditional Judaism, even a part of our soul is deeply connected to the physical body and its desires.) Like the Israelites, we want meat, not the ethereal manna of G-d. We do not want to give up the physical comforts of the life we know, no matter how trapped we may feel by it.

And if we make some progress in overcoming these first two obstacles, we generally encounter the third example given in this chapter. Miriam and Aaron inflate their own stature and begin to self-righteously judge Moses. For one of the common hallmarks of early spiritual commitment is self-inflation, seeing ourselves as somehow better than other people and judging them harshly.

Such judgment, such inevitable human failure, is followed by punishment, as Miriam is first made leprous and then exiled from the camp for seven days. In reading Leviticus, we interpreted the Torah's examples of leprosy as representing serious spiritual impurity. Given that, we can easily also understand Miriam's exile not as punishment as much as the inevitable sense of G-d's absence that we experience when our own transgressions move us away from the Divine.

But we can always get past this error and reconnect with the Divine Presence, as both Aaron and Miriam do by the *parshah's* end.

For Formal Practice: Today, I'd like to explore what this *parshah* says about how we cut ourselves off from awareness of the Divine Presence. When you are ready, sit in silence with your breath. Let your mind hover over the question about ways in which you enslave yourself in seeking physical satisfactions: through food, sex, shopping, etc. Or, let your mind hover over your own tendencies toward judgment and self-righteousness.

At some point, let yourself go to thankfulness for the gifts that you have been given—perhaps, family or friends or health. Or the sound of birdsong outside your window right now. Or the breath of life itself. I could go on forever, for the miracles of the Divine Presence are expressed in every bit of the physical world, from the thunderbolt to the ant. The miracles permeate every moment of existence.

If you like, use the phrase "I give thanks before you." If you prefer Hebrew, the phrase is *Modeh* (feminine is *Modah*) *ani l' fanecha*.

In My Own Practice: *I go at once to my recurrent obsession: My neighbors are too close to me. I see their presence whenever I go outside.*

I knew they were close when I bought my house, but both of their lots were wooded at that time. One neighbor later cleared most of his property, and both have put up very visible, ugly metal fences and other structures.

Immediately, I go to greed. To the equivalent of wanting meat. How I focus on what I don't have, on what more I want, on the privacy I used to have. How I envy all the people I know who have no neighbors nearby. In my envy, my mind skitters through what's wrong with their properties, why they don't really have it better.

And then my mind jumps to all of the people in the world who live in poverty— how undeservingly rich I am compared to most of the human race.

I return to my breath and sit with my desire, my greed, my envy, my embarrassment.

Nothing changes, and I turn to giving thanks for what I have. The houses I envy cost more than I could spend. I can afford my house. I can pay my bills.

I'm making a beautiful garden. And I have a bog in the far back that I love in winter. My heart expands slightly.

And then the thought appears in the silence: I am making judgments. It is not up to me to decide who has more and who has less, or to weigh each person's lot in the balance scale.

What is just is. People do not have equal shares. Life is not fair. It never was.

What is just is. I can let go of judgment.

In that moment, I let go of the sense of failure, the underlying sense that I should somehow make my house perfect.

It's not my job to make perfect choices.

I sit with my breath and open up to the freedom and serenity of the deep silence of the Divine Presence.

Numbers/*B'midbar*, 4, "Send"/*Sh'lach L'cha*
(Num. 13:1–15:41)

"And YHVH spoke to Moses, saying, 'Send men and let them scout the land of Canaan that I'm giving to the children of Israel....' "

—Num. 13:1

Interpretive Overview: The twelve scouts report back to the Israelites that the Promised Land is indeed wonderful, but inhabited by monstrous, semi-human giants. As the terrified people talk of returning to Egypt, G-d angrily declares that they will now have to wander for forty years in the wilderness, until the whole generation of slaves is dead. At the deeper level, the narrative is describing our horror of confronting the demons and giants within ourselves as we advance on our spiritual path.

Summary of *Parshah:* G-d tells Moses to send scouts from each tribe to see the Promised Land. They get as far as Hebron,[1] where they reconnoiter the area and cut down a huge branch with a single cluster of grapes (for it is the season for grapes), and also take back some pomegranates and figs. At the end of forty days, they report back to Moses and Aaron, and to the people.

The scouts say that Canaan is indeed a land of milk and honey, but ten of the twelve declare it filled with many powerful tribes in well-fortified, large cities. Caleb, the eleventh scout, interrupts to say that the Israelites can overcome the tribes and should go forward, but the other ten insist that the tribes are too strong for the Israelites. (Joshua, the twelfth scout, is silent at this point.) Then they say that this is a land "that devours its settlers,"[2] that the inhabitants are all of great size, and that they even saw the giant *Nephilim* there.[3] They conclude, "And we looked like grasshoppers to ourselves, and so we must have looked to them."[4]

231

The whole community is terrified. They blame Aaron and Moses yet again for bringing them out of the safety of Egypt, wailing that they would have been better off to die in Egypt or in the wilderness than to die in "that land to fall by the sword."[5] When they tell one another that they should head back to Egypt, Moses and Aaron are in despair.[6] Both Caleb and Joshua tear their clothes in mourning and exhort the Israelites to go forward and not rebel against G-d's wishes by turning back. When the community threatens to stone Caleb and Joshua, YHVH's presence descends upon the Tent of Meeting.

Incensed at their lack of trust despite all the signs of Divine protection given to them, G-d tells Moses that they will be struck with pestilence and disowns them, offering to start afresh with a lineage from Moses. But Moses turns aside YHVH's anger, saying that Egypt and the other nations will believe that G-d slaughtered the Israelites because the Divine was too weak to bring them into possession of the Promised Land. And then he pleads once more for mercy. Indeed, he uses the famous self-description that the Divine gave him in Exodus at the cleft in the rock, saying, "The Eternal! slow to anger and abounding in kindness; forgiving iniquity and transgression … Pardon, I pray, the iniquity of this people according to Your great kindness, as You have forgiven this people ever since Egypt."[7]

The Divine Presence agrees not to kill the Israelites, but adds that none of the adults who witnessed the miracles in Egypt will enter the Promised Land, except for Caleb and Joshua. Then G-d tells Moses the people should begin the march into the wilderness the next day by way of the Red Sea,[8] avoiding the Amalekites and the Canaanites in the valleys.

In yet another angry passage, YHVH adds that the people will get what they asked for: they will die in the wilderness. They will wander for forty years, G-d says, corresponding to the forty days that the land was scouted, until the whole generation of slaves dies. Only their children will enter the land that they rejected.

Then comes the interposition that ten of the scouts die of plague. Only Joshua and Caleb survive.

After this, Moses reports G-d's words to the people, who try to make atonement by setting out the next morning to the Promised Land. In their grief, they do not take the route the Divine commanded, and Moses tells them that they are again disobedient and will be killed because the Divine will not be with them. Again they do not listen, and the Amalekites and Canaanites slaughter them.

The narrative is then broken by a serious of instructions involving ritual practice.[9] These begin with a brief description of the kinds of offerings to be made after entering the Promised Land, with the reiteration that a stranger in residence[10] shall follow the same ritual. The Israelites are also told to offer up to YHVH some of the bread they bake from their first grain harvest.

After this come instructions for making expiation through ritual sacrifice for an unwitting failure to observe any one of the commandments[11] given to Moses, whether by the whole community or by individuals. But, says the text, if the lapses by an individual are in deliberate defiance of G-d, that person shall be cut off from the community.

A story then interrupts the instruction, telling about the Israelites coming upon an [Israelite] man gathering wood on the Sabbath. Brought before Moses, Aaron, and the whole community, the man is then placed in custody because no one knows what to do. But the Divine tells Moses he should be stoned to death outside the camp by the whole community, and so they do as commanded.

And finally, YHVH tells Moses to tell the people to make fringes on the corners of their garments with a cord of blue in the fringe at each corner.[12] This fringe shall be worn to remind them "to observe all My commandments and be holy to your G-d. I the Eternal am your G-d, who brought you out of the land of Egypt to be your G-d: I the Eternal am your G-d."[13]

Parshah **Interpretation:** In the last *parshah,* we'd already met obstacles on our inward path of transformation, for we began to regret leaving the safety and routine of our "normal" life. Already, we yearned for the simple material comforts of that life (as represented by wanting meat and other Egyptian food). As we moved further out on our journey, we arrived at a place of judgment and criticism of others (as Miriam and Aaron criticize Moses), feeling ourselves better than other people, somehow more highly developed.

In this *parshah,* we have started forward again. We are, in fact, on the edge of the Promised Land, which is not really such a surprise, for it always there waiting for us. The symbolic narrative is quite clear, for the scouts go directly to Hebron, the place where Abraham tented, and the place where the angels came to tell him that he would have Isaac and that his lineage would multiply and thrive in covenant with G-d. Here Abraham sat under the oaks of Mamre, a holy site for prophecy. Here, also, Abraham argued for mercy for Sodom and Gomorrah, just as Moses argues with G-d in this *parshah.*[14]

In the narrative, there are also allusions to Noah and Mount Sinai—for the scouts return after forty days, just as the rains came down in the flood for forty days, and just as Moses spent forty days atop Mount Sinai. The scouts bring back the branch of a grape as the dove brought Noah an olive leaf. All these references—to Abraham, Noah, and Mount Sinai—are resonant of new possibility, of new beginnings in covenant with the Divine.

This *parshah,* in its very title, also suggests a reference to our internal spiritual life, just as the corresponding title in Abraham's *parshah* suggested going inward for his journey. In the same way that Abraham was told to *lech l'cha*: to "go [in]to yourself," we are told to *sh'lach l'cha*: to "send [in] to yourself"; that is, to go inward to the Promised Land. To explore the interior Garden where the Divine dwells. To find the Divine as we plumb our own depths.

But looking inward also requires us to become aware of negative aspects of ourselves that would turn us from a path of holiness; to recognize aspects of ourselves that we'd rather keep in darkness, out of our consciousness. In the literal narrative, ten of the scouts are afraid to go forward; at the metaphoric level, we may fear going on with the inward self-examination necessary for spiritual change. In the surface narrative, the scouts are afraid not simply of the human tribes they will have to overcome, but of the *Nephilim*, creatures described in Genesis 6:1–4 as descended from divine beings who mated with human women. As giants who are only part human, they seem to stand for a kind of alien power, perhaps for what we would now think of as unconscious, primitive forces in ourselves. We don't want to know these aspects of ourselves. We never do. Better to turn back, the Israelites say.

And the price is disconnection from the Divine. Rather than read it as punishment, read it as simple fact: if you don't do this work, if you don't face your demons, you will be cut off from the Divine Presence, you will wander in a spiritual desert. Also, if you try to face your demons while asking for guidance, you can do it; but if you spurn that help and try to do it egoistically, as the Israelites do when they march against G-d's will, you are likely to fail.

The Promised Land—awareness of the Divine Presence permeating your existence in every moment—is always possible. You can always come to it later down the road, just as the children of the Israelites will. And when you have these moments of awareness, the symbolic text says, make sure to recommit yourself to the service of YHVH (i.e., in the literal text, offer up your sacrifices). And give thanks for the miracles of your life, as represented in the harvest bread. Also, remember that such actions are called for by anyone in such a state of awareness no matter where they come from (i.e., even a stranger).

Furthermore, the text next says—as it does over and over—that we will inevitably fail in our quest because we are human and far from fully conscious, and that we can always recommit ourselves. But deliberately rejecting the Divine is different. We do not know what the literal meaning is of the punishment to be "cut off from the midst of his people,"[15] but when we remember that the word *Israel* stands for "G-d wrestler," the punishment sounds at the symbolic level like spiritual exile from the community of G-d wrestlers.

Then comes a bit of narrative that is shocking to the modern, Western ear: stoning the man caught gathering wood on the Sabbath. But at the symbolic level, he is breaking the prime commandment: he is doing, working, keeping too busy to commune with G-d. Too busy to emulate YHVH through simple *being*-ness, through opening to the Divine silence. Perhaps, the stoning that follows represents some kind of pulverizing of our impulses to keep busy, to keep doing in order to escape the fear of what we will discover within ourselves if we try to simply *be*.

And finally, the *parshah* ends with instructions to wear a garment whose fringes help us remember to follow G-d's commandments, keeping us conscious of how we must act when we would otherwise fall back into forgetfulness and unawareness. For no matter how we feel internally, whether open to G-d or not, following the commandments to act with loving-kindness keeps a pathway open within us for manifesting and communing with the Divine force that is the source of all existence. We can even think of ourselves as simply being part of G-d, with this entire world akin to being YHVH's body as G-d manifests in the physical realm.[16]

For Formal Practice: The intention (in Hebrew, the *kavanah*) of this contemplative meditation is to begin to explore the demons deep within you. When you are ready, follow your breath until you begin to have some moments of silence. In that silence, let yourself glimpse the deep sources of your resistance to following the spiritual path. (If you try to regularly meditate but seem unable to consistently practice, ask what keeps you away.)

If you like, use the following phrase as you need: "G-d is with me, I shall not fear." (In Hebrew: *Adonai li, lo eerah.*)

In My Own Practice: *I begin the meditation knowing that I have gone back this week to my default state of being overly committed, of signing myself onto too many projects. I feel harried and tense as I begin. I try to focus on some sense of the demons within my being, but I keep returning to my need to be in action. I feel like the man who was stoned for gathering wood on the Sabbath, unable to rest, to simply be still and open to the is-ness of the Divine Presence.*

I keep returning to the breath. Begin to have moments of quietness. The thought arises: what does the endless doing feel like? The answer arises: service. Service to others.

Another feeling arises in opposition—a feeling of wanting only to rest, to be without working.

Then another thought bubbles up. I need to serve. I need expiation. And with this thought appears a conversation I had the night before with a friend. I had calmly told him that I couldn't remember where my late mother-in-law was buried, because I'd killed her.

I'd explained that she'd called me to say her big toe hurt and I'd told her to take some aspirin. When my husband came home two days later from the conference he'd been at, I relayed the story. He immediately called his mother, but it was too late. Her leg was amputated some time later because of a blood clot, and, ultimately, she died. I'd known she had Reynaud's syndrome, a disease involving blood circulation, I explained, but it had never crossed my mind when she called that it was serious, that she might have a blood clot.

I sit now with the memory of my mother-in-law's call. She was cognitively impaired, but even so, she could have called her doctor instead of me. Or explained to me why she was worried. But I know, deeply know, that she did the best she could.

I return to following my breath.

Soon, the thought bubbles up: I also did the best I could. Maybe her death was preventable, but blaming myself has a note of grandiosity. Bad things happen. Bad things happen all the time.

I need to think about—off the cushion—expiation and guilt and grandiosity. And then a last thought arises in the silence: guilt feels better than powerlessness. Guilt offers some phantom of possible control.

The guilt immediately drops away. Relief washes over me. I return to the silence.

Numbers/*B'midbar,* 5, "Korach"/*Korach*
(Num. 16:1–18:32)

"And Korach ... got up in front of Moses—and two hundred fifty people from the children of Israel, chieftains of the congregation...."

—Num. 16:1–2

Interpretive Overview: This *parshah* seems to conflate two different rebellions against Moses and Aaron. Korach, who is their first cousin, is jealous of both their closeness to G-d and their power; while the revolt of Dathan and Abiram seems to be more purely political, simply motivated by a craving for power. At a deeper level, this *parshah* continues to explore the obstacles we encounter as we move forward in our spiritual practice. For we may come to desire closeness to the Divine not just for its own sake, but at least partly for the power such closeness confers upon us; or we may simply desire the privileges of power.

Summary of *Parshah:* The *parshah* begins with one of the most famous rebellions in the Bible, led by Korach—a great-grandson of Jacob's son Levi[1]—and by Dathan, Abiram, and On[2] —great-grandsons of Jacob's son, Reuben. These four men, along with 250 well-respected chieftains of the community, tell Moses and Aaron they have unlawfully raised themselves above the rest of the community. "You have gone too far!" they say. "For all the community are holy, all of them, and the Eternal is in their midst."[3]

In despair, Moses answers that G-d will make known who is holy and close to the Divine; and he tells Korach and his 250 followers to bring lit incense burners to the Sanctuary the next day to test whom YHVH chooses as High Priest. He also asks Korach why he is not satisfied with the position he already has, as a Levite serving in the Sanctuary. Why does he seek the priesthood as well?

When Moses sends for Dathan and Abiram, they refuse to approach, asking what right he has to lord it over them, particularly since "you brought us from a land flowing with milk and honey to kill us in the wilderness."[4] A furious Moses tells G-d that he has wronged none of them, and repeats his order to Korach and the 250 others to bring incense pans to the Sanctuary. (Only the priests are allowed to burn incense, so this will test their claim to the priesthood.)

The next day, Korach brings the whole community out against Moses and Aaron, YHVH's glory comes down, and YHVH once again seems ready to destroy all the Israelites in punishment. Aaron and Moses plead that retribution should be limited to the actual rebels. The Divine relents, but tells Moses that everyone had better move away from the tents of the rebel leaders.

The community backs away, and Moses proclaims that the rebels' deaths will not be his doing but G-d's. Then the earth opens its mouth and swallows Dathan and Abiram so that they go down—alive—to *Sheol,* the land of the dead, along with their children, households, and all their possessions. Meanwhile, the 250 followers of Korach are consumed by Divine fire as they hold their incense pans. (It is not clear from the text whether Korach is himself consumed by fire or is swallowed up.)[5]

After this, YHVH says that Aaron's son Eleazar should hammer the incense pans into sheets for plating the altar[6] as a reminder that none but priests can offer incense in the Sanctuary. But the people continue to miss the point that Moses and Aaron have not chosen themselves as leaders; it is G-d who has chosen them. When they accuse the two brothers of having killed G-d's people, the Divine sends yet another plague; and Moses tells Aaron to burn incense in atonement for the community's sinfulness. As Aaron stands in the midst of the plague "between the dead and the living,"[7] with his lit incense, the plague ends.

Then YHVH tells Moses to have each of the twelve tribes bring a staff on which is written the name of their chief, with Aaron's name on the

Levites' staff. Moses is to place all twelve staffs in front of the Ark in the Sanctuary; the staff that blossoms will belong to the man G-d has chosen as High Priest. Of course, it is Aaron's staff that flowers and bears almonds, and YHVH commands Moses to place it by the Ark to remind the rebels of G-d's choice, to end their mutterings so that they do not die. But the people are again terrified, saying that now they will die if they come even near the Tabernacle.

The *parshah* ends with a section on the responsibilities and rights of priests and Levites.[8] Most striking is the reiteration that neither group has any rights to land. Without crops or cattle of their own, therefore, they eat and drink only the holiest of food, taken from the sacred offerings in the Tabernacle.[9]

***Parshah* Interpretation:** Many Torah interpreters have said that this *parshah* conflates two distinct and separate accounts of rebellion, one religious and one secular.[10] Thus, Korach represents the religious sphere by wanting to be as close to G-d as Moses and Aaron—and by challenging their place as YHVH's representatives. Dathan and Abiram represent a more simple political rebellion, in which they just want to be the ones in charge.[11]

Torah commentators have sometimes seen Korach's deep yearning to be closer to YHVH in a positive light,[12] pointing to the statements that he is an ancestor of the prophet Samuel,[13] that the incense pans of his followers are beaten into copper plates to cover the Ark, and that Korach's sons are believed to have composed eleven of the psalms, one of which is read at morning synagogue services every Monday.[14]

But tradition more often emphasizes Korach's desire for what is not his, in his craving for the personal power and authority that proximity to G-d might bring. This emphasis is implicit in the paragraph that immediately precedes his rebellion, at the very end of the last *parshah,* which has YHVH's commandment to put fringes on the clothing so that "you shall not stray after your heart and after your eyes, after which you go whoring."[15]

Korach's clan is responsible for transporting the most sacred objects in the Sanctuary; as clan leader, he ranks just below the priests. Thus, he is representative of someone far advanced on the spiritual path, and he displays a defect that is all too often encountered in such people—a corrupting desire both for greater closeness to the Divine and for the power that goes with such closeness.

The two hundred and fifty leaders (and, probably, Korach) are consumed by G-d's fire just as Aaron's sons were consumed when they brought unpurified incense to G-d. The punishment is ironically fitting: craving closeness to the Divine, they themselves become burnt offerings, turned to smoke as they go up to G-d.

On the other hand, Dathan and Abiram seem more simply political, challenging G-d by seeking to replace Moses' leadership with their own. In response, they are swallowed up by the earth, taken down alive to the realm of the dead along with their families and all they own. Everything that has defined them in the material world disappears along with them: possessions, descendants, accomplishments. As with the rebels who go up in smoke, their punishment has an ironic humor alongside its macabre quality. It is as if G-d is saying, "So you want power? Well, take your possessions to the land of the dead for all the good it will do you. But here on earth, it is as if you have been wiped out. Nothing of you remains."

Whether they die by fire or by the earth's swallowing them, the rebels' death is described as punishment for their sinfulness in ignoring G-d's will. But we can also interpret what happens as cause and effect, in the terms used in Leviticus. For the raw power of the Divine Presence is overwhelming, dangerous for mere mortals to intrude on, particularly when we are still defiled by the ego's desires for dominance. It is one thing to seek to experience some of the *being*-ness of the Divine, or to be overcome by the compassion of the Source of All. It is quite another to seek to enhance one's own authority by plugging oneself into that life force, like Korach and the 250 rebels, or to steal that life force for one's own use, like

Dathan and Abiram when they try to take the power that G-d has given to Moses for themselves.

In all the ancient shamanic traditions, it is dangerous to challenge the forces of the spirit world to obtain power for oneself, for the forces of that world can turn against one all too easily. It does not matter whether we talk of the spirit world or of G-d: the danger is the same (since the spirit world is subsumed to G-d's realm). And so we have the image of the rebels being consumed by fire or consumed by the open mouth of the earth, possessed by the forces of the underworld, of *Sheol*.

Therefore, we can choose to see this narrative as a warning about striving too hard to get close to the Divine Presence when we want to use such closeness for our own purposes. The purity discussion at the end of this *parshah* is all about the priests and Levites—those nearer to G-d—having no secular holdings and thus none of the secular power that goes with such holdings. Instead, they are simply to serve the Divine. Revelation may come, but it is not ours to force, particularly if we are still contaminated by the desire for control and supremacy.

For Formal Practice: When you are ready, let yourself focus on the scene outside the Sanctuary. The two hundred and fifty rebels with Korach are lined up with their smoking incense pans at the entrance of the Tent of Meeting. They stand upright, stiff with pride. And Dathan and Abiram stand in front of their tents with their wives and children and infants.

The rebel leaders have stated their case. Let the sense of their words reverberate for you: "All the people are holy. What makes you believe that you can lord it over us?"

Let yourself sit with the scene as you follow your breath.

Go to the experience of one person lording it over another. Try to stay with the experience and see what arises.

In My Own Practice: *I have had a lot of difficulty going anywhere with this meditation until today. I see power in terms of creativity—having the means and the authority to bring something into being. The something can be a clean kitchen, a meal, a work of art, or a program of social change. The something doesn't matter.*

I try to focus on the tone of their words: "What makes you think you can lord it over us? " I go to the feeling of being lorded over. I think of someone I once worked with, someone I thought less capable than me, but someone who had more power. Whenever she persuaded me to her point of view, I had no problem doing what she asked. But when we continued to disagree, I was angry if I had to surrender to her will. More than angry if I really cared about the decision. Furious.

Now I see the army of rebels standing upright in front of the Tent of Meeting. I hear the arrogance of Korach and the others.

Suddenly, I get it. They see the world in terms of domination. They experience Moses and Aaron as dominating them, they resent the domination, and they want to exchange places, to be the ones at the top of the power heap.

They do not understand that power is to be used for service, for transforming the world into a Sanctuary. They do not see that those in power are meant to be, like the rest of us: servants. They see the exchange in terms of Moses and Aaron lording it over them.

They do not see the acts of service, the goals strived for; they feel only the authority, only the lash of a whip. They understand the world from the perspective of a slave, not of a free human being.

Numbers/*B'midbar*, 6, "Law"/*Chukat*
(Num. 19:1–22:1)

"The Eternal One spoke to Moses and Aaron, saying: 'This is the ritual law that the Eternal has commanded.' "

—Num. 19:1–2[1]

Interpretive Overview: This *parshah* brings us almost to the end of the forty-year trek through the wilderness, for it closes with the Israelites encamped on the steppes of Moab, overlooking the Jordan River and the Promised Land. At the metaphoric level, the *parshah* seems similarly to be near the end of the Book of Numbers' accounting of the successive obstacles encountered on the path of spiritual growth. For now it is Moses who stumbles, momentarily believing himself to be as powerful as G-d in the famous passage in which he strikes the rock for water at Meribah. Once again, the stories that surround the main narrative seem concerned with spiritual purification as we carry on with our inner journey.

Summary of *Parshah*: The narrative begins with instructions for re-purification of people and possessions that have become impure after contact with dead bodies, a process that involves burning an "unblemished red cow,"[2] and then mixing the cow's ashes with flowing water to sprinkle on—and thus purify—them.

Then comes the bare statement that the people continue traveling and that Miriam dies and is buried at Kadesh, followed by a sentence that says there was no water. Immediately, the thirsty people declare, yet again, that Moses and Aaron have taken the community out of Egypt to die in the wilderness. YHVH tells Moses to take the staff (apparently the staff of Aaron that flowered in the last *parshah*), assemble the community, and order the rock to yield water.

245

In a very famous scene, Moses says, "Listen, you rebels, shall we get water for you out of this rock?"[3] and twice strikes the rock with the staff instead of verbally passing on G-d's command to it. Water gushes out and everyone drinks, but the Divine Presence is angry. Exclaiming that neither Moses nor Aaron will enter the Promised Land because they failed to trust YHVH to bring the water, the Divine names the site the Waters of Meribah, which means "the waters of quarreling [with YHVH]."

As the trek continues, they come to the territory of Edom (i.e., of Esau's descendants). Calling him brother, Moses twice asks the king's permission to pass through, promising not to stray from the road, and even to pay for the water they and their cattle drink. But when the king refuses and blocks the way, the Israelites turn toward Mount Hor instead.

The narrative of the journey is now interrupted when the Divine tells Moses that Aaron is to go up Mount Hor to die, since he will not be allowed to enter the Promised Land because of what happened at Meribah (just as Moses will be denied entrance). Moses is to take both Aaron and his son Eleazar up with him, and then strip Aaron of his vestments and put them on Eleazar. Moses does this, Aaron dies, and the community mourns for thirty days.

After this comes a brief account of an attack by the Canaanite king of Arad, and a battle in which the Israelites win and destroy the Canaanites and their cities. They then set out from Mount Hor, avoiding Edom. By now, the people are impatient, but this time they are not only bitter toward Moses but—for the first time—toward both Moses and YHVH, complaining even of the manna on which they depend. In response to their complaints, the Divine sends down serpents, and many die of the bites. The people acknowledge their sin in speaking out against both G-d and Moses, and ask Moses to intervene. When he does, G-d tells him—in an anomalous statement that seems to involve a kind of idol, and therefore contradict all the edicts against making idols—to make a statue that looks like a serpent and set it on a standard so that anyone who is bitten can look at it and be cured.

Then comes more marching and fighting, with fragments of very ancient text inserted along the way, including one called the *Book of the Wars of God*. But they have defeated the Amorites by the end of this *parshah,* and are encamped in the steppes of Moab, just across the river Jordan from Jericho and the Promised Land.

***Parshah* Interpretation:** The last *parshah* seemed to be addressing a particular kind of impurity often seen in those who are on a serious spiritual quest, as they are tempted to conflate Divine Power with an inflated sense of their own authority. At a symbolic level, the chapter seemed to be commenting on both the lure and the destructive force of self-aggrandizement as one moves forward in one's spiritual growth.

This *parshah* now begins with a ceremony for purification from contact with death, in which the burnt ashes of an unblemished red cow are mixed with "living water,"[4] a term that is used elsewhere to refer to YHVH. Once more, the metaphoric narrative seems to be saying that we will inevitably lose our way on the spiritual journey, for we are merely human. If anything, progress on the spiritual path almost guarantees a lapse into self-aggrandizement and an encounter with spiritual death—even if briefly. So here is a ceremony for us stumbling, self-aggrandizing G-d wrestlers, which returns us from the side of death—and from the side of G-d as the bringer of death—and puts us on the side of the Divine Presence as the force of life.

But after this opening section on re-dedicating ourselves to continued wrestling with this boundless, unnamable Divine Presence, the narrative continues its exploration of self-aggrandizement as we witness a catastrophic lapse by Moses himself.

Once again, the Israelites have confused his power with YHVH's, blaming him for taking them out of Egypt when their release was not achieved through Moses' strength but by the power of the Divine. And in his fury at them for yet again complaining, he makes the same error as they: like the people, he confuses his power with G-d's, indicating that it is he—rather than G-d—who brings water from the rock. For he says, "Listen, rebels, shall we bring water out of this rock for you?" And then "Moses lifted his hand and struck the rock with his staff twice."[5]

For once, he has not acted humbly before the Divine Presence. In an instant of inattention and distraction that is driven by righteous fury, Moses has instead felt more than human, elevated to G-d's stature. Although we are likely to feel that denying him entry to the Promised Land is too harsh a penalty for this momentary blunder, a few Torah commentators have pointed out the similarity between Moses' striking the rock and the much earlier episode of his striking the Egyptian taskmaster and killing him.[6] Perhaps, then, he is kept from the Promised Land because of the homicide he committed in his youth, when he killed an Egyptian overseer who was beating a Hebrew slave. He was driven by righteous anger then, just as he is driven by righteous anger now; and he usurped the role of YHVH then, assuming G-d's power for himself in taking human life, just as he usurps the role of the Divine now.

In any case, YHVH's denying him entry into the Promised Land can be read as statement of fact rather than as penalty. The Promised Land is a metaphor for the state of surrender of self, of letting go of all self-concerns before the Divine Presence. Even if Moses only momentarily saw himself rather than YHVH as the miracle maker (or the avenging angel), he was not ready to fully let go of ego, to be a pure channel for Divine will.

As to the rest of the *parshah,* all of it concerns our final approach to the Promised Land, struggling against the remaining forces of egoistic self-centeredness.

Old wounds of rivalry and deceit are re-opened as Edom (Esau's descendants) refuse to let the Israelites (Jacob's descendants) pass. But the Israelites manage to remember their kinship with Edom in an astonishing moment of acceptance and forbearance, choosing not to fight even as

Edom denies them passage. In another moment of acceptance, this time of the inevitability of death, we see Moses prepare Eleazar to replace his dying father, Aaron, as priest.

At the literal level, the next-to-last section has the Israelites overcoming the Canaanite king Arad and utterly destroying his towns. But the Hebrew word for this destruction implies that all of the booty was consecrated to G-d,[7] suggesting that we must not only destroy our remaining resistances (as symbolized by the Canaanite kingdom), but convert whatever remains of them into holy service.

And yet, even after everything seems to have been converted to such service, we again show doubt as we come to the very edge of the Promised Land. In the narrative, the Israelites have moved much farther on their journey, for, at last, they comprehend that it is YHVH, and not Moses, who has brought them out of enslavement—and that it is YHVH who has all power. But they still lack trust, even criticizing the manna that has sustained them all these years. So G-d sends down serpents to bite them, and then commands that a statue be made of a snake to heal those who are bitten.

At a symbolic level, the snakes take us back to the Garden of Eden in Genesis. For it is the serpent who provokes doubt, so that Eve eats of the Tree of Knowledge, and we become consciously separate from YHVH, exiled from Eden, and prey to fear and craving. We are now on the very edge of the Promised Land, looking down upon the metaphoric Garden of Eden to which we are returning. But the serpent is still present in our minds, because we still have doubt about surrendering to the Divine will to become a channel for G-d.

For Formal Practice: The intention of this meditation is to acknowledge how much your own achievements have been controlled by forces outside your control, whether you call the forces fate or chance or life, or whether you see them as Divine will.

When you are ready, put yourself in Moses' place, striking the rock. Feel the sense of power as you hit the rock. Notice your sense of power as you see the water flow.

Now let yourself notice some of your achievements. They can come from any time in your life and refer to anything you have done, including the buildings you made out of blocks when you were three. Feel your pride in them.

Now let yourself contemplate how much your achievements, like Moses', have also depended on factors outside your control.

Just let the experiences come to you without thinking about them.

If you become distracted, return to the moment of striking the rock.

In My Own Practice: *I strike the rock and feel such pride. I think of the program I directed in New York City that recruited psychiatrists to provide care for mentally ill homeless people.*

It had started as a volunteer program, but sometime after I was hired, I was able to greatly expand it. I got us contracts with most of the training hospitals in the city to give us their psychiatry residents for a half day or more a week. I feel deep pride about that.

But they didn't just give us their young psychiatrists out of the goodness of their hearts. They were able to do it because we paid them.

Suddenly, I realize what a fluke it was to have that money. It had never been there before, but that year, and for years afterward, it came through the city from the federal government. HUD gave the city a billion dollars one year just for homeless programs. And the city got so much money because they'd created the best system in the nation for grant applications to HUD.

Without that money, we might never have grown to be more than a small organization of volunteer psychiatrists. Wonderful but small. Without that money from HUD and the city, it wouldn't have mattered how many times I struck the rock. It wouldn't have mattered how hard.

And I had nothing to do with creating that stream of available money in the first place.

And more. I got the job because I was already a friend of the psychiatrist who'd created the volunteer program. I couldn't have even struck the rock if I hadn't already known her.

I still feel deep pride in my accomplishment. I also see how imbedded my work was in a frame completely independent of anything I did.

Numbers/*B'midbar*, 7, "Balak"/*Balak*
(Num. 22:2–25:9)

"And Balak, son of Zippor, saw everything that Israel had done to the Amorite."

—Num. 22:2

Interpretive Overview: As the Israelites camp just outside the Promised Land, King Balak asks the famous pagan magician Balaam to curse them. Balaam, however, repeatedly says that he can do only what YHVH wants, despite what seems to be some ambivalence on his part. At the metaphoric level, we ourselves are Balaam (as well as the Israelites), and are far enough along in our spiritual development that we generally behave well—offering blessing rather than curses. But we are still ambivalent at times, distracted by worldly concerns. The tale plays gently with our awareness that we can never be perfect, for ambivalence and loss of focus are inevitable aspects of being human.

Summary of *Parshah:* When the narrative begins, the Moabites are frightened by the Israelite conquest of the Amorites and terrified by the sheer size of their encampment. Therefore, the king of Moab, named Balak, sends messengers to the famous pagan magician and prophet, Balaam, asking him to curse the Israelites so that they can be defeated despite their numbers. As in other parts of Torah, the text seems to indicate that other powers beside YHVH may exist.[1]

The messengers, who come from Moab and Midian, are themselves elders who, according to the text, are versed in divination. But now the surface story begins to lead to its main point, that G-d's power is supreme. For Balaam tells them he must ask G-d what to do, and during the night, G-d tells him not to curse the Israelites. In the morning, Balaam tells the messengers that G-d will not let him come.

King Balak sends new messengers who promise great reward, and Balaam again says he can only do as ordered by G-d. This time, the Divine tells him to go, stressing that he must follow G-d's commands. In the morning, Balaam leaves with them, riding on his donkey. Without explanation, the text then says that G-d is enraged at Balaam and sends an angel to block his path. We can speculate that YHVH is angry because Balaam doesn't simply reject the king's request and instead keeps asking G-d the same question, as if in hope of a different answer.

As Balaam rides with his two servants, he does not see the angel holding a sword, although his donkey sees and swerves aside. After Balaam beats the animal, the angel moves even closer. The donkey lies down rather than go forward, Balaam continues to beat her, and G-d enables the donkey to speak in protest. When G-d also uncovers Balaam's eyes so that he too sees the angel, Balaam asks if he should turn back, but the angel repeats that he must do whatever is commanded. When King Balak goes out to meet Balaam on his arrival, Balaam once again says that he can utter only the words that G-d will allow.

After offering the first sacrifice, Balaam goes off to seek omens. G-d tells him to tell Balak that the Israelites are to be blessed. So he gives blessings in a fairly long poem that horrifies the king, to whom Balaam repeats that he can only say what G-d puts in his mouth. King Balak then moves them to another site, saying that if Balaam cannot see the whole Israelite horde, but only part of it, he may provide the curses that Balak has asked for. After the sacrifice, Balaam again goes off looking for omens, only to come back with an even stronger blessing.

When Balak asks him to neither curse nor bless, Balaam reminds him that he has already said that he can only say the words G-d gives him. But Balak is still hoping that G-d may give him a different judgment, and takes Balaam to the top of Mount Peor, overlooking the wilderness. This time, Balaam is so certain of YHVH's views that he simply turns his face toward the Israelites' encampment. And the Divine spirit enters him so that he blesses Israel and curses Israel's enemies at even greater length.

A furious Balak says that he's asked three times for curses but instead has been given blessings, and that G-d has denied Balaam his reward by interfering. Balaam answers that he's said that he could only do what G-d wanted. They then part, each of them going home. As Balaam leaves, he prophesizes the triumph of the Israelites over Balak's people, the Moabites, as well as victories over many others.

The *parshah* ends with the note that the Moabite women begin to seduce the Israelite men into having sex with them and into offering sacrifices to their gods. Incensed, the Divine tells Moses to have the ringleaders publicly impaled. Just then, an Israelite man brings a Midianite woman to have sex with her in front of the whole community,[2] where the people are mourning Aaron in front of the Tent of Meeting. Phinehas, son of Eleazar, the High Priest, spears them together through the belly (or, possibly, her genitals), stopping the plague that G-d has sent down as punishment, so that only 24,000 die.

Parshah Interpretation: As we come near the end of the Book of Numbers, we are approaching the metaphoric Promised Land, the Garden Within that refers to the state that we sometimes call enlightenment. In large part then, this *parshah* elaborates on the theme being developed in the prior chapter: there is only one Divine Presence behind all existence, behind everything and everyone in the whole physical world. The *parshah* also reminds us that we will at times become distracted from that awareness, seduced by worldly concerns for self-protection and self-care onto a path of negativity. But we will be jolted back from that distraction and negativity, blocked by an inevitable awareness—call it an angel—that tells us we have strayed from a place of blessing to one of curses.

The specific story of Balaam is a comedy about spiritual resistance in a great seer and prophet who is not an Israelite believer, but a member of an enemy group. Yet he is so great a prophet that he refers to YHVH as "my G-d"[3] and he speaks directly to the Divine Presence, questioning, receiving clear answers, and serving as a channel for compassion and blessing—indeed, he is incapable of proclaiming curses. Still, even he gets distracted at times; and so he lives in Moab rather than in the Israelite encampment, and appears to hope that he can do as his king wants, perhaps for the promised rewards.

The story deliberately compares the power of this soothsayer and his king with that of the Egyptian Pharaoh and his magicians, who also fought a losing battle against G-d in regard to the Israelites' future. Thus, the chapter uses some of the same language as is found at the start of the Book of Exodus, with the Israelites described in terms of being loathsome in their insect-like swarming.

In reality, Balaam is too spiritually developed to utter curses. But he is still in conflict, like the Israelites who are now approaching the Promised Land themselves. In this metaphoric narrative, we play the parts of both Balaam and the Israelites, at times blind and resistant, even when we are well on the path of psychological and spiritual change. But whatever our momentary state of being, we are being told that our awareness of the world's holiness is now more powerful than the forces of resistance within us, so that we will be released from distraction and able to offer and receive blessings and love far more than curses and negativity.

In our symbolic narrative, we have overcome most of our egoistic resistance to surrendering to the Divine, so that we are finally at the edge of the interior Garden. Although some blindness remains, we are more often channels for love and compassion; we are also awakening to the blessings being showered upon us as we struggle toward the light. To phrase it another way, that part of us which is most aware that there is nothing but G-d is now strong enough to overcome the remaining resistance that we have to such awareness.

And, of course, by the end of the *parshah,* we already slide backward.

For Formal Practice: The intent of this meditation is to open us to the experience of being awakened and given guidance when we become distracted and caught up in negativity, so that we turn back onto our path of change and transformation.

When you are ready, put yourself in the place of Balaam's ass, with the angel standing in front of you, blocking the path. Remember that in Torah, G-d and angels are interchangeable.

Notice the angel in front of you. Let yourself become aware of times that you became distracted from your devotional path only to be turned back by chance, or accident, or what we call fate—or G-d.

Just notice what arises when you think of angels in your path. If nothing arises, note the moments when you become distracted from the contemplative exercise and then come back to awareness. For this mysterious moment of re-awakening can also be thought of as an angel turning you back from distraction.

In My Own Practice: *I see the angel in front of me. Blocking my path. Moving me out of the path I was trying to take.*

Then I see the pages of this book erupting from behind the angel. They flutter into the air, two pages at a time, like butterflies. They are also partly burnt, singed brown at the edges, for they are a sacrifice, an offering to the Divine.

Immediately, I see that they are utterly dependent on my being open to the guidance of the Divine Presence.

And more: I came to this path through a woman I met at a workshop that I went to after my husband died. I was looking for magic at the time, with no interest in Judaism.

The woman I met told me that I ought to move to Woodstock when I sold the house I had in New Jersey. She told me about the rabbi, Jonathan Kligler, who was to become my teacher even though I'd never before belonged to a congregation. Later, she even set me up to rent her sister's house near Woodstock, so I could see what living so far from a major city felt like. I'd never have come without her.

Still later, she sent me a brochure about the Chochmat Halev *Training Program, which would lead me to become a teacher of Jewish meditation, which was the backdrop for this book. Then she disappeared from my life. Like an angel, pointing the way, then gone. No longer visible.*

Perhaps, this is what Divine guidance often looks like.

Numbers/*B'midbar,* 8, "Phinehas"/*Phinehas*
(Num. 25:10–30:1)

"And YHVH spoke to Moses, saying: 'Phinehas, son of Eleazar son of Aaron, the priest, has turned back My fury from the children of Israel....' "

—Num. 25:10–11[1]

Interpretive Overview: The Israelite presence at the edge of the Promised Land can be taken as symbol of our own proximity to enlightenment as we each have progressed on our personal path. Thus, Phinehas keeps the Sanctuary from defilement without needing Moses' direction, just as we are to be able to observe ourselves and rectify our lapses without external pressure. The new census is another reference to who we have now become, while other parts of the narrative refer to the unique flavor of each person's development.

Summary of *Parshah:* This *parshah* opens by continuing the narrative of the last section. Phinehas, son of Eleazar the High Priest, has ended the defilement of the Tabernacle by killing the offenders, who are a prince of Israel and a princess of Midian.[2] His action stops the plague that has been sent as punishment, while he is awarded G-d's eternal friendship and the promise that his descendants will carry on the priestly line.[3]

In the next part of this *parshah,* G-d calls for a new census to be taken, of those over twenty years of age, to serve in the army. YHVH also declares that each tribe shall be assigned territory in the Promised Land (except for the Levites, as said earlier), according to their size, and by random lot. And then the count is given clan by clan within each tribe, with a note that none of those alive at the time of the first census, except Caleb and Joshua (and, of course, Moses) are still alive.

After this, the daughters of Zelophehad (who have not appeared in the text before this) ask to inherit their father's land since they have no brothers to carry on their father's name, and YHVH agrees, making the general ruling that land is to be allotted to daughters if there are no sons.[4]

Next, YHVH tells Moses to go up to the mountain of Abarim to see the Promised Land and die. Moses speaks to G-d for the last time in the Torah,[5] asking for a man to be appointed as his replacement to shepherd the people. G-d chooses Joshua, who is then consecrated by the priest Eleazar, son of Aaron. The old generation of ex-slaves has died out, but Moses himself does not yet die.

And now, the narrative is interrupted with detailed commands for required sacrificial offerings throughout the year. This calendar starts with the daily burnt offerings, and then moves to the burnt offerings for the Sabbath, and to the burnt offerings and sin offering at the beginning of each month and on the four festivals between spring and autumn, beginning with Passover and ending with The Festival of Booths (i.e., *Sukkot*).[6]

***Parshah* Interpretation:** The Book of Numbers opened with G-d's call for a census before beginning the march to the Promised Land. We understood the poll to mean that each of us is to be held individually accountable for our behavior as we move through life. Successive *parshot* then recounted some of the obstacles along the path of spiritual development, after which the last chapter, "Balak," reiterated the point made to Pharaoh at the beginning of the Book of Exodus: that YHVH is the source of all existence, the deep reality behind the physical world.

But at the end of "Balak," we failed once again to keep to the path of holiness, defiling ourselves by turning to other idols (to be interpreted as meaning whatever we worship, whether luxury, power, possessions, or anything else). In the literal narrative, we were then struck by G-d's plague; in the metaphoric reading of the text, we die spiritually as we turn away from G-d.

In the current chapter, something new has happened: we finally have enough self-awareness to strike down our impulses to worship false idols.

In the literal narrative, this righteous, self-aware part of us is represented by Phinehas, grandson of Aaron.

As the *parshah* unfolds, a second census is taken—that of the new generation, for the old one has died out. This census is to take account of who we have become, now that we have left behind those parts of ourselves that were enslaved by egoistic fear and self-aggrandizement. Then, with the count completed, we are told that each of us will be allotted a place in the Promised Land that is uniquely fitted to each of us: so that "with larger groups, increase the share, with smaller groups reduce the share."[7] The implication is that our spiritual development will somehow be matched to our needs.

The next section seems to imply that there are many spiritual paths. In the literal text, the daughters of Zelophehad ask for their father's inheritance so that his lineage not be lost, and G-d agrees, saying that daughters can substitute if you have no sons to carry your name. And if no daughters, then brothers, or uncles or any other relative who is close to you: there is no straitjacket into which everyone must fit.

After this, G-d tells Moses to go up on the mountain, where he will die in sight of the Promised Land without being allowed to enter it. Since Moses does not die for quite a while yet, this bit of narrative seems yet another reminder that no one reaches spiritual perfection, not even Moses.

And when the *parshah* closes with a calendar of requirements for sacrificial offerings, day by day, throughout the year, the implication is that we are to continually recommit ourselves to serving G-d, knowing that we need to consciously turn to the Divine precisely because of the inevitability of our lapses.

For Formal Practice: When you are ready, let yourself notice some of the past steps of your spiritual journey. If you can, try to notice the particular flavor of your path, or how it is somehow characteristic of you. You may want to picture a light at the center of your being, and look at the quality of that light as compared to the light that you can see in other people. Ask to see how the Divine Presence is imbedded in your awareness. If you wish, offer yourself up to the Divine: "Here I am." *Hineinei.*

In My Own Practice: *Once again, I have enormous trouble with this at first. I keep remembering a meditation teacher saying that I was someone searching for truth. I didn't know what he meant then and I still don't.*

I sit, following my breath, looking at the light in my center.

Pain. I come from pain.

But pain seems to be the common denominator for most people that I meet on the meditation path. I follow my breath and wait.

Suddenly, I feel myself at age eleven. I feel the self-loathing and despair.

I come from blackness, from a place of death. Images of the Holocaust pass before me, images I was raised with. Photographs my father took when he was one of the soldiers liberating Auschwitz. Stories my mother told of the death camps and the earlier pogroms, heard from G-d knows where.

Other images of death, starting with my newborn brother.

And then the heavy silences of anger and depression that formed the backdrop of so much of my childhood.

My path has been a search for light. For the revelation that Divine glory pours into the world in every direction, permeating all existence.

For a G-d who tells us to choose life, not death.

For a path that celebrates life and joy and laughter, despite the inevitability of pain and loss. That is the truth of my path.

Numbers/*B'midbar*, 9, "Tribes"/*Matot*
(Num. 30:2–32:42)

"And Moses spoke to the heads of the tribes of the children of Israel, saying, 'This is the thing that YHVH commanded: "A man who will make a vow...." ' "

—Num. 30:2–3

Interpretative Overview: The surface narrative begins with rules about making vows and goes on to the conquest of the Midianites and distribution of booty. It ends with Moses' agreeing to let the tribes of Reuben and Gad settle outside the Promised Land of Canaan, but only once they vow to fight alongside the other Israelites for its conquest. The chapter can be read metaphorically as a discourse on our continued need to overcome and extirpate parts of ourselves, even as our spiritual life greatly deepens. Even at the edge of the Promised Land, we have inevitable limitations as long as we are still in a physical form that has desires and needs for protection.

Summary of *Parshah:* Although it appeared that Moses was to die in the last *parshah,* the text now opens with him giving the Israelites G-d's injunctions about keeping vows. Then follow restrictions on these injunctions for a woman.[1]

After that, G-d tells Moses to have the Israelites attack the Midianites to get revenge (presumably for seducing the Israelite men into having sex and worshipping idols).[2] Led by Phinehas, they kill the five Midianite kings and the prophet Balaam, who turns out to have directed the Midianite women in their program of seduction. They also kill all the males and burn their settlements.

But Moses is furious that they have taken captive the women who enticed the Israelites into idolatry, as well as the children. So, on his own initiative, in a command horrifying to the modern reader, he orders the death of all male children and all women who are not virgins (although the text does not indicate whether this happens).

After this, instructions are given for purifying the soldiers and any contaminated possessions, giving half of the plunder to the noncombatant Israelites, and for tithing to the priests and Levites. Detailed accounts of all the plundering follows. Then the officers (but not the rank and file) tell Moses that they are freely offering to YHVH, in addition, all the gold jewelry or ornaments they have taken as spoil, because no Israelite soldier has died in the battle. Moses and Eleazar bring the gold to the Tent of Meeting.

In the last part of the *parshah,* the tribes of Reuben and Gad ask Moses for permission to settle on the east side of the Jordan, just outside the Promised Land of Canaan, because the land offers excellent pasture for their large herds of livestock. At first, Moses angrily assumes that they will not fight alongside the other tribes in the conquest of Canaan. In addition, he accuses them of behaving like the scouts who'd refused to enter the land forty years before, and says that YHVH will doom all the Israelites because of them, just as G-d had doomed the earlier generation to wander for forty years and die in the desert.

But the tribes of Reuben and Gad vow to fight in the vanguard of the army, leaving their families and livestock behind until victory is achieved. Moses now agrees, and commands Eleazar and Joshua to carry out the agreement.

When the two tribes repeat their vow, Moses apportions land on the east side of the Jordan to them and to half the tribe of Manasseh (the latter apportionment is not explained in the text). The chapter concludes with accounts of their conquest of this eastern land and their naming of the new cities they build.

Parshah **Interpretation:** The narrative reads like a history of the preparations to enter the Promised Land (although we know it to be archeologically inaccurate). But we can choose to also understand each section of the account symbolically, in terms of our continued struggle with ourselves despite our considerable spiritual progress. In these accounts, different protagonists represent different aspects of our psyche, as we have seen in other *parshot.*

The chapter begins by saying that vows must be kept, except in the case of their annulment by a woman's husband or father. Although it may be farfetched to interpret this ruling metaphorically, we can perhaps understand that a husband or father, in the patriarchal society of the time, stands for a more responsible part of us, which we should listen to before making a vow that might commit us to an unwanted course of action.

In the next section, YHVH commands an attack on the Midianites, who have tempted the Israelites into idolatry. The literal narrative is appalling to most of us, as it goes on to Moses' enraged order to kill women and children. But we can understand it as symbolizing the effort to extirpate parts of ourselves that are once again—even so late in the game—tempted to some form of idol worship.

As the spoils of combat are distributed in the next section, the text seems to imply differences in intensity of commitment to the Divine, even at this stage. Sometimes, we are like those in the army, ready to give our very lives to the service of G-d; at other times, we are more passive, like civilians who are ready to accept YHVH's bounty but are far from fervent. We also understand that we may vacillate even when we reach the highest levels of devotion. For the common soldiers keep whatever of their booty is not tithed, while the army officers freely, in thanks, turn over to G-d all the gold ornaments that they have taken as spoil. In the literal narrative, gold that once served to ornament the idolatrous Midianite is now to be melted down into sacred vessels for the Tabernacle. At the metaphoric level, we, too, can be like the officers rather than the common soldier, becoming selfless and thankfully consecrating to the Divine everything that is ours, including what might once have been used in the service of the ego.

The chapter ends its exploration of human limitation by having the tribes of Reuben and Gad ask to stay on the east side of the Jordan, just outside the Promised Land. They can help the others move forward, but they want to stay where their livestock (i.e., their beasts or their more animal selves) can be nurtured.

So we have taken our vows and committed ourselves to the service of the Divine, but even now, just outside the Promised Land, we are not fully ready to open ourselves completely to G-d. After all, we are not angels.

The next-to-last *parshah* of *B'midbar* offers a final comment on our nature as human beings who are made of both the dust of the earth and of the Divine breath. We can struggle to be pure channels for the Divine, but we remain bound in earthly form. It is understood that we are not angels, that we never will be angels. That we *cannot* be angels; neither is that expected of us.

For Formal Practice: When you are ready, picture yourself encamped on the border of the Promised Land. What would it mean to cross that border? This time, as you follow your breath going in and out, let your attention include both your breath and your bodily sensations.

Let your mind hover over the idea that we are not angels and cannot be angels. How then do we cross into the Promised Land? How do we reach the interior Garden?

In My Own Practice: *I read somewhere that an angel's legs are fused, making a kind of pedestal. Well, they don't need to separate; they have no sex organs. In Torah, angels have no personalities either. They are merely messengers, existing only long enough to carry out their missions.*

But we have personalities. In fact, people that I've met who seem furthest on this path are all very different from one another. If anything, their personalities seem to be unusually distinct. And they laugh a lot.

I used to think that I'd have to give up my very essence as I committed to serving the Divine. I was afraid of that. But it hasn't worked out that way at all.

I've given up a lot of fear and a lot of what once seemed to be needs and now seem merely preferences. And I have a lot less chatter going on in my head. Often, I go about my business in the world with only silence in my mind.

Often, I don't know what I'm going to say until I hear my words, yet I say the right things and sound like me—a nicer me, a kinder me, a more fearless and playful me, but still recognizably me.

This me is often simply present to what is happening, without judgment. In these moments, I have crossed into the Garden.

*"These are the travels of the children of Israel who went out from the land of
Egypt by their armies by the hand of Moses and Aaron."*

—Num. 33:1

Interpretive Overview: At the literal level, this final *parshah* of *B'midbar*
begins with a recitation of the path that has been taken across the
wilderness, after which G-d commands the Israelites to dispossess the
inhabitants of the Promised Land and destroy all their idols. After this,
G-d gives instructions for allotting the conquered land among the different
tribes and specifies that cities be set aside for the Levites, of which some
will provide refuge for those who have killed another. At the metaphoric
level, the text is commenting on how far we have come on a complicated
journey, and it reminds us that our minds still have many different, even
self-defeating facets that must be recognized and dealt with.

Summary of *Parshah:* In this final *parshah* of *B'midbar,* the text traces
the long journey from Egypt across the wilderness, and names forty-three
stopping places.[1] Then YHVH once again tells Moses that the Israelites
are to take possession of the Promised Land from the groups already living
there, destroy all their idols, and distribute territory by lot, with each tribe
getting an amount proportionate to its size. Further, G-d tells him that
if they do not dispossess those living there, they will find them to be like
"sticks in your eyes and thorns in your side,"[2] and that, as well, G-d will
do to the disobedient Israelites what was planned for their enemies.

After that, G-d delineates the borders of the territory to be taken.[3] Moses
repeats which tribes are staying east or west of the Jordan, and names the
tribal chieftains who will be responsible (alongside Joshua and Eleazar) for
allotting the land within each tribe.[4]

G-d also tells Moses that the Levites are to be given forty-eight cities for themselves, to be taken out of the other tribes' holdings. Six of the forty-eight are also to be cities of refuge for any Israelite or resident alien who is fleeing a blood feud after killing someone.

Rules are then given for how the assembly is to judge whether such a person has truly committed murder as opposed to unintentionally causing someone's death.[5] If a trial finds him guilty of intentional harm that has resulted in killing, the penalty is death, and he is to be turned over to those seeking vengeance. If the assembly finds him guilty only of an accidental death, he is to be returned instead to the city in which he has sought refuge. He can return to his landholding only after the High Priest dies; if he leaves before, he is subject to the vengeance of the blood feud.

Finally, there must be more than one witness to a killing in order for the assembly to assign a verdict of murder. And whether the verdict is of murder, with a death sentence, or of inadvertent manslaughter, with a sentence of exile to a city of refuge, money cannot be paid in lieu of the sentence being carried out.[6] Moreover, YHVH adds that all shedding of blood contaminates the land, and that the Israelites are forbidden to shed blood in the Promised Land, for it is G-d's dwelling place as well as theirs.

The *parshah* closes with the Israelites clarifying that the daughters of Zelophehad (and other daughters who inherit) must marry within their fathers' tribes in order to keep their landholdings from passing out of the tribe. For this would change the original apportionment among the tribes in a way that could not be fixed at the Jubilee (the fiftieth year Great Sabbath, when all holdings were supposed to go back to the line of the original owner).

B'midbar then closes with the statement that "these are the commandments and regulations that the Eternal enjoined upon the Israelites, through Moses, on the steppes of Moab, at the Jordan near Jericho."[7]

Parshah **Interpretation:** Our journey never ends. But in this final chapter of *B'midbar,* we look back to see how far we have come from the moment in which we first became aware of the desire to be freed from enslavement to our fears and cravings. In the mystical understanding of Torah, this is the moment that we began to leave Egypt.

Like the Israelites, we look back on our wanderings and on the places we stayed awhile, mainly looking back in pain but sometimes glimpsing freedom and enlightenment. In reviewing the past, we can see more clearly how every part of our experience has contributed to who we are right now.

We are hoping for complete freedom from our imperfections, so that we can fully become vessels for the Divine, able to make this earth and our own lives upon it truly holy. We are hoping for what some of us might call a final stage of enlightenment. But the text warns that we must continue to be on guard against parts of ourselves that inevitably still exist. In the literal text, we must dispossess the groups already in the Promised Land or they will poison it for us; in the metaphoric text, we must continue to root out those parts of ourselves. For we never reach perfection.

The rest of this *parshah* can be seen as offering commentary on what we are to do about our remaining shortcomings. We are reminded, first, that each of us possesses different sides of ourselves, something that we become only more aware of as we try to change in the course of our spiritual journey. The different sides are each allocated territory within us, but the placement and size of each territory varies, just as it does for the twelve tribes.[8] Sheer randomness also plays a role in who we are, just as the tribal territory is determined by lot.

The esoteric text then continues with questions about how we ought to view ourselves now that we have arrived at this moment. The literal text goes to the gravest of sins (other than ritual desecrations), exploring what should be done with one who kills another. But our question is what the text might mean if we are still talking about rooting out parts of ourselves. What does it mean to kill part of oneself?

In the literal text, one who deliberately commits murder must die in turn, for murder is an act of total violation of the will of G-d. At the symbolic level, self-murder occurs if one deliberately turns one's back on the spiritual journey, choosing instead to remain enslaved to the ego.

And what about inadvertent killing? If we think of it symbolically, we can inadvertently kill aspects of our being by way of denial, suffocation, or an accumulation of small transgressions. In the text, such an inadvertent killer is placed in the care of the Levites in a city of refuge.

Instead of condemnation for the inevitable sins that we commit along our journey, the text is asking for compassion. The more spiritually advanced aspects of ourselves, the Levites, are called on to protect and nurture far less developed parts. For we need nurturing and self-compassion if we are to let go of our remaining cravings and fears, be able to be simply present to Divine *being*-ness, and become capable of serving as a conduit for holiness.

Finally, the odd coda on the daughters' inheritance in respect to their tribe may be yet another comment on balancing our own needs with those of the larger community. It may also remind us that we owe it to ourselves to acknowledge where we have come from in our long process of growth, as well as who we have been.

For Formal Practice: When you are ready, let yourself appreciate for a moment how far you've come on your spiritual journey.

Now let yourself remember that the Promised Land is directly in front of you, accessible with the next breath. Remember that you can step into it at any moment, merely by shifting your awareness.

Now let yourself become aware of the ways in which you turn your back on Eden.

Let your attention hover over the question about ways in which you still turn away from the forces of life, clinging instead to fear and craving.

If you can, let yourself feel what it might be like to change sides and fully embrace life. Let yourself feel what the Garden means to you.

In My Own Practice: *I immediately realize that I'd like to take a walk, that I want to be outdoors, but that I choose to work instead. Work is my demon, capturing my spirit. I don't take enough care of my body either. I too often treat it like a machine that needs necessary maintenance, but I don't treasure its aliveness enough. I suddenly feel the memory of climbing up a high steel-mesh fence as a child: the pleasure of finding each toehold, of keeping my balance as I climb. With my weight against the fence, I feel the movement of air around me.*

Why do I work so much? Another part of me answers: to prove that I am good.

It is time to let go. The Garden has movement, dancing, music, friends, other people. I suddenly see the others, see the twisting path each person is taking through time and space, and each one is dancing, filled with life. There is no judgment.

And also, I remember walking in the woods yesterday, feeling the ache in my left knee and a different kind of soreness in my right ankle, sensing the air come into my nostrils and lungs as my body inhales, feeling the swing of hips and torso with each step, seeing the glory of the dark trees silhouetted against the twilight sky. This is the Garden.

I call a good friend later to arrange to meet, and feel the rush of pleasure in my body at the sound of her soft voice. This moment, too, is the Garden.

Or, sitting with a patient today in a psychotherapy session, feeling his suffering, sharing a moment of connection. This also is the Garden. It is always right here.

Interpretive Summation of Numbers/*B'midbar*

While the Book of Numbers seems like history when read literally, *B'midbar* is also the story of our spiritual lives as we free ourselves from the constrictions of the ego, or *Mitzrayim*. The text traces the parts of ourselves we need to let go of as we travel on this path, moving from fear, to craving for what we have lost, to craving to unite with the Divine, to craving for power, to ultimate acceptance that all power is YHVH's.

In this metaphoric reading, we are shown a path of progressively higher levels of purity, a path we must travel if we are to truly live with the awesome, boundless, indefinable, and fundamentally unknowable Divine force, which is known in Hebrew by the deliberately unpronounceable letters YHVH. This force is sometimes described as the Ground of All Being, the Source of All, or the Mystery, with the letters of its unpronounceable name referring to simple *being*-ness—to existence without concept or form.

If we are to open ourselves to the awareness of this YHVH, says the text, we must be free of craving and fear, able to simply *be* in each moment as it occurs. And in such a state of simply being, we naturally feel compassion and loving-kindness, loving our neighbors and ourselves. But we cannot force such awareness. The process takes time and commitment as we gradually discover our weaknesses and let go of our own particular idols—with many lapses along the way.

As we near the end of our journey, we can look back and see the experiences that have led us to this place. The journey has been difficult, and we are never going to be done. In fact, we can still fail and spiritually die through inadvertence and lack of continued attention.

On the other hand, we must have compassion and mercy for our failings even as we try to root them out, for there is neither a single path to enlightenment, nor a straight line. Each of us, in Numbers and in the world, is imbedded in the larger community, playing our roles beneath the banners of our tribe. Yet, each of us is also an individual, making our own choices and following our own unique path, however convoluted it may seem.

5

General Framework of Deuteronomy/ *D'varim*

Numbers described our long journey through the wilderness, not only in terms of the historical vision of the Israelites, but also in terms of the way each of us seeks to draw closer to the mystery of the Divine Presence, overcoming the psychological obstacles in our path.

Now, in Deuteronomy, the narrative shifts. Instead of being *about* the people of Israel—or about each of us—it is being spoken directly *to* the people of Israel, and, likewise, to each of us G-d wrestlers today. The style is rhetorical and persuasive, and the Hebrew title *D'varim* means "Words," from the opening sentence, "These are the words Moses spoke...."

At the simple level, we are at the end of the journey begun forty years before, when Moses led his band of slaves out of Egypt. Although the people of Israel are encamped on the border of the Promised Land, Moses is about to die without crossing over it. Having named Joshua as his successor, Moses' last act of leadership is to speak to his people to prepare them for a future he will not share. The Book of Deuteronomy—and with it, the whole Pentateuch—will end with his death.

Most of Deuteronomy consists of Moses' long speech to the children of the slaves who died in the course of the forty years. He begins by saying that their trek need only have taken eleven days—a shock to the reader and possibly to the people themselves—if only they had been ready. Then he recounts the history of their travels, and their failures; repeats some old laws along with new; and outlines the blessings they will receive if they choose to follow G-d, along with the curses that will follow upon rejection of the Divine. Mainly, he warns them that their commitment to the Divine will have to be made and remade continually if they are to possess the Promised Land and remain in it. Indeed, he even says they will lose their possession because of their failures, but that they will regain it when they return to G-d.

At the literal level, Moses is telling his people how they must behave if they are to keep YHVH's favor and hold onto the land of Canaan after their conquest of it.[1] But the phrasing of his rhetoric deliberately confuses past and present. As he stands at the borders of the Promised Land, the whole generation of slaves has died; yet Moses speaks as if everyone is able to remember with him all that happened in Egypt and afterward. Moreover, he talks as if all future generations were also present, listening to him in a timeless, eternal moment.

And so, he is speaking to us today, giving us guidelines for building a society that would manifest G-d's love for all of us. Ultimately, Moses clarifies what is implicit elsewhere in Torah, as he explains the meaning and relevance to our lives of the commandments and laws that have, until now, been presented largely without comment.

In his speech, he creates a new context for our understanding. At the ethical level, the Book of Deuteronomy stresses compassionate action to all—and particularly toward those who are powerless. For we were slaves in Egypt, says Moses, and we recognize what it means to be without power.

Our choices are not abstract or theoretical. The decisions around choosing G-d—around being with G-d—come in the nitty-gritty acts of daily life. Moses insists that almost every action we take involves a choice between the Divine Presence and false idols. While the surface narrative speaks of worshiping other gods, the metaphoric narrative refers to the idols of wealth, achievement, power, beauty, approval, and so on.

But these idols can never truly satisfy or protect us, and then we reap the consequences of our choices, for good or ill, in what naturally follows. Although Moses speaks of our bringing down G-d's blessing or curse, we can interpret blessing and curse in terms of the inevitable unwinding of cause and effect in our own lives and over the eons of history.

Furthermore, Torah commentators have for millennia understood that the Promised Land is not merely a physical place. Neither can it be reduced to a blueprint for a world that humans have yet to create; for it is also a metaphor for the internal state of connection with the Divine, and for the feeling of protection that comes with such connection, despite the vicissitudes of life. While the surface text speaks of blessing or curse in terms of life or death, the deeper meaning refers to inner freedom regardless of life circumstance. The Promised Land is a metaphor for that place of inner freedom, just as Egypt is understood to be a metaphor for the state of enslavement to our needs for self-protection and self-aggrandizement.

Deuteronomy is written with deliberate timelessness, its language formed with the intent of having Moses speak directly to each of us. From the distant past, he presents a choice for today: we can have the Promised Land at any moment, the blessing of closeness to YHVH and paradise on earth; or we can turn away from the commandments to worship idols, live in the cursed state of disconnection from the Divine life force, and face inevitable chaos and disaster.

Deuteronomy/*D'varim* Week by Week

Deuteronomy/*D'varim*, 1, "Words"/*D'varim*
(Deut. 1:1–3:22)

"These are the words that Moses spoke to all of Israel across the Jordan in the wilderness … eleven days from Horeb…. And it was in the fortieth year, in the eleventh month, on the first of the month…."

—Deut. 1:1–3

Interpretive Overview: In this first part of Moses' final speech to the Israelites, he reveals that the entire trek across the wilderness could have been done in eleven days. But it took forty years because the people were not ready. At the metaphoric level, we are being told that we, too, can reach the internal Promised Land, the interior Garden, by a slow route or a faster one, depending on our courage and our commitment to the practices of the devotional path.

Summary of *Parshah*: In the opening of this *parshah*, forty years after the beginning of the journey through the wilderness, the text states that the entire crossing could have been completed in only eleven days. After that bald statement, upon which no comment is made, Moses begins his long farewell speech to the children of Israel by recounting some of their history during the forty years. As the people wait at the border of Canaan, he talks to them as if they had actually lived through all that happened.

He begins by recounting G-d's telling them to leave Mount Sinai (here and elsewhere called Mount Horeb) for the Promised Land, after which Moses appointed judges other than he to hear their disputes, so as not to be overwhelmed by all their cases.[1] Then he describes the scouts spying out the Promised Land and coming back with tales of fearful giants, so that the already frightened people became even more afraid despite his reminders to them of G-d's protection. It was then, Moses says, that YHVH decreed they would wander for forty years, because they would not trust in the Divine.

Moses also says something not found anywhere else in the Torah: that G-d was angry with him because of the people's failings (rather than because of his own behavior),[2] and has denied him entry to the Promised Land because of them.

After this, he recounts the rest of their travels, with some of the details not being the same as in the narrative in the Book of Numbers.

***Parshah* Interpretation:** Deuteronomy opens as Moses begins to talk to the people of Israel, who are standing at the entrance to the Promised Land "in the fortieth year, in the eleventh month, on the first of the month."[3] In a shocking statement offered without further commentary, he says that they are only "eleven days" from the starting point.[4] So the whole frame of Deuteronomy is that they have wandered in circles through the desert for forty years, when, in fact, the Promised Land was only eleven days away.

The news is like an arrow through the heart: they (and by implication, we) could have been here long ago, if only they had truly listened to YHVH.

Deuteronomy is written in the form of a speech by Moses that is addressed not only to the Israelites at the time, but to each of us today. Coming after the first four books of the Torah, this opening chapter of Deuteronomy goes directly to the point. If we read the term "Promised Land" as a metaphor, we see it as the state of being open to G-d's presence, letting go of our self-protective shields to be simply present to the I Am That I Am of the Divine. Again and again, the Torah teaches that YHVH is ever present, always available; all we need do to reach the Divine is let go of the false idols of the greedy, fearful ego and of the stories that we tell ourselves. We live in the preconceptions and habits of our self-protectiveness, in the past of "what was" and in the future of "what might happen," hiding from

G-d behind barriers of regret, worry, and planning. But we are rarely in the present, in the now of "what is happening in this moment," without interpretation. When we are in this state, in the brief moments of pure being, we are aware of the Divine permeating all.

For Formal Practice: The intent of this meditation is to allow us to deeply recognize that the Promised Land is right in front of us all the time.

When you are ready, let yourself stand before Moses as he speaks.

Feel the desert light pouring down on you. Feel the heat of the air as you inhale. Feel the sandy rock beneath your feet.

Look up and see the cloud in front of you. The Divine is present.

Let the thought hover that it is only your resistance that keeps you from awareness of the Divine Presence, which is with you now as you sit in meditation.

Ask for help in letting go of your resistance.

Let your heart soften to the Divine Presence as you sit.

As you try to open your heart, notice the sensations that arise in your body.

Let yourself sit in the silence.

If you become distracted, return to the intention to soften your heart and let go of resistance. Let yourself yearn for the Divine Presence.

In My Own Practice: *At first, I sit in silence. My mind is quiet as I sit with the breath. There is only sensation and peacefulness. Nothing special, nothing overwhelming, simply being present to this moment, accepting it as it is. Then* *a feeling of peace and light as my body seems to become transparent and far away, unimportant.*

But then an image appears of an animal being tortured. My heart constricts, and I try to shut it out, then stop. As I look, I do not see the Divine. G-d is not here. Not in acts of cruelty. Those are ours alone, done with free choice.

My mind goes to a conversation with a dear friend earlier today. My heart expanded while we spoke. It expands again at the memory of being with her. G-d was present then. G-d is present as I remember.

The Divine is present whenever the heart expands. In those moments, we are one with the Divine Presence. In moments of reaching out, of love, of compassion. This statement is neither metaphor nor sloppy thinking; it is simply a statement of fact.

The Divine is always present, although we are often shut away from that Presence. But when our hearts are open, we are in the Promised Land.

Deuteronomy/*D'varim*, 2, "And I Implored"/*Va-et'chanan* (Deut. 3:23–7:11)

"And I implored YHVH at that time, saying, 'My Lord, YHVH, You've begun to show Your servant Your greatness and Your strong hand....'"

—Deut. 3:23

Interpretive Overview: In this long *parshah,* Moses continues to talk as if his audience had been with him at Mount Sinai. In what will be the refrain of Deuteronomy, he tells them that the Promised Land is theirs if they serve G-d by following the Divine commands that he will soon reiterate; but he warns that they will be destroyed if they turn instead to false idols. At the metaphoric level, Moses is speaking to each of us G-d wrestlers today. If we do not serve YHVH by our ethical actions, we will be exiled from the metaphoric Promised Land.

Summary of *Parshah:* Moses begins by referring to G-d's refusal to let him enter the Promised Land despite his pleas. He then tells the people to follow their covenant with the Divine as it is epitomized in the Ten Commandments "so that you'll live,"[1] and possess the Promised Land, and thus demonstrate YHVH's greatness through the wisdom and understanding of their laws.

Speaking as if the people in front of him had been at Mount Sinai, he stresses that it was a G-d without form who spoke to them that day, giving them laws from the midst of fire; and that they must guard themselves against accepting idols instead of this nameless G-d. Yet he also says that they will come to worship idols, so that they will perish from the land to be scattered among other nations—but that they will once again be protected if they return to YHVH with all their heart and soul.

In the next section, Moses talks at length about G-d's power and greatness, beginning with the story of creation and going up to the miraculous freeing of the Israelites from the great nation of Egypt. The Israelites have been chosen to experience this miracle, he says, so that they comprehend that there is only one G-d, whose laws and commandments they must follow if they are to prosper. After this comes an insertion in which Moses sets aside three cities of refuge for those who kill another inadvertently.

Then he becomes even more emphatic about the covenant having been made with the living to whom Moses is now speaking, as he says, "YHVH did not make this covenant with our fathers but with us! We! These! Here! Today! All of us! Living!"[2] After this, he repeats the Ten Commandments (with some slight variations from the original presentation).[3]

Finally, he recites the first paragraph of what has become the central prayer of Judaism (called the *Shema,* the word for "Listen"), which is the call to the Israelites to obey the commandments given by YHVH:

> Listen, Israel YHVH is our G-d, YHVH is one. And you shall love YHVH, your G-d, with all your heart and with all your soul and with all your might. And these words that I command you today shall be on your heart. And you shall impart them to your children, and you shall speak about them when you sit in your house, and when you go in the road, and when you lie down, and when you get up. And you shall bind them for a sign on your hand, and they shall become bands between your eyes. And you shall write them on the doorposts of your house and in your gates.[4]

The *parshah* closes with Moses saying that G-d will help them take possession of the Promised Land, whose inhabitants they must destroy[5] along with all their idols, and that they must stay on guard never to worship any false gods. For G-d has freed them to serve only the Divine.

Parshah Interpretation: The metaphoric essence of this *parshah* seems quite straightforward as soon as we realize that Moses' speech is intended not merely for the Israelites standing in front of him, but for each of us on our own spiritual journey. We are to remember that YHVH is always here, speaking to each of us today as if we had been at Mount Sinai, reminding us to obey the Divine commands for loving-kindness and justice; reminding us that we have been freed from the constrictions of the self-serving ego in order to love and serve G-d with all our heart and all our soul and all our might; and reminding us that we must be on guard against ourselves, for we will inevitably forget, turn away, and suffer the loss and emptiness that follows. Yet we can always return.

Moses says that we have seen the fire coming out of the mountain, and heard the words, and seen that G-d has no form. And so we must never confuse G-d with anything we can name—not with any kind of form whatsoever. And if we forget, we will be destroyed, he says, "Because YHVH, your G-d: He is a consuming fire, a jealous G-d."[6]

Going to the metaphoric level, we understand that we can worship the unbounded, unnamable YHVH, the Mystery beyond all our knowing, or instead choose an idol that can be measured and named and known, whether that be power, money, looks, achievement, or something else. G-d is called "jealous" because, in fact, we can't choose both.

For Formal Practice: When you are ready, see yourself standing at the foot of Mount Sinai, listening to Moses as he speaks directly to you.

Feel the sun pouring down its heat. Feel the light burning your eyes as you stand on the sandy rock. Look up and see the cloud in front of you.

As Moses speaks, ask yourself what it means to you to follow false idols instead of loving the Divine.

What are your idols? See if you can meditate on your experience of following your idols.

In My Own Practice: *As I begin to sit, I remember a moment this morning in which someone I was sitting with in my meditation group opened her heart in pain. My first reaction was withdrawal, putting up a wall against her feelings.*

And yesterday, when I went to another meditation group, I thought of kissing the leader and his wife hello as I often do, as most of us do, but somehow I held back, feeling cool.

This is my idol: coolness. A slight distance that keeps me safe. If I do not reach out, no one can find me. I am invisible and safe. I can control who enters.

But my heart is closed when I am cool like this, and the Divine Presence disappears.

I cannot enter the Promised Land when I am cool, because then I am not loving. I do not embody G-d's compassion and loving-kindness. Instead, I am estranged.

"And it will be because you'll listen to these judgments and observe and do them that YHVH....."

—Deut. 7:12

Interpretive Overview: Using the singular form of the word *you* in this *parshah,* Moses emphasizes that each of us will be protected by the Divine when we observe the commandments, for the Divine has the power to give us all our needed sustenance and safety. But each of us forgets that everything that we have comes ultimately from the Divine, even our very abilities to take action in the world. At the metaphoric level, protection refers to the psychological experience of feeling G-d's bounty, and destruction to exiling ourselves from that awareness.

Summary of *Parshah:* Moses begins by saying that "you" need have no fear about entering the Promised Land because G-d will honor the covenant, offering abundance, prosperity, and protection from all enemies, just as "you" were protected from the power of Egypt as long as "you" followed the commandments of YHVH.

Then he reiterates the command to destroy all foreign idols when taking possession of the Promised Land, to have no other gods or idols.

Next, Moses says that the years in the wilderness have been a test to see whether the people would follow the commandments when confronted with their total dependence on the Divine for survival.[1] For our dependence was to show us that "a human doesn't live by bread alone, but [that] a human lives by every product of YHVH's mouth."[2]

Then Moses repeats that the Divine is offering possession of the Promised Land only on condition of observing the commandments. And that we each will forget that all comes from G-d, even our very power to build up wealth. "And you'll say in your heart, '*My* power and *my* hand's strength made this wealth for me....'³ "And it will be, if you'll *forget* YHVH ... and go after other gods and serve them and bow to them ... you'll *perish*.' "⁴

Moses goes on to say that G-d will give the Israelites victory over the inhabitants of the Promised Land not because of their virtue (because they constantly rebel), but because other peoples behave even more badly than they do. Moses then recounts at great length much of the rebellious history of the Israelites from the time they left Egypt. He focuses most on the episode of the golden calf, when the people made an idol even while Moses was on Mount Sinai receiving the Ten Commandments, with Moses then protecting them from G-d's enraged wish to destroy them.

The *parshah* closes with Moses saying that we can now possess the Promised Land if only we commit to love and serve the Divine, and follow the commandments; and the only specific commands given in this section are about accepting no bribes and taking care of the widow, orphan, and stranger. The final sentences of this chapter include the second paragraph of the central prayer of Judaism, the *Shema*,⁵ telling us each to love G-d with all our heart and soul and might, so that we will prosper in the Promised Land.

Parshah Interpretation: In this *parshah*, the focus is on the idea that Divine power pours forth ceaselessly, creating in each moment air to breathe, the possibility of food and water, and the existence of the physical world and life itself.

But we tend not to notice G-d's bounty when things go well, attributing our successes purely to our own efforts. Most often, we only open our hearts to the Divine in times of trouble, as we trek through the desolate places of our lives and are forcibly confronted with our fundamental helplessness.

We are being asked to stop seeing ourselves as the controlling force in the world in both bad times and in good, instead acknowledging our dependence on YHVH's gifts in each moment, and turning to G-d in love, ready to serve through acts of loving-kindness.

At the societal level, the world we would thus create would be a kind of paradise. And if we don't, the text says that "YHVH's anger will flare at you, and the Divine will hold back the skies and there won't be showers, and the earth won't give its crop, and you'll perish quickly from the good land that YHVH is giving you."[6] In an era of global climate change, weapons of mass destruction, and multiple acts of hatred, it is impossible not to read this as simple truth.

At the individual level, the metaphoric reading also proposes that we can feel YHVH's protection and bounty internally, no matter what might be threatening us in the physical world. We can feel safe if we renounce our self-centered striving and egotistical belief in our own capacity to have things come out the way we want; if, instead, we become vessels for expressing Divine compassion in the world. For the Promised Land is not a geographic place, but the experience of being present to the Divine force that is the living source of all existence—the bedrock of reality and the fount of compassion.

For Formal Practice: When you are ready, let yourself contemplate how little control you actually have over what befalls you. Whether you go to moments of helplessness or moments of apparent control, open yourself to the awareness that all comes from G-d.

In My Own Practice: *The first memory that appears today is of the time I lost control of my car while going around a curve on a mountain road. There was a truck coming toward me, and my car spun around as I tried to brake; my young son was now trapped on the side of the car that was going to hit the truck. I wanted to change places with him, but there was nothing I could do. And, somehow, both car and truck stopped, only inches short of the impact.*

There are so many of those near misses.

So many factors led up to the moment of crisis. That led me to be driving on that road at that moment, that led the truck there also. That kept us from being a foot closer when I spun out, so that we were both able to stop before crashing. None of it was mine to control.

Each moment of life is a gift, imbedded in the tapestry of all that's gone before. Everything is interconnected across time and space.

Then memory shifts to a sudden thought about my writing this book. It has taken a long time. But I am not invested in outcome. I will do what I can to sell it, and I'd certainly like it to be read. But my inner eye sees the whole process imbedded in so many strands of determinism and choice—which involve so many other people and situations—that my own role feels profoundly limited. And my acceptance of that limitation frees me to simply be present to what comes next, to each step of the process as it arises.

That is what my late husband did in the last weeks of his life. He had fully accepted his inability to determine whether he lived or died. He continued with his medical treatment, doing what he could, but he no longer felt responsible for the outcome. He wanted to live, but the decision wasn't up to him. In those final weeks, he was kind and funny and at peace. On the last day of his life, I heard him laughing as I walked toward his room in the hospital. He was listening to a recording of a favorite comedian.

Deuteronomy/*D'varim*, 4, "See"/*R'eih*
(Deut. 11:26–16:17)

"See, this day I set before you blessing and curse...."

—Deut. 11:26[1]

Interpretive Overview: The *parshah* begins with Moses setting before us the choice of blessing or curse, depending on whether or not we follow the commandments. He then mandates a number of ritual and ethical practices, most of which have to do with celebrating and sharing G-d's bounty. At the metaphoric level, blessing and curse again refer to our inner experience, while our continued spiritual practice turns us from enslavement and idolatry to the awareness of YHVH's unbounded love in each moment, pouring down abundance upon us that we are to commemorate and emulate.

Summary of *Parshah*: The *parshah* begins with a famous phrase: "See, this day I set before you blessing and curse...."[2] The use of the phrase "this day" once again emphasizes the timelessness of the text, referring equally to the past and to those of us reading it now.

Most of the remaining section then lists commandments. The first of these involves destroying all the idols and sites of idol worship in the Promised Land. Then comes a brand new command restricting ceremonial sacrifices to only one Tabernacle in all the Promised Land—which will become known as the Temple of Solomon in later times—to be located at "the place" (in Hebrew, *hamakom*)[3] that G-d will choose.

There is also a new statement that animals may be slaughtered secularly, so that those who live far from that single Tabernacle can have meat.[4] Then Moses reiterates the command to make offerings only at the one Tabernacle, which is to be sited at "the place" that YHVH chooses.[5]

After this, Moses once more tells the Israelites not to follow after the gods of those about to be displaced in the Promised Land, for these nations, he says, commit abhorrent acts, even burning their sons and daughters as sacrifices. This is followed by a warning that the Israelites must put to death any false prophet or diviner, for such a person is a test of their commitment to YHVH. He similarly demands death for anyone else who might lead us astray, no matter how close a relative or friend, and he commands that any Israelite town that turns to false gods be destroyed—set afire and never rebuilt—and its inhabitants killed.

Then come a variety of other rules, starting with a repetition of the ritual rules for what might and might not be eaten. After this, we are told to tithe all our produce, turning it over to G-d in "the place"[6] the Divine chooses, and eating there in celebration. Then we see a number of strict ethical rules about providing for the indigent according to need and about tithing for the poor, the alien, and the Levite (who has no portion of his own). In addition, we are to remit all loans every seventh year,[7] and free any Israelite slave (unless he or she refuses to go), providing for them adequately as they leave, out of remembrance of our own slavery in Egypt. Then comes a note on consecrating every unblemished firstborn from the flock and herd for sacrifice to G-d.

The *parshah* ends with commandments for going to the central Tabernacle on three pilgrimage festivals throughout the year, to appear before the Divine at "the place"[8] the Divine chooses. The first of these festivals commemorates Passover and the exodus from Egypt; the second, seven weeks later, is for celebrating the first harvest with the Festival of Weeks; and the third, for the fall harvest with the Festival of Booths. In the last two pilgrimages, we are to come with our whole household and with "the alien and the orphan and widow who are among you."[9]

Parshah Interpretation: A central motif of Deuteronomy begins to appear in this *parshah* as Moses presents us with the choice of blessing or curse. "See,"[10] he says, you will be blessed if you fulfill the commandments of the

Divine Presence and cursed if you abandon them. But this *parshah* does not indicate what either blessing or curse looks like. Instead, the focus is on a small set of commandments.

In essence, we must destroy all idol worship; accept only one Tabernacle as a place to offer sacrifices; never be seduced by others toward idols, and away from G-d; ingest only that which is considered pure; tithe a portion of the bounty of our harvest to G-d for sacrifice and celebration; remit debt and free slaves every seventh year; and come three times a year to the central Tabernacle, both to remember that we have been freed by G-d from servitude and to rejoice in G-d's bounty with our families and those in need.

By now, we understand that idol worship refers to anything we substitute for the Divine Presence, whether this means putting our faith in the power of money, possessions, or even food, or believing that we will protect ourselves through fame, accomplishments, authority over others, or other idols. We understand that we can be easily seduced into idol worship by those we live with, by political leaders, by commercials, and by the expectations of the society within which each of us is embedded.

And we can understand many of the commands of this *parshah* as offering strategies to untangle us from the seductiveness of idol worship. We are asked to share our wealth with those who are more needy; to let go of our accumulated possessions in the seventh-year Sabbath; and to go to the Tabernacle, "the place" where G-d appears, for spring and fall festivals that commemorate G-d's bounty and our escape from slavery. All of these actions bring us out of our normal state of enslavement to self-concerns, into a state much closer to purely being in the moment with an open heart, which is "the place" (in Hebrew, *hamakom*) where the Divine dwells. For this *parshah* emphases this phrase, and in traditional Torah understanding, *hamakom* is not a physical space, but is rather the place within each of us where we can find the Divine as soon as we expand our consciousness and open our heart.[11]

In such a state of deep awareness, as we enter the Garden Within, we automatically act as channels for the Divine to manifest in the world. Aware of G-d's bounty pouring down on us, we celebrate. Aware that we rest in G-d, we share whatever we have and turn to others with compassion and loving-kindness.

To say it in slightly different language, we know, when we are in this state, that we are manifestations of the Divine, coming from G-d and returning in the end to G-d. Power, possession, and achievements are not G-d, are not even valuable in themselves. Instead, we can simply *be*, experiencing and savoring each moment as it comes.

For Formal Practice: See if you can be aware of G-d's presence everywhere you turn, pouring forth bounty in each moment. When you are ready, follow your breath for a few minutes as it goes in and out. Let yourself relax into the breath.

Then, open yourself to the goodness of your experience, beginning with your moment-to-moment awareness of your breath, your body, your sitting in this room meditating—of the goodness of having a place to come to. Notice as other thoughts arise about something that may be flawed, not good, or somehow needing to be fixed or improved. The thought may be some idea you have of how you ought to be meditating differently. It may be about something that happened recently or in the more distant past. It may be about a relationship with which you are struggling or a conflict you are engaged in.

Notice, as these thoughts arise, how your body feels. Notice where it contracts, where it tightens.

Notice how these critical thoughts take you away from the sense of YHVH's presence being with you.

Be open to seeing your experience in a different light. Ask to see YHVH's presence and notice what arises. If you become distracted or lost in thought, return to the breath and the goodness of this moment.

In My Own Practice: *My meditation goes to the walk I took this morning with my very elderly dog. She is deaf and almost completely blind. Periodically, her front legs give way, and she stumbles onto her belly. I find myself, again and again, focusing on her dying, on her fragility, on her weakness, on the pain of seeing her stumble.*

And then I realize that the day was beautiful, the sun was shining, and I was having the joy of taking my aged dog, who has been my beloved companion for more than sixteen years, out into the sunshine on yet another walk. Her tail was wagging and she was happy; and I am grateful, and I feel YHVH's grace was pouring down on us as it always is doing.

The bounty is always there, waiting for me to notice. It is I who turn to the negative, to the place of constriction.

Deuteronomy/*D'varim*, 5, "Judges"/*Shof'tim*
(Deut. 16:18–21:9)

"You shall put judges and officers in all your gates...."

—Deut. 16:18

Interpretive Overview: As part of the ongoing command that we serve YHVH, Moses provides instructions for attaining justice in those situations in which the covenant has been, or might be, broken. Instead of emphasizing expansive loving-kindness, this *parshah* recognizes the need to set up rules and boundaries in a world of inevitably imperfect humans. It can also be interpreted at the level of the individual, in terms of the internal process of self-assessment and self-judgment that we go through as we struggle forward on our spiritual journey.

Summary of *Parshah:* The focus of this *parshah* is on the pursuit of justice as being central to the covenant, as summarized by the well-known line: "Justice, justice you shall pursue, so that you'll *live*, and you'll take possession of the land that YHVH, your G-d, is giving you."[1]

Moses begins with the instruction to create judges and officers of the law in every settlement; prohibits acceptance of bribes or any preferential treatment in deciding cases; and again forbids idolatry or the sacrifice of any animal that is blemished.[2] He calls for at least two witnesses before a judge can convict an idolater, with the witnesses taking personal responsibility for a death verdict by casting the first stones, after which the whole community then follows. At this point, a phrase is used that first appeared in the previous *parshah* and that reappears in essentially the same form throughout this one: "So you shall burn away what is bad from among you."[3]

The insistence on justice continues with the command for a higher court[4] to interpret the law in difficult cases, with the statement that the court's decision must be obeyed under penalty of death "so you shall burn away what is bad from Israel."[5]

Later in the *parshah,* we read that at least two witnesses are needed before an accused can be found guilty of any crime, not just idolatry. And a lying witness must receive the punishment that would have been meted out to the one who was falsely accused "so you shall burn away what is bad from among you."[6] Also, three cities of refuge must be created for those who kill another unintentionally, but deliberate murderers must die, in accordance with the comment "and you shall burn away the innocent blood from Israel, and it will be well with you."[7]

On a national scale, the people can choose to create a king—as other nations have—but the king must himself copy from the Levite priests the instructions Moses has given, and he must "read them all the days of his life ... so that his heart will not be elevated above his brothers, and so he will not turn from the commandments, right or left...."[8]

Finally, Moses gives some rules having to do with warfare. In phrases that have received centuries of commentary, he says that men are exempted from the army if they have built a new house but not lived in it, planted a vineyard but not harvested it, are betrothed but not yet married, or are simply fearful. Also, a city that offers to surrender must be taken peacefully (although its inhabitants will be subject to forced labor), but a city that resists can be pillaged. And a city of idolaters must be destroyed. The *parshah* closes with what seem to be a few odds and ends.

Parshah **Interpretation:** Once again, we must remember that the Promised Land is not synonymous with a geographic location. At a deeper level, the Promised Land stands for the paradise we could create on earth if we were to follow the commandments for behaving toward others with compassion, each of us becoming at long last our brother's keeper. For the central commandment is to love your neighbor as yourself, and it is followed by the command to love the stranger as yourself.

We never reach this paradise because we never meet these ideals; thus Deuteronomy ends with us overlooking the Promised Land but not yet living in it. The Torah provides these commandments for us to work toward, to give us direction for our behavior, but it recognizes that they cannot be the only guidelines for human society. Instead, the commandments to love one another sit on one side of the balance bar, while limit-setting rests on the other.[9] Both are essential to the individual and to the larger society, because the reality is that unlimited love and compassion belong only to the realm of the Divine, the infinite, inexhaustible Source of All. In contrast, we are constrained by our physical bodies and physical needs. We must set boundaries because our resources—material, psychological, and spiritual—are finite.

Furthermore, we seldom offer love with anywhere near our full capacity. Much of the time, we don't even have the best of intentions. For we will misuse authority; get into conflicts on an individual and societal level; even steal, cheat, and lie. And so we need instructions for how to manage our inevitable failings. We need ways to resolve disputes, and we need to use punishment, at least some of the time, to discourage bad behavior.

So this *parshah* addresses issues of equity, fairness, and justice because both our resources and our commitment to loving-kindness are limited. It calls for impartial judges who know the law, a higher court for difficult cases, two or more witnesses to find someone guilty of a crime, punishment for perjury, refuge for those who kill unintentionally, etc. These directives are imbedded in the larger context of renouncing false idols and committing ourselves to the service of the Divine Presence that demands that we behave with compassion—and they are necessary because of our inevitable limitations.

At yet another level of interpretation, the instructions in this chapter have often been interpreted as referring to an internal process of self-assessment and judgment. Thus, we set up internal judges who are fair and impartial, and who know what should replace both perfectionism and negligence.

We call on different aspects of ourselves to speak truth and stand for different sides of the case, so that we judge ourselves neither too easily nor too harshly. We distinguish between unintentional acts and deliberate ones, regardless of outcome. And we do our self-assessment in the context of trying to commit ourselves to the service of the Divine Presence, manifesting loving-kindness in the world as best we can, approaching the metaphoric Promised Land.

In Jewish practice, this *parshah* is read as we approach the New Year of *Rosh Hashanah*, for which we are supposed to prepare by just such a process of careful self-evaluation. For only by such careful examination can we actually make the changes that G-d requires.

For Formal Practice: Our starting place for this week's meditation is the phrase at the start of the *parshah*: "Justice, justice you shall pursue, so that you'll *live*, and you'll take possession of the land that YHVH, your G-d, is giving you."[10]

When you are ready, let yourself follow your breath for a few minutes. Let your mind begin to empty. If you become distracted, just return to your breath.

As you continue to sit, let your mind hover around these questions: "Have I been just? Where have I been unjust? What does justice even look like?"

See what surfaces as you think about your relationships in the last year, with those closest to you, with those less intimate, with strangers.

Don't let yourself think about it. Instead, let the questions simply hover in awareness without judgment.

Just breathe in and out, and see what arises. If you get distracted, return to the hovering questions as you breathe.

In My Own Practice: *As soon as I ask the question about what is meant by justice, the answer pours into me in a burst of swirling, deep blue waves so filled with compassion that I begin to cry.*

The Divine is only love. Justice is for humans; it is on the human scale.

Humans need justice because we cannot hold love in our hearts well enough. Justice is second best, an attempt at equity and fairness, when society should simply share all resources equally. I realize that this is why the justice of this parshah has so much compassion mixed into it. Because compassion is always the goal.

I breathe in and out, still crying, my body shaken by the feeling of being completely loved. Then my mind returns to self-judgment, to self-assessment.

It skitters back to the animal experiments I did for my PhD dissertation. I'd cut out a part of the brain of my rats to see how their behavior changed. Back then, it was the only way to find out how different parts of the brain worked. I loved playing with the questions, with the emerging data, but I hated the experiments once I was face to face with them. I felt like a torturer, like the commandant of a concentration camp.

The rage of one of the rats comes back, his body splayed against the door of his cage as he leaps to get at me, teeth bared, desperate to attack. A totally ruined animal, for this breed of lab rat was incredibly gentle if the brain was intact. I had lived with one as a beloved companion at home.

I am crying again, seeing this rat. Destroyed by me.

I suddenly realize that I feel like the rat, that somehow I see the scene from behind his eyes as well as from behind mine.

I have wanted to destroy someone who was tormenting me. I have felt rage as intense as that.

In this moment, I see that, somehow, we are all the same—different physical forms but one being. Logic tells me that I don't really know this animal, but I am seeing him from his side of the cage. He no longer feels alien.

I see how trapped I was then. I couldn't see my way to freedom any more than he could. I didn't even know that I had a choice.

I go back to the breath, calmer. Somehow, the rat is now inside me, enfolded by me, gentled back to calm. Perhaps, I can finally forgive myself.

Deuteronomy/*D'varim*, 6, "When You'll Go Out"/*Ki Teitzei* (Deut. 21:10–25:19)

"When you'll go out to war against your enemies…."

—Deut. 21:10

Interpretive Overview: Much as in the prior chapter, the commandments of this *parshah* center on developing discernment and creating boundaries, even though the assorted ritual and ethical commandments have no obvious unifying theme at the literal level. At the metaphoric level, the text can be understood as reiterating that our spiritual journey requires us to separate ourselves from our unacceptable cravings so that they do not dominate us, even though we can never fully obliterate these parts of ourselves. The section ends with a warning about the dangers of doubt.

Summary of *Parshah*: Most of the commands (in Hebrew, *mitzvoth*) in this chapter are new, although they may expand upon a general principle found elsewhere in the Torah. The first command has to do with the treatment of women captured in war and then taken as wives (specifically not as slaves), and particularly about granting them a respectful waiting time before having sex with them.[1] It ends with the phrase "Since you had your will of her, you must not enslave her."[2]

The second has to do with granting your firstborn his rightful inheritance even if you love him less than another son, saying that "the birthright is his due."[3]

The third is about having a wayward son stoned to death for defying his parents, if the elders of the community find him guilty (a penalty that we have no record of being carried out, and that the rabbis forbade in practice). It ends with the words "Thus, you will sweep out evil from your midst: All Israel will hear and be afraid."[4]

The fourth is about taking down a body that has been impaled for one day after an execution for a capital crime, "for an impaled body is an affront to G-d: you shall not defile the land that the Eternal your G-d, is giving you to possess."[5]

After this come a variety of commandments that seem to fall under the rubric of loving-kindness. One of the more well-known tells us to return a lost sheep or ox or ass or garment, "or any lost thing of your brother's … that you find. You shall not be able to ignore it."[6]

The remainder of the *parshah* has a mixture of commands. A few seem to involve keeping category boundaries intact and thus are ritual in nature. These include commands forbidding cross-dressing as well as mixing different seeds in a vineyard, or linen and wool in a garment, or an ox and an ass at plow. Several others involve judgments about sexual issues in regard to divorce or punishments for adultery and rape. Here are some other examples from the *parshah*:

"You shall not turn over to the master a slave who seeks refuge with you from that master."[7]

"You shall not abuse a needy and destitute laborer, whether a fellow Israelite or a stranger in one of the communities of your land."[8]

"You shall not subvert the rights of the stranger or the fatherless; you shall not take a widow's garment in pawn. Remember that you were a slave in Egypt and that the Eternal your G-d redeemed you from there; therefore I do enjoin you to observe this commandment."[9]

You must have completely honest weights and measures. For "everyone who deals dishonestly, is abhorrent to the Eternal your G-d."[10]

And, finally, you must remember how Amalek "surprised you on the march, when you were famished and weary, and cut down all the stragglers in your rear."[11]

Parshah **Interpretation:** Like the *parshah* before, this one seems a hodgepodge of many specific directives, although they are given in the context of the overall demand that we create a just and compassionate society. This is sometimes hard for us to see today, because so many of the commands are built around societal norms we find objectionable, such as the acceptance of slavery, the subordination of women, and the death penalty for adultery or (extreme) defiance of parents. But the intent of these ancient directives is always to treat others with a degree of respect and concern that is rooted in the awareness that all humans are made in the Divine image. And many of the commandments in this chapter do not come with the baggage of an ancient society; these are more clearly universal in their application, and more transparently about fairness and loving-kindness

Other commands (or *mitzvoth*) address issues of ritual and purity, and so may seem entirely irrelevant to creating a just or compassionate society. But Torah mixes together what we think of as ethical and ritual *mitzvoth* because they both function the same way in our spiritual life, requiring that we let go of our egoistic concerns as we concentrate on performing the commandment. Carrying out *mitzvoth* transforms us as the new practice begins to become second nature; and the habit of serving G-d instead of ego can transform the larger society, whether the *mitzvoth* appears to be about justice, morality, or what we may think of as *merely* ritual.

In fact, the deep reading of this *parshah* takes us repeatedly to the inner spiritual journey, particularly if we generalize the commandments beyond their specific situations. The first two directives, for example, can be easily interpreted as our placing brakes on our desires, instead of simply giving in to them. The captive woman in war cannot be raped. No, we must take her into our home, give her time to mourn what she has lost, marry her, and treat her well. And we cannot turn away from the son we love less, despite our preference; he must be treated fairly and given what is due him. In this reading, the examples are most meaningful as illustrations of a larger principle: that we must delay or inhibit satisfaction of our lusts and desires and cravings if we are to build a world of respect, compassion, fairness, and justice.

The particular object of our desire or craving is irrelevant; what matters is our relationship to our desires as we learn to separate ourselves from our cravings, recognizing them as part of us but not letting them dominate. In this interpretation, the delinquent son can be seen as another component, a defiant aspect that does not want to give in and obey YHVH, a part of our being that we must stifle—even erase—as much as possible.[12]

Finally, this part of the metaphoric discussion closes with the command that we not have contempt for ourselves as we struggle with our imperfections, just as we must (at the literal level) treat the body of the executed criminal without contempt, cutting it down and burying it.

Many of the other commandments can be similarly interpreted in terms of a purely internal process that Torah describes in concrete language. In this reading, the end of the *parshah* seems to recognize that we will be exhausted at times by the demands made upon us for change and transformation. For the last commandment warns us to "remember what Amalek did to you on your journey, after you left Egypt—how ... he surprised you on the march, when you were famished and weary, and cut down all the stragglers in your rear. Therefore ... you shall blot out the memory of Amalek from under heaven. Do not forget."[13]

In traditional interpretation, Amalek stands for doubt.[14] Amalek stands for the moments when we stand exhausted on the spiritual journey, when faith fails, when the Divine feels far away or even a nonexistent myth. Amalek stands for our desire to give up when the wilderness seems endless, and the path through it to the Promised Land too hard and demanding.

Amalek strikes when we are already weakened, lost, and disheartened, when we feel spiritless, sunk in ennui or fatigue. However demanding they feel, the commandments are the lifeline then, the threads to cling to and follow in the darkness. We must follow them, whether we feel like it or not, whether or not, in this moment, we are believers. If we do, we will find ourselves aware, at some point, of being safe in the presence of the Divine. For the Divine is waiting for us as we leave behind the tyranny of the ego, moving out from the narrow straits of slavery and leaving *Mitzrayim.*

For Formal Practice: The focus of this meditation is on experiencing the various commandments as paths toward developing discernment and toward creating boundaries that separate us from our all-too-human weaknesses.

When you are ready, follow your breath for a few minutes, letting your body relax and your mind begin to empty of thought.

Then let any one of the commandments given in this chapter of Torah come into your mind.

Without thought, let your attention hover around the idea that following this commandment leads to holiness. If you are comfortable with Hebrew prayer, you can use the equivalent Hebrew phrase *Baruch atah, YHVH, eloheynu melech ha'olam asher kideshanu bemitzvotav vetzivanhu....* ("Blessed are thou, YHVH our G-d, who has made us holy by commanding us to....")

In My Own Practice: *As I begin this meditation, I am overcome with thankfulness for being given guidelines for loving-kindness. Specifics to help me remember how to act.*

My mind is particularly struck by the command to return to the owner anything I find of his that that he has lost—indifference is forbidden. But at the same time, I am also struck by the limits in the guidelines that protect me from my tendencies toward unrelenting standards of zealousness. If the owner lives too far away, or is unknown to me, I can hold his possessions until he shows up. I don't have to obsessively search him out.

Another commandment: When I harvest, I go around the field only once. Whatever is left standing, I leave for those in need—but I take my harvest. So I needn't give up all I own because others have less. I am asked only to give up that which is somehow extra, somehow discretionary. I have obligation to give—that demand never changes—but I can put limits on what I offer in time, energy, resources.

I have been meditating on the Amtrak train. I have an empty seat next to me and I would love to keep it empty for the comfort and isolation. Almost everyone on the car feels the same way, and so people put their briefcases, purses, even their carry-ons on these seats, to discourage anyone from asking if the seat is free.

But this space is truly extra for me today. I feel well, I've done most of my writing for the day, and I can easily move over to let another person sit. There aren't enough single seats to go around; some of us will have to double up.

I clear the space, with just my purse partly in the spot. A woman stops and asks if she can sit. I smile and say of course she can. She is apologetic, and I say, "I just happened to get to this seat before you. I don't own it." She smiles and relaxes.

As I sit here, I am grateful for being offered this path to the Divine. For in emulating YHVH's compassion and justice, I have become inexplicably happier in my skin. Fewer things bother me, and I take other people's behavior much less personally. And, yet, I am also clearer about what I want and what I am willing to do. Less judgment of others and of myself, and more compassion toward us both.

Deuteronomy/*D'varim*, 7, "When You'll Come"/*Ki Tavo*
(Deut. 26:1–29:8)

"And it shall be, when you'll come to the land that YHVH, your G-d, is giving you...."

—Deut. 26:1

Interpretive Overview: Reaching across the generations to the present listeners, Moses expands on the theme of choosing blessing if we serve the Divine, or curse if we turn away, with detailed descriptions of the consequences of each choice. At the metaphoric level, we understand that reaching the Promised Land is our choice each day, dependent on our choosing to serve G-d rather than remaining enslaved to our egoistic concerns.

Summary of *Parshah:* In words that move not only across the eons but between the Israelites' present and future, Moses now comes to the end of the laws he has been presenting since the fourth *parshah* of Deuteronomy.[1] He closes this section by telling the people to celebrate their commitment to G-d once in the Promised Land by bringing some of their first crops to the *mishkan.* He then gives the exact words G-d wants them to recite there about their experiences in Egypt and their emancipation by YHVH, and he adds that they must tithe their produce to share with the poor.[2] Then he formally declares that the people and G-d have each committed themselves to the other "this day."[3] *Today,* the Israelites have agreed to listen to G-d and to observe G-d's laws, and G-d has agreed to protect them as a treasured, holy people as long as they do so.

Turning to what must be done on the very day they enter the Promised Land, Moses commands the Israelites to inscribe his teaching[4] upon large stones that they are to cover with plaster and set up on a mountain (Mount

Ebal). Then, they are to build an altar and offer sacrifice, after which they must perform a ceremony in which six of the tribes are to stand on one mountain (Mount Gerizim), as the Levites call out the blessings that he is about to enumerate.[5] The other six tribes are to stand on Mount Ebal as the Levites call out of the curses.

In describing the ceremony, Moses recites a short and assorted list of forbidden behaviors, which he says the Levites will proclaim at the start, and to each of which the Israelites will assent by calling out, "Amen." He begins with, "Cursed be anyone who makes a sculptured or molten image"[6] and, "Cursed be the one who insults father or mother,"[7] and he ends by calling out, "Cursed be whoever will not uphold the terms of this Teaching and observe them."[8] (The phrase is ambiguous, for the Hebrew implies that it may refer to the entire Torah and not merely to the commandments just cited or to any other subset of laws.[9])

After this, Moses recites the blessings the Levites will proclaim, beginning with, "Blessed shall you be in the city and blessed shall you be in the country,"[10] and, "Blessed shall be the issue of your womb, the produce of your soil, and the offspring of your cattle, the calving of your herd and the lambing of your flock."[11]

Then he itemizes the long list of horrific curses (three times as many curses as blessings), proclaiming, among others, "The Eternal will let loose against you calamity, panic, and frustration in all the enterprises you undertake, so that you shall soon be utterly wiped out because of your evildoing in forsaking Me."[12] And:

> The Eternal will strike you with consumption, fever, and inflammation, with scorching heat and drought, with blight and mildew; they shall hound you until you perish. The skies above your head shall be copper and the earth under you iron. The Eternal will make the rain of your land dust, and sand shall drop on you from the sky until you are wiped out.[13]

The *parshah* closes with Moses saying that the people have seen what YHVH did in the land of Egypt to Pharaoh and all his land, and in the forty years since then in the wilderness, but that only now do they have "eyes to see and ears to hear."[14]

Parshah Interpretation: This *parshah* is profoundly confrontational as it speaks to each of us today. Enumerating blessings for those who obey the laws of the Divine Presence and curses for those who do not, the text has frequently been read as a literal threat of punishment versus reward. In our time, the curses can also be read—and often they are read this way—as a prophetic indictment of what our choices have brought upon us in this age of war and profound climate change.

Or we can choose to absorb Moses' words at the personal and metaphoric level. In this understanding, this *parshah* can be read as saying the following: when you are aware of the presence of the Divine in your life moment by moment, then you will rejoice at the bounty being poured out upon you at all times; you will recognize your release from the slavery of the ego; and you will practice loving-kindness. In this frame, it is simple fact that you who have been rescued from *Mitzrayim,* from the place of constriction and ignorance, you G-d seekers wherever you are, you have now glimpsed YHVH and are aware of the Divine permeating all existence. In this state, you automatically become a channel for the Divine to manifest compassion in the world.

And if you want to maintain your awareness of Divine Presence within and around you, you must continue to give thanks and offer yourself up for service. You must continually reaffirm your commitment to G-d in your behavior.

If you don't, you will inevitably lose your sense of ever-present Divinity and be exiled to a world of deficit, deprivation, danger, alienation, and aloneness. This is the fundamental curse and punishment, for all the specifics of "curse" in this *parshah* can be read as symbolically expressing what it feels like to lose the experience of G-d's presence once you have known it. At the mystical level, the emphasis of this *parshah* is on the experience of abandonment reserved for G-d wrestlers, for those of us who have become aware of Divine Presence and then lose that connection, because the experience of loss, abandonment, and exile is very different from the experience of never feeling G-d's presence at all.

For Formal Practice: The intention is to offer yourself to the Divine for service and notice what happens as you sit with that commitment.

When you are ready, let yourself soften into your breath. As you continue to sit, offer yourself up to the Divine, offer yourself wholeheartedly for service. As you breathe, notice how your body relaxes, notice any sense of peace or equanimity.

If you can, offer thanks for whatever comes to mind.

In My Own Practice: *I have been working hard all week as a volunteer, arranging for landscaping for my synagogue. This morning, I spent several hours helping in the garden itself.*

For weeks, I've been obsessed with worry about the outcome of the upcoming national election in the United States. But in the last few days, my fear has somehow moved to another part of my awareness. I am as committed as ever to my candidate, and I still plan to volunteer time for his campaign, but my panic has, at least for the moment, gone to the side.

Today, the recent financial crisis has been added to the mix, once again making clear to me that there truly are no certainties in life. Yet I feel surprising calm and equanimity as I follow my breath going in and out. Somehow, my grasping, fearful "I" has been subdued by the experience of service this week, of subsuming myself to this landscaping effort. I even feel joyous as I sit with my meditation group, thankful for their presence, for the day, for the silence, for the garden taking shape outside.

It is hard to describe the feeling of equanimity, for it sits side by side with complete consciousness of possible looming disaster. Somehow, my emotions are not activated. Instead of feeling fear (which may yet come), I somehow feel safe in the bounty of the Divine Presence.

Deuteronomy/*D'varim,* 8, "Standing"/*Nitzavim*
(Deut. 29:9–30:20)

"You're standing today, all of you, in front of YHVH—your G-d...."

—Deut. 29:9

Interpretive Overview: In extremely powerful language, Moses' speech culminates in a call for us to choose blessing over curse, and therefore, life over death. Most of all, he says that he is speaking to those who are not standing in front of him (i.e., to each of us now) and that the capacity to choose blessing is not miraculous but immediately available—"in your mouth and in your heart."[1]

Summary of *Parshah:* In the previous *parshah,* Moses rciterated that he was speaking to us *today.* In this one, he makes this point even more emphatically. In an astonishing phrase, he says that the covenant with G-d is being made *today* not just by the people standing before him (as stated in the opening paragraph) but also by those "who are not with us here this day."[2]

Then, in blistering language, he says that some of us who are listening will turn away from YHVH to serve false idols, even though we've seen the exodus from slavery to freedom and know that the idols that others worship are not for us. And, as a result, we will be cursed.

From there, he refers again to the whole children of Israel turning away from the Divine to worship idols, with the resultant destruction of the Promised Land and their exile from it, all to be witnessed by later generations.

In another famous line, he adds, "The hidden things belong to YHVH, our G-d, and the revealed things belong to us and to our children forever, to do all the words of this instruction."[3] After this, he speaks of the Israelites' eventual return to the service of the Divine, with G-d welcoming them back, gathering them up, and returning them to the Promised Land to prosper under Divine protection. He adds that YHVH will also open their hearts, sensitizing them to the Divine, "so as to love YHVH, your G-d, with all your heart and with all your soul so that you'll live."[4]

Then comes another astonishing phrase: that the commandment to observe G-d's laws is not too far or wondrous. It is not in the skies or across the sea, Moses says, "But the thing is very close to you, in your mouth, and in your heart, to do it."[5]

In the final paragraph, Moses' language continues to speak to us across millennia as he says, "See: I've put in front of you today life and good, and death and bad."[6] And, "I call the skies and the earth to witness regarding you today: I've put life and death in front of you, blessing and curse. And you shall choose life, so that you'll live, you and your seed…."[7]

***Parshah* Interpretation:** Once again, we must remember that the Torah is a spiritual workbook for each of us, an extraordinarily complex narrative that must be read at the metaphoric level for its deepest meanings. At this level, the Promised Land is the state of mind in which we are aware of YHVH—whatever that Mystery means to us—permeating the fabric of existence in every moment. We can sometimes enter that state unexpectedly, as if by G-d's grace; but the Torah insists that we can reliably reach that state by committing ourselves, each of us, to loving YHVH with all our heart, and by then emulating Divine compassion and loving-kindness in our behavior.

When we are in that state of awareness, we are no longer enslaved by the constrictions of the ego, by the fears and needs of the self that exists to protect our vulnerable bodies and to satisfy its cravings. We are then freed from the slavery of *Mitzrayim*. In this state of freedom, we are totally alive, present to the possibilities of the moment as it is, liberated from preoccupations with the past and fantasies about the future. In the last part of his speech, Moses offers the culmination of the theme he opened early in Deuteronomy,[8] as he exhorts us to become totally alive, to "choose life"[9] by committing to the path of loving service.

G-d may be a mystery to us, completely beyond our awestruck comprehension, but G-d calls out to us, and is always present if we open our hearts and listen to the commands for compassion and loving-kindness. Thus Moses exclaims, "The hidden things belong to YHVH, our G-d, and the revealed things belong to us and to our children forever, to do all the words of this instruction."[10] For the path is not esoteric; it has been laid out in Moses' teachings, awaiting us whenever we choose it.

In the breathtaking leap of the mystic, Moses makes his teaching universal by explicitly speaking *today*, and to those "who are not with us here this day."[11]

Of course, the *parshah* also recognizes the universal inevitability of human failure: in the metaphor that was given at the start of Genesis, we are made of both the dust of the earth and of the Divine breath. Although we yearn to love G-d and feel G-d's presence, we will always slide back, returning to the worship of the false idols of greed, power, lust, achievements, and other aspects of *doing* rather than *being*. But we can always return to the love and service of the Divine Presence. G-d is always there to welcome us back, to welcome us to being fully alive in the moment, without fear or longing.

Choosing YHVH is to enable ourselves to live fully in the moment, without fear. But turning away from the path of G-d is to be internally cut off from the source of aliveness, and to deaden ourselves. The root word *shuvah*, meaning "return," is the crucial word of this *parshah*, repeated over and over. Moses asks us to choose life, to turn to the Divine with love, and to follow the ways of YHVH with all our hearts and souls.[12]

For Formal Practice: Let us focus on the intent to choose life by following the command to emulate Divine compassion and loving-kindness in the acts of daily life.

Begin by following your breath for a few moments. When you are ready, think of someone whom you find hard to treat with compassion and loving-kindness. This could be someone close to you or not so close. Or, choose someone not in your personal life at all—perhaps, a public figure. Just choose someone you now speak of without compassion and loving-kindness.

Now let your yearning focus on changing your behavior toward this person. Open your heart as you ask for help with your struggle. Notice how much of your resistance is rooted in your fear, your memories of the past, and your fantasies about the future.

If you become distracted, follow your breath for a few moments. Then go back to your craving to return to the presence of the Divine by following G-d's path of love and compassion. Let your heart open as you ask for help in seeing others with G-d's eyes.

If you like, go into silence as you open your heart.

In My Own Practice: *Someone new has come to my meditation group today, a woman I've never met before. Her hair a dull gray, she is probably in her sixties. She walks laboriously with a cane and speaks quite slowly. It is obvious that she has been ill, perhaps is even recovering from a stroke. Yet, I was aware that my first impulse was to dismiss her as uninteresting—perhaps slow-witted—on the basis of her physical appearance. I was also aware of not wanting to open up to her because I feared she might cling to me in neediness.*

In fact, I spoke with her before we began the group's formal meeting and saw how far wrong my inclination had been.

But I am still aware of the impulse in me to judge, to discriminate, to decide who is more worthy and who less. Now I sit with her face in front of my closed eyes, asking for help in seeing her through G-d's eyes.

After a few moments, I am surprised to begin to see her as fully distinct from me, with the line of her life stretched out behind and in front of her. It is like a rope, turning and looping. I realize that when I open up to someone, I generally lose a sense of separation from them, somehow merging in my own consciousness with them. This time is very different.

I see the rope of her lifeline and the rope of mine, and hers is clearly different from mine. The two intersect in this moment only, in this room right now. I ask for help to see the others in the meditation group as well, and now the ropes twist past each other, crossing and re-crossing as I look backward and forward. I know this is a visual metaphor, and I am certain that I am not reading the future. Yet the vision both exhilarates and frightens me, for it seems utterly real.

For a moment, I see an immense tangle of lines for everyone in the world: humans, trees, ants. I feel freed of my body and at the same time dizzy. It is too powerful a vision. For the rest of the meditation, I dip into it and out again.

Deuteronomy/*D'varim*, 9, "And He Went"/*Vayeilech*
(Deut. 31:1–30)

"And Moses went and spoke these things to all Israel. And he said to them, 'I'm a hundred and twenty years old today. I'm not able to go out and come in anymore. And YHVH said to me, "You shall not cross this Jordan." ' "

—Deut. 31:1–2

Interpretive Overview: As Moses prepares to die, he presents Joshua to the Israelites as their new leader, writes down his teachings,[1] and commands that these be read to the people every seven years. Predicting that they will worship false idols in the Promised Land, so that G-d will turn away from them, the Divine gives Moses a song for the people to learn as witness to this future. At the symbolic level, the text informs us that teachings and teachers are available, but that we are ready to take responsibility for ourselves; and adds that it helps to know that regression and exile are an inevitable part of the spiritual journey. Finally, the *parshah* implies that YHVH will be most accessible to us when we acknowledge the fragility of our own control and when we are simply "being," rather than actively doing, as in the seventh Sabbath year.

Summary of *Parshah*: Known in Hebrew as *D'varim* or "Words," Deuteronomy has Moses speak directly to us across millennia. Now, he comes to the final part of his speech.

In this very short *parshah,* he reminds the people that G-d will lead them across the Jordan to the Promised Land under the leadership of Joshua, Moses' successor. For G-d has told Moses that he cannot cross the Jordan or lead the people any further. Assuring them that G-d will support them in overcoming their enemies, he tells both the people and Joshua to "be strong and be bold."[2]

Then Moses writes down his teaching and gives it to the priests in charge of the Ark of the Covenant and to the elders, commanding them to read it

316

to the whole people every seven years, the Sabbatical Year,[3] at the autumn Festival of Booths, or *Sukkot*. In this way, Moses says, even those not yet born will know what G-d wants of them, and do it.

After this, G-d tells Moses to bring Joshua to the Tent of Meeting, for Moses' death is near. When the two men reach the Tent, G-d appears in a cloud and tells Moses yet again that the people will forget G-d's ways because of their "inclination,"[4] turning to false idols once they are in the Promised Land. The Divine will be angry and hide from them despite their cries when things begin to go badly for them; twice the phrase "I'll hide My face"[5] appears. Then G-d tells Moses to write down the song that appears as the next *parshah*, prophesying what will happen after the Israelites enter the Promised Land; and the Divine tells Moses to have the people memorize it so that it will be a "witness"[6] for them in the future.

Moses does as commanded, telling Joshua once again to be strong and bold. Then he adds the song to the rest of the teaching he has given and tells the priests to place the whole teaching by the Ark of the Covenant, where it will serve as witness of G-d's warning. After this, he tells them that he fully knows how rebellious and stiff-necked they are, that they have disobeyed G-d so many times already, that he knows how "corrupted"[7] they will be after his death. Finally, he sings the song that makes up the next *parshah*.

***Parshah* Interpretation:** As this *parshah* begins, Moses reminds us once again that we can enter the Promised Land, where we can feel safe and protected in the awareness of G-d's presence. We also hear from G-d that it is inherent in our nature as human beings to stray from the path leading to that state of consciousness, so that we find ourselves lost and desolate, with G-d hidden from us. As Moses' death approaches, we are given his teachings and the song we read in the next *parshah* to serve as witnesses to help us stay on the path.

Thus we are told to memorize the song and do a public reading of the teaching every seventh year at the festival of *Sukkot*, one of the three yearly pilgrimage festivals "when all Israel comes to appear before YHVH."[8]

Sukkot is the festival in which we give thanks for the bounty of G-d's earth while dwelling for seven days in temporary shelters that are open to the wind and rain. *Sukkot* reminds us, on the one hand, of impermanence and our own lack of ability to control what happens to us, and on the other, of the inexhaustible gifts and miracles of the Divine that would be visible if we'd each just open our eyes and consciousness.

Furthermore, the *Sukkot* festival on the seventh year would be a particularly powerful time, for the seventh year is the one in which debts are to be remitted and fields lie fallow. It is a year of rest, a Sabbath year, a time in which we are finally not struggling for control, in which our accumulation of wealth is at least partly nullified; in which we are sent back to a state of simply *being*. In that yearlong Sabbath, we can be open to the awareness of G-d, moment by moment.

We are being prepared to take responsibility for ourselves in the absence of Moses. It is understood that our human inclination is to forget the covenant and turn away from service to the Divine, and so both the required public reading of Deuteronomy and the song that YHVH has dictated for posterity are spiritual tools to help those who do not live with Moses or with the obvious face of the Divine.

Moses' death at this place and time is a reminder that we must each approach G-d individually. Each of us houses a Sanctuary for G-d deep within our being; and each of us must ultimately find the way to that Sanctuary by ourselves. We need teachers and guides to point the way and to help us when we fall back, but no one else can take the path for us. In the end, we are each given responsibility for ourselves.

For Formal Practice: The focus of this meditation is to ask yourself what it means to take responsibility for your own spiritual path, knowing that you will have moments of forgetfulness.

When you are ready, let yourself sit in silence, allowing your breath rise and fall.

Let the question hover in your awareness as you breathe in and out.

In the metaphor of Genesis, you are made of the dust of the earth. And yet you are also made in the Divine image, able to emulate YHVH's compassion.

In the light of this metaphor, what does it mean to take responsibility for your own spiritual path?

In My Own Practice: *The answer comes immediately. I can do only two things. I can choose to be present to my experience, and I can choose to behave with loving-kindness.*

If I am present, I can pay attention to how my heart feels, whether it is open or constricted. That helps me let go of my resistance and act as a channel for Divine compassion.

And the more I follow this path, the less fear I have, the less I feel limited to physical form, the more I see a moving tapestry of time and space around each moment, and the more I am aware of YHVH permeating all existence.

That is all I can do. And it is more than enough.

Deuteronomy/*D'varim*, 10, "Listen"/*Haazinu*
(Deut. 32:1–52)

Listen, skies, so I may speak
And let the earth hear what My mouth says.
Let My teaching come down like showers;
Let My saying emerge like dew,
Like raindrops on plants
And like rainfalls on herbs.

—Deut. 32:1[1]

Interpretive Overview: G-d presents the Israelites' future history in a prophetic song that recounts G-d's great love for the Israelites, contrasts it with their predicted betrayal of the Divine, and portray G-d's angry abandonment and later resumption of the role of their protector. At the metaphoric level, we can read the song as saying that our human vulnerability leads us to behave badly, while simultaneously closing us to the awareness of the Divine. In our estrangement, we experience the world, both outside and within us, as being filled with destruction and chaos.

Summary of *Parshah:* According to Robert Alter in *The Five Books of Moses: A Translation with Commentary*, the song may date to the eleventh century BCE; it is certainly far older than the bulk of Deuteronomy. Because of its age, it contains a number of unusual words that cannot be translated with assurance. It also has sections that appear to have been miscopied—accidentally or not—in the course of centuries of handwritten transmission.

The song opens with statements of YHVH's goodness and perfection as contrasted with the flawed nature of humans. Quickly, it traces the Divine's love for the children of Israel, starting with finding and guarding them in the wilderness, which is characterized as a "formless place."[2] Here the text uses the same word (*tohu*) that is found in Genesis for the formless chaos that existed before creation—a word not used since. Using another phrase from Genesis that has not been seen again until now, YHVH is described as having protected the children of Israel like an eagle that "hovers over its young, spreads its wings, takes it, lifts it on its pinion."[3]

In the song, which is written all in past tense, G-d leads the people to the Promised Land of milk and honey, only to have them then turn away to worship demons and foreign gods, forgetting the Divine Presence. Incensed, G-d turns away, sending down punishment and destruction. The song suggests that YHVH might even erase them entirely if not for the fear that their enemies would believe the extermination was their doing and not G-d's.

Then YHVH's tone shifts to protection of the now powerless Israelites and destruction of their enemies, who are without understanding and like the people of Sodom and Gomorrah. In closing, the Divine asks rhetorically where the other gods are, and says that only G-d has power. "*I* cause death and give life, *I've* pierced, and *I'll* heal. And there's no deliverer from My hand."[4]

After that, Moses again tells the people to pay attention to everything he has said so that they will tell their children to observe and do it all. Then, in a famous culminating phrase, Moses proclaims, "For this is not a trifling thing for you: it is your very life; through it you shall long endure on the land that you are to possess upon crossing the Jordan."[5]

Immediately after this, we read that YHVH tells Moses to go up to Mount Nebo in the land of Moab to look over at the Promised Land—the land of Canaan. For the Divine says, again, that Moses cannot himself come there, any more than his brother Aaron could, because of the sin they committed at Meribah, when Moses struck the rock and commanded water.[6]

Parshah **Interpretation:** At the literal level, this song is supposed to prophesy the future history of the Israelites; at the metaphoric level, it is once more about us. In this reading, the text yet again says that we will inevitably turn from serving the Divine through the path of loving-kindness. Instead, we will return to the service of the fearful ego, worshipping false idols; consequently, we will no longer find ourselves in the Promised Land in which we feel enfolded by the miracles of each moment, but instead will be back in the wilderness, alone and frightened in a threatening world.

In wonderful wordplay, the Divine tells of rescuing the Israelites from a wilderness that is described as a formless chaos, just as there was before creation. Through this wordplay, G-d reminds us that rejecting the commandments to love both your neighbor and the stranger creates a culture in which *anything* can happen, a world of potentially limitless chaos. More than that, to lose the connection to the Divine is to be cast adrift in a "formless place,"[7] in a state of mind in which there is no meaning or purpose. It is in this sense that we can read Moses' saying, "For this is not a trifling thing for you: it is your very life…."[8]

To make the point even clearer, the Israelites are referred to as Jacob, rather than by the usual name, "Israel." For when G-d came to Jacob in the wilderness, in the Book of Genesis, Jacob had just stolen his brother Esau's blessing and birthright, and was fleeing into exile to escape Esau's revenge.[9] More than anyone else in the Torah, Jacob represents our own aspirations and failures. In the moment in which he first encounters G-d, he is absolutely rudderless and lost. Not only has he behaved badly, he has no knowledge of the commandments that are to be given at Sinai generations later.

Having no compass for spiritual guidance, he is truly in a place of formless chaos.

For Formal Practice: The focus of this contemplative meditation is on the consequences of falling back into selfishness and fear.

When you are ready, let your awareness hover on the experiences of chaos, meaninglessness, and desolation that are the consequences of following a path dominated by self-concerns.

As you continue to sit, turn instead to the consequences of becoming a channel for Divine compassion to manifest in the world. As Moses says, "For this is not a trifling thing for you: it is your very life...."[10]

In My Own Practice: *The instant I begin to meditate, thoughts arise that revolve around the current economic meltdown. People moving in with relatives, the lines at food banks, the homeless men sleeping in the subway. The collapse has happened because of unregulated greed throughout the financial system, and the unchecked worship of money and possessions.*

As I sit, more concrete images inevitably appear—of children desperately seeking water in Darfur, of women being gang-raped in Bosnia, of Holocaust Jews dying of suffocation in boxcars, even before they reach the death camps. The images are endless.

Images of chaos, of desolation. Of pointless pain inflicted.

I go to personal experience. Consequences of my own acts of cruelty.

I see my mother asking me to write to a second cousin who is almost my age; her parents, Auschwitz survivors. They had only just recovered her from the Polish family who'd hidden her through the war and had fought in court to keep her afterward. I was very young—and jealous of a child loved by two families, by two sets of parents.

When I refused to write, my mother was angrier than she'd ever been.

As I sit, I feel compassion for the child self whose refusal came from pain. And all I gained was more sense of desolation. Wandering in circles in the chaotic desert of my mind.

Who knows what our letters to each other might have led to?

Worse, suddenly there's a new thought: who knows what my refusal meant to cousins who had already lost everyone else in their family?

Deuteronomy/*D'varim*, 11, "And This is the Blessing"/ *V'Zot HaB'rachah* (Deut. 33:1–34:12)

"And this is the blessing with which Moses, the man of G-d, blessed the children of Israel before his death."

—Deut. 33:1

Interpretive Overview: In this *parshah*, we come to the end of the Torah, the Five Books of Moses. After blessing each tribe separately and assuring them of victory over their enemies, Moses goes up Mount Nebo where G-d shows him the Promised Land that he cannot enter. Then he dies, and the Israelites accept Joshua as their new leader. At the metaphoric level, we can see Moses' blessings to each tribe as referring to the gifts we have each received on our individual spiritual journey. But the Torah ends before we enter the Promised Land because we are all still struggling, moving sometimes forward and sometimes back, as we seek to become transparent channels through which Divine compassion can manifest in the human realm.

Summary of *Parshah*: In this final, short *parshah*, Moses blesses the different tribes of the children of Israel and yet again says that YHVH will bring them victory over their enemies. Then he goes up Mount Nebo, where G-d shows to him all of the Promised Land, reiterating that the Divine had promised it "to Abraham, to Isaac and to Jacob,"[1] and to their descendants; and that Moses may not enter.

Moses, "YHVH's servant,"[2] dies and is buried (although it's not clear whether G-d buries him or the people of Israel) in an unnamed place. He is a hundred and twenty years old. The people mourn for thirty days, and then turn to their new leader, Joshua, whose wisdom, the text says, has been passed to him by Moses.

The Torah ends by saying there was never again a prophet like Moses, who knew G-d face to face; neither were there ever again the wonders and miracles by which Moses led them out of Egypt.

Parshah **Interpretation:** The blessings appear to be very old, having been written sometime after King David's reign, possibly around 900 BCE,[3] and translators are uncertain of the meaning of many of their words and phrases. In general, however, it seems that each tribe receives a blessing that focuses on the tribe's specific qualities in following YHVH's ways of virtue and justice, with the whole people of Israel (consequently) keeping the Promised Land against its enemies under G-d's protection.

The blessings can also be read metaphorically, aligning them with the rest of Deuteronomy's deep teachings. In this reading, Moses is blessing each one of us as we struggle with our tendencies to behave badly because of our enslavement to fear and neediness. This is our natural inclination, and it is our enslavement to these emotions that is the metaphoric enemy.

The blessings, then, refer to those characteristic strengths that are uniquely our own as we struggle to overcome our enemy and return to the Edenic state in which we are channels for G-d to manifest loving-kindness. These qualities derive from a mixture of genetics and environment as we grow from infancy into, and through, adulthood, with each decision we make along the way becoming the foundation for further character development. Moment by moment, we create ourselves. With each of our actions, we choose blessing or curse, life or death, the chaotic wilderness in which we feel estranged from G-d or the Promised Land in which we feel the Divine Presence permeating our existence.

For Formal Practice: As we come to the end of the Torah, the focus of this contemplative meditation is on the gifts that we have been given to overcome our internal enemies, so that we can reach the Promised Land.

When you are ready, follow your breath for a few moments. As you continue to sit, open your awareness to the gifts you have received that give you strength on your spiritual quest, and that help you manifest loving-kindness in the world.

Remember that some of these gifts may be bittersweet. They may not seem like gifts. They may even be gifts you would rather not have.

If you begin to think, go back to your breath for a bit. Then let yourself return to the focus. What are my strengths? What blessings have I been given? Let answers come to you without thought.

In My Own Practice: *As soon as I open myself to the question, the image appears of a particularly unpleasant night almost twenty years ago. In the memory, I am sitting at home in front of my new computer with stacks of books piled all around my chair.*

I had finished writing my second book. But my old computer had crashed and taken with it all the references for my footnotes. The computer had been built by a company that had gone out of business, and my backups couldn't be read by either PC or Mac programs.

So I'd had to recreate all the references, and I'd been up for twenty-four hours, sitting at that new computer. I was going through my manuscript, page by page, finding every place in the text with a footnote and tracing down the reference. It was pure grit and determination at work, going painstakingly, one by one.

But it had to be done, and I was the only one who could do it.

The scene is so clear, although, at first, I don't understand why I'm seeing it. Then I get it: grit and determination. Perseverance. Plodding ahead, step by step.

I don't tend to think of myself as a plodder. But it rings true as I sit in meditation. That really is one of my main characteristics. I keep going, step after slow step.

Plodding. Persevering. The peaks of exaltation and awe may happen, but what sustains me is the step-by-step practice. It sustains me during the dry spells, when the Divine Presence is hidden and the world goes flat and dry. It makes the dry periods a little shorter. Plodding along, decision by decision, from one choice-point to the next. Choosing blessing instead of curse as I head out of slavery, aiming for the Promised Land on the far side of the wilderness.

Final Interpretive Summation

The Book of Genesis sets the stage for our spiritual journey. Our nature is inevitably conflicted, for we are made of the dust of the earth, yet filled with the Divine breath and able (to some extent) to choose how we behave. Genesis then recounts our disconnection from the Divine, our loss of Eden, and numerous acts of lust, rage, greed, and fear as it demonstrates the problem of being in bodies that need satisfaction and self-protection.

It is not as if we are to devalue the world, for G-d labels all of creation "good" at the beginning of Genesis. It is rather that we are to find a balance between satisfying our own needs and satisfying the needs of the others, with whom we share the planet. Our physical needs are essential, propelling human invention and creativity, even civilization itself. Without our physicality, we would not even reproduce, and the human race would vanish from the scene. But we are not to become so trapped in the desires of the flesh that we turn away from service to the Divine and ignore the needs of others, particularly the less powerful.

Perhaps this is why Genesis ends as it does. Egypt has offered Joseph's family sustenance—life—but they have been given more than survival, for they thrive while the Egyptians are reduced to serfdom in order to stay alive. Although many commentators have been troubled by this turn of events,[1] the narrative can once more be approached as metaphor. For the accumulation of wealth and power too easily becomes an end in itself, a snare that turns the ego away from the Divine and into enslavement in *Mitzrayim,* just as Joseph's descendants become enslaved.

So Exodus begins with our enslavement, with us as unconscious as insects and caught in the web of our passions and fears; and it continues with descriptions of our initial escape, our immediate backsliding, and our recommitment to G-d at Mount Sinai. The stories of Genesis have made clear that we need a map if we are to be freed from ourselves; and, at Sinai, we are given clear guidance for the first time—rules for how to behave each day. We are fearful in Exodus, and half ready to turn back from the spiritual path, but we pledge ourselves to G-d anyway. We even build a Sanctuary in which the Divine Presence can dwell both in our community and in our own hearts.

Leviticus then calls a temporary halt to action as it deeply explores the question of what it means to truly live in the presence of G-d. It provides even more ethical guidelines, culminating in the command to love our neighbors—and even strangers—as ourselves. And it provides rituals by which we can intensify our commitment and focus, and by which we can cleanse our spirits when we falter, make mistakes, and miss the mark. It also accepts the hard reality that G-d is the source of death as well as of life—not just a fount of protection and love but a fearful, awesome, and overwhelming Presence.

Numbers brings us back into time, as we start forward again. We have moved from our starting place in *Mitzrayim;* our commitment and focus are intense. We've been given directions for maintaining that intensity, but we are far from our goal. Numbers catalogues both the sequence of spiritual obstacles that we must yet overcome and our many reversals of direction. Our progress is real, but our journey is long, and each person's path has its own challenges and flavor. Numbers ends with us at the edge of the Promised Land.

Then comes Deuteronomy, composed of a series of speeches by Moses that contain both a reprise of our journey and an insistent call to each of us today to open our hearts to the Divine Presence. Deuteronomy addresses each of us individually, taking account of our particular strengths and weaknesses, with full awareness that we are each constrained by our inheritance, by our history, and by the endless tangles of cause and effect in which our lives are imbedded.

But we still have some freedom of choice, and we will reap the consequences of our decisions. In the outer world, we can wreak havoc on ourselves and on the earth itself, or we can create a heaven on earth. And in the inner world, we can experience safety even as we walk through the Valley of the Shadow of Death, if we have made our hearts a home for the Divine. This is one of the central messages of Torah.

Each one of us is asked to wrestle with the Divine, even though no one is likely to surrender all concerns of self. For we are merely human, inevitably conflicted, caught between the needs of our physical being and the call of the Divine, within and without. Thus, we stand just outside the Promised Land even when Deuteronomy ends, for we have not yet made it our home.

The core of the Hebrew Bible, the Five Books of Moses, ends with the Israelites encamped on the steppes of Moab overlooking the Jordan valley; they are still outside Canaan. In the symbolism of Torah, we are not expected to ever reach a state of permanent enlightenment. We move forward on our path, and we have moments of enlightenment, but even the best of us don't live in that state all the time. Not even Moses, who dies at the end of Deuteronomy.

Yet Deuteronomy/*D'varim*/"Words" offers us the chance to return to Paradise—both in the society we create here on earth, and in our internal experience—by following the commandments that center around our loving our neighbor, the stranger, and ourselves in equal measure, and in this way serving the Divine. In Deuteronomy, this is the path to enlightenment.

The more we let go of our resistance, the more time we spend in the Edenic state of attunement with the Divine Presence. And we can always shorten the journey, coming home to G-d at any moment, for enlightenment is to be found neither in the furthest heavens nor in the deepest ocean. As Moses says,

But the thing is very close to you, in your mouth, and in your heart, to do it. See: I've put in front of you today life and good, and death and bad, in that I command you today to love YHVH, your G-d, to go in G-d's ways and to observe G-d's commandments....[2]

This state of being is always available to us, ours to experience each time we recognize the Divine Presence now, manifesting as all that is in each moment of existence, forever and ever.

Book II

6

Suggestions for Exploring the Formal Meditations in This Book

If you choose to do the formal meditations in this book, you are very likely to find that your consciousness changes, so that you become more loving, less judgmental, and more at peace with yourself and others. You are likely to have many profound experiences of Divine Presence as well.

If you've never meditated before, begin with five to ten minutes a day in which you will not be disturbed by any interruptions. Because our minds are amazingly resistant to the work of meditation, it is easier to develop a daily routine if you begin with such small doses of practice. As you get comfortable with the time you are spending, increase it in small increments. Forty minutes a day is an excellent long-term goal.

If you can meditate at the same time each day, it will be easier for the practice to become habitual; it will also be easier if you can meditate in the same place. It's helpful to pick a room where you will not be distracted. (Sitting at your office desk or the kitchen table is generally a no-no.) And if you can make a small area of that room welcoming to meditation, either aesthetically or by having particularly meaningful objects in it, go for it. Even the most experienced meditators have days in which they don't feel like sitting or can't concentrate, so anything that makes your practice easier is worth doing.

For the meditation itself, I recommend beginning with what is known as a body scan, particularly if meditation is new to you. Instructions for the body scan are in Appendix A if you're unfamiliar with the exercise; once you get used to doing a body scan, you can tailor the sequence for yourself. The whole process looks longer in the reading than it is in the doing, should need only a few minutes, and makes focusing the mind much easier when you begin the meditation.

I also recommend doing each meditation for a week. But if you find that there are some you wish to spend more time on, go right ahead. They are calling out to you for a reason.

7

The Bible We Don't Know

The Five Books of Moses (The Torah/Pentateuch) are basic to Western civilization, forming the heart of our shared Wisdom book, with many of its phrases known to us all. But if you are like most of us, you've been exposed to its words only as a child in religion class, in the course of listening to sermons, or both. And some us haven't even had this much instruction. (Most of my own ideas about it originally came from crayoning in the pages of a large coloring book of Bible Stories.)

Even if we go regularly to services, we are generally offered a more or less literal reading of the text, with its inconsistencies, gory details, and boring rituals either ignored or treated as incomprehensible. While some congregations have been offered allegorical interpretations that get around a few of these problems, most American Jews and Christians have been exposed only to the surface layer.

At this stratum, the books may seem to be a jumble of myth, magic, history, law, ethics, and cultic practice. For some of us, this apparent jumble may coexist with what seems true religious writing, even revelation, while others of us may see only the jumble. Even if we feel that some of the writing is applicable today, we may find many of the descriptions of human behavior demoralizing, certainly not to be imitated.

In fact, many of us, if not most, do not find the Torah/Pentateuch a book that we regularly turn to. Feelings of awe and a sense of the world's holiness may be part of the fabric of our lives, but these feelings may not seem to be related to the Bible. Some of us don't even have a formal religious affiliation; and others have turned to other spiritual traditions because our own does not speak to us, exploring Buddhism, Sufism, Hinduism, or variants of Native-American and other shamanic cultures.

However, educated Jewish practice has, for more than two millennia, looked beneath the surface narrative to uncover hidden meaning, on the assumption that the text must be decoded before its deep spiritual messages can be fully appreciated. In this tradition, we have three levels of interpretation beyond the literal, or *p'shat,*[1] with each level revealing matters more subtle than the last.

The two levels above *p'shat* are *remez*[2] and *drash.*[3] At these two levels, commentators look for implied meanings, discover allegory and metaphor, explore subtle connections between different parts of the text, and use or create a variety of legends and stories from outside the Torah to illuminate what feels contradictory or incomplete.[4] The fourth and deepest level is called *sod,* which means "secret, mystery, hidden." This is the mystical level of understanding.

The most famous mystical reading is the *Zohar*[5] of the thirteenth century, and it is mainly the *Zohar* and teachings in its lineage that have come to be identified with the mystical teachings known as Kabbalah.[6] While some of the framework for our exploration comes out of Kabbalah, most of it belongs with the earlier, multileveled tradition of interpretation; almost every one of the teachings in this book can be found in traditional interpretive and mystical commentaries.[7]

How is the Torah Different from the Hebrew Bible and Christian Old Testament?

The Torah/Pentateuch is limited to the Five Books of Moses: Genesis, Exodus, Leviticus, Numbers, and Deuteronomy. When Deuteronomy ends, the Israelites are camped in the plains of Moab, east of the Jordan River, waiting to enter the Promised Land. Not only is there no temple built, the people haven't even set foot in the land to which they've been traveling for forty years.

The Hebrew Bible (in Hebrew, the *Tanakh*)[8] is essentially the same as the Christian Old Testament.[9] Both contain The Five Books of Moses and two additional volumes called Prophets[10] and Writings.[11] While the Torah ends by the Jordan River, Prophets and Writings give the history of the Israelites after they cross the Jordan into Canaan, along with poetry, prophecy, and purely religious and philosophical texts. Some of the history is unsubstantiated or appears to be historically inaccurate. But for many spiritual seekers, historicity isn't the point anyway. (Both Moses and Christ, for example, are equally absent from contemporaneous historical records.)

The Role of Divine Revelation in the Torah/Pentateuch

The Five Books of Moses are the keystone of the Jewish religion, the core of the Hebrew Bible. They are also basic to Christianity, as well as a sourcebook for many of the Koran's teachings. For most Orthodox Jews and fundamentalist Christians, this Torah is literally the word of G-d, spoken unambiguously to Moses at Mount Sinai by the Divine Presence. To many other religious Jews and Christians, this part of the Bible has its roots in Divine revelation, perhaps to a man named Moses, perhaps to a series of different sages, but it is not the literal word of G-d because human language cannot fully convey Divine meaning.

These believers point to a number of different traditions, each of which had roots in an experience of Divine revelation that was then translated into human speech. In their belief, the various traditions come from different time periods and were gradually written down over centuries; some, perhaps, were written down as early as the tenth century BCE. They were ultimately re-edited and spliced together into a final document about 2500 years ago, at approximately the same time that the culture of classical Greece reached its height. For these believers, the Torah has been compiled by humans, no matter how spiritual they may have been; inevitably, therefore, it has insertions, contradictions, and gaps that come not from G-d but from our incomplete understanding.

For at best, we are imperfect conduits for revelation. As in the fable of the blind men with the elephant, some of us see only the trunk, some the legs, and so on—and we add details, even without knowing it, to make a better story, so that some elephants wear circus tights.

But the range of beliefs about the nature of Torah goes even further. While some of us with only a passing knowledge of the text may doubt it to be rooted in Divine revelation, there have been very serious Torah scholars who have had these same doubts—about part, or even all, of it. Many of these scholars have believed that some parts of the text were deliberately written by certain groups to bolster a particular point of view or to enhance political power, with Divine revelation playing no role. Other scholars have believed the whole document was produced without any Divine intervention whatsoever. For them, the Torah is a compilation of many centuries of history, political polemic, ethics, mythology, shamanic belief, and theology.

The most well-known revisionists have been a number of largely non-Jewish, generally Protestant Biblical scholars over the last 150 years, who have debated versions of what eventually came to be called the "documentary hypothesis." For these researchers, the Torah has incorporated different oral and/or written traditions not only from different time periods, but from competing political factions, with specific threads of writing traceable to specific groups. Usually, they refer to the *J, P, E,* and *D* threads,[12] originating in different source documents and put together in the Torah we know. Sometimes, they also refer to the *R* source, standing for the editor(s), or redactor(s), who put the various pieces together and perhaps made some changes in the process.

In more recent years, the "documentary hypothesis" has been complemented by a contrasting approach, largely, but not entirely, in the Jewish world, which assumes that the apparent contradictions are often deliberate editorial choices that function as implied pointers to deeper meaning or the need for commentary. (This is also part of ancient Jewish interpretive tradition, except that the ancient tradition assumes that the whole Torah is literally the word of G-d.) While all scholars agree that there are different threads woven through Torah in what often looks like contradiction, many now feel that it does not matter so much whether a paragraph comes from the *J*, *P*, *E*, or *D* source. Instead, we should ask what meaning the final editor(s) wanted to convey by the selection and placement of each passage.

Perhaps, these scholars say, we have been asking the wrong questions as we seek to deconstruct the text into its component threads. What if the original material had hidden meanings that we have overlooked? And what if we accept the possibility that the finished product is a carefully constructed tapestry of threads, deliberately woven to carry these meanings, and perhaps some new ones as well? The eminent anthropologist Mary Douglas, following on the seminal work of Jacob Milgram,[13] has recently expanded our understanding of Leviticus and Numbers in just this way.[14] For she reads these books in terms of ancient literary styles that shape narrative to a very different formal structure than we are used to—not into beginning, middle, and end at all. More than that, her anthropological training carries an understanding of shamanic practice that adds yet more depth of meaning to these newly structured narratives.

In this book, I have suggested that there is the additional possibility that the redactors were deliberately writing a continuous narrative concealed behind the surface story, creating a mystical manuscript whose final form uses words to go beyond words, applying imagery, symbol, and metaphor to communicate the essentially nonverbal experience of Divine revelation.

Because many of the apparent inconsistencies vanish when we read the text metaphorically, I have even wondered if the redactors didn't always care that much about the literal reading. Perhaps they were focused instead on writing a more or less seamless text at the deeper, esoteric level without worrying too much about whether this left them with contradictions at the surface. Perhaps, they were even writing a hidden story for initiates, for we know that mystery cults existed throughout the ancient world, their knowledge passed on by word of mouth, concealed from outsiders. And we know for sure that such a tradition existed in Judaism later.

But what they had in mind doesn't, in reality, make much difference to us. For this book is following an ancient tradition that holds that the interpretations have as much weight as the original words (as will be outlined in the next chapter).

Revelation From Prehistory to Rome

The Torah is very old, some of it even deriving from oral traditions that belonged to a people attuned to living out in the open, using the stars as a clock and the sun as a compass, alert to changes in weather and the turn of seasons, aware of the characteristics and character of each plant and animal in their world. As best we know from nonliterate tribes that have been studied by modern anthropologists, the world for such peoples is alive with the presence of Divinity and is intrinsically sacred. In their world,[15] time is fluid, nonlinear, often cyclical; and ceremonial rituals and taboos re-enact what has happened in the mythological past, or have meaning at a cosmological level. In this shamanic worldview, nothing is simply what it looks like in the physical world.

Many of us today are drawn to shamanic traditions, particularly those of Native Americans. Yet the truths expressed by these traditions are not limited to shamanic cultures. While they are most clearly imbedded in the texture of everyday life in these societies, they are to various degrees what is experienced by the individual mystic, the practiced meditator, and the deeply and genuinely religious person caught up in the rituals and rites of his or her particular sect. Mircea Eliade, the scholar of comparative religion who is famous for his seminal works on shamanism, myth, symbol, and ritual, considers these experiences to belong to the general religious life of humanity, to all those he calls "religious man" as opposed to secular or "profane."[16]

But the religious, mystical, meditative, or shamanic experience—whatever we call it—is essentially nonrational and nonlogical; in fact, it is comfortable with what the intellect sees as paradox or inconsistency. Its sensibility is often uncomfortable for us, for we live in a world whose intellectual heritage has been shaped by the rationality of Greek civilization.

It is hard for us to grasp the feeling-tone of text that comes out of a time predating Athens, for we are imbedded in a rationalist and secular worldview, inherited essentially from the Greek philosophers (and further developed with the Renaissance and, later, the Age of Enlightenment). Our world assumes the value of linear thinking and logical analysis in all areas, including religion.

So we tend to be tone deaf when it comes to the archaic underpinnings in Torah. Moreover, these undertones were already becoming foreign to those who put the Torah into its final form, even before the ascendancy of Greek thought throughout the Middle East. For these editors did not belong to a nomadic people living under the desert sky, but to a people clinging to a precarious existence among large and powerful monarchies, struggling to retain their identity amidst the politics and armed conflicts of those around them.[17]

Conquered first by Assyria and then by Babylonia, their Temple was destroyed in 586 BCE[18] and their surviving ruling class exiled to Babylonia.[19] We don't know for certain if the Torah was completed before or after the return of the exiles, which began about fifty years later,[20,21] when King Cyrus of Persia succeeded his father and allowed the exiles to go home, reestablish their kingdom under Persia, and begin to build the Second Temple. The most recent scholarly opinion, however, suggests that the Torah was completed in the fifth century, around 450 BCE, considerably after King Cyrus' decree.[22]

But whenever it was done, the Israelites were influenced by their exile. For their life in exile was urban and worldly, exposed to many different traditions and religions as a result of the ongoing trade of objects and ideas throughout the Middle East and even into India. Most of the old teachings seemed archaic or did not take account of the loss of their kingdom and of the domination of the Assyrians, Babylonians, and Persians. The Israelites were struggling to put their traditions into a form that spoke to them as exiles and returnees, making the ancient teachings relevant to who they now were.

Most Jewish commentators assume that those who put the Five Books of Moses into final form were, in fact, deeply religious men. Some mystical Jewish traditions even claim that the Torah was edited into the book we know by a group of seers who were adept at spiritual practice. Many of them may indeed have been mystics, able, therefore, to discern hidden spiritual depths in the texts they were combining.

So the question remains: "What might the redactors of Torah have been trying to say when they rewove their traditions into the lives they were now leading, using the literary forms available to them? And what were they saying that modern, more rationalist scholars, imbedded in their own nonmystical worldviews, have missed? "

For whatever else Torah may be, it is, to believers, a record of a series of encounters with the Divine Presence, and it is permeated with that profound spiritual experience. Whether humans have distorted some of that experience or not in recording it, the text remains such a powerful guidebook because it is a testament to our enduring relationship with the Divine.

8

Making the Bible Relevant to Each Generation by Adding Oral Torah to the Written Text

Interpretation began with the long process of putting the Torah into final form, but it didn't end there. For there are actually two parts to Torah. The "Written Torah" generally refers only to the Five Books of Moses, while the "Oral Torah" refers to later commentaries about these books at the literal, metaphoric, allegorical, and mystical levels. In Judaism, the Oral and Written Torah are equally important, and Jews generally mean both when they refer simply to "Torah" or "Torah study." (In fact, many Orthodox Jews believe that the Oral Torah was given by G-d to Moses at Mount Sinai just as the Written Torah was.)

Although some Protestant sects read the Pentateuch literally, the Catholic Church and some Protestant churches read much of the text allegorically (although, generally, in terms of it prefiguring the coming of Jesus Christ or other Christian teachings); early Catholic teachings also made considerable use of interpretation. However, one of the main differences with Christianity is that *all* the major movements in Judaism have insisted that the Written Torah *must* be interpreted, because too much of it seems self-contradictory or obscure if we limit our reading to the surface of the text.

Furthermore, the laws given in Torah needed to be discussed and fleshed out in detailed case law even in ancient times; in the absence of interpretation, they could not adequately serve as the basis for justice in the community. Continuing interpretation was also needed to keep the text relevant as cultural perspectives shifted. For Greek thought penetrated society as the Jews continued to live in Israel and the rest of the Middle East. Many became assimilated first into Hellenistic and then Roman life. Others struggled to live in both the pagan and Jewish worlds simultaneously.

Then, in 70 CE, when the central Temple at Jerusalem was destroyed by Rome, much of Torah, with its detailed descriptions of sacrifices and ceremonies at the Temple, simply became irrelevant as it stood. In a brilliant move, Rabbi Johanan Ben Zakkai then ordained that G-d did not wish for animal sacrifice. What was really wanted, he said, was service to the Divine through prayer, study of Torah, and acts of loving-kindness.[1]

With this shift in devotional practice, a book, rather than cult rituals, became the centerpiece of the religion. Instead of focusing on a central Temple dedicated to priestly acts of sacrifice and ceremony in the service of the Divine, Judaism now focused on studying and contemplating the words of Torah, and on further interpreting these words in ways that made them spiritually relevant to the new problems and dilemmas being confronted.

Here the issue became less about uncovering hidden meaning than about interpreting text to match entirely new situations. Traditionally, the Oral Torah refers to two major groupings of these interpretations. The first is the *Mishnah,*[2] which was compiled around 200 CE by Rabbi Judah haNasi from oral teachings handed down by word of mouth for as long as six hundred and fifty years, from the fifth century BCE. The other is the *Gemarah,*[3] which is composed of some of what he left out, along with later commentary offered over the next three hundred years. Together, they make up the *Talmud,*[4] which exists in two slightly different versions—the Babylonian Talmud, which is later and more extensive, and the Palestinian.

Most Talmudic interpretation is about legal matters, because the Written Torah was the source of Jewish law. Like the judges of the United States Court of Appeals or Supreme Court, judges and lawgivers of the time often disagreed and wrote complex arguments to bolster their opinions of the meaning of a phrase or of the scope of a law. As they tried to make sense of what they read, they might also note how a line over here seemed to reverberate to a line over there; sometimes they even clarified what was obscure by adding a story to fill in the text. Their legal commentary and debates in the course of eight centuries became the core of the Talmud, and is called *Halakhah,* which means "walking," as in "walking the path."

However, other aspects of the Talmud expand on the written text in ways that are more emotive and mystical than legalistic. Many of these teachings are hidden in story and allegory that, together, are referred to as *Aggadah.*[5] Thus there are, for example, many stories about why Moses is reluctant to take leadership of the Israelites when G-d speaks to him at the burning bush: in some, he is unwilling to take precedence over his older brother Aaron, while in others, he does not want to fight Pharaoh because Pharaoh is his adoptive grandfather. In still others, Moses' reluctance is a mirror of our own ambivalence about opening up to G-d's voice, an ambivalence that is developed throughout the Torah. In all cases, the story, or *midrash,* makes its point through narration instead of intellectual argument.

Strict Jewish tradition restricts Oral Torah to the writings of the Talmud, but later commentaries are also considered indispensable. Some of the most famous include those of Rashi (twelfth century in France), Maimonides (eleventh century in Alexandria), the Kabbalists (fourteenth century in Palestine), and Hasidim (starting with the Baal Shem Tov in the eighteenth century in Lithuania). And in most Jewish tradition, all of these are part of Oral Torah.

In fact, central to much Jewish thought is the idea that each generation must reinterpret Torah for itself, so that its deepest teachings can be revealed with full relevance. What is rather recent is the idea that commentary can be made not only by scholars and rabbis but also by ordinary people. In most branches of current Judaism, anyone studying Torah is contributing to the Oral Torah with his or her comments and interpretations. The comments may never be known outside a small study group, but they are still Oral Torah. Each of us makes Torah our own in this way.

9

Jewish Meditation Practice in Overview

Every religious tradition that I know of offers a number of paths for those seeking to feel G-d's presence in their lives as real, direct experience. Since the destruction of the Second Temple by Rome in 70 CE,[1] traditional Judaism has offered three primary paths: prayer, acts of loving-kindness, and study of Torah. Building on teachings from as early as the fifth century BCE,[2] Rabbi Johanan ben Zakkai transformed Judaism forever in convincing Jews that they did not really need the Temple and its ritual sacrifices. Instead, he taught, the Divine Presence cared less about the sacrifices offered there than about the intent that lay behind the offering: to commit to a covenant with the Divine and to open oneself to G-d's presence.

It is worth noting that most, if not all, spiritual traditions would agree that prayer, loving-kindness, and study of spiritual texts[3] all provide doorways to the direct experience of the Divine. But it is also true that each of these paths to G-d can come to feel arid or even meaningless. Prayer as recited from a liturgical service may come to be a rote repetition of words that have little personal meaning, uttered without feeling or belief. Even acts of loving-kindness can become routine, performed not because the heart is the channel for G-d's compassion but because the will says it ought to be done. And study of spiritual texts, including Torah, can likewise become divorced from the heart, transformed into feats of intellectual prowess that are interesting, even powerful, but without the force of actual revelation.

Therefore, a fourth path exists in most traditions, both Western and non-Western, and in Judaism, too. This is the path of meditation: a straight line to the experience of Divine Presence.

For meditation is neither secondhand nor simply intellectual. While there may be periods of boredom in meditation practice (which certainly happen often enough), or distraction (which is more interesting than boredom, but hardly uplifting spiritually), there are other moments—which are always staggering in their impact—of opening to the awareness of the Divine.

Authenticity of Meditation Practice in Judaism

When I tell someone that I've been trained to teach Jewish meditation practice, the response is almost always, "Jewish meditation practice? I never heard of it." Sometimes, the comment is added, "It's New Age, right?"

In fact, meditation practice seems to have been part of Jewish spiritual life almost as long as there have been Israelites, although references to early practice are fragmentary or written long after the period in question. There is an often quoted allusion, in writings of the third century CE, to meditation practice being done five hundred years before, in the second century BCE. The allusion goes like this: "The Hasideans would be still one hour prior to each of the [three] prayer services, then pray for one hour and afterwards be still again for one hour."[4]

According to Aryeh Kaplan, there is another well-known allusion to meditation practice that existed yet earlier, before the time of the Babylonian exile in 586 BCE, near the height of classical Greece. In that reference, the Talmud even states that one million people were practitioners, although this sounds grossly exaggerated to the modern ear.[5]

As we move even further back in time, evidence is still more fragmentary, but there are what seem to be references in the Bible to ongoing meditation practices as far back as the time of King David (about three thousand years ago, around 1000 BCE), or at least at the time the Psalms were written.[6] And translations from the Hebrew seem to indicate acts of meditation practice in various places in Torah, even in Genesis, such as when "Isaac was meditating in the field."[7] But we do not know how these references relate to actual practice at any given time.

Still, we do know for certain that there have been a number of distinct branches of Jewish meditation practice, of which the three described below are probably the best known. The first, *Merkabah* mysticism, is rooted in ancient mystical studies thought to date from the time of the Second Temple, with the core text for these studies being Ezekiel's vision of the chariot.[8] By the second century CE, these studies had evolved into esoteric meditative practices that practitioners used in order to come near to G-d for perhaps a thousand years, until the ninth or tenth century CE.[9]

Revealed only to initiates who had sufficient moral qualities and certain physical attributes, *Merkabah* meditation involved the seeker's ascent to G-d,[10] as the Divine sat on the Throne-Chariot (i.e., the *Merkabah*) surrounded by the heavenly chorus of angels and cherubim. The process involved days of fasting, recitation of certain hymns and songs, and maintenance of a particular posture (with the head between the knees), all of which were designed to produce an altered state of consciousness. The journey itself progressed through seven levels of the heavenly domain, with its interior and chambers, such as those of a palace. The meditator obtained access to each successive level only after giving the correct magical words— which involved secret names of G-d—to the terrifying celestial gatekeepers on each side of the doorways. The secret names were progressively more complex and longer as the adept progressed through the levels, while his senses were assaulted by false and misleading perceptions; a mistake at any doorway would lead to his painful destruction. The visualizations, or guided meditations, were detailed and intense, with the goal to see for oneself the awesome Divine, G-d as king of the universe. In addition, the meditator could have one request granted by the Divine upon reaching the final chamber.

Although the practice was linked with magic and obtaining of magical powers, adepts understood the passage through the seven levels to be far more than a matter of reciting the correct ritual incantation (or having one's wish granted); instead, it involved progressively stricter purification of the soul. Thus, the saintly Rabbi Akiva (who was ultimately martyred by the Romans in the second century CE) was believed to have been able to make the ascent and return safely.[11] According to later writing, another adept was the Rabbi Johanan ben Zakkai himself,[12] the mystic who helped Judaism recreate itself after the destruction of the Second Temple two thousand years ago.

Ultimately, many of the concepts of *Merkabah* practice and belief were absorbed into Kabbalah as it arose in southern France and northern Spain in the twelfth and thirteenth centuries. A complex system of thought about the nature of G-d and our relationship to the Divine, Kabbalah is also the source of the second major branch of meditation in Judaism.

The first Kabbalistic techniques were created by Abraham Abulafia in the thirteenth century.[13] Calling for intense intellectual focus and the development of the capacity for concentration through constant practice, Abulafia's meditations involve permutations of the letters of the Hebrew alphabet; for these letters, in traditional belief, are the building blocks of creation, since G-d spoke the world into being. By chanting certain combinations of the letters (as well as specified words and phrases), and coupling the chants with particular head movements and control of the breath, practitioners could, Abulafia taught, reach an altered state of consciousness and the experience of the Divine Presence.[14] He even believed that his techniques led to prophesy.

In the sixteenth century, under Isaac Luria's seminal influence, Kabbalah provided a new way of thinking about G-d and the nature of the material world. In Luria's understanding, holy sparks of Divinity were scattered at the time of creation, in a primordial catastrophe that left the world at the mercy of evil from then on. Humans were to heal the world by gathering up these holy sparks and reuniting them with the Divine, not only through living lives of holiness based on Torah but through an intense meditation practice called *unification*.[15]

Luria's approach required strenuous spiritual preparation, including the elimination of anger and other negative emotions from the self, as well as the practice of purifying rituals and penitential acts. The meditations themselves were reminiscent of Abulafia's in that they involved complex permutations of different names of G-d and the letters composing these names.[16]

The third distinct category of meditative practices comes out of eighteenth century Hasidim, a branch of Judaism that was developed in Eastern Europe by the Baal Shem Tov (i.e., "Master of the Good Name"). In an era in which more purely intellectual approaches were dominant among traditional Jewish scholars, and with many of the Jews in Eastern Europe desperately poor and illiterate, the Baal Shem Tov wanted to reduce intellectual demands in Jewish religious practice and, instead, bring forward the heart. His approach emphasized the path of music and dancing, particularly the rhythmic humming of wordless melodies,[17] to create an altered state of consciousness that led to an ecstatic embrace of the Divine. One of his followers, Rabbi Nachman of Brazlav, also instituted a form of contemplative prayer done in isolation, a meditative technique of speaking aloud to G-d in a solitary place, pouring out one's heart to the Divine and awaiting a response, in a practice called *hitbodedut*.[18] This practice also required an hour spent in solitude to empty the mind of all but yearning for G-d before beginning to pour out one's heart.

However, most of the meditation practices in Judaism were not separated from the rest of religious observance and daily life. As Rabbi David Cooper has commented in the *Handbook of Jewish Meditation Practices:*

The essence of meditation is an integral part of traditional Jewish daily life, ritual, prayer, study of Torah, Talmud, and celebration of the Sabbath and the holy days. Indeed, meditation techniques are so fully integrated into traditional Jewish life that they were not separated out as unique practices of themselves.[19]

For traditional religious life in Judaism is rooted in the idea of constant communion with G-d, of always feeling G-d's presence as immanent in the world and even in oneself. This goes way beyond seeing the Divine as an awesome being on the throne of heaven; instead, it involves feelings of love as well as awe, and an awareness of attachment to G-d—what in Hebrew is known as *devekut.*

The practice of *devekut* goes back to the command in Deuteronomy 6:4-9, which became the opening of the central prayer of Judaism, the *Shema:*

Listen, Israel: *YHVH* is our G-d. *YHVH* is one. And you shall love *YHVH*, your G-d, with all your heart and with all your soul and with all your might. And these words that I command you today shall be on your heart. And you shall impart them to your children, and you shall speak about them when you sit in your house and when you go in the road and when you lie down and when you get up. And you shall bind them for a sign on your hand and they shall become bands between your eyes. And you shall write them on the doorposts of your house and in your gates.[20]

The goal is to be aware of the Divine Presence at each moment of waking life, from morning to night. And the effort to translate these words into practice in the centuries after the destruction of the Second Temple gradually led to an integrated lifestyle in which every instant became an opportunity for expansion of consciousness. For Judaism not only had thrice-daily prayer services, plus the Sabbath and other holy days to devote to G-d, but provided rules for every aspect of behavior at each moment, from the well-known laws about permissible foods and their preparation, to rules governing all aspects of interpersonal relationships and personal behavior. Rooted in Torah, these rules and commandments—along with required daily study of Torah—enveloped Jewish communities in a way of life designed to promote not only constant affirmation of the commitment to serve G-d, but a mystical state of consciousness involving constant awareness of G-d's presence. While it didn't always achieve this end, it was a life that is hard for most of us to imagine today in our fragmented and secular world.

And now, finally, we come back to the study of Torah as a way of opening to the Divine Presence. Because the Five Books of Moses are traditionally understood to be rooted in Divine revelation—YHVH's calling out to us—their study is absolutely central to Jewish spiritual life. (Although as stated earlier, it has always been understood that the words need to be interpreted, that they cannot just be taken literally.)[21] But there is more.

For study goes beyond intellectual work to contemplative practice, in which the language of the Five Books of Moses permeates the being of the meditator so that the voice of G-d may come through from behind the words, providing a direct experience of the Divine.

Such contemplative study is so basic that it has always been part of Judaism.

In this understanding, focus on Torah is the way to G-d, and so the words of Torah are to constantly fill the mind, even when one is not sitting down to formal study. Torah becomes the ever-present context within which daily life transpires. When study does take place, it is done with a devotional attitude and an opening of the heart. Set times should be dedicated to it, and a particular place set aside; one traditionally prepares for study through prayer, confession of sins, and emptying the mind of all but yearning to serve the Divine and cleave to the Divine Presence. Above all, one opens the heart so as to see more than what the intellect alone can apprehend.

The great twelfth century scholar and expounder of Torah, Moses Maimonides, is generally portrayed to us as a rationalist, but he was, in fact, a mystic who thought he had achieved the lower levels of prophesy through his contemplative study of Torah. He writes:

> … cause your soul, whenever you read or listen to the Torah, to be constantly directed—the whole of you and your thought—toward reflection on what you are listening to or reading. When this too has been practiced consistently for a certain time, cause your soul to be in such a way that your thought is always quite free of distraction and gives heed to all that you are reading … so that you aim at meditating on what you are uttering and at considering its meaning.[22]

Why Jewish Meditation is so Unfamiliar

Although meditation has been part of Judaism for millennia, the tradition has always been fearful of encouraging people to seek direct experience of G-d except as part of communal prayer and communal life. For in traditional understanding, the Divine is too powerful and too overwhelming for most human minds to approach one on one. Moreover, what people come back with can be dangerous. After all, we can believe that G-d has told us to kill the infidel without mercy, even for the sake of saving his soul. We can believe that we are called up to martyr ourselves, and even our children, in the name of religion. We may even believe that G-d tells us to take a shotgun and kill our neighbors—or family. (Some readers may think of the story of Abraham at this point.)

The issue is real. How do we know that what we experience as Divine Presence is accurate? How do we know it can be trusted? Too much evil has been done worldwide in the name of religion—everyone's religion.

For these reasons, Judaism has always hedged specific meditation techniques with strictures: they should be taught only to those already immersed in Torah study, in ethical practice, and in self-reflection. One should always have a reputable teacher, one should never violate the Ten Commandments, and one should be imbedded in the community.

Because the teaching of such techniques was restricted to a more or less select group—and carefully kept secret from outsiders—the instructions were often not written down, but remained dependent on a living chain of teachers and students through the centuries. Thus, many of these practices never reached a wider audience. And we, as Americans, are not likely to have heard of those that were in fact put into writing. Most documents have been lost anyway, in various periods of persecution or chaos, or simply in the natural course of history. Many others are still in museums and libraries in old scripts that are hard to read even once located—and even those published have often not been translated into English. Moreover, after the middle of the eighteenth century—the Age of Enlightenment— Judaism wanted to appear more Western and rational. As a result, almost all references to meditation disappeared from mainstream Judaism, even among the Hasidic writers for whom it was so recent and central, and even in Kabbalistic works published after 1840.[23] Finally, we have the decimation of Judaism in the Holocaust, with the death of about half the Jews in the world and the destruction of almost all the traditional Jewish communities of Europe, along with their rabbis and teachers.

That is all changing today, for meditation practices have become an overt part of Jewish practice, although still in a limited way, in the last thirty years. A generation of teachers who were hungry for spiritual pathways began to explore Eastern meditation practices in the 1960s and 1970s. As they brought these teachings back to Judaism, they mingled them—particularly Buddhist and Sufi practices—with still extant Jewish traditions, including some from surviving and even resurgent Hasidic communities. Meanwhile, Aryah Kaplan reintroduced the Jewish world to its own ancient, meditative approaches in his 1978 book, *Meditation and the Bible*. And here we are.

Basic Varieties of Meditation

There are only a few basic forms of meditation practice. One is *focused meditation,* in which all of one's attention is fixed on a single something, which fills all of the mind's space. The something can be a word, a phrase, a chant, a dance movement, the breath. As one practices such focus, everything else disappears from awareness, and there may be an experience of deep relaxation as well as a sense of safety. With enough practice over time, the initial focus of concentration may vanish, leaving only an experience of spacious emptiness and Divine Presence, which is impossible for me to convey in words.

We generally think of meditation as a sitting tradition, in which we hold our bodies still, remaining in one position. In fact, the meditation period is often called a *sit*. But many of us cannot begin with sitting practice. Our minds just go all over the place once we force our bodies to be quiet. If you find you are one of those who can't settle down if you sit, you might try what is called *walking meditation*. In this practice, you walk very, very slowly, taking small steps and focusing your attention on the feeling within your feet and legs as you shift your weight from one foot to the other, moving forward.

It is also possible to meditate simply by focusing awareness on the sensations of the body. This approach, which is sometimes called *mindfulness meditation,* is particularly useful for simple tasks like cleaning, peeling vegetables, or gardening. This kind of focus can also be turned on when waiting in line at a store, for an elevator, or for a friend at a restaurant. The practice is to focus simply on sensation, bringing oneself fully into the present moment without ideas about ways the moment ought to be better or different—just simply being present to what *is*. As earlier parts of this book indicate, this goal of bringing oneself into the moment without judgment or thoughts is one of the ways to approach the Divine and open oneself to the presence of G-d.

Focused meditation is often the easiest way to begin. But another basic approach is through what is called *awareness meditation,* in which one opens wide the lens of attention, without focusing on anything in particular. As one sits in silence, with the eyes closed, awareness can simply open to whatever is happening from moment to moment. As with mindfulness meditation, one can be aware of sounds or smells or other sensations, or of whatever else impinges on consciousness. Most often, this meditation goes to thought, image, and feeling, registering the mental experience without hanging on to it. When awareness is turned toward the mind's contents in this way over many meditation sessions, we gradually begin to separate our experience of self—of our essence—from the clutter of everyday consciousness.[24]

While the practices of awareness and mindfulness have become the most well-known forms of meditation in the United States, a third kind of practice is central to Judaism: contemplation.[25] As stated earlier, this calls for focusing all attention on an idea or concept, usually taken from the Bible or the prayer service, so that it fills the mind to the exclusion of all else. However, we don't *think* about the idea or concept. We let it hover in our awareness as our consciousness circles around and around it. Images may arise about the concept, or thoughts; but we observe them and let them go while continuing to maintain focus. As with the other kinds of meditation, the mind may eventually become empty of all but the awareness of Divine Presence.

We have been doing all three kinds of meditation in the formal practice offered in this book, but contemplative meditation on a particular section of the Torah has been our chief approach.

10

A Final Personal Comment

With each reading, I am more stunned by the wisdom and depth of the Five Books of Moses, and by the relevance of its teachings for each day, even each hour, of my life. Many of my friends and acquaintances have told me that I've changed markedly in the course of working with it these last years, becoming more open, warmer, calmer, less critical, and more spontaneous. As is always the case, the hardest work has been in my most intimate relationships; but even here, the changes are striking.

I'm also aware that my sense of who I am has altered: in fact, there is no one being inside my head who is "me." Instead of a single entity, that "me" seems to be an uneven collection of mood states, preferences, and habits of feeling and behaving. Sometimes one dominates, sometimes another, and some states of being occur more often than others. The specific combinations of states are what seem to characterize me as an individual, but I don't feel defined by any one of them. And somehow, this awareness frees me from being bogged down in self-defensiveness.

With this awareness has come another experience—that of seeing this shape-shifting "me" imbedded in a process that spans all of space-time. I am a kind of impermanent concentration of energy and mass that can be located in this moment at this location, but I will pass like every other such concentration, whether human or dinosaur. Nothing persists, and, somehow, quite mysteriously, that is all right.

At the same time, I am aware of some component in myself that does seem both permanent and at the core of what I call "me." It is the component that observes and notices the shape-shifting, and it seems to be genderless and simply aware. When I really pay attention, it seems to be an intimation of G-d, my own limited awareness of the infinite awareness of the Divine Presence within my own being.

Apparently, this awareness goes deep. For about half of 2011, I had a devastating illness requiring multiple hospitalizations. At one point, I was unable to move even to ring for a nurse because the slightest movement caused unbearable pain. The doctors could not agree on a diagnosis or predict what was going to happen next, but worst of all was my total helplessness as I lay there. To my amazement, I remained rather calm throughout the experience, feeling myself in the presence of something larger than myself that I can only call G-d, as I kept repeating the meditation that goes *Adonai li, lo eerah,* which means "G-d is with me, I shall not fear."

Nothing of the physical world persists, and at the same time, nothing of this world exists in isolation. All is imbedded in the flow of time, all connected in one space across the universe, and all a manifestation of G-d. And when I pay attention, everything I look at pulses with life and sensuality, even the supposedly inanimate rock. Everything shimmers with radiance, with glory.

Everything and everyone is holy.

I am intensely grateful for these years spent immersed in studying the Five Books of Moses. I wish for you the perception of this glory and holiness as you follow your own spiritual path to the Edenic Garden Within.

Appendix A

Instructions for a Body Scan

This is a technique to induce some degree of relaxation and release from distractions. As it becomes habitual to meditation practice, it can, by itself, begin to induce an altered state of consciousness that involves a relaxed focus on the inner experience. The whole exercise need take no more than five minutes.

Begin by shutting your eyes and paying attention to your breath. Just notice your breath going in and out.

When you are ready, let your awareness move to the top of your head. Notice any sensation there.

Breathe.

Let your awareness move to your forehead. Notice any sensation there and relax whatever tension you can.

And breathe.

Now let your awareness move to the muscles around your eyes. Notice any sensation there and relax whatever tension you can.

And breathe.

Let your awareness move to the muscles around your mouth. Notice any tension there and relax what you can.

And breathe.

Let your awareness move to the muscles at your jaw. Notice any tension there and relax what you can.

And breathe.

If you pay attention, you may even notice tension at the root of your tongue. Relax what you can.

Breathe.

After a while, notice any tension in your neck. If you can, stretch so as to release tension there.

Breathe.

Now let your awareness move down your arms. Into your elbows. Your forearms. Your hands. Wiggle your fingers for a moment.

Breathe.

Let your awareness move into your shoulders. Notice any tension or tightness there. If you can, shrug to help release some of the tightness.

Breathe.

Let your awareness move to between your shoulder blades. If you feel able, stretch to release some of the tension there.

And breathe.

After a while, notice tension as you move down your back, releasing what you can as you move into your middle back and then your lower back.

Breathe.

Notice your bottom against the chair.

And breathe.

After a while, let your awareness move down your legs. Past your thighs. Past your knees. Past your calves and shins. Past your ankles. Into your feet. Wiggle your toes for a moment.

And breathe.

Notice your breath going in and out.

Now, however you see it, imagine yourself opening a space at the top of your head to the level of your forehead, to let energy flow in.

And breathe.

Now open that space further, to the level of your throat, to let the energy flow down to there as well, however you imagine this. Notice any release of tension in your throat as you do this.

And breathe.

When you are ready, open the space to the level of your heart, to let the energy flow down to there, however you imagine this. Notice any release of tension.

And breathe.

Now open the space to the level of your belly to let the energy flow down to there, however you imagine. Notice any release of tension as you do.

And breathe.

Finally, open the space to the level of your groin to let the energy flow down to there and then out, however you imagine this. Let the energy that comes in with your breath mix with the cells of your body before flowing out to rejoin the rest of the universe. Let it flow into you, mixing with the cells of your body and then flowing out.

Breathe.

Just notice your breath going in and out.

And when you are ready, begin the meditation for the *parshah* you've chosen.

Appendix B

Visualization of the Hebrew Letters *yud, heh, vuv,* and *heh* for Meditation Practice

As you look at each letter, try to see it as clearly as you can. Trace its outline in your mind, feeling its height and width, feeling the way it holds itself on the page. Close your eyes and see if you can trace it in your mind's eye. Once you can do this, you can meditate without looking at the page. But you can begin the meditation even if you need to look at the page.

Now, begin the meditation practice by inhaling as you picture the *yud,* exhaling on the *heh,* inhaling on the *vuv,* and exhaling on the *heh.*

You may recite the names of the letters as you go, if this makes it easier. But if you can, let go of naming to simply see each letter in your mind's eye as you breathe in and out: *yud* as you inhale, *heh* as you exhale, *vuv* as you inhale, and *heh* as you exhale. If you use this meditation often, you will eventually be able to see each letter clearly and even place it on yourself or people or objects around you, to see YHVH permeating all of you.

Hebrew Letters for the *Yud-Heh-Vuv-Heh* Meditation
(Written from right to left)

Hebrew Calligraphy from *The Book of Letters* by Lawrence Kushner
Woodstock, Vermont: Jewish Lights, 1990.

Appendix C

Glossary

B'midbar. Translates as "In the wilderness" and refers to the third book of the Hebrew Bible, known in English as Numbers.

B'reishit. Translates as "In the beginning" and refers to the first book of the Hebrew Bible, known in English as Genesis.

D'varim. Translates as "Words" and refers to the fifth book of the Hebrew Bible, known in English as Deuteronomy.

Garden Within. This term refers to the state of mind in which we reach deep inside ourselves to find the Mystery that we call G-d. The reference alludes to the Garden of Eden, in which humans lived with G-d at all times.

Kadosh. Holy.

Kavod. G-d's glory; also, a characteristic of G-d that we can perceive.

Klippot. The internal obstacles we must overcome once we have committed ourselves to the spiritual path. In metaphor, they cluster around the Divine spark at the center of our being, hiding it from our view.

Mishkan. The Sanctuary, or the holy building where G-d somehow dwells (even though G-d is also unbounded by time or space). In the desert, the *mishkan* was a portable structure; later, it was part of the First Temple, built by Solomon, and then part of the Second Temple. In more mystical understanding, the *mishkan* is also found deep within each one of us.

Mitzrayim. At the surface level, this is the word for Egypt, but it means "the place of constriction, the narrow straits." Therefore, in metaphoric interpretations of Torah for more than two millennia, *Mitzrayim* refers to a state in which our spirit is constricted, in which our narrowness of vision leads us to be trapped in our habitual fears and desires.

Parshah (plural *parshot*). The division of the Torah/Pentateuch into fifty-four sections, which are traditionally read in sequence in synagogues, one each week (with some doubling up).

P'shat. A literal reading of the Torah. In traditional teachings, this is also the simple level, appropriate for children.

The Promised Land. At the literal level, this is the land of Canaan, which G-d has promised to the Israelites. At the metaphoric level, it is the state of mind that we call enlightenment.

Shema. The central prayer of Judaism, which begins with the words "Listen O Israel, You must love G-d with all your heart and all your soul and all your will." *Shema* translates as "Listen."

Sh'mot. Translates as "Names" and refers to the second book of the Hebrew Bible, known in English as Exodus.

Vayikra. Translates as "And [G-d] called" and refers to the third book of the Hebrew Bible, known in English as Leviticus.

Yisrael. Translates as "G-d wrestler." It is the name that Jacob is given after wrestling with the man/angel/G-d, and then the name given to his descendants. In recent years, Rabbi Arthur Waskow has also generalized the name to anyone who wrestles with G-d.

Appendix D

Bibliography

Alter, Robert. *The Five Books of Moses: A Translation with Commentary.* New York: W. W. Norton, 2004.

Ariel, David S. *The Mystic Quest.* Paperback Edition. New York: Schocken Books, 1992.

Armstrong, Karen. *The Great Transformation: The Beginning of our Religious Traditions.* New York: Alfred Knopf, 2006.

Cooper, Rabbi David A. *The Handbook of Jewish Meditation Practices: A Guide to Enriching the Sabbath and Other Days of Your Life.* Woodstock, Vermont: Jewish Lights, 2000.

_____ *God as a Verb: Kabbalah and the Practice of Mystical Judaism.* Paperback Edition. New York: Riverhead Books, 1997.

_____ *Ecstatic Kabbalah.* Sounds True, 1995.

Douglas, Mary. *Leviticus as Literature.* Paperback Edition. Oxford: University Press, 2000.

_____ *In the Wilderness: The Doctrine of Defilement in the Book of Numbers.* Oxford: University Press, 2001.

Efros, Israel L. *Ancient Jewish Philosophy.* Paperback Edition. New York: Block, 1976.

Eliade, Mircea. *The Sacred and the Profane: The Nature of Religion,* trans. Willard R. Trask. Paperback Edition. San Diego: Harcourt, 1987.

Epstein, Mark. *Thoughts without a Thinker: Psychotherapy from a Buddhist Point of View.* Paperback Edition. New York: Basic Books, 1995.

Friedman, Richard Elliott. *Commentary on the Torah with a New English Translation and the Hebrew Text.* Paperback Edition. New York: HarperCollins, 2003.

Gefen, Nan Fink, *Discovering Jewish Meditation: Instruction & Guidance for Learning an Ancient Spiritual Practice.* Woodstock, Vermont: Jewish Lights, 1999.

Gold, Rabbi Shefa. *Torah Journeys: The Inner Path to the Promised Land.* Teaneck, New Jersey: Ben Yehuda Press, 2006.

Jacobs, Louis, Ed. *The Schocken Book of Jewish Mystical Testimonies,* 2nd Edition. New York: Schocken Books, 1996.

Kaplan, Aryeh. *Meditation and the Bible.* Paperback Edition. York Beach, Maine: Samuel Weiser, 1988.

_____ *Jewish Meditation: A Practical Guide.* Paperback Edition. New York: Shocken Books, 1985.

Kugel, James L. *The Bible As It Was.* Cambridge: Belknap Press/Harvard University Press, 1997.

_____ *How to Read the Bible: A Guide to Scripture, Then and Now.* Paperback Edition. New York: Free Press/Simon & Schuster, 2008

Kushner, Lawrence, *The Book of Letters.* Woodstock, Vermont: Jewish Lights, 1990.

Matt, Daniel. *God and the Big Bang: Discovering Harmony Between Science and Spirituality.* Paperback, 4th Edition. Woodstock, Vermont: Jewish Lights, 2006.

Milgram, Jacob. *Leviticus: A Book of Ritual and Ethics, A Continental Commentary.* Minneapolis: Augsburg Fortress, 2004.

Plaut, W. Gunther, ed. *The Torah: A Modern Commentary.* Revised Edition. New York: URJ Press, 2005.

Sholem, Gershom G. *Major Trends in Jewish Mysticism.* Paperback Edition. New York: Schocken Books, 1961.

Van Der Toorn. *Scribal Culture and the Making of the Hebrew Bible.* Paperback Edition. Cambridge: Harvard University Press, 2007.

Verman, Mark. *The History and Varieties of Jewish Meditation.* Northvale, New Jersey: Jason Aronson, 1996.

Zornberg, Aviva Gottlieb. *The Beginnings of Desire: Reflections on Genesis.* New York: Image/Doubleday, 1996.

_____ *The Particulars of Reason: Reflections on Exodus.* Paperback Edition. New York: Image/Doubleday, 2002.

Endnotes

Introduction

1. For ease of reading, I will, at times, refer to the Torah as the Bible, for it is that part of the Bible that is the focus of this book. I will also use the word *Torah* rather than *Pentateuch* most of the time.

2. The term *Common Era* is abbreviated as CE when used with dates, such as 70 CE, and it is equivalent to AD.

3. Sixteen of the fifty-four sections are grouped into eight "pairs," which can be combined as needed to match the number of weeks in that year. (The lunar month is 29.5 days, and the Jewish year usually has twelve lunar months, or 354 days, which makes for 50 weeks. To match the solar calendar of 365.24 days, leap months are added as needed.)

4. Actually, the more accurate translation is "In the beginning of," which translation plays a significant role in Kabbalistic interpretations of the text.

5. Richard Elliott Friedman, *Commentary on the Torah with a New English Translation and the Hebrew Text,* Paperback Edition (New York: HarperCollins, 2003).

6. W. Gunther Plaut, ed. *The Torah: A Modern Commentary*, Revised Edition (New York: URJ Press, 2005). All rights reserved.

7. Karen Armstrong, *The Great Transformation: The Beginning of our Religious Traditions* (New York: Alfred Knopf, 2006).

8. From http://www.torahjourneys.com referred to in n. 8. I also checked in regularly with http://torah.org and http:chabad.org. Both of these sites have numerous interpretations for each *parshah*.

9. Friedman, *Commentary on the Torah*; Plaut, ed. *The Torah: A Modern Commentary;* Robert Alter, *The Five Books of Moses: A Translation with Commentary* (New York: W. W. Norton, 2004). When taking translations of quotes, I have chosen

translations that seemed to best convey the feeling tone I want. The English titles of each *parshah* all come from Friedman, *Commentary on the Torah.*

10. Aviva Gottlieb Zornberg, *The Beginnings of Desire: Reflections on Genesis* (New York: Image/Doubleday, 1996); Zornberg, *The Particulars of Reason: Reflections on Exodus,* Paperback Edition (New York: Image/Doubleday, 2002); Mary Douglas, *Leviticus as Literature,* Paperback Edition (Oxford: University Press, 2000); Douglas, *In the Wilderness: The Doctrine of Defilement in the Book of Numbers* (Oxford: University Press, 2001); Jacob Milgram, *Leviticus: A Book of Ritual and Ethics, A Continental Commentary* (Minneapolis: Augsburg Fortress, 2004).

11. Rabbi Shefa Gold at her website http://www.torahjourneys.com (which was later published as *Torah Journeys: The Inner Path to the Promised Land* (Teaneck, New Jersey: Ben Yehuda Press, 2006).

Chapter 1. Genesis/*B'reishit*

General Framework of Genesis/*B'reishit*

1. Gen. 4:9, Alter, *The Five Books of Moses.*
2. Gen. 1:27, Ibid.
3. Gen. 2:15. In Hebrew, the word is *leshamrah.* It has often been translated as "keep" rather than "guard."
4. The story of G-d's command to Abraham to sacrifice his son, Isaac, will be discussed in this context.

Gen. 1, "In the Beginning"/*B'reishit*

1. Gen. 4:3, Plaut, *The Torah: A Modern Commentary.*
2. Gen. 4:4, Ibid.
3. Gen. 4:9, Alter, *The Five Books of Moses.*
4. Gen. 3:9, Ibid.

Gen. 2, "Noah"/Noach

1. Gen. 6:9, Friedman, *Commentary on the Torah.*
2. Gen. 8:21 Alter, *The Five Books of Moses.*
3. The text also gives humans dominion over all the animals and allows them to eat meat, which seems not to have been the case in the Garden of Eden (but the new rules still forbid humans to consume an animal's blood). Eventually, the text was enormously elaborated by the rabbis into what is known as the Noachide rules of behavior. In Judaism, the Noachide rules are believed to apply to all humans, everywhere.

4. The text says that Ham "saw his father's nakedness" (Gen. 9:22), which is sometimes a Biblical euphemism for sexual relations. Since Ham is the purported ancestor of the Egyptians, and his son of the Canaanites, this appears to be a subtle polemic against Israel's enemies, as descendants of perverts. But the story is confusing. See Plaut, *The Torah: A Modern Commentary,* p. 74. See also, Alter, *The Five Books of Moses,* n. 20–27, pp. 52–53.

5. Gen. 1:31, Friedman, *Commentary on the Torah.*

Gen. 3, "Go"/*Lech L'cha*

1. Gen. 12:1, Friedman, *Commentary on the Torah.*

2. It is here that Melchizedek the priest of "God Most High" blesses Abram in Gen. 14:18–20; Plaut, *The Torah: A Modern Commentary.*

3. Ibid. See n. 15:10, p. 98. Also, see Friedman, *Commentary on the Torah,* n. 15:10, p. 57.

4. When Hagar is given to Abraham, she is called his wife in the Hebrew, just as is Sarai. However, her status in regard to Sarai does not change; the Hebrew is clear that she is Sarai's slave girl. See Plaut, *The Torah: A Modern Commentary,* n. 16:3, p. 99.

5. Gen. 16:6, Ibid.

6. Gen. 16:6, Friedman, *Commentary on the Torah.* YHVH has just referred to the future Egyptian slavery of Abraham's descendants. Now we have an ironic echo of that slavery in the mistreatment of Hagar. Not only is she referred to as both Egyptian and a slave, but the language used is the same as that in the story of Israel's enslavement in Egypt: "Egypt degraded them" (Exod. 1:12), and "they fled" (Exod. 14:5). And note that, like Israel, Hagar is fleeing to the "*wilderness*" (Gen. 16:7, 8). Emphasis is Friedman's, n. 16:6, p. 59.

7. G-d appears under the name of *El Shaddai,* the meaning of which is in dispute, although all agree that it is an ancient name. It is sometimes said to derive from the Akkadian word for mountain, and thus to an ancient mountain god. One translation that I like, which I've heard from Rabbi Arthur Waskow, is that it refers to breasts, which in Hebrew are *shaddayim.* This translation takes us back to the era of the earth goddess, known throughout the Middle East and predating the patriarchal religions (Lecture, Woodstock Jewish Congregation, 2011).

8. The phrase *G-d as verb* owes a debt to the seminal book by Rabbi David Cooper, *God is a Verb: Kabbalah and the Practice of Mystical Judaism,* Paperback Edition (New York: Riverhead Books, 1997).

Gen. 4, "And G-d Appeared"/*Vayeira*

1. Friedman, *Commentary on the Torah*. Friedman actually writes, "And He Appeared," which is implicit in the Hebrew. Since I am avoiding the word *He* in reference to the Divine Presence, I've substituted the word *G-d*. I will do the same throughout this book.

2. The oaks of Mamre appear to refer to an ancient sacred site, as does the Oak of Moreh where Abram builds an altar immediately after starting on his journey in the last *parshah*.

3. Gen. 18:19, Plaut, *The Torah: A Modern Commentary*.

4. At the other extreme, Friedman, a modern interpreter, sees it as an example of Middle Eastern negotiation, in which the offer is never intended to be taken seriously. See *Commentary on the Torah*, n. 19:8, pp. 66–7.

5. Gen. 19:31, Friedman, *Commentary on the Torah*.

6. Gen. 21:10, Plaut, *The Torah: A Modern Commentary*.

7. Gen. 21:22, Ibid.

8. Gen. 22:1, Ibid.

9. Gen. 18:23, Ibid.

10. In fact, Abraham's concern seems to be for Ishmael alone.

11. Gen. 22:2, Plaut: *The Torah: A Modern Commentary*.

Gen. 5, "Sarah's Life"/*Chayei Sarah*

1. This is the relationship described in the text. So she is Abraham's great-niece through her father, Bethuel, who is Abraham's nephew, the son of Abraham's brother Nahor. But Rebecca's father is also related to Abraham's other brother, Haran, through his mother Milkah, Haran's daughter and thus, Abraham's niece. So Bethual is his great-nephew as well as his nephew, and Rebecca his great-great-niece.

2. Gen. 24:63, Friedman, *Commentary on the Torah*.

3. Gen. 24:67, Alter, *The Five Books of Moses*.

4. Indeed, these descendants were to become the semi-nomads of the trans-Jordan region and the Arabian peninsula. See p. 127, n. 1, Ibid.

5. Some commentators have argued that Keturah is actually another name for Hagar, with Abraham coming back to her after Sarah's death. See Plaut, *The Torah: A Modern Commentary*, n. 25:1 with citation, pp. 161–2.

6. Abraham is sending them away with gifts to ensure Isaac's inheritance. Ibid, n. 25:5–6, p. 162.

7. The text adds that Isaac is then blessed by G-d and goes to live at the site of the well where Hagar was told that she would give birth to Ishmael, perhaps hinting at further reconciliation of the half-brothers.

8. Ishmael's story is somewhat different because G-d reassures Abraham of his safety—but still, from Ishmael's perspective, he is sent away to die by his father.

Gen. 6, "Records"/*Tol'dot*

1. Friedman disagrees with this translation, saying that it is utterly ambiguous which of the brothers shall serve the other. *Commentary on the Torah*, n. 25:23, p. 88.
2. Gen. 25:27, Ibid.
3. Gen. 25:27, Ibid.
4. The birthright would have included the family name and titles, the bulk of the inheritance, and the position of the family leader upon the death of the father.
5. At the literal level, he is doing this because Abimelech's people stopped up the wells in their jealousy of his prosperity. At the metaphoric, the text seems to be stressing Isaac's inability to create a full existence for himself.
6. Gen. 26:28, Friedman, *Commentary on the Torah*. The emphasis is Friedman's.
7. Gen. 26:35, Ibid.
8. Gen. 27:19, Plaut, *The Torah: A Modern Commentary*.
9. Gen. 27:37, Freidman, *Commentary on the Torah*.
10. Gen. 27:38, Friedman, *Commentary on the Torah*.
11. See also Aviva Zomberg, *The Beginnings of Desire: Reflections on Genesis*, Paperback Edition (Image/Doubleday, 1996), pp. 144–79.
12. Gen. 27:19, Plaut, *The Torah: A Modern Commentary*.
13. Gen. 25:23, Ibid.

Gen. 7, "And He Left"/*Vayeitzei*

1. Gen. 28:12, Friedman, *Commentary on the Torah*.
2. Gen. 28:13, Ibid.
3. Gen. 28:14, Plaut: *The Torah: A Modern Commentary*.
4. Gen. 28:16, Alter, *The Five Books of Moses*.
5. Gen. 28: 21, Ibid.
6. Gen. 29:2, Friedman, *Commentary on the Torah*.
7. Gen. 29:25, Ibid.
8. See Plaut, *The Torah: A Modern Commentary*, n. 30:3, p. 199.
9. Gen. 31:11, Friedman, *Commentary on the Torah*.
10. These figurines, called *teraphim*, are thought to refer to some kind of household worship related to ancestors, common throughout the Middle East at the time.
11. Gen. 28:16, Alter, *The Five Books of Moses*.

Gen. 8, "And He Sent"/ *Vayishlach*

1. The children of Israel are the descendants of Jacob, whose other name is Israel or "G-d wrestler." Jacob gets the name of Israel after he spends the night wrestling with a man/angel. But angels in Torah have no separate identity; they are understood to be temporary manifestations of G-d. So when the text is understood as saying that Jacob wrestles with an angel, traditional commentators understand that to mean "G-d wrestling." Some commentators, however, have felt the being is to be understood not as an angel but as a demon or spirit of Esau, or as an externalization of all that Jacob contends with within himself. See Alter, *The Five Books of Moses*, n. 27, p. 180.

2. Gen. 32:29, Plaut, *The Torah: A Modern Commentary*.

3. Gen. 32:31, Ibid. Emphasis is by Plaut.

4. Gen. 33:1, Friedman, *Commentary on the Torah*.

5. Gen. 33:9, Ibid.

6. Gen. 33:10, Ibid.

7. Gen. 33:11, Ibid.

8. There have been many efforts to explain this story by later commentators. See, for example, James L. Kugel, *The Bible As It Was* (Cambridge: Belknap Press/ Harvard University Press, 1997), pp. 233–244 for ancient commentary. More modern Biblical scholars also believe that the story may involve insertion of a tale that originally had nothing to do with Jacob in order to explain Jacob's later condemnation of Reuben and Levi. James L. Kugel, *How to Read the Bible: A Guide to Scripture, Then and Now*, Paperback Edition (New York: Free Press/ Simon & Schuster, 2008), pp. 169–175.

9. These may be figurines captured from Shechem, but they may also belong to members of Jacob's household, like the figurines taken by Rachel from Laban's house.

10. The brother of his mother Rebecca.

11. It seems worth noting that he continues to be called by his old name of Jacob despite having been given the new name of Israel, as if he's not really ready to take on this new identity.

12. Gen. 33:11, Friedman, *Commentary on the Torah*.

Gen. 9, "And He Lived"/*Vayeishev*

1. The translation of the first line of the *parshah* comes from Plaut, *The Torah: A Modern Commentary*.

2. Gen. 37:9, Ibid.

3. Gen. 37:14, Ibid. This is the word Jacob used for himself after he had the vision of angels climbing up and down the ladder to the heavens, when he agreed to make YHVH his G-d only if his journey ended with him *shalom*.

4. Gen. 37:13, Ibid.

5. Gen. 37:15, Ibid.

6. Gen. 37:27, Alter, *The Five Books of Moses*.

7. Gen. 38:9, Plaut, *The Torah: A Modern Commentary*.

8. This story is the source of the misunderstood "sin of Onanism." The issue is that he refuses to produce a child who would be his brother's legal heir, maintaining his brother's line through his widow. According to Alter, his action actually refers to *coitus interruptus* rather than masturbation. See *The Five Books of Moses*, n. 8, 9, p. 215.

9. Judah plays a major role in the Joseph story, appearing as an extraordinarily compassionate man as well as a just one. As the ancestral father of the line of King David through Tamar, he is also in the line of descent to the messiah in both Jewish and Christian belief. His importance to the Joseph saga may also play a political purpose, since it is his tribe that ruled the southern kingdom of Israel while it was Joseph's (through his son Ephraim) that ruled the northern. It should also be noted that the word *messiah* connotes Jesus Christ to the modern reader; but the Hebrew word for messiah is *mashiach,* which does not have the same meaning of a savior. In Jewish tradition, the *mashiach* is a charismatic leader, but human.

10. Gen. 39:2, Friedman, *Commentary on the Torah*.

11. Gen. 40:15, Ibid.

12. Gen. 40:15, Ibid.

13. See Zornberg, *The Beginnings of Desire,* pp. 263–276.

14. We are reading this chapter at the darkest time of the year (at least in the hemisphere in which the story arose), and Jews are reading it at the time of the holiday of Hanukah, with its parallels to Joseph's story. For it, too, commemorates the experience of apparent hopelessness, of darkness much like Joseph's, which is followed by change.

Gen. 10, "At the End"/*Mikeitz*

1. The translation of the first line of the *parshah* comes from Plaut, *The Torah: A Modern Commentary*.

2. Gen. 41:38, Ibid.

3. The text says she is the daughter of Poti-phera, priest of On. Joseph marries the daughter of a foreign priest, just as Moses does later, in Exodus.

4. Gen. 41:51, Emphasis is Plaut's, *The Torah: A Modern Commentary*.

5. Gen. 41:52, Ibid. Emphasis is Plaut's.
6. Gen. 42:4, Ibid.
7. Gen. 42:6, Friedman, *Commentary on the Torah.*
8. Gen. 42:13, Ibid.
9. Gen. 42:22, Ibid.
10. Gen. 43:29, Ibid.
11. Gen. 44:16, Ibid.
12. Another reason given by these traditional commentators was that Joseph was merely obeying G-d's will in waiting to reveal himself. Kugel, *The Bible As It Was,* pp. 265–9.

Gen. 11, "And He Went Over"/*Vayigash*

1. As Pharaoh's second in command.
2. Gen. 45:27, Friedman, *Commentary on the Torah.*
3. Gen. 32:29, 35:21–22, Ibid.
4. Gen. 46:1, Ibid.
5. Gen. 46:2. In Hebrew, *Hineinei,* Ibid.
6. The number includes Jacob, Joseph, and Joseph's two sons but doesn't count wives, who are in-laws. Of course, seventy is a symbolically significant number, as a multiple of seven.
7. This passage has many confusing features. See Alter, *The Five Books of Moses,* n. 2–6b, pp. 271–2; Plaut, *The Torah: A Modern Commentary,* p. 298; Friedman, *Commentary on the Torah,* n. 47:3, pp. 152–3.
8. Gen. 47:9, Friedman, *Commentary on the Torah.*
9. Gen. 38:26, Ibid. Here he takes responsibility for fathering Tamar's child.
10. Many traditional commentators, beginning with Rashi, have argued that Joseph never contacted his father to say he was alive because he would have had to tell Jacob how he came to Egypt as a slave in the first place, a truth that would have been too devastating to his father. When his brothers appeared before him, the problem remained, and he could only reveal himself when he had some acceptable way of framing what they did. See Zornberg, *Beginnings of Desire,* pp. 333–4.

Gen. 12, "And He Lived"/*Va-y'chi*

1. It is generally believed that Jacob's blessings date from an early period in Canaan, before the monarchy. See Kugel, *How to Read the Bible,* pp. 192–4.
2. Later parts of the Torah seem to contradict this part of Jacob's speech. The tribe of Simeon is given land later on; and while the Levites remain landless, they have

the great honor of serving in the Sanctuary. Indeed, both Moses and Aaron are Levites, and the priestly line, which runs through Aaron, is all Levite.

3. Because this is not in the text, we have no way to know whether this is to be taken as true.
4. Gen. 48:15, Friedman, *Commentary on the Torah.*
5. Nan Gefen taught this meditation in the *Chochmat Halev* training program for teachers of Jewish Meditation. See Nan Fink Gefen, *Discovering Jewish Meditation: Instruction & Guidance for Learning an Ancient Spiritual Practice,* Paperback Edition (Woodstock, Vermont: Jewish Lights 1999).

Chapter 2. Exodus/*Sh'mot*

General Framework of Exodus/*Sh'mot*

1. From its first sentence: "And these are the names of the children of Israel who came to Egypt." Exod. 1:1, Friedman, *Commentary on the Torah.*
2. Kugel, *How to Read the Bible,* pp. 204–208.
3. Gen. 4:9, Alter, *The Five Books of Moses.*

Exod. 1, "Names"/*Sh'mot*

1. Exod. 1:7, Alter, *The Five Books of Moses.*
2. Exod. 1:8, Ibid.
3. Exod. 2:11, Friedman, *Commentary on the Torah.*
4. Exod. 2:14, Ibid.
5. This is the name that has been translated into English as Jehovah.
6. Exod. 1:7, Alter, *The Five Books of Moses.*
7. Zornberg, *The Particulars of Rapture,* pp. 18–23.
8. Exod. 2:23, Plaut, *The Torah: A Modern Commentary.*
9. Exod. 2:24, Ibid.
10. Exod. 2:5, Alter, *The Five Books of Moses.*
11. Exod. 2:11, Ibid.
12. Exod. 2:11, Ibid.
13. Exod. 3:2, Ibid.
14. Exod. 3:3, Ibid.
15. Exod. 3:4, Ibid.
16. Exod. 3:7, Ibid.

Exod. 2, "And I Appeared"/*Va'eira*

1. Exod. 6:12, Friedman, *Commentary on the Torah.* Emphasis is Friedman's.

Exod. 3, "Come"/*Bo*

1. Friedman, *Commentary on the Torah*, n. 5:26, p. 585. In *The Five Books of Moses*, Alter also comments that the three different verbs used for what happens to Pharaoh's heart all convey being "stubborn, unfeeling, inflexible" (n. 3, p. 345).

Exod. 4, "When He Let Go"/*B'shalach*

1. This is also translated as "The Reed Sea," which may refer to a marshy area in northeastern Egypt. As best I can tell, it is often just unclear what body of water is being talked about when the Red Sea is mentioned in Torah.
2. Exod. 15:20, Alter, *The Five Books of Moses*.
3. Miriam has neither been mentioned by name before, nor called a prophetess. Presumably, she is the same sister who approached Pharaoh's daughter when she took Moses from the river, recommending Moses' mother to her as a nurse. There are many *midrash* about her powers in Oral Torah.
4. Exod. 16:31. In Numbers 11:8, the manna is also described as tasting like "something creamy made with oil." Alter, *The Five Books of Moses*.
5. G-d also sends quail that morning, but nothing more is said of that in the text.
6. Here, and in other parts of the text, it is called Mount Horeb rather than Mount Sinai.
7. See, for example, Rashi, as quoted in Zornberg, *The Particulars of Reason*, p. 237.

Exod. 5, "Jethro"/*Yitro*

1. Exod. 18:12, Friedman, *Commentary on the Torah*.
2. Exod. 19:5, Ibid.
3. Exod. 19:6, Ibid.
4. Exod. 19:8, Ibid.
5. Exod. 20:19, Ibid. Emphasis is Friedman's.
6. Exod. 19:5–6, Alter, *The Five Books of Moses*.
7. Exod. 19:8, Friedman, *Commentary on the Torah*.
8. Exod. 20:2–14, Plaut, *The Torah: A Modern Commentary*.
9. Exod. 19:16, Friedman, *Commentary on the Torah*.
10. Exod. 19:18–19, Ibid.
11. Exod. 20:2–3, Plaut, *The Torah: A Modern Commentary*.

Exod. 6, "Judgments"/*Mishpatim*

1. The translation of the first line of the *parshah* comes from Plaut, *The Torah: A Modern Commentary*.

2. The first set of these rules is about offering freedom to male slaves, but not to their families if the wife has been given the slave by his master. In the same section, rules are also given for the treatment and freedom of female slaves, including those taken as concubines. In a general way, the Hebrew slave was something like an indentured servant. And a woman taken as a concubine had considerable rights that had to be observed, or she went free.

3. In Exod. 21:23–5, the phrase is used, "life for life, eye for eye, tooth for tooth, hand for hand, foot for foot, burn for burn, wound for wound, bruise for bruise," in referring to penalties for hurting a pregnant woman in the course of a fight with her husband. This enumeration of equal retribution is believed to have been part of the phrasing known in the ancient Near East that actually referred to specified fines for particular damages. See Plaut, *The Torah: A Modern Commentary*, pp. 528–9.

4. "If you will happen upon your enemy's ox or his ass straying, you shall *bring it back* to him. If you will see the ass of someone who hates you sagging under its burden, and you would hold back from helping him: you shall *help* with him." Friedman, *Commentary on the Torah*, Exod. 23:4. Emphasis is Friedman's.

5. The text is explicit in requiring this *because* the Israelites were strangers in Egypt. See Exod. 22:20, Ibid.

6. Exod. 24:3, Ibid.

7. Exod. 24:7, Ibid.

8. Hur seems to be an important personage, but he disappears without explanation after this. Traditional teachings have offered various explanations of who he was. See, for example, Kugel, *How to Read the Bible*, pp. 282–3.

Exod. 7, "Donation"/*T'rumah*

1. Plaut, *The Torah: A Modern Commentary*.

2. Exod. 36:22, See Friedman, *Commentary on the Torah* for the Hebrew.

3. Exod. 36:25, Ibid.

4. Exod. 36:27, Ibid.

5. Exod. 36:31, Ibid.

Exod. 8, "Command"/*T'tzaveh*

1. Exod. 28:36, Alter, *The Five Books of Moses*.

2. The altar for the sacrificial offerings was in the outer courtyard, before the entrance to the Tent of Meeting. All the Israelites could enter the courtyard, but only the priests could go beyond it, into the Tent itself. The whole structure, including the courtyard, was part of the Sanctuary, or *mishkan*, but the courtyard itself was uncovered.

3. Exod. 30:9, Alter, *The Five Books of Moses.*
4. Exod. 29:46, Ibid.
5. Exod. 28:36, Ibid.
6. Deut. 6:8, Plaut, *The Torah: A Modern Commentary.* During morning prayers, many Orthodox Jews wear hand and head phylacteries (in Hebrew, *t'fillin*), which are small boxes attached to head and hand by straps, and which contain parchments on which are written the words of the *Shema* as well as other Biblical verses.
7. Deut. 6:5, Friedman, *Commentary on the Torah.*

Exod. 9,"When You Add"/*Ki Tisa*
1. Exod. 32:4, Friedman, *Commentary on the Torah.*
2. Exod. 32:20, Ibid.
3. Exod. 32:24, Ibid.
4. Exod. 32:26, Plaut, *The Torah: A Modern Commentary.*
5. While it is clear from the text that the tablets will contain the Ten Commandments, it is a tenet of many Orthodox Jews that the tablets contained not only the Ten Commandments but the whole Torah and commentary upon it. At least one *midrash* says that the first tablet contained only the Ten Commandments, and the rest was added to the second set because our making of the golden calf indicated the need for more guidance. See *Midrash Rabbah* as quoted in http://www.chabad.org for this *parshah.*
6. Exod. 34:6, Friedman, *Commentary on the Torah.* Emphasis is Friedman's.
7. Exod. 34:27, Ibid. The text itself is somewhat confusing. Instead of G-d writing the commandments on the tablets, the instructions change to have Moses do it. Moreover, there is some confusion between the commandments that G-d proclaims as part of the new covenant, and the Ten Commandments.
8. It is usually assumed that Moses' face became so radiant with [G-d's] light that he could not be directly looked at. The passage was erroneously translated in medieval times, and is the source of the belief that Moses had horns of some kind, as in Michelangelo's *Moses.* It may also be that Moses face was in some way disfigured by exposure to the Divine, rather than radiant. Ibid., n. 34:29, p. 294.
9. The text is generally read as if they were once again worshiping a pagan god or gods as the source of their salvation and exodus from Egypt. But many recent commentators have said that it is more likely they were following the custom of the Middle East at that time in creating an image not to be worshiped for itself but to be treated as a platform through which to focus prayer. See, for example,

Plaut, *The Torah: A Modern Commentary,* pp. 598–9. Note that the Israelites exclaim, "These are your gods ...." because the calf gives them entrance to the various gods of the god realm; if they were truly praying to the calf, the words would be in the singular. But this still means that they were not praying to YHVH. See Alter, *The Five Books of Moses,* n. 4, p. 494.

Exod. 10, "And He Assembled"/*Vayak'heil*
1. Exod. 35:5, Friedman, *Commentary on the Torah.*
2. Exod. 35:10, Ibid.

Exod. 11, "Accounts"/*P'kudei*
1. Exod. 40:38, Friedman, *Commentary on the Torah.*
2. Exod. 40:36–38, Ibid.

Interpretive Summation of Exodus/*Sh'mot*
1. Exod. 40:38, Friedman, *Commentary on the Torah.*

Chapter 3. Leviticus/*Vayikra*

General Framework of Leviticus/*Vayikra*
1. There have been innumerable commentaries on the text of Leviticus, most of them legalistic. As an English speaker interested in other approaches, I am particularly indebted to the modern scholars Jacob Milgram, for his book *Leviticus: A Book of Ritual and Ethics,* and Mary Douglas, *Leviticus as Literature.* (In particular, see Introduction, n. 6.)
2. In fact, the text does not clearly specify that the High Priest can only enter once a year. Jacob Milgram, *Leviticus: A Book of Ritual and Ethics,* p. 167.
3. Lev. 19:18, Friedman, *Commentary on the Torah.*
4. Lev. 19:34, Ibid.
5. Babylonian Talmud, *Shabbat* 31a. See http://en.wikiquote.org/wiki/Hillel_the_ Elder.

Lev. 1. "And G-d Called"/*Vayikra*
1. The translation of the first line of the *parshah* comes from Plaut, *The Torah: A Modern Commentary.*
2. The offering of well-being also called the peace offering or the communal offering. The grain offering is also known as the meal offering. In general, it may be that the meal offering was essentially a way to have even the poorest member

of the congregation afford a holy sacrifice (Lev. 5:7). In a similar way, the animal offerings often allow the substitution of a smaller, less expensive animal, such as a bird, for a larger, more expensive one (Lev. 5:11).

3. In rabbinic tradition, it has always been essential to kill the animal painlessly by slitting its throat with an extremely sharp knife. Although not stated in the Written Torah, Oral Torah assumes the sacrifices were killed in the same way. See Milgram, pp. 105–6.

4. For comments, see Milgram, *Leviticus: A Book of Ritual and Ethics,* pp. 103–5; Plaut, *The Torah: A Modern Commentary,* p. 785.

5. If the sacrifice is of a bird (restricted to a turtledove or pigeon), the priest kills it by wringing the neck and prepares the body after the congregant brings it forward (Lev. 14–15).

6. Lev. 1:9, 13, 17. If the burnt offering is of birds, the priest does not burn the "crop with its feathers" (Lev. 1:16) but throws them into the ashes beside the altar. If the burnt offering is grain, most of it is set aside for Aaron and his sons to eat, for it is the "holy of holies" (Lev. 2:3, 10), having been consecrated to G-d. See Friedman, *Commentary on the Torah.*

7. Only the kidneys, a part of the liver, and the layer of hard suet fat under the skin and around the inner organs were burnt. Along with the heart, the kidney was considered the seat of emotions, thought, and life itself. The part of the liver sacrificed was particularly used in divination. The suet is the fat that can be readily peeled away, and it includes the fat tail of sheep, which is explicitly named in the text as part of the sacrifice. See Milgram, *Leviticus: A Book of Ritual and Ethics,* p. 29.

8. It is also called the purification offering.

9. There is a strict gradation of ritual atonement that depends on the importance of the sinner in defiling the Tabernacle. When the High Priest has committed the sin, the sacrifice must be a bull. The priest dips his finger in the blood, sprinkles the blood seven times just outside the innermost chamber that holds the Ark, and then puts some of the blood on the horns of the incense altar in the middle chamber. Only then does he spill all the rest at the base of the altar in the outer courtyard.

   If the whole community has sinned, then the congregation brings forward a bull, with all the elders placing their hands on the bull's head before slaughtering. The rest of the ceremony is the same as when the High Priest sins.

   If it is only a single chieftain who has sinned, he brings forward a goat. The priest, who again takes the blood on his finger, places some of it on the horns of the altar in the outer courtyard, spilling the rest at the base of the altar, but not approaching either the middle or innermost chambers of the Tabernacle.

The ceremony is the same if the sinner is an ordinary member of the congregation, except that the goat is now female instead of male, and the person can bring a female lamb instead. If he is too poor, he can bring two turtledoves or pigeons instead, one of which is to be a burnt offering. If still poorer, he can bring a meal offering (Lev. 4:1–13).

10. Milgram, *Leviticus,* p. 46. Also, the sacrificial animal in these cases was to be a ram.

11. In Hebrew, the word for a sacrifice is *korban,* which translates as "something brought near" (i.e., to G-d's altar). Plaut, *The Torah: A Modern Commentary,* p. 674.

12. Douglas, *Leviticus as Literature,* pp. 67–86. Also, see Milgram, *Leviticus: A Book of Ritual and Ethics,* p. 29.

13. It is unknown why only some of the organs were chosen as an offering to the Divine. Perhaps it was recognized that we needed to keep some of our passions in order to live in the world.

Lev. 2, "Command"/*Tzav*

1. The parts to be sacrificed include the suet, kidneys, and lobe of liver (as in the offering of well-being), plus the right thigh, which would normally be reserved for eating. Here it is burnt, with only the ram's breast saved as food. (Moses holds it up as his elevation offering, but does not burn it.)

2. Lev. 6:10, 18; 7:1, Friedman, *Commentary on the Torah.*

Lev. 3, "Eighth"/*Sh'mini*

1. Lev. 10:1–2, Plaut, *The Torah: A Modern Commentary.*

2. Lev. 10:20, Ibid.

3. The Israelites can eat land animals with split hooves who chew their cud. This eliminates the camel, the rock-badger, the hare, the pig, and presumably others not named. Creatures of the water must have fins and scales, while a variety of birds are named as unacceptable as food (but the translations of the bird names are not definite). Also forbidden are all flying, swarming creatures that have four legs, unless the legs are jointed, as with locusts. Finally, creatures that swarm on the earth like the rat, the mouse, the lizard, and so on, are distinguished as forbidden, as is every swarming creature, whether it moves on its belly or on legs. For some explanations, see Plaut, *The Torah: A Modern Commentary,* pp. 718–21. In *Leviticus as Literature,* Douglas suggests that the categories have to do with G-d's beneficence toward what has been created, pp. 137–75.

4. Lev. 11:45, Friedman, *Commentary on the Torah.*

5. Plaut, *The Torah: A Modern Commentary,* pp. 725–6.

Lev. 4, "She Will Bear Seed"/*Tazria*

1. For reasons not given in the text, the length of her period of impurity is twice as long if she gives birth to a female rather than a male.

Lev. 5, "Leper"/*M'tzora*

1. Both ceremonies take eight days; the leper, like the priest, is sprinkled with blood; blood (and holy oil) are then placed on his right earlobe, thumb, and big toe; and, finally, an elevation offering is made to G-d before any sacrifices go on the fire. While the blood in the priestly consecration comes from a ram, the blood used in the leper's purification comes from a sacrificed bird. Its blood is put into a clay pot with spring water (called "living" water. See Lev. 14:5 in Friedman, *Commentary on the Torah*), and a second bird is then dipped into the blood, along with a mix of cedarwood, scarlet yarn, and hyssop. Bloody bird plus bloody mix are sprinkled seven times on the leper, after which the live bird is let go into the fields (presumably carrying off the impurity), and the leper washes himself and his clothes, shaves all his hair, and returns to camp, although he does not return to his tent for seven more days.

   Then on the eighth day, the leper makes a guilt offering, a sin offering, a burnt offering, and a grain offering. When the guilt offering is made, the animal's blood (and holy oil) are placed on his right earlobe, thumb, and big toe, with the rest of the oil spilled on his head. In another ritual reminiscent of the priestly consecration, the guilt offering is raised up before G-d as an elevation offering before anything goes on the fire.

2. Emissions that occur during intercourse are included here.
3. Lev. 15:31, Plaut, *The Torah: A Modern Commentary*.
4. Moreover, the purification ceremony, which involves the sacrifice of one bird and the release to the wild of a second, is very reminiscent of the solemn communal ceremony of the scapegoat who carries off the whole group's sins each year at Yom Kippur (to be described in the next chapter).

Lev. 6, "After the Deaths"/*Acharei Mos*

1. Milgram comments that the text doesn't actually limit Aaron to this one day. See *Leviticus: A Book of Ritual and Ethics,* p. 167).
2. Lev. 16:16, Plaut, *The Torah: A Modern Commentary*.
3. Milgram, *Leviticus: A Book of Ritual and Ethics,* pp. 168–9.
4. Aaron has chosen two rams to be burnt offerings at the start of the ceremony. The text does not explain why only the suet of the two sin offerings is burnt and

not the usual internal organs as well; the text only says that all the rest of each sin offering was burned outside the camp.

5. Lev. 17:11, Plaut, *The Torah: A Modern Commentary*. This command against eating blood was also expressed in the rules given by G-d to Noah after the Flood, but the relation of blood to the life force that belongs to G-d was not as yet stated overtly. See n. 3 for Lev. 1, "And G-d Called"/*Vayikra*. See also Milgram, *Leviticus: A Book of Ritual and Ethics*, pp. 104-5.

6. Lev. 18:21, Friedman, *Commentary on the Torah*.

7. For example, Milgram, *Leviticus: A Book of Ritual and Ethics*, p. 170.

8. Kugel, *The Bible As It Was*, pp. 442–4.

Lev. 7, "Holy"/K'doshim

1. Lev. 19:18, Friedman, *Commentary on the Torah*.
2. Lev. 19:14, Plaut, *The Torah: A Modern Commentary*.
3. Lev. 19:16, Ibid.
4. Lev. 19:32, Ibid.
5. Lev. 19:18, Friedman, *Commentary on the Torah*.
6. Lev. 19:34, Plaut, *The Torah: A Modern Commentary*.
7. Milgram, Leviticus: A Book of Ritual and Ethics, pp. 233–236.

Lev. 8, "Say"/Emor

1. Lev. 22:3, Friedman, *Commentary on the Torah*.
2. Lev. 22:9, Ibid.
3. Lev. 22:32–33, Ibid.
4. Lev. 23:2, Plaut, *The Torah: A Modern Commentary*.
5. In the tradition of Oral Torah, *Shavuot* also commemorates G-d's giving of the Ten Commandments and even of the whole Torah at Mount Sinai.
6. In Hebrew, *Rosh Hashanah*, "The Head of the Year," not named as such in the text.
7. It should be noted that the Israelites do not act independently, but are following G-d's orders. More to the point is the metaphoric reading of this passage, as discussed in the *parshah* interpretation.

Lev. 9, "In the Mountain," B'har

1. To my knowledge, it's not known whether the Great Sabbath, or Jubilee, was really observed.
2. All land sales during the intervening forty-nine years are to be priced with an adjustment for this return, as well.
3. Lev. 25:23, Plaut, *The Torah: A Modern Commentary*.

4. Lev. 25:55, Plaut, *The Torah: A Modern Commentary*. We've seen elsewhere in Torah that slavery is accepted for non-Israelites, but that there are many restrictions on the slave owner's power when compared to Egyptian slavery or to that in other nations. In this part of Leviticus, the discussion is limited to Israelites who sell themselves out of necessity, and are to be treated not as slaves but as indentured servants.

5. Lev. 25:19, Friedman, *Commentary on the Torah*.

6. Lev. 25:23, Plaut, *The Torah: A Modern Commentary*.

7. Lev. 25:55, Ibid.

8. Lev. 26:1, 2, Ibid.

Lev. 10, "If You Follow My Laws"/*B'chukotai*

1. The translation of these lines comes from Plaut, *The Torah: A Modern Commentary*.

2. Lev. 26:13, Friedman, *Commentary on the Torah*.

3. Lev. 26:46, Plaut, *The Torah: A Modern Commentary*.

4. A famous mystic and teacher, Rabbi Akiva helped lead the rebellion against the Romans in 135CE. He was executed by having his flesh removed by red-hot iron combs.

Interpretive Summation of Leviticus/*Vayikra*

1. Lev. 11:44, 19:2, Friedman, *Commentary on the Torah*.

Chapter 4: Numbers/*B'midbar*

General Framework of Numbers/*B'midbar*

1. Num. 1:1, Friedman, *Commentary on the Torah*.

2. Kugel, *How to Read the Bible: A Guide to Scripture*, p. 373–385.

3. Friedman, *Commentary on the Torah*, p. 423.

4. In current scholarship, the Written Torah appears to have perhaps been put into final form before the Buddha appeared rather than afterward. If that is so, the influence may have gone from West to East. Of course, there may also have been early precursors to the Buddha's teaching that influenced the redactors of Torah.

5. Mark Epstein, *Thoughts Without a Thinker: Psychotherapy from a Buddhist Point of View*, Paperback Edition (New York: Basic Books, 1995).

Num. 1, "In the Wilderness"/*B'midbar*

1. The translation of these lines comes from Plaut, *The Torah: A Modern Commentary*.

2. The timing conflicts with Exod. 38:26, which describes the same census but places it a month earlier.
3. This is essentially the same number of men, given as "about 600,000" in Exod. 12:37.
4. There are three groups of Levites, descended from Levi's three sons, Gershon, Kohath, and Merari. Moses and Aaron are also Levites through Kohath. Num. 3:4 states that neither Nadab nor Abihu had sons.
5. Both the Levites and their animals belong to G-d; they serve as substitutes for the firstborn in all the other tribes, who were claimed by G-d the year before, at the time of the final plague that killed all the firstborn in Egypt.
6. Exod. 1:7, Alter, *The Five Books of Moses*. The text reads "were fruitful and *swarmed* and multiplied …."

Num. 2, "Add Up"/N*aso*

1. Num. 5:3, Alter, *The Five Books of Moses*.
2. In the trial, the priest mixes a drink made from holy water and dust from the Sanctuary floor, and recites a curse that will befall the woman if she has committed adultery; the woman says, "Amen, amen," after which the priest writes the curse on a scroll and then rubs the writing off into the water for her to drink. Since it is the water that carries the curse, she is proven innocent if she remains unharmed (Num. 5:12–31).
3. When the term of their vow is over, they are to bring a variety of offerings to the sanctuary. After the priest places these offerings on the altar, the Nazarite shaves his or her head at the entrance of the Tent of Meeting and adds the hair to the other sacrifices. The ceremony ends with a final elevation offering (which was similarly made when the priests were consecrated) and the drinking of wine by the Nazarite.
4. Num. 6:24–26, Friedman, *Commentary on the Torah*. Note that Friedman uses the phrase "His face" and I have changed it to "the Divine face."
5. Each offers one silver dish and one silver basin, both filled with fine flour that is mixed with oil for a grain offering; one gold pan filled with incense; one bull, one ram, and one lamb in its first year for a burnt offering; one goat for a sin offering; and two oxen, five rams, five he-goats, and five year-old lambs for a peace offering.
6. In Orthodox Judaism, the priestly blessing can only be offered by someone of the priestly lineage, as are those with the last name of Cohen.

Num. 3, "When You Put Up"/B*'haalot'cha*

1. Already described in Exod. 25:37.
2. The priests were already consecrated in Lev. 2.

3. Exod. 12:47–50 says that the rules include the requirement for the stranger to be circumcised.
4. Num. 9:14, Plaut, *The Torah: A Modern Commentary.*
5. Num. 9:15, Ibid.
6. Jethro is here named "Hobab, the son of Reuel the Midianite." Elsewhere he is called by the name Reuel. The text makes no comment on the different names. Presumably, they come from different narrative traditions regarding the Israelites and the Midianites.
7. Here Moses seems to be turning to a human for guidance rather than to G-d. Alter suggests that this may reflect genuine history involving Midianite help. *The Five Books of Moses,* n. 31, p. 732.
8. Num. 11:4, Plaut, *The Torah: A Modern Commentary.*
9. Num. 11:4–6. Ibid. In the next sentences, the manna is described as being gathered by the Israelites, ground up, boiled, and made into cakes that tasted like rich cream.
10. Num. 11:14, Ibid.
11. Num. 11: 20, Ibid.
12. Num. 11:23, Ibid.
13. In an apparent interruption of the narrative, two men named Eldad and Medad also speak in ecstasy. And Moses says, "Would that all the Eternal's people were prophets, that the Eternal put [the divine] spirit upon them!" See Num. 11:29, Ibid.
14. Num. 11:33, Ibid.
15. Torah commentators differ as to whether this refers to his wife Zipporah or to a second unknown woman. See Friedman, *Commentary on the Torah,* p. 465.
16. Num. 12:2, Plaut, *The Torah: A Modern Commentary.*
17. Num. 12:3, Alter, *The Five Books of Moses.*
18. Num. 12:8, Plaut, *The Torah: A Modern Commentary.*
19. Num. 12:13, Ibid.

Num. 4, "Send"/*Sh'lach L'cha*

1. The site where Abraham was visited by the three angels who told him he would have a son (Gen. 13:18), the place where the patriarchs and matriarchs are buried (Gen. 23:19), and the place from where Jacob sent Joseph to find his brothers. See Friedman, *Commentary on the Torah,* p. 470.
2. Num. 13:32, Plaut, *The Torah: A Modern Commentary.*
3. These are the giants referred to in Genesis 6:4 as descended from the union of divine beings and human women.
4. Num. 13:33, Plaut, *The Torah: A Modern Commentary.*
5. Num. 14:3, Ibid.

6. The text says that they "fell on their faces before all the assembled congregation of Israelites." See Num. 14:5, Ibid. Also see comment in Alter, *The Five Books of Moses*, n. 5, p. 750.
7. Num. 14:18, 19, Plaut, *The Torah: A Modern Commentary*.
8. The route is actually not clear.
9. The final part of this *parshah* has one of those seemingly senseless breaks in the narrative that are disconcerting to our ear, although Mary Douglas has argued that the alternation of narrative and rules for ritual practice is precisely the literary structure of *B'midbar*. In fact, she argues that the structure not only involves such a deliberate alternation of narrative and laws, but that such alternation forms a larger structure in which the book is divided into two halves that mirror each other, section by section, lining up against each other to explore the same underlying subject. See *In the Wilderness: The Doctrine of Defilement in the Book of Numbers*, Paperback Edition (Oxford University Press, 2001).
10. In all cases, the "stranger" refers to a non-Israelite who is residing in the community, a resident alien. According to Alter, it was common throughout the Middle East to have a resident alien participate in the religious activities of the community in which they lived. See *The Five Books of Moses*, n. 15, p. 757.
11. This refers to all the commandments, not merely the Ten Commandments.
12. A piece of clothing that fits this purpose is still worn under regular clothing by the most orthodox Jews.
13. Num. 15:40-41, Plaut, *The Torah: A Modern Commentary*.
14. This is not only the place where Abraham was visited by the three angels (Gen. 13:18), but is also where the patriarchs and matriarchs are buried (Gen. 23:19), and the place from where Jacob sent Joseph to find his brothers. See Friedman, *Commentary on the Torah*, p. 470.
15. Num. 15:30, Alter, *The Five Books of Moses*.
16. This idea of the world being akin to G-d's body has long seemed to me a powerful way to approach the experience of oneness with the Divine. Recently, I also saw this idea in Daniel Matt's book, *God and the Big Bang: Discovering Harmony Between Science and Spirituality*, Paperback, 4th Edition (Woodstock, Vermont: Jewish Lights, 2006).

Num. 5, "Korach"/*Korach*

1. Korach is the son of Izhar. Izhar is Moses' uncle, a brother of his father, Amram. Moses, Aaron, and Korach are all great-grandsons of Levi. See Exod. 6:20 for the genealogies and length of lives. Although the Israelites were in Egypt for over four hundred years, only a few generations have gone by, perhaps because

each generation lived so long and had children late in life. Or it is simply a contradiction in the text.

2. On immediately disappears from the story and is not mentioned again. Plaut comments that the name is believed to be a scribal error. See n. 16:1, p. 1003, *The Torah: A Modern Commentary*.

3. Num. 16:3, Ibid.

4. Num. 16:14, Friedman, *Commentary on the Torah*.

5. It does seem that that Korach's children are not swallowed up, unlike the children of Dathan and Abiram. Later, the text states that they did not die (Num. 26:11).

6. The pans have become holy because they have been touched by G-d's power.

7. Num. 17:13, Friedman, *Commentary on the Torah*.

8. Priests are even closer than the Levites to G-d, and therefore need even greater purity and have greater privileges, as the section indicates.

9. The Levites serve the priests in the Sanctuary and also offer a portion of what they receive as a tithe to the priests.

10. For example, see Plaut, *The Torah: A Modern Commentary*, p. 1012.

11. But I was fascinated to find that some Buddhist teachings would be in complete agreement with *B'midbar* in placing both rebellions together—as occurring in that realm on the Wheel of Life that holds the obstacles for those who have advanced partway on the spiritual path. As I understand it, in these Buddhist traditions, their stories would be intermingled as they are in this *parshah,* with Korach's desire for union with the Divine belonging to what is simply called *The God Realm;* while Dathan and Abiram would be dwelling in *The Realm of the Jealous Gods* (which is often placed within The God Realm), where they aggressively pursue the ego's craving for dominance. See Mark Epstein, *Thoughts Without a Thinker: Psychotherapy from a Buddhist Perspective,* Paperback Edition (New York: Basic Books, 1995), pp. 3–36.

12. For example, www.chabad.org, *Parshah Korach,* From the Chasidic Masters, "Who is Korach?" from the teachings of the Lubavitche Rebbe.

13. I Chron. 6:16

14. See Plaut, *The Torah: A Modern Commentary*, pp. 1013–1014.

15. Alter, *The Five Books of Moses.*

Num. 6, "Laws"/*Chukat*

1. The translation of these lines comes from Plaut, *The Torah: A Modern Commentary.*

2. Num. 19:2, Friedman, *Commentary on the Torah.*

3. Num. 20:10, Plaut, *The Torah: A Modern Commentary.*

4. Num. 19:17, Friedman, *Commentary on the Torah*. The phrase refers to fresh flowing water, as from a well or other source. See n. 19:17, p. 492.
5. Num. 20:10–11.Traditional commentary tends to focus simply on his disobedience in striking the rock rather than just speaking. I am indebted to Alter's citation of Jacob Milgram, in *The Five Books of Moses*, n. 10, p. 783 for confirming my sense that Moses' sin is rather about believing the power is his rather than G-d's.
6. See Aviva Zomberg, *The Particulars of Rapture: Reflections on Exodus*, Paperback Edition (Image/Doubleday, 2002, n. 106, p. 242.
7. See Alter, *The Five Books of Moses*, n. 2, p. 788.

Num. 7, "Balak"/*Balak*

1. The ancient Israelites seems to have believed originally that more than one god exists, but that their god was the only one worthy of worship. This belief is called "monolatry," and indications of it can be found in many parts of Torah prior to the Book of Deuteronomy; traces of this belief can even be found in the traditional Jewish liturgy. See, for example, Exod. 7:11–13, or Exod. 12:12.
2. Some commentators think they may have gone into the Tabernacle itself to have sex. The story is unclear, with several apparent contradictions, such as the conflating of the Midianites and Moabites. See n. 1,2 for *Parshah Phinehas*.
3. Num. 22:18, Alter, *The Five Books of Moses*.

Num. 8, "Phinehas"/*Phinehas*

1. Friedman does not capitalize the word *My*. I have done so to maintain consistency of style.
2. It appears that they were defiling the Sanctuary by an act of public sex in it. This is ritual sacrilege, calling down Divine wrath, and it is over and above the people's sinfulness in committing idolatry with the Moabite women.
3. As stated in the first note for *Parshah Balaam*, this episode has numerous internal discrepancies. However, in now naming the man and woman whom Phinehas kills as Zimri, son of an Israelite chieftain, and Cozbi, daughter of a Midian chieftain, the text indicates how widespread and serious the Israelites' intermingling with the tribes of Canaan and their gods was. Again, it should be noted that Moab and Midian seem to be used interchangeably. Alter suggests that they may, in fact, have been assimilated with one another. See his notes on this chapter in *The Five Books of Moses*, pp. 817–18.
4. And if there are neither sons nor daughters, then the land goes to the father's brothers or progressively more distant relatives until an heir is located. Later on, in Num. 36:1–10, the text states that daughters must marry within the tribe if they inherit, so that the land remains in the tribe.

5. The next book, Deuteronomy, consists of the speech Moses makes to the people just before his death.

6. The festivals are Passover, or *Pesach;* First Fruits, or *Shavuot;* and the Holy Assembly in the seventh month (now called *Rosh Hashanah* and *Yom Kippur*); and then The Festival of Booths, or *Sukkot,* on the seven days that immediately follow *Yom Kippur.* These festivals also call for one or two days set aside for worship, without working.

7. Num: 26:54, Plaut, *The Torah: A Modern Commentary.*

Num. 9, "Tribes"/*Matot*

1. Her father or husband can annul her vows, although he then bears the guilt for whatever comes of that annulment. But no one can interfere with the vows of a widow or divorcee.

2. The text here seems to confuse Midianite and Moabite.

Num. 10, "Travels"/*Mas'ei*

1. Many sites are listed for the first time, and others that have been named before are not mentioned.

2. Num. 33:55, Friedman, *Commentary on the Torah.*

3. The description of the boundaries doesn't match the borders given in Joshua and Ezekiel, and they don't seem to correspond well with the borders as we understand them historically. See Alter, *The Five Books of Moses,* n. 3–12, p. 856.

4. The reader may have noticed that the tribes are being counted differently than originally. As stated earlier, the Levites don't get land and are therefore are not counted for land distribution, while the tribes of Manasseh and Ephraim are counted separately rather than together. This keeps the number of tribes to the original twelve.

5. The text only distinguishes between intentional and accidental acts of harm. It appears that causing death is considered murder even if the intent was not to kill, but only to hurt.

6. It was common throughout the Middle East to pay a fine in lieu of another penalty. It is understood that the bloody sounding "eye for an eye," etc. was, in fact, not what was done. Instead there were standard payments for different sorts of injuries. See n. 2 for Exod. 6, "Judgments"/*Mishpatim.*

7. Num. 36:13, Plaut, *The Torah: A Modern Commentary.*

8. It is interesting to remember here that the twelve tribes have often been thought to have astrological significance, for astrology also uses the idea of different aspects of the psyche taking up territory.

Chapter 5. Deuteronomy/*D'varim*

General Framework of Deuteronomy/*D'varim*

1. To the modern reader, Biblical descriptions of the conquest of the Promised Land may sound uncomfortably like ethnic cleansing. It is worth remembering that the text is ancient and comes from a time of very different sensibilities. Although we may not behave any better today, we do seem to be more uncomfortable with mass murder. It is also important to realize that the text may be very misleading. As discussed in n. 1 to Deut. 2, "And I Implored"/*Va'etchanan,* the conquest of the Promised Land may never have happened, and certainly not in the way the text describes here.

Deut. 1, "Words"/*D'varim*

1. In the original story in Exod. 18:13–23, he was told to do this by his father-in-law, Jethro.
2. In Num. 20:12, G-d denies Moses entry to the Promised Land because of his striking the rock at Meribah instead of simply commanding it to produce water, as the Divine had told him to do. G-d says that Moses showed a lack of trust and failed to affirm G-d's holiness by taking matters into his own hands in striking the rock with his rod.
3. Deut. 1:3, Friedman, *Commentary on the Torah.*
4. Deut. 1:2, Ibid.

Deut. 2, "And I Implored"/*Va'etchanan*

1. Deut. 4:1, Friedman, *Commentary on the Torah.*
2. Deut. 5:3, Ibid.
3. This is a slightly different version from that given in Exod. 20:1–17. One difference is that Moses now says that we are to "observe" the Sabbath (Deut. 5:12), whereas the phrase in Exodus was "remember" the Sabbath (Exod. 20:8). The reasons given for the Sabbath are also different. In Exodus, it is a commemoration of the creation and of G-d resting on the seventh day; in Moses' speech, it is in commemoration of G-d taking the Israelites out of Egyptian slavery. Ibid., n. 5:7–5:17, pp. 582–4.
4. Deut. 6:4–9, Ibid.
5. However, there are internal inconsistencies in the Books of Joshua and Judges that indicate that conquest was actually slow and limited, with the Israelite tribes often only loosely allied with one another, and frequently assimilated with the local inhabitants. Archeological evidence also suggests that the history of the

area is very complex, and that there may have been a very gradual process of emigration and settlement by a group that became known as the Israelites, with some conquest and some intermingling with the local inhabitants of Canaan. All conclusions are provisional at this time.

6. Deut. 4:24, Friedman, *Commentary on the Torah*.

Deut. 3, "Because"/*Eikev*

1. As with a few other statements of Moses, there is no place in Torah in which G-d says this. In traditional understanding, we would assume it to be true because Moses says it is.
2. Deut. 8:3, Friedman, *Commentary on the Torah*.
3. Deut. 8:17, Ibid. The emphasis is Friedman's.
4. Deut. 8:19, Ibid. The emphasis is Friedman's.
5. Deut. 11:13–21 provides the second paragraph of the *Shema*. The first section of the *Shema* was in the last *parshah*, Deut. 6:4–9. The third paragraph is found in Num. 15:37–41.
6. Deut. 11:17, Friedman, *Commentary on the Torah*.

Deut. 4, "See"/*R'eih*

1. The translation of this line of the *parshah* comes from Plaut, *The Torah: A Modern Commentary*.
2. Ibid.
3. Deut. 12:4.
4. They are commanded to spill the blood of the animal on the ground and drain it before cooking the meat, for the blood contains the life force that belongs to G-d; however, meat is no longer to be obtained only through a holy act in which the sacrifice (from which the meat comes) symbolizes our commitment to serve G-d.
5. Deut. 12:5
6. Deut.14:23
7. Although Torah interpreters have taken so many of the commandments as referring to all people (particularly to love one's neighbor as oneself), it appears that many, if not most, were initially more restricted. Thus, foreigners may not be necessarily treated in the same way as nonforeigners, as is the case here, where loans to foreigners were not to be remitted. Indeed, it is extraordinary that so many laws in Torah specifically say that foreigners who are permanent residents of the community are to be treated no differently from Israelites. It should also be noted that it is not clear how much the command about remission of debt was indeed carried out.

8. Deut. 16:16
9. Deut. 16:11, Friedman, *Commentary on the Torah*.
10. Deut. 11:26, Ibid.
11. We first see the word *makom* when Jacob "came upon a certain place" (Gen. 28:10) while fleeing from his brother Esau after cheating him of his blessing and birthright. Jacob sleeps and dreams of angels climbing up and down a stairway that reaches from the earth to the skies. When he wakes from the dream, he says, "Indeed, the Lord is in this place and I did not know." (Gen. 28:16) For both quotations, see Alter, *The Five Books of Moses*.

Deut. 5, "Judgments"/*Shof'tim*

1. Deut 16:20, Friedman, *Commentary on the Torah*. Emphasis is Friedman's.
2. In the metaphor of Levitical sacrifice, offering a blemished animal is the same as holding back from G-d, not committing oneself wholeheartedly to serve the Divine. And the text continues in the same vein by stating that idolaters who reject YHVH must die.
3. Deut. 17:7, Friedman, *Commentary on the Torah*.
4. The text says "levitical priests or the magistrate in charge at the time" (Deut. 17:9), which has been interpreted to mean that an official other than a priest might officiate if no priest was available or if the priest was unfit. See Plaut, *The Torah: A Modern Commentary*, n. 9, p. 1295.
5. Deut. 17:12, Friedman, *Commentary on the Torah*.
6. Deut. 19:19, Ibid.
7. Deut. 19:13, Ibid.
8. Deut. 17:19, 20, Ibid. It's not clear whether these instructions refer to the full law code of Deuteronomy or to the laws that specifically apply to the king, which are in this *parshah*.
9. In medieval Kabbalah, unbounded love, or *chesed*, is balanced on the Tree of Life by judgment, or *gevurah*. In this formulation, *chesed* is expansive, infinite love pouring forth without restraint; and it must be tempered with *gevurah*, or judgment, which is a constricting force, setting boundaries, rules, and limits.
10. Deut. 16:20, Friedman, *Commentary on the Torah*.

Deut. 6, "When You'll Go Out"/*Ki Teitzei*

1. According to many traditional Torah interpreters, this may refer to a ritual mourning period, in which the woman can shed her prior life and become ready to take on her new role as an Israelite wife. When one places this alongside this section's other requirements in regard to captured women, its humanity is quite striking. See, for example, Friedman, *Commentary on the Torah*, n. 21:11 p. 629.

2. Deut. 21:14, Plaut, *The Torah: A Modern Commentary*.
3. Deut. 21:17, Ibid.
4. Deut. 21:21, Ibid.
5. Deut. 21:23, Ibid.
6. Deut. 22:3, Alter, *The Five Books of Moses*. In another insertion of pragmatism, we are told we can hold the item until the owner calls for it, if the owner lives far away or is unknown.
7. Deut. 23:16, Plaut, *The Torah: A Modern Commentary*.
8. Deut. 24:14, Ibid.
9. Deut. 24:17–18, Ibid.
10. Deut. 25:16, Ibid.
11. Deut. 25:18, Ibid.
12. We recognize that complete obliteration is impossible, just as no one expected an actual stoning of the delinquent son.
13. Deut. 25:17-19, Plaut, *The Torah: A Modern Commentary*.
14. Each Hebrew letter has a numerical value. The letters of Amalek sum to the same number as the letters for "doubt," which is *safek* in Hebrew. This is the foundation for a host of rabbinic teachings, in the Talmud and afterward.

Deut. 7, "When You Come"/*Ki Tavo*
1. Deut. 12:26–16:16
2. Deut. 26:12–15.This command refers to tithing every third year, and not to the immediate ceremony of the first fruits.
3. Deut. 26:16, 17, 18, Plaut, *The Torah: A Modern Commentary*.
4. The teaching that Moses tells them to inscribe on stone in this section (Deut. 27:3) is thought by Torah interpreters to refer either to the code of laws just given by him in the last several chapter (i.e., Deut. 12–26) or to the entire Book of Deuteronomy. See, for example, Alter, *The Five Books of Moses*, n. 3, p. 1008.
5. One of the six tribes is the Levites. The Levites are also listed separately as the tribe pronouncing the blessings and curses. The text doesn't specify whether it is just the Levitical priests who do this part.
6. Deut. 27:15, Plaut, *The Torah: A Modern Commentary*.
7. Deut. 27:16, Ibid.
8. Deut. 27:26, Ibid. Capitalization is Plaut's.
9. While this reference may refer to the list of curses just given, or perhaps to the prior laws in Deut. 12–16, or even to the entire Book of Deuteronomy, traditional interpreters have taken it to refer to the whole Torah, for the word for instruction is the word *Torah*. See, for example, Ibid., n. 26, p. 1355.

10. Deut. 28:3, Ibid.
11. Deut. 28:4, Ibid.
12. Deut. 28:20, Ibid.
13. Deut. 28:22–24, Ibid.
14. Deut. 29:3, Ibid.

Deut. 8, "Standing"/*Nitzavim*
1. Deut. 30:14, Friedman, *Commentary on the Torah.*
2. Deut. 29:14, Plaut, *The Torah: A Modern Commentary.*
3. Deut. 29:28, Friedman, *Commentary on the Torah.* See n. 29:28, p. 657.
4. Deut. 30:6, Ibid.
5. Deut. 30:14, Ibid.
6. Deut. 30:15, Ibid.
7. Deut. 30:19, Ibid.
8. In Deut. 4:1, Ibid., Moses says, "And now, Israel, listen to the laws and to the judgments that I'm teaching you to do, so that you'll live...." The rest of Deuteronomy can be seen as an explication of what it means to live.
9. Deut. 30:19, Ibid.
10. Deut. 29:28, Ibid.
11. Deut. 29:14, Plaut, *The Torah: A Modern Commentary.*
12. This *parshah* is always read in synagogues just before the High Holy Days of Rosh Hashanah, which is itself all about *shuvah,* or returning to G-d. So it has particular resonance for Jews. But my hope is that G-d wrestlers of many faiths will read this book and respond to Moses' call to choose life. It's also worth remembering that such a return can occur at any time of year. In fact, it should take place again and again through the year because we lose our way so readily.

Deut. 9, "And He Went"/*Vayeilech*
1. According to Friedman in his *Commentary on the Torah,* his teachings refer to Deut. 12–26, plus the blessings and curses in Deut. 28. By the rabbinic period, Friedman writes, the *teachings* were understood to refer to the whole Torah, which is still the accepted belief among Orthodox Jews. See n. 31:9, pp. 661–2.
2. Deut. 31:6, Friedman, *Commentary on the Torah.*
3. This is a year in which no farming is to be done, Hebrew slaves are to be freed, and all debts are to be remitted. It is a year dedicated to starting over, letting go of acquisition, and, by implication, remembering the Divine; thus it is an appropriate year for reading Moses' teaching. The command to do this reading

appears to be the source of the Jewish custom of reading the entire Torah every year or every three years (depending on the congregation), in weekly portions.

4. Deut. 31:21, Friedman, *Commentary on the Torah*.
5. Deut. 31:17,18, Ibid. Friedman does not capitalize the word *My*. I've capitalized it for consistency of style.
6. Deut. 31:19, Ibid.
7. Deut. 31:29, Ibid.
8. Deut. 31:11, Ibid.

Deut. 10. "Listen"/*Haazinu*

1. Friedman does not capitalize the word *My*. I have done so to maintain consistency of style.
2. Deut. 32:10, Friedman, *Commentary on the Torah*.
3. Deut. 32:11, Ibid.
4. Deut. 32:39, Ibid. The emphasis is Friedman's. However, he did not capitalize the word *My*. I did so for consistency of style.
5. Deut. 32:47, Plaut, *The Torah: A Modern Commentary*.
6. Deut. 32:51. As I wrote earlier in this book, many commentators have written that the real sin was Moses speaking as if it were he, rather than the Divine, who had the power to create miracles.
7. Deut. 32:10, Friedman, *Commentary on the Torah*.
8. Deut. 32:47, Plaut, *The Torah: A Modern Commentary*.
9. This is when Jacob had his vision of angels climbing up and down a ladder to the heavens and woke saying that G-d was in that place and he had not known it (Gen. 28:16).
10. Deut. 32:47, Plaut: *The Torah: A Modern Commentary*.

Deut. 11, "And This is the Blessing"/*V'Zot Ha B'rachah*

1. Deut. 34:4, Friedman, *Commentary on the Torah*.
2. Deut. 34:5, Ibid.
3. And the tribe of Simeon is left out, perhaps because it is already absorbed into Judah See Plaut, *The Torah: A Modern Commentary*, p. 1429.

Final Interpretive Summation

1. Plaut, *The Torah: A Modern Commentary*, pp. 298–9.
2. Deut. 30:14–16, Friedman, *Commentary on the Torah*.

Chapter 7. The Bible We Don't Know

1. *P'shat* means "simple." In traditional teachings, it is the level for children.
2. *Remez* means "hint."
3. *Drosh* means "inquire, interpret."
4. These stories are what are meant by the Hebrew word *midrash,* familiar to many Jews.
5. *Zohar* means "splendor, radiance."
6. *Kabbalah* means "received," as in "received tradition."
7. In general, however, most traditional commentary focuses on a single line or phrase and not on the entire Torah portion. The only approach that I've seen that consistently takes an overview of the entire *parshah* is that by Rabbi Shefa Gold, on her website at http://www.torahjourneys (which has been published as *Torah Journeys: The Inner Path to the Promised Land* (Teaneck, New Jersey: Ben Yehudah Press, 2006).
8. The word *Tanakh* is an acronym, referring to its three parts: Torah, Prophets, and Writings. In Hebrew, the three are: *Torah, Nevi'im* (meaning "Prophets"), and *Ketuvim* (meaning "Writings"), written as *TaNaKh.*
9. The ordering is slightly different for different Churches, and the Catholic and Greek Orthodox Churches have added a few more writings to their canon.
10. Prophets include nine books of mixed history and religious writing: Joshua, Judges, Samuels I and II, Kings I and II, Isaiah, Jeremiah, and Ezekiel.
11. Writings is made up of eleven books: Psalms, Proverbs, Job, The Song of Songs, Ruth, Lamentations, Ecclesiastes, Esther, Daniel, Ezra/Nehemiah, and Chronicles.
12. Sometimes Lev.17–26 is referred to as the Holiness Code, also referred to as "the *H* thread."
13. Milgram, *Leviticus: A Book of Ritual and Ethics* (Minneapolis: Augsburg Fortress, 2004).
14. Douglas, *Leviticus as Literature,* Paperback Edition (Oxford University Press, 1999); *In the Wilderness: The Doctrine of Defilement in the Book of Numbers,* Paperback Edition (Oxford University Press, 2001). The work on Numbers has been received less enthusiastically by Bible scholars.
15. In Hebrew, the key words are *kadosh,* or "holy," and *kavod,* or "glory." The root meaning for *kadosh* speaks to separation or separateness, and it is used in *kadoshim,* the sense that the Divine exists in a sphere other than our own, distinct and apart. It is in this sense that we separate the holy world from the secular. But the term *kavod,* or "glory," refers to the absence of separation, to

the bursting through of G-d's essence in every expression of the physical world, including the most mundane— as in Isaiah's vision, where the seraphim call out, "and the whole world is filled with G-d's glory." (Isaiah 6:3, quoted by Israel L. Efros in his discussion of *kadosh* and *kavod, Ancient Jewish Philosophy,* Paperback Edition (New York: Block, 1976, p. 10).

16. Eliade, *The Sacred and the Profane: The Nature of Religion,* trans. Willard R. Trask, Paperback Edition (San Diego: Harcourt, 1987).

17. Initially they were in exile in Babylonia, which was then conquered by Persia. When they returned from exile, their land was part of the Persian Empire. They were not only at the mercy of the power struggles of Mesopotamian nations but were geographically placed between the rival empires of Egypt and Mesopotamia.

18. BCE stands for "before the Common Era" and is equivalent in its dates to "BC." CE stands for "the Common Era" and is equivalent to AD in giving dates.

19. Their kingdom had split in half after King Solomon's death in about 922 BCE, and ten of the tribes had disappeared after the Assyrians conquered the northern half (Israel) in 722 BCE. The tribes of Judah, Benjamin, and Levi survived in the southern kingdom (Judah) until it was conquered by the Babylonian king, Nebuchadnezzar, 135 years later, destroying the First Temple and exiling the upper classes to Babylonia. After the return from exile, tribal distinctions seem to have disappeared, except for the Levites.

20. Kugel, *How to Read the Bible,* pp. 8–9.

21. As a matter of fact, most of those exiled apparently chose not to return.

22. Karel Van Der Toorn, *Scribal Culture and the Making of the Hebrew Bible,* Paperback Edition. (Cambridge: Harvard University Press, 2007), p. 250.

Chapter 8. Making the Bible Relevant to Each Generation
by Adding Oral Torah to the Written Text

1. Rabbi ben Zakkai is credited with saving Judaism altogether. The Romans had not only destroyed the Second Temple but laid waste to Jerusalem. Rabbi ben Zakkai won an agreement with the Roman commander Vespasian (later to be emperor), to allow the founding of a school, or *yeshiva,* in the town of Yahveh, for the purpose of studying Torah, as long as it remained apolitical. Between his creation of the *yeshiva;* reconstitution of the counsel of sages (the *Sanhedrin*); and his teachings about replacing Temple sacrifice with prayer, acts of loving-kindness and study of Torah, Rabbi ben Zakkai was the primary force in giving Judaism the form it still has, with the teacher of Torah, the *rabbi,* becoming

the community's religious leader. Also see n. 2 for Ch. 9. of this book, "Jewish Meditation Practice in Overview."

2. which means "repetition," from a verb meaning "to study or review."

3. which means "debate, discussion."

4. which means "learning, instruction."

5. *Aggadah* means "tales, lore."

Chapter 9. Jewish Meditation Practice in Overview

1. The Second Temple was destroyed when Jews lost what is called The Great Revolt against the Roman occupation. But when Hadrian vowed to create a Roman city at the site of the Temple, complete with a temple to Jupiter, the Jews revolted again under the leadership of Bar Kochbah, who claimed to be the messiah. He actually held Jerusalem for over two years, but was defeated by a huge Roman army in a war with massive losses on both sides in 135 CE. Destruction was enormous through much of Israel, and Jerusalem itself was barred to Jews by the Roman victors; many Jews left for other lands.

2. For the source of Rabbi ben Zakkai's formulation, the Talmud cites Simeon the Wise, naming him as a member of the Great Assembly that took charge of the Jews and Judaism after their return from Babylonian exile. According to the Talmud, Simeon taught that, "The world rests on three things: on Torah, service of G-d, and acts of loving-kindness (*Pirkei Avot.* 1:2). For text, see htt://www.chabad.org under *pirkei avot.*

3. It must also be acknowledged that acts of loving-kindness are sometimes restricted to co-religionists, or to certain ethnic or racial groups, or certain social classes, etc.

4. *B. Berachot,* 32b, quoted in Mark Verman, *The History and Varieties of Jewish Meditation* (Northvale, New Jersey: Jason Aronson, 1996), p. 8.

5. *Megilah,* 14a, *Shir HaShirim Rabbah* 4:22, *Ruth Rabbah* 1:2. Quoted in Aryeh Kaplan, *Meditation and the Bible,* Paperback Edition (York Beach, Maine: Samuel Weiser, 1988), p. 152. Kaplan actually refers to these millions as taking part in the prophetic mystery school of the period.

6. Kaplan, *Meditation and the Bible,* pp. 5–10. A particular reference on p. 10 is to Psalms 16:8, with the phrase "I have set G-d before me always." The phrase has become a standard source of meditation practice.

7. Gen. 24:64. According to Aryeh Kaplan, the Hebrew word for "meditate" that is used in this phrase is *suach.* It appears only in this place in the Bible, and is a common translation. It is related to other Hebrew words (*siyach* and

sichah), which are also translated as having to do with meditation. See Kaplan, *Meditation and the Bible,* pp. 103–110.

8. Ezekiel 1:1–2:2. Ezekiel's vision occurred in 592 BCE, shortly after the Babylonian conquest of Jerusalem in 597BCE, but before the Babylonian destruction of the First Temple in 586 BCE. Mystical speculation, both about this vision and about the story of creation in Genesis, were combined at some point, perhaps by the time of the destruction of the Temple. It appears that Rabbi Johanan ben Zakkai was very involved in these mystical studies, along with his disciples.

9. The practice is also referred to as *Hechalot* mysticism. When this term is used, the focus is on the various chambers of the heavenly palace that are being explored.

10. The journey is actually described as a *descent* in much of the literature.

11. My understanding is that Rabbi Akiva descended more than once. But there is a famous story in the Talmud of the dangers. In the tale, four mystics enter Paradise, in what seems to be a reference to *Merkabah* practices. The four are Ben Azai, Ben Zoma, Aher, and Rabbi Akiva. Of these four, Ben Azai dies, Ben Zoma becomes insane, Aher becomes a heretic, and only Rabbi Akiva returns safely. The story comes from the Babylonian Talmud, *Hagigah* 14b, and the *Tosefta Hagigah* 2:1, as quoted, for example, in David S. Ariel's *The Mystic Quest,* Paperback Edition (New York: Schocken Books, 1992, p. 20).

12. The references to Johanan ben Zakkai are found in the writings called *The Greater Hekaloth,* some of whose material may date to the second century CE. See Gershom G. Sholem, *Major Trends in Jewish Mysticism,* Paperback Edition (New York: Schocken Books, 1961, p. 47 and n. 13, p. 357). Gershom indicates that the naming of Johanan ben Zakkai may be inaccurate.

13. Abulafia's teachings were not well received by the Kabbalists of his era, immersed as they were in the Zohar; neither were they well received by the more traditional Jewish community. It was only in the sixteenth century, after Kabbalah had been much changed by Isaac Luria, that Abulafia gained in popularity.

14. Despite the intense focus required for any of these meditations, some of Abulafia's meditations are relatively easy to learn, at least at a basic level. In his recent book *Ecstatic Kabbalah* (Sounds True, 1995), Rabbi David Cooper has made available many of them, particularly those meditations that concentrate on permutations of the four letters of the unnamable name of the Divine—in Hebrew, *yud, heh, vuv,* and *heh*—which are represented in English by the letters YHVH.

15. In Hebrew, *yechudim.*

16. In Kabbalist understanding, Torah can be understood to be composed of a web of complex symbols for different names of G-d.

17. These are called *niggunim.*
18. The word comes from the Hebrew root *bdd,* meaning "to be isolated." See Kaplan, *Meditation and the Bible,* p. 2. Isolation for purposes of contemplation seems to have always been part of Judaism, rooted in the statement earlier mentioned that Isaac was "meditating in the field" when his wife-to-be, Rebecca, first appeared to him. What was new was talking aloud to G-d, pouring out one's heart.
19. Rabbi David A. Cooper, *The Handbook of Jewish Meditation Practices: A Guide to Enriching the Sabbath and Other Days of Your Life* (Jewish Lights, 2000, p. 5).
20. Friedman, *Commentary on the Torah. Shema* means "Listen," which is the first word of the prayer. In traditional practice, this passage is recited before going to sleep and upon arising, and also as one's last words before dying. The phrase "Listen, O Israel, G-d is one and G-d's name is one," is also used as by itself as a focus of meditation practice.
21. As already stated, it is traditionally believed that all the words of Torah were literally spoken to Moses by the Divine Presence. Jews who are less traditional believe that G-d's words have been filtered through imperfect human beings who were limited by their own needs and agendas as they tried to translate experiences beyond the human sphere into human concepts and language. But Torah is still understood to be a book rooted in revelation.
22. Louis Jacobs, Ed., *The Schocken Book of Jewish Mystical Testimonies,* 2nd Edition. (New York: Schocken Books, 1996), p. 52.
23. Aryah Kaplan, *Jewish Meditation: A Practical Guide,* Paperback Edition (New York, Shocken Books, 1985, p. 41).
24. This approach is central to the Buddhist meditation practice known as *vipassana.*
25. Contemplative practice is also a traditional approach in Christianity; and contemplative meditation of paradoxical statements, called *koans,* is an essential practice in Zen Buddhism.

Made in the USA
Middletown, DE
13 October 2017